THE WAITING GAME

THE WAITING GAME

The Untold Story of the Women Who Served the Tudor Queens

NICOLA CLARK

PEGASUS BOOKS

NEW YORK LONDON

THE WAITING GAME

Pegasus Books, Ltd.
148 West 37th Street, 13th Floor
New York, NY 10018

Copyright © 2025 by Nicola Clark

First Pegasus Books cloth edition January 2025

ISBN: 978-1-63936-809-9

10 9 8 7 6 5 4 3 2 1

Printed in the United States of America
Distributed by Simon & Schuster
www.pegasusbooks.com

To all my female friends

Contents

Note on Money, Dates, Names and Titles

In sixteenth-century England, money was calculated predominantly in pounds, shillings and pence. There were twelve pence in a shilling, and twenty shillings to a pound. In contemporary financial accounts shillings were usually abbreviated to 's' and pence to 'd' for the Latin 'denarii'. I have kept to this usage, for example £39 13s 4d. Medieval and Tudor England also calculated in marks. A mark was worth two-thirds of a pound. Where comparison between the two currencies is required, I have converted marks to pounds. Currency equivalents have been sourced from the National Archives currency converter.

The beginning of the year during the Tudor period could be calculated in several ways now unfamiliar to us: sometimes on 25 March, 'Lady Day', sometimes by regnal year (under Henry VIII, 25 April) and sometimes on 1 January. I have used 1 January as the beginning of the year throughout.

Names and titles were confusing even for contemporaries, because individuals could change title over the course of their lives. This was even more complex for women, who changed surnames as well as titles. For the sake of narrative clarity, I have referred to all noblewomen by their natal surname and by the title that they used at any given time, e.g. Elizabeth Stafford, Countess of Surrey between 1514 and 1524, and Elizabeth Stafford, Duchess of Norfolk thereafter. I have anglicised the names of well-known individuals, e.g. Catherine of Aragon, and have used nicknames to aid differentiation between individuals, e.g. Bessie (rather than Elizabeth) Blount.

Sixteenth-century spelling was not uniform, and I have leaned into this where it aids clarity. Individuals with the same name have been given different spellings or different versions, e.g. Isabella, Queen of Castile and her daughter Isabel, Queen of Portugal; Catherine of Aragon, Katherine Howard and Kathryn Parr. These choices are made for the ease of the reader and do not necessarily reflect historical reality.

Cast of Main Characters

María de Salinas, Lady Willoughby (c.1490–1539)
  Spanish attendant of Catherine of Aragon

Elizabeth Stafford, Duchess of Norfolk (c.1497–1558)
  Wife of Thomas Howard, 3rd Duke of Norfolk and aunt of
  Anne Boleyn; lady-in-waiting to Catherine of Aragon

Mary Howard, Duchess of Richmond (1519–c.1555)
  Daughter of the above; wife of Henry Fitzroy, Duke of Rich-
  mond (illegitimate son of Henry VIII); lady-in-waiting to Anne
  Boleyn

Gertrude Blount, Marchioness of Exeter (c.1502–1558)
  Lady-in-waiting to Catherine of Aragon; wife of Henry VIII's
  first cousin

Jane Parker, Viscountess Rochford (c.1505–1542)
  Sister-in-law of Anne Boleyn; in service with Catherine of
  Aragon, Anne Boleyn, Jane Seymour, Anna of Cleves and
  Katherine Howard

Anne Basset (c.1520–c.1558)
  Maid of honour to Jane Seymour, Anna of Cleves, Katherine
  Howard and Kathryn Parr

Katherine Willoughby, Duchess of Suffolk (1519–1580)
  Daughter of María de Salinas; friend of Kathryn Parr

Preface

On 5 June 1536, Diego Hurtado de Mendoza, Marquis of Cañete and Viceroy of Navarre, sent a letter to his friend and colleague, Spanish royal secretary Juan Vásquez de Molina. In it he said that he had recently heard some news from England. 'As I am the son of a former governess of Queen Catalina,' he wrote savagely, 'there is no punishment that could descend upon that King that would not make me happy.'[1] Mendoza's news was the alleged adultery and execution of Queen Anne Boleyn, which had happened two weeks previously, and which he thought a fitting penance for King Henry VIII. Anne Boleyn's predecessor, Queen Catherine of Aragon – Mendoza's 'Queen Catalina' – had died five months before this in January 1536, sad, sick and alone in a damp fenland castle, ignominiously cast aside by her husband the king. Unlike most people in England, Mendoza placed the blame for her death squarely on Henry VIII's shoulders. This was a common Spanish viewpoint, but Mendoza had extra insight beyond his people's anger at Queen Catalina's treatment: his mother had been Francisca de Silva, one of the women who had come to England in attendance on Princess Catherine long ago in 1501.[2]

The loyalty of ladies-in-waiting was not to be underestimated, nor their capacity for hatred of those who wronged their mistress. We don't know how long Francisca stayed in England with Catherine. She may not have witnessed Henry VIII's attempts to annul their marriage and his increasingly poor treatment of his wife at first hand. But she had clearly seen enough to carry indignation back across the ocean to Spain, and to inculcate it in her children. Rage against Henry VIII became part of their family story. Mendoza himself, the oldest son, was a royal advisor whose opinions on foreign monarchs carried weight, and thus Francisca's experience continued to affect Spanish royal policy. The reach of ladies-in-waiting was long.

Contemporaries knew this. Protestant writer John Foxe frequently sought out ex-ladies-in-waiting as sources of information for his famous *Book of Martyrs* during Elizabeth I's reign. We, however, seem to have forgotten this. It's not that we never see them at all. Ladies-in-waiting are a ubiquitous presence in fiction, in TV and in films about the Tudors, a phalanx of pretty faces and velvet dresses ranged behind the queen. You'd notice if they weren't there, probably, but you don't notice them especially when they are. A lot of Tudor political history perpetuates this view, focusing on male ministers and aristocrats to the exclusion of the women with whom they shared the royal court. But we know that this isn't how power works. Opinions are swayed and decisions made as commonly in the pub after work as in the office boardroom, and 'soft power' is as crucial as formal hierarchical structures. A quiet word behind the scenes, an appropriately timed gift, a well-negotiated marriage alliance – the general management of the human networks so necessary in early modern society were all forms of political agency wielded expertly by women.[3]

Every queen had ladies-in-waiting. Their role was to serve the queen in any way she required. Not servants, strictly speaking, they might nevertheless be called on to perform what we would nowadays consider to be menial tasks for women of such upper-class backgrounds. Yet even holding a bowl for the queen to spit into was a source of honour and prestige when it was done for a member of the royal family.[4] They were her confidantes and her chaperones. Only the queen's ladies had the right to enter her most private chambers, spending hours helping her to get dressed and undressed, caring for her clothes and jewels, listening to her secrets. Catherine of Aragon's ladies-in-waiting spied for her during the divorce crisis, risking disgrace and even death. Anne Boleyn's women, on the other hand, were rumoured to have brought her flirtatious behaviour into the open, ultimately causing her execution.

Ladies-in-waiting were never not there. That means that they were intimate and underused witnesses to one of the most tumultuous periods of pre-modern history. Henry VIII's reign saw the rise and painful consolidation of a new royal dynasty as successive queens strove to produce the male heir he so desperately sought. As they failed, so their own ladies-in-waiting jostled to step into their shoes. The gossip that ensued drove the creation of more treason legislation during Henry VIII's reign than any other.[5] This led not only to the first and second executions in the history of queens consort, but to the legal persecution of the women around them who had enabled their alleged scandalous activities. At the same time, the king's break with Rome and creation of the Church of England produced religious division on a previously inconceivable scale.

Henry VIII's penchant for marrying also meant that his court experienced the highest turnover of queens consort ever seen in a single reign. Four of his six wives were English subjects rather than foreign princesses. Each was irrevocably embedded in England's aristocracy, weighed down and buoyed up by ties and loyalties to families that were not part of the Tudor dynasty. A new queen's women were there to show her the ropes, but also to be her companions. How did Henry's wives negotiate the need for experience with the desire for friendship? What did this do to the delicate balance of factions at court?

To be a lady-in-waiting, therefore, was to be forced to make difficult choices. What was most important – her birth family, marital family, children or her mistress the queen? Or perhaps her religious convictions, or sense of right and wrong? What was she to do if these conflicted, as they inevitably did as Henry's reign wore on? The Tudor court was an increasingly tough environment in which to exist. The queen's women were trying to forge individual paths through difficult circumstances, just like everybody else, but they were forced to do so amid a set of pressures and competing loyalties for which there was no precedent.

This book explains how they navigated such a dangerous tightrope. The ladies-in-waiting of Henry VIII's six consorts have never been considered as a discrete collective, with experiences and opportunities beyond the rest of their class and gender.[6] Part of the reason for this is the state of the surviving source material. Where a king had only a single consort, or where the reigning monarch was a queen regnant, there is often a wealth of material about the workings of their households: wage lists, account books, correspondence, wardrobe records. But since Henry VIII went through wives like a knife through butter, there was sometimes scarcely time for clerks and household officers to make such records, and little point in preserving those of his previous queens – meaning that the archive for the households of Henry's consorts is woefully small by comparison with, for instance, Elizabeth I's.[7]

Simply finding the names of the six wives' ladies-in-waiting is not a task that can ever be 'finished'. A careful gleaning across many different kinds of sources in many different locations yields hundreds of names, but so many records have been lost or destroyed that we will never know them all. The age of digitisation has meant that we can now access many original sources with reasonable ease, but in some areas we are still reliant on 'calendars', short summaries of original documents compiled by men during the nineteenth and twentieth centuries before the study of women was considered a serious pursuit. Those men were not interested in summarising women's letters, nor were they always interested in accurately representing women in their indexes. In this they were only following the norms of a long-standing patriarchy. Women had long been hidden in official records as a result of the legal doctrine of coverture, under which our ladies-in-waiting operated. Until the Married Women's Property Act of 1870, married women didn't exist in the eyes of the law: they were chattels, owned by their husbands, 'covered' by his legal identity and with none of their own. Married women couldn't file lawsuits, make wills or administer property in their own names.[8] That makes them very difficult to find in archives. Research is done backwards, reading the archive 'against the grain', looking for the men around a woman rather than the woman herself.[9] For women of the highest status – duchesses, countesses, baronesses – this is not so difficult.

For those of more obscure gentry origins – still elite, just not top-drawer elite – it can be almost impossible to identify an individual with certainty.

It's not all doom and gloom. Even with the restrictions of the archive, there is plenty of information about pre-modern women just waiting to be uncovered. *The Waiting Game* is designed partly as an example of what we might learn when we pay attention to those who spent much of their time in the background and who were never supposed to leave much trace behind. I've tried to preserve the sense of the queen's women as a distinct group while teasing out the stories of certain individuals, following the course of their lives and their service and using them as a lens through which to understand their unique collective position. The book carries the reader from 1501 to 1547 in three parts. Part One follows young ladies-in-waiting María de Salinas and Elizabeth Stafford, Countess of Surrey and later Duchess of Norfolk, alongside some of their more experienced colleagues as they settled into the service of Catherine of Aragon. By 1529, though, the peaceful, quasi-medieval atmosphere of Henry's court had begun to change, and our ladies faced a difficult situation: what did you do when one of your number was elevated above you? Part Two poses this question with greater urgency as we meet more women in the competing households of Queen Catherine of Aragon and Queen Anne Boleyn, like teenager Mary Howard, Duchess of Richmond, Gertrude Blount, Marchioness of Exeter and Jane Parker, Viscountess Rochford. Then, a shock: the world was turned upside down with Queen Anne's execution for high treason. Part Three documents the dizzying speed with which our ladies-in-waiting changed employer. Maid of honour Anne Basset kept her place through the last four consorts and two short periods of unemployment, and was joined by Katherine Willoughby, Duchess of Suffolk, who was the daughter of our first lady-in-waiting, María de Salinas.

While we follow the ups and downs of royal service in a chronological format, the book also explores the daily lives of ladies-in-waiting, revealing the secrets of recruitment, costume, what they ate, where (and with whom) they slept. It uncovers the advantages of court service – four ladies-in-waiting became queen of England – but also the inherent risk: two of those ladies ended up with their heads on the block. As Henry changed wives, and changed the country's religion besides, these women had to make choices about loyalty that simply didn't exist before and would never exist like this again. By the end of Henry's reign, being a lady-in-waiting was far more dangerous than it had been at the beginning.

Part One: 1501–1529

1

Brittle Fortune

The ladies could hear carousing in the distance, excitement and nerves drawing closer until the two were indistinguishable. Inside the chamber, Princess Catherine of Aragon was as ready for her wedding night as they could make her. The room itself had taken several hours to prepare – quite why is unclear – and now the freshly made bed stood in its candlelit centre like a solemn symbol of duty, a threat and promise alike. The room was full of ladies-in-waiting, from Jane Vaux, Lady Guildford, one of Queen Elizabeth of York's attendants, to teenager María de Salinas, raised in the Castilian royal household and sent with the princess to England. Women were at the heart of this, the most significant of national events, as they were for every intimate occasion at court.

The chamber door opened to reveal Prince Arthur, who had been carried bodily from the hall by a host of raucous young men of dubious sobriety. The wedding breakfast, hosted by the Bishop of London in his palace next to St Paul's Cathedral, had lasted all afternoon and most of the evening. While the ladies had been readying the princess, the men had continued to roister. Now, both Catherine and Arthur were placed together in the bed and blessed by bishops. Spiced wine was passed around – though whether the male members of the party really needed any more alcohol was questionable – and then the ladies and gentlemen retired to their own chambers, leaving the royal couple to their duty.[1]

It had been a long day, and an even longer road to this wedding. When it had first been planned twelve years ago in 1489, Jane Vaux had not been long married herself. Her husband was Sir

Richard Guildford, one of Henry VII's most trusted advisors. But Jane's own court pedigree was substantial without him. She had been raised and educated in the household of the king's mother, the formidably intelligent Lady Margaret Beaufort, and had served Queen Elizabeth of York before becoming Lady Governess to the latter's two daughters, Princesses Margaret and Mary.[2] Now, at almost forty years of age, she knew Henry VII's court, its personnel and its ceremonies intimately. Small wonder that she had been chosen to go to Plymouth with other noblewomen to meet Princess Catherine and escort her to London.

This damp, muddy, autumnal progress through the lush green English countryside was the first opportunity for the princess and her household to begin to learn how things were done here, how to follow the small unwritten social rules of a new court and avoid faux pas, all things that ladies-in-waiting were supposed to teach a new queen or princess. Cultural differences were already apparent. The food, particularly, would take some getting used to; there was more meat here and less fruit, especially citrus, and the spices were different. Even their clothes marked them out. The Spanish wore the *verdugado*, a hooped skirt like an early farthingale, and platform shoes called *chapines*, to lift them clear of street dirt. Jane, in her more closely fitted gowns and flat-heeled shoes, would have found them strange.[3] Language was a more immediate issue. None of Princess Catherine's women could speak English, and neither Jane nor any of her colleagues could speak Spanish, but there were workarounds, and this might have been why Jane was there. As the daughter of a French lady-in-waiting, Jane could speak French and Latin as well as English.[4] Queen Isabella of Castile's court was more of a hothouse for learned women than almost anywhere in Europe, and so the Spanish were not behindhand with languages. The queen had famously struggled hard to learn Latin as an adult, and she provided tutors not only for her daughters but for all the ladies-in-waiting.[5] The English had not welcomed a foreign princess for a royal marriage for over fifty years, and, helped by this mixture of languages, they did so now in style, with local nobility and dignitaries on hand to escort her ceremonially everywhere she went.

On the way to London, Jane would have met María de Salinas, one of Princess Catherine's young Castilian attendants. Around sixteen years old, the same age as the princess, María could speak to Jane in Latin, and probably French as well. Not much is known in English scholarship about María or any of her Spanish colleagues. Even María's parentage is routinely mistaken, but Spanish sources reveal that she had been steeped in the tradition of royal service since birth just as much as Jane.[6] María's father, Juan de Salinas, had been secretary and chamberlain to Catherine of Aragon's older sister Isabel, Queen of Portugal, and her mother, Inés de Albornoz, one of her most senior ladies-in-waiting. When her father died in 1495, María and two of her sisters had moved into the royal household with their mother, serving first Queen Isabel of Portugal, then her short-lived son Prince Miguel, and finally Queen Isabella of Castile.[7] The family were not titled, but they were certainly professional courtiers of considerable standing, trusted by the Castilian royal family, and so María's social status was as good as that of most of the women in service at the English court, and her education arguably better.

While Princess Catherine had known since childhood that she would one day cross the sea to England and probably never return, María hadn't had nearly as long to ready herself materially or emotionally for the journey. A list of the household was first made in October 1500, a mere seven months before departure, and there were only fourteen women listed by name, though most of these would have had their own female servants to swell the ranks. María, listed as 'the daughter of Inés de Albornoz', was placed near the bottom in a position akin to what would later be called the 'maids of honour' in England, young, adolescent women at court to finish their education and make a good marriage.[8] Perhaps María was excited at the prospect of foreign travel, or perhaps not – the evidence doesn't say – but in either case her sojourn in England was not likely to last forever. Most foreign ladies-in-waiting returned home eventually.

As an unmarried woman, María might not yet have known the details of what her mistress would undergo in the bedchamber deep in the Bishop of London's palace, but she knew how important it was to the futures of both countries. Nobody braved the Bay of Biscay so close to winter unless for a good reason. Driven back once by bad weather, their ships had taken five wet, freezing, nightmarish days to cross the sea amid 'great hugeness of storm and tempest'.[9] María was used to travelling – the Spanish court routinely covered far more ground in its peregrinations between palaces than the English court did – but she had never attempted it in an English autumn before. Their progress from Plymouth was not slow, but it was not as fast as King Henry VII liked. He waylaid them at Dogmersfield in Hampshire: he would see the princess, he insisted, even if she was in bed. This went against Spanish protocol, but since they weren't in Spain any more there was nothing to be done. The prince and princess were introduced and spent an awkward, but pleasant, afternoon together. That evening, someone called for music, and the ladies came to life: it was not yet appropriate for the couple to dance together, even if they had known the same dances, and so Jane partnered the young prince while a Spanish lady – perhaps María – danced with the princess.[10]

Lying in bed in the bishop's palace, María could still smell London. It was inescapable. Even before travellers entered the city walls they were engulfed by the stench of rotting meat, sewage and all manner of dangerously disgusting things dumped into ditches, back streets and the river. The flat, sprawling metropolis was twice the size of most of the cities that María knew, and the dampness of the air made the stink all the worse.[11] The city authorities had tried to clean up the main thoroughfares for the princess's entry. The unevenly paved streets had been laid with gravel and sand, and barriers were erected to keep the common people – and perhaps the city's free-roaming pigs – away from the procession.[12] The many liveried servants, attending their gorgeously apparelled superiors, did distract the eye, and the cold November light made gold embroidery and polished weapons glint. María and the other Spanish women wore their black lace dresses, their hair loose, but were quite literally outshone by the English ladies decked out in shimmering cloth of gold. They rode in pairs, one English lady to each Spanish, but side-saddle in England was the opposite way round to that in Spain and so it looked as though the ladies were deliberately facing away from one another, back to back against the press of the crowd.[13]

Amid the sea of faces was a young lawyer, eagle-eyed and sharp-tongued. Writing afterwards to a friend, he compiled a deeply unflattering list of the Spanish entourage: 'hunchbacked, tattered, barefooted, Ethiopian, pygmies', remarks that at least partly referred to those of African or Arab origin in the princess's household.[14] Slavery existed formally in Spain in a way that wasn't yet the case in England. María had grown up with enslaved people; her family owned several. The household list made for Princess Catherine in 1500 included 'two slaves to wait upon the maids of honour'.[15] Their inclusion in the princess's retinue was most likely considered by the Spanish monarchs to be an advertisement of Spanish military achievements. That the marriage between Catherine and Arthur was a means of enlarging the black population in England was probably not something that had been foreseen by contemporaries, and the young lawyer's attitude was, alas, a forerunner of widespread racism.

The wedding itself might have been an anticlimax after the overwhelming sounds and sights of the entry into the city and its welcoming pageants, but the crowds at St Paul's were just as vast. A platform had been erected for the prince and princess so that everyone might see them exchange their vows. María and the others were dressed in the Spanish fashion, with farthingales over their skirts and wide, pleated sleeves that soon became all the rage in England.[16] Walking slowly two by two along the raised walkway behind the princess's white satin train, they could see only a wall of faces in every direction. Ten-year-old Prince Henry, escorting his sister-in-law, was dressed in silver with gold roses, and – characteristically – he glittered nearly as much as the ostentatious display of jewel-encrusted gold plate that surrounded the high altar. The vows were exchanged during the customary matrimonial mass, and then as minstrels played joyful music everybody of significance processed back to the Bishop of London's palace for the feast.[17]

It had been a tiring day, and many of the princess's attendants must have been glad to retire to their own beds and leave her alone with Arthur. At least, we assume that they were left alone. Ladies-in-waiting were chaperones as much as confidantes, and there's some evidence to suggest that under previous monarchs a royal servant may have stayed in the bedchamber while the king and queen lay together, presumably to ensure that marital relations were indeed taking place.[18] Jane would have known about this; her own mother may even have performed this service in her capacity as one of Queen Margaret of Anjou's closest ladies. So far as the record shows, nobody did this for Catherine and Arthur. That consummation occurred was – at the time – taken on trust.

María may have known better. Jane, Lady Guildford would much later testify that she had been there that night, had left the couple in bed together and returned in the morning to find them there still; but she did not have access to Princess Catherine's chambers over the next few days.[19] The mood there was sombre. Prince Arthur might have left the room boasting about his night 'in the midst of Spain', but the women did not share his confidence.[20] Francisca de Cáceres, another of María's colleagues with whom the princess was close, told the rest of the women derisively that Arthur hadn't been able to perform. For the whole day, Catherine remained in her chamber with her Spanish attendants, granting access to nobody.[21]

This wasn't necessarily an immediate disaster. Both were young. English ladies at court spoke significantly to one another about the five or so nights that the pair did spend together.[22] After the majority of the Spanish party returned home on 29 November there was more serious discussion. Prince Arthur must return to Ludlow Castle on the Welsh border, to act as an extension of the Crown there as Prince of Wales. Should Catherine and her women go with him? Or should she stay in London?

There was disagreement even within her own household. The people in charge – *mayordomo*, or Lord Steward, and the *camarera mayor*, head lady of the bedchamber – were a married couple: Don Pedro Manrique and his stern, proud wife, Doña Elvira Manuel. She relished her position of power and did not think she would be able to hold onto it if the princess's household merged with the prince's. In company with King Henry VII, she also did not think too much sex was good for adolescent boys. María, as a much more junior member of Catherine's establishment, would not have been asked for her opinion, but the prospect of travelling to Wales was probably not one that appealed. In the event, the princess herself convinced the king that separation would be cruel.[23] Regardless of Doña Elvira's frowns, they were sent together to Ludlow Castle. María and the other Spaniards went too; Jane, Lady Guildford remained with the royal household in London. Some English women, though, did join the princess's establishment. Margaret Plantagenet, Countess of Salisbury, long-faced with sharp black eyes, a wry smile and a royal pedigree to rival the Tudors', was the wife of the prince's Lord Chamberlain, and so it made sense for her to join the household.

If England had seemed cold and damp thus far, this was nothing compared with a winter on the Welsh Borders. The castle was set on a hill overlooking the town. The walls were thick, the apartments made as cosy as possible in the innermost part of the castle, but even so it must have felt very isolated; unsurprisingly, Princess Catherine and Countess Margaret became close friends over long winter evenings spent in front of the fire. What María made of Ludlow is not recorded, but for Queen Isabella of Castile it was 'that unhealthy place', and so it proved.[24] In March 1502 sickness struck, and it struck with unusual virulence. Both the prince and princess were taken ill, but anxiety soon turned to tragedy: Prince Arthur weakened and died within only a few days. So many others were still ill that his funeral at Worcester Cathedral in early April 1502 was poorly attended.[25] Princess Catherine, weak, convalescent and heartbroken, was eventually fetched back to London in a litter sent by her solicitous mother-in-law, the equally heartbroken Queen Elizabeth of York.[26]

What now? To be a widow at sixteen was a harsh fate, but

María, almost the same age and fresh from a Ludlow winter, must have wondered whether this might not be a blessing in disguise. Royal widows did not usually remain in their marital country. They were sent home, that their parents might direct their dynastic duty in a new direction. If that happened, Princess Catherine's Spanish ladies would return home too. Soon, perhaps, she would see Castile again.

It was not to be. In December 1504, María de Salinas was still in England, still with the now-dowager Princess Catherine, still under the dictatorial household management of the unbending Doña Elvira Manuel, and terrible news had just arrived: Queen Isabella of Castile was dead.

Those in England already felt abandoned by the Spanish monarchs, and now it could only get worse. After Prince Arthur's death, Princess Catherine had been installed at Durham House in London. Doña Elvira had put the household into full Spanish mourning and kept them largely isolated from the royal court. Both the English and Spanish monarchs had been keen to hold onto their alliance in order to keep France at arm's length. By July 1503 Catherine was betrothed to Prince Henry, now heir to the throne at twelve years old, and the marriage was due to take place on 28 June 1505, the day that Henry would turn fourteen, which meant that María and the others could not go home yet.[27] But things were not secure. Catherine's dowry for her marriage to Arthur had not been fully paid by her father King Ferdinand of Aragon, and so King Henry refused to allow her access to her jointure, the income set aside to support her in the event of her widowhood. Who, then, should pay for her household in England? As María would write home a little later, 'the king our lord says that the king here has to provide it; the king here says that the king our lord has to provide it. So in this way we stop.'[28]

'Stop' they had. The £100 that King Henry allowed them per month did not go far for a princess who had obligations of patronage and magnificence to consider as well as feeding, clothing and paying her staff; Queen Elizabeth of York had three times as much to spend.[29] Under such difficult conditions the household became quarrelsome. Doña Elvira Manuel ruled the establishment with a rod of iron and a hefty streak of self-interested interference. Her husband, though nominally also in charge, was evidently not a man of comparable force. Not surprisingly, the other Spaniards resented this, and resented the Spanish monarchs' continued insistence that everybody must do as Doña Elvira ordered.[30] Princess Catherine – still only a teenager – was unable to control them. In the summer of 1504 she had even asked her father-in-law King Henry to intervene, which he wisely forbore to do.[31]

Though Doña Elvira was trusted by the Spanish monarchs, she had her own agenda, and it wasn't the same as theirs. It's easy to think of a foreign princess's household as divorced from politics back home, as though the geographical separation were mental and emotional as well as physical. This was emphatically not the case. Doña Elvira came from a family with strong links to Philip, Duke of Burgundy, who was married to Catherine of Aragon's elder sister Juana. With Queen Isabella's death, Juana would now inherit the crown of Castile. Queen Isabella had stipulated that King Ferdinand of Aragon should rule as governor on Juana's behalf, because of her 'fragile' state of mind. Duke Philip, naturally, wanted to use her as a puppet and rule in her stead. Between 1504 and 1506, therefore, Castile became the centre of a power struggle between Duke Philip and King Ferdinand.

Doña Elvira was well aware of this. Her brother, Juan Manuel, was Duke Philip's advisor on Castilian matters.[32] This put her in a difficult position. She did not want to lose her influence in England, or at the Spanish court, and must have feared that this would happen if King Ferdinand remained in power in Castile; if her brother's activities on behalf of Duke Philip were known, she herself would no longer be trusted. For her own and her family's sake, therefore, Duke Philip must win. Elvira now began encouraging her mistress, Princess Catherine, to support Duke Philip against her own father King Ferdinand. Catherine – young, impressionable and very much under the older woman's thumb – soon became extraordinarily pro-Burgundian.[33] Encouraged by Doña Elvira, in

August 1505 she proposed a meeting between Henry VII and Duke Philip.[34] Doña Elvira and her brother knew that if such a meeting took place an alliance would likely be concluded. Catherine, in an unusual display of density, apparently did not realise that this would be to the detriment of her father and by extension to herself. For if King Ferdinand no longer controlled Castile, Catherine's own inheritance would be lessened and her value on the marriage market would plummet: why should King Henry VII uphold her betrothal to Prince Henry under those circumstances?

Others were quicker than Catherine. Spanish ambassador Dr Roderigo González de la Puebla was appalled. He tried everything to prevent the princess sending a message to Henry VII about the proposed meeting, but to no avail. He then confronted Doña Elvira. In the face of his wrath at the potential ruin of years of his work shoring up the alliance between Henry and Ferdinand, she promised to prevent the princess from sending the message; but, away from him, immediately broke her word. Puebla felt that he was left with no choice. Tears streaming down his face, he went to the princess and told her everything. Horrified, she wrote a letter to King Henry at his dictation, and he ordered his messenger to overtake hers. Wary of Doña Elvira, Puebla then warned Catherine to continue to appear eager for the meeting, lest news to the contrary reach Duke Philip. He wrote to King Ferdinand with the whole story, asking the king not to trust the advice of Doña Elvira.[35]

King Ferdinand was already well aware of the Manuels' duplicity, as he saw it. He had written to Henry VII back in June 1505 warning him not to confide anything to Elvira, because she could not be trusted: her brother Juan was a traitor to both of them.[36] Doña Elvira has been labelled a villain, as so many women of strong character are. But the surviving sources give us only others' impressions and not her own voice. She was also a victim of the complex loyalties facing ladies-in-waiting. Elvira was not acting in Spain's interests or in Princess Catherine's interests, but in a world where women's interests rarely counted for much, one can hardly blame her for trying to capitalise on the connections that she had elsewhere in her life. She wasn't seeking to change the course of diplomacy for its own sake, but for her own and her family's gain, and in that she was no different from any other courtier.

By early December 1505, Doña Elvira's departure from Princess Catherine's service was in train, though who arranged this is unclear. Catherine herself was given an excuse: Elvira told her that she needed to go to Flanders in order to see an eye specialist to save her sight, which was failing. As Catherine said, 'if she were blind she could not serve me', and so acquiesced to her leaving.[37] Later she returned to Castile with her husband, but there's no evidence that she ever served in a royal household again. Some ladies-in-waiting proved themselves too dangerous – too intelligent, and too influential – to be allowed near the centre of politics.

María de Salinas was desperate. 'I am the loneliest person in the world without him,' she wrote to her brother-in-law. 'He's one of the most honest people I have ever seen in my life . . . I had no other pastime but to see him come every day with stories of the English to tell us, and he's so measured and so sincere that he made me laugh with pleasure.'[38] It sounds like a love affair, but it wasn't romantic love that made her write this way. The man she referred to was a letter bearer, most probably a merchant or low-ranking courtier come from Castile to England on business, bringing letters from home to María and the other Spaniards marooned in Princess Catherine's household. It is a pity that we don't know his name. That his mere presence brought such joy paints a correspondingly sad picture: María and the other ladies-in-waiting were so bored and so lonely that even a humble messenger was a bright spot in their lives.

It was 1507, and things had only got worse. Though the death of Philip, Duke of Burgundy at the end of 1506 had unexpectedly placed Castile back into the hands of King Ferdinand of Aragon, he was so preoccupied with his new wife Germaine de Foix and with holding onto his Italian territories that he had no time or inclination to spare for his daughter in England and he remained utterly blasé about settling his debts with King Henry

VII. Princess Catherine's dowry remained unpaid, she remained unmarried, and King Henry had stopped paying for all but the most basic food and lodging for her household, knowing that the louder she complained to King Ferdinand the more likely it was that the dowry would be paid.[39] In 1505 she wrote in desperation that she was forced to borrow money or starve. The next year she was 'in the greatest anguish, her people ready to ask alms, and herself all but naked'.[40] It's sometimes thought that she was exaggerating for effect, to bounce her father into a response, the more so since these are years in which we are relatively archivally 'blind' in England where the princess's household is concerned. There are no surviving financial accounts for her establishment, and those for the king's yield only sparse information. We are usually forced to rely on the princess's own letters.

Yet she was not the only one to pick up a pen. Most of the Spaniards probably wrote home, but unlike most – so far as we currently know – some of María de Salinas' letters have survived, tucked away amid other family papers in Spain.[41] Unused by English-speaking historians, and underused by Spanish scholars, they reveal María to us as a vibrant, straight-talking, astute young woman. They also give us a new lens through which to see these otherwise shadowy years. María is usually described as the epitome of the loyal lady-in-waiting, at her mistress's side through thick and thin. That might have been true later, but it wasn't true in 1507. María was desperate to leave.

Most of her letters were written to her brother-in-law Ochoa de Landa, who was treasurer in the household of Catherine's older sister Juana, Queen of Castile.[42] They weren't formal petitions but frank, engaging epistles, full of in-jokes, snide remarks and even an occasional upbraid, all written in her own round, somewhat sprawling hand. María's letters show that the princess was not the only one who was suffering, and she was not exaggerating. In July 1507 María explained that 'since we have come to this land we have never been paid for our living, in which I think you would marvel at the way we support ourselves'.[43] The princess herself was repeatedly and vocally concerned about the plight of her ladies-in-waiting. In 1505 she asked her father to pay María de Salazar, because she was unable to, and noted that six of her women had served her devotedly without any remuneration.[44] In 1507 she again pleaded with Ferdinand for money for them, explaining that by now she had only five women in her service and that 'they have never received the smallest sum of money since they were in England [. . . I] cannot think of them without pangs of conscience'.[45]

Their increasingly tattered clothing was at odds with the glory of their surroundings. In response to Princess Catherine's plea for money, King Henry had reduced her household and moved them into his newly built palace of Richmond, both part of and yet separate from the rest of the royal court.[46] María had seen Richmond before; the court had celebrated there in the days after the wedding of the prince and princess in 1501. It was a triumph of modern architecture and the pride of the king's heart. Built in white stone, the skyline of the new lodging range was a mass of endless towers, each topped with a dome and gaily decorated weathervane. The Tudor rose, Beaufort portcullis and Henry's red dragons and greyhound badges were in evidence everywhere that the eyes might rest. Inside were costly tapestries, curtains, cushions and carpets, the furniture the best that craftmanship could offer or money buy.[47] María and her colleagues could walk in the gardens, or under the covered galleries that encircled them if it rained. They could play cards – though probably not for money, given their straitened circumstances – sing, dance and sew. Needlework was a comfort. It was calm, peaceful, familiar and it brought them together. They could gossip, or pray, or read aloud as they worked intricate 'Spanish blackstitch' patterns onto collars and cuffs.[48]

But for María and the other Spanish women, Richmond must have felt like a gilded cage. Their household was kept in comparative isolation even from others living in the palace, and there was little to do but wait for the tides of fortune to turn.[49] Not surprisingly, she was desperate to return home. She reminded her brother-in-law Ochoa repeatedly that she had no intention of

remaining in England after her mistress's marriage, and declared
that 'this is not a land to stop [in] unless necessary'.[50] She was so
unhappy that she could not bear to contemplate the glory of going
home in case it did not come true: 'I want my departure so much
that I cannot receive it except as a mockery.'[51]

Part of her desperation was homesickness. Most of María's letters contain complaints that her relatives did not write frequently
enough and that she didn't receive family news in a timely fashion.
Sometimes she gave her sharp tongue free rein, writing with biting
sarcasm that her brother Juan had done no more for her than if he
were dead.[52] On another occasion she wrote of her joy at hearing
news of their youngest brother Alonso, and about her sister Inés'
betrothal, but was annoyed that Juan hadn't bothered to tell her
these things himself, exclaiming 'I find on my own account that
I am the most loving of you all.'[53] Though she berated them from
time to time, it's clear that María's family network was close and
strong. She remained in individual contact with her older brother
Juan, brother-in-law Ochoa and sisters Isabel and Inés, was eager
for information about their youngest brother Alonso, asked her
nun sister Teresa to pray for her, and regularly sent her good
wishes to their grandmother. In the face of English intransigence
she held fast to her Spanish identity, insisting that 'I am as Spanish
as the first day I came to this land', even though Ochoa teased
her about adopting English customs: 'I say it because you always
send me to make you kiss my mouth.'[54] Though nowadays the
English are usually thought reserved and not particularly tactile,
this wasn't the case in the sixteenth century, when commentators
from other European countries were both horrified and amused
by the English propensity for kissing; Dutch philosopher Erasmus
wrote that 'When you go anywhere on a visit, the girls kiss you.
They kiss you when you arrive. They kiss you when you go away.
They kiss you when you return. Once you have tasted how soft and
fragrant those lips are, you could spend your life there.'[55]

María must have devoured letters from home. Her own make it
clear that there was not much affection to be found in the English
court. Though they spent every day in one another's company, she

and the princess were not especially close. She mentioned Catherine frequently, but it was usually in somewhat hopeless relation to her marriage to Prince Henry: it will be after Easter, before Christmas, 'the princess is not yet married, nor do we know when'.[56] María did occasionally mention some of the girls who served with her, but not in overtly positive terms. She had tried to stay in touch with María de Rojas, for instance, who had gone home to marry in 1506, but was annoyed that she'd received no reply to her letters.[57]

Perhaps she'd hoped for advice. There was only one way for María to get out of England and return home: marriage. In Spain, ladies-in-waiting received a dowry from their royal mistress when they married. For many, including María, it was the reason they went into service in the first place.[58] Princess Catherine, unable even to feed and clothe her household adequately, was consumed with anxiety over this. Ordinarily she could have expected marriages to occur between her women and the English nobility, for this was one way in which women acted as peace-weavers, strengthening alliances between countries. Back in 1504 it had looked as though María de Rojas would go down this path, having attracted the young and extremely wealthy heir to the earldom of Derby, and both she and Catherine were pleased because it would allow Rojas to continue to serve at court.[59] This, alas, had been stymied by the interfering Doña Elvira, who had wanted Rojas to marry her own son.[60] The dismissal of Elvira and her family had meant that this did not happen either, and finally Rojas' family arranged a Spanish marriage for her in 1506.[61] The rest of the princess's women were reliant on the goodwill of King Ferdinand, and on their own families.

Therein lay María de Salinas' problem. For a while there was talk of a match with a man from a wealthy Castilian merchant family.[62] But arranging marriages was a complex business even when all parties were in the same country. The family member who should have dealt with this for her was her oldest brother Juan, who since the death of their mother and uncle in 1503 had been the nominal head of the family. Unfortunately, he was either subject to continual bad luck where his sisters' marriages were concerned, or he simply wasn't very good at this. María wrote scathingly of his inaction, asking her sister to make sure that nobody furthered the negotiations 'until they write of his person and what he has', because the honour of the family was at stake – apparently she did not trust Juan to guard it properly.[63] She was absolutely clear that it was no good marrying somebody who was not suitably well off and of good birth, and this was not María being mercenary: her future standard of living and social status would depend upon those of her husband.

María tried sarcasm on her brother: 'Pray God for those well married, whoever they have for husbands.'[64] She badgered the rest of her family for information. She even asked the interfering Manuels, Doña Elvira and her husband, for help, and Juan apparently protested, probably because the Manuels had come back to Spain in such disfavour with King Ferdinand. María reassured him that she knew what she was doing and implied that in fact she had no choice, since Juan himself told her so little about what was going on. Impatient, she effectively told her brother what to do, revealing expert knowledge of Spanish officials and patronage ties despite her absence: 'And if for this, my lord, you have need of help, we think that they will help you, and since Juan López is so much your lord, and this is by way of discharge, you should put it in his hands.'[65] López, in charge of the king's payments, could indeed expedite any warrant for remuneration.

When her sister Isabel was married to Ochoa de Landa in May 1506, María took immediate advantage of having another adult male in the family. Soon she was writing frankly to him, telling him all of her doubts and worries about her marriage, her future and her brother's uselessness. In 1507 she begged him to be blunt with her, suspecting that those involved now thought the match unsuitable but didn't dare to tell her.[66] He may have done so; the one-sided nature of the surviving correspondence means that we can only infer his replies from María's own. The wealthy merchant was mentioned no more.

By the end of 1507, María was in greater despair than ever. This was a difficult year all round. Princess Catherine's marriage to

Prince Henry at first looked plausible: King Ferdinand was once more in nominal control of Castile, which meant access to funds for her dowry, but then less so; he remained in Naples until June 1507 and couldn't meet the original deadline, asking for a delay in payment.[67] King Henry VII betrothed his youngest daughter Mary to Ferdinand's nephew and heir to Castile, the future Charles V; what use for the marriage between Catherine and Henry now? And yet he refused to cancel it entirely. The princess's spirits and circumstances fluctuated accordingly. María was undoubtedly affected by the tense atmosphere and frustrated by the lack of progress on her own marriage. In a letter filled with despair, she told Ochoa defiantly that she would either return to Spain with the proper honour or not at all, no matter what her brother Juan did or did not arrange: 'Do what you will, for I will choose what is best for me, and with this I console myself.'[68]

2

So Much Loyalty

María de Salinas was suspicious. Francesco Grimaldi was hounding her for an answer that she wasn't convinced she wanted to give. Every day he told her there was a messenger ready and waiting to carry her consent to her family in Spain. Every day, so far, she smiled and dissimulated and concealed her thoughts, and wrote home demanding more information. Grimaldi wanted to marry her, and it was getting harder to hold him at bay.

He had arrived in February 1508 with the new Spanish ambassador Don Gutierre Gómez de Fuensalida, both of them commissioned to conclude the financial arrangements for Princess Catherine's marriage with Prince Henry. Ambassador Fuensalida was to lead the negotiations; Grimaldi, a banker originally from Genoa, was to put up the money for the rest of the dowry on behalf of King Ferdinand of Aragon.[1] Apparently he had another, more personal, mission on his mind. He was on the hunt for a wife, and María's letters reveal for the first time that she was his target. In fact, her brother-in-law Ochoa de Landa had suggested the match to Grimaldi before he ever left Spain. Ochoa was a royal treasurer and Grimaldi a financier; they knew and worked with one another. Ochoa had extolled María's virtues, had shown Grimaldi her letters – she wasn't pleased about this – and evidently told him to go and see for himself. But Ochoa had told María nothing about any of it. Faced now with Grimaldi's ardent proposals she felt blindsided, her trust in her family shaken. Maybe Ochoa had thought it would be best to let Grimaldi speak for himself and win her over, but if so he reckoned without María's quick intellect and courtier instincts.

In April she took up paper and ink to ask Ochoa what he had done behind her back – 'you are the beginning of this business' – and told him frankly that for her to say yes there would need to be more family discussion and she would need to be part of it.[2] It was true that there was much to recommend him. Despite his Italian origin, Grimaldi must in some ways have been a reminder of home. He had long been involved with the Spanish court in matters of finance, and King Ferdinand trusted him, insofar as King Ferdinand trusted anybody where money was concerned. He could speak to her in Spanish; he knew her family. Though not noble or a courtier, he was respectable. And María was still desperate to find a way to get home.

Thus she prevaricated. With Grimaldi, she played a game of doublethink. She knew that he knew that she knew that he had spoken to her family, that marriage was under discussion, but she played her cards close to her chest. She wrote briskly to Ochoa that 'he is very willing to do it [marry], and I conceal everything from him as I tell you'.[3] She was careful with correspondence and letter bearers, telling Ochoa not to forward her letters to Grimaldi and to use a different route and courier to send his replies, because she did not want them to come into Grimaldi's hands. With her family she played the role of dutiful sister, anxiously trying to do what was best for their collective honour. The acerbic, pointed remarks that she dripped into her letters, though, show that this was not the whole truth. She was annoyed at the position they had put her in, writing a little waspishly, 'I am forced to do what was given to you gentlemen', meaning that she had to deal with Grimaldi personally instead of referring him to a male relative.[4]

Trust was in short supply at royal courts, and María was a courtier to her bones. She sensed that her family was hedging its bets, perhaps waiting for her to make a decision, and she was extremely wary. Her uncle and sister had both written to her promoting Grimaldi's suit, but she knew that they did this only because Ochoa told them to. She asked for more information, for an explicit instruction to go ahead, but despite her relatives' recommendations she continued to behave as though she had not received this. While her normally anxious tone was surely not fabricated – this must all have been intensely stressful – it bought her time to work out just what was going on and where her own loyalties should lie.

Part of the problem was that she didn't trust Grimaldi. She didn't even like him very much. She said nothing complimentary about his person or personality, only that 'he seems to me to be good for the little that I know of him'.[5] Her considerations were of a purely practical nature, focusing on the things that would affect her the most as his wife; she noted approvingly, 'of everything else, as I am told, both in lineage and in property, he is not lacking'.[6] She was also concerned, or chose to appear concerned, about Princess Catherine's reaction. When Ochoa suggested she speak to Princess Catherine she was loath to do so, 'because I did not know the manner in which it was to be carried out', and because she did not want to go to the princess 'without some cause that I could put before her, telling her that you had already arranged the marriage for me and showing her the letter in which you told me so that she would do it willingly'.[7] María was not going to go to the princess with a 'maybe'.

Her instincts proved unerringly accurate. Grimaldi, though intense, had a short attention span. He wanted to marry a lady-in-waiting, probably because he thought that this was a good way to gain influence at the royal court, but he was not particularly fussed about which one. Princess Catherine's household had become a place of power struggle once more, and this time the source was her charismatic, conniving, domineering confessor, Fray Diego Fernández. At this point in her life Princess Catherine was clearly someone who responded willingly, even blindly, to moral authority, however dubiously contrived, and the friar amply filled the gap left by the departure of the similarly dictatorial Doña Elvira Manuel. He wanted the princess's entire loyalty and resented those who claimed any part of it. Particularly he disliked the lady-in-waiting whom he perceived to be her closest confidante, Francisca de Cáceres. According to Ambassador Fuensalida, Francisca saw Fray Diego for what he was; suspicious of his 'ambition and pride and lightness', she tried to mitigate his influence with the princess.[8] Marrying Francisca off would get her out of the way, and there was Grimaldi wanting a wife. If Fray Diego knew about the match between Grimaldi and María, he did not care. He turned matchmaker and brought the princess on side.

Fuensalida wrote nothing about Francisca's feelings, but it's likely she was as desperate to leave England as María was. We know almost nothing of her family situation in Spain, which may well mean that her parents were not of very high status or favour. A good marriage would have been difficult to arrange and Grimaldi's offer too good to turn down. Francisca is usually presented as domineering and scheming purely because she chose to marry a man instead of remaining with her mistress.[9] But loyalty was difficult for all of these women, and for Francisca especially, because Francisca was a spy. She sent news to the Spanish monarchs through letters written in cipher. According to an account written by her descendants, her skill at Latin meant that she acted as the princess's secretary, and was thus privy to more information than the other women. But her position came at a cost. She would wait in dread 'for hours' lest her letters be discovered, and she was allegedly threatened by Prince Arthur when he suspected her of writing about the princess.[10] It's easy to think of this as a betrayal of the princess's trust, and to paint Francisca as a villain. We prefer to think of ladies-in-waiting as entirely dedicated to their mistresses. But what had loyalty to Princess Catherine brought Francisca, María, or any of them? Seven years, so far, of poverty and isolation.

And so when Grimaldi flirted with Francisca over long summer days in 1508 she returned his attentions, and it was probably at this point that the match between him and María died a death. María's suspicions about Grimaldi were well founded, for he proved more than willing to turn the situation to his own advantage in a way that ultimately cost Francisca her position. When pushed to propose, Grimaldi asked Fray Diego how he was supposed to marry Francisca when he did not yet know what her dowry would be? The friar, most reprehensibly, told him to simply make out a warrant for however much he wanted, the princess would sign it and all would be well. Grimaldi thought he might as well try it on, and a warrant for 4,000 ducats was duly signed.[11]

Fuensalida was horrified. The princess's mother Queen Isabella, he said, had never given more than 2,000 ducats to any lady-in-waiting as dowry.[12] Francisca then wanted to have the wedding at court, as befitted her status as one of the princess's ladies. Fuensalida thought this was not such a good idea, since the princess didn't have the means to host those sorts of celebrations, and suggested that they have the wedding at his lodgings in London instead, which they did. This went down poorly with Fray Diego. He and Francisca had a stand-up row in public in front of the princess. Francisca then refused to make her confession to the friar, choosing instead to confess to Henry VII's own chaplain, an extremely public snub.[13]

This so infuriated the princess that she dismissed Francisca that very day. In her own version of events the princess claimed that the marriage had taken place against her will, and that Grimaldi had threatened to take her own dowry money if she did not promise an unusually large sum to Francisca.[14] Whether this was true or not is debatable. Grimaldi would have found it difficult to explain his actions to King Ferdinand had he done this, and evidence shows that he only ever received 1,000 ducats of the 4,000 promised.[15] Regardless, María had skilfully sidestepped an extremely volatile situation. If she had said yes to Grimaldi it might have been she facing the princess's wrath, not to mention finding herself married to such an unscrupulous opportunist. And yet this was cold comfort through another lonely winter. She had been deprived of yet another potential route home. Like her mistress, María was still unmarried; like her mistress, she was losing hope.

The wheel of fortune never did remain steady, and by 1510 María thanked God for it. The long, dark winter of 1508 had been King Henry VII's last. April 1509 had seen the kingdom rejoice at the accession of his son, the golden prince, King Henry VIII. The sticking points over Princess Catherine's dowry had only ever been plays for time; finally, she and her women could have their happily ever after. Even the sudden and violent rainstorm that soaked their gowns during the procession from the Tower of London to Westminster for the coronation could not dampen their spirits for long, for by now they were used to taking their blessings with a little salt.[16] The coronation ceremony – unfamiliar to María and the other Spaniards, since coronations had not been performed in Spain since the fourteenth century – had gone without a hitch.[17] Under the vaulted ceiling of Westminster Abbey, amid the soaring voices of the choristers and singing men, they knelt as one to their new queen, weighed down by their heavy crimson velvet gowns. The crowd were asked whether they would accept their new king and queen; shouts of 'Yea, yea!' filled the air. It must finally have sunk in that they were going to be ladies-in-waiting to the queen of England, fulfilling the role for which they had been sent here all those years ago.

Within a month, the many years of poverty were like a bad dream. King Henry VIII paid £840 in wages to 'the Spaniards', as well as £1,000 for the queen's debts.[18] The queen's household swelled to include English ladies-in-waiting, many of them very experienced. Having spent years moving between the many royal female households during King Henry VII's reign, they knew English court ceremony, factions and administrative processes inside out. While Catherine of Aragon and her Spanish women had eked out a miserable existence waiting for their lot to improve, her sister-in-law Princess Mary had been the principal royal woman at court, taking in many of her mother Queen Elizabeth of York's ladies after the latter's death in 1503. Now Queen Catherine's household took that place, and many of those same ladies-in-waiting came to join her.[19] Female experience like this played a vital role in the formation of a new queen's establishment. Catherine and her Spanish women were not entering this new phase blind and unaided.

By 1510 the household was no longer really Spanish at all. María herself had written in 1507 that she had no intention of remaining in England after the princess was married, and clearly others were of the same mind.[20] The majority of the Spaniards departed shortly after the coronation.[21] María's colleague Inés de Vanegas, daughter of the queen's old governess of the same name, remained, but almost immediately married an English nobleman, William Blount, Lord Mountjoy. This was a positive move – Henry VIII wrote to King Ferdinand of Aragon that he considered it 'very desirable that Spanish and English families should be united by family ties' – but it did mean that Inés most probably left the queen's service.[22] Another, Catalina Fortes, went home to become a nun in early 1510.[23] The only Spanish names routinely found amid ladies-in-waiting from this point are 'Elizabeth' Vergas – probably originally 'Isabel' – and María de Salinas herself.[24]

We don't know why she stayed. None of her letters from this period have survived. If her family were still trying to arrange a marriage for her in Spain, it did not materialise. Being one of so few Spaniards left placed María in an intimate position with the new queen. At this point there were three ranks of ladies-in-waiting, corresponding broadly with social status: the 'ladies', usually peeresses; the 'gentlewomen', who might be the wives of knights or gentry; and the 'chamberers', the lowest status and most menial position, usually women of gentle but not aristocratic status.[25] María was among the gentlewomen.[26] While we might expect a queen's closest friends (insofar as a queen could ever enjoy simple friendship) to be her highest-status ladies, this wasn't necessarily, or even usually, the case. María and Queen Catherine don't seem to have been especially close before 1509, but now it was a different story. Shared experience bound them together. María was one of the few women left who could remember Catherine's mother, and indeed Catherine probably remembered María's parents too. They could reminisce in Spanish, teach the English women their intricate 'blackwork' embroidery and, as wardrobe accounts show, María could tell English tailors and seamstresses how to make a proper pair of Spanish sleeves.[27]

Such intimacy could open ladies-in-waiting to deeply traumatic experiences. The winter of 1510 was a severe one, and even in palace rooms cocooned in woollen tapestries, carpets, velvet cushions and fur-lined coverings it was difficult to keep out the sharp frost. Ladies-in-waiting like María routinely shared a room and sometimes a bed with their mistress the queen when the king was not with her, especially in seasons of such icy cold. In the small hours of 31 January 1510 María found herself woken by groans of pain. Queen Catherine appeared to be in labour; but this was all wrong. She was only about seven months pregnant.[28] She hadn't even withdrawn into confinement yet, so nothing needful was ready. The queen's confessor later wrote that it was kept secret, and that the only people who knew of it were himself, the king, a physician and two Spanish women, one of whom was almost certainly María.[29] This means it must have happened overnight, before the queen rose in the morning, before there was anybody else to see her in pain and distress. This was just as well. For queens, miscarriages and stillbirths were shrouded with shame. What good was a queen who could not birth a live child? Such things were always her fault, not her husband's, and were considered suggestive of physical or even moral or spiritual defect.[30]

The court was at Westminster, and the queen's chambers were on the opposite side of the palace from the king and the rest of the court.[31] Nobody would hear or see anything that they should not, but this also meant there was some distance to go for help. No doubt the three women consulted in panic, and one flew for the physician. María must have been terrified. As an unmarried woman she had probably never witnessed a birth before, never mind known what to do. What would happen if they were the only ones present and the queen of England died?

It was kept secret. Only the king was told. 'Her Highness brought forth prematurely a daughter,' her confessor Fray Diego would write later, but what happened next was almost as heartbreaking.[32] Catherine's belly remained round and so she was told, and believed, that she was still pregnant with a twin of her lost daughter, a fiction that remained in place even though her periods resumed. Either Catherine didn't know enough about her own body to realise how unlikely this was, or she was so desperate to give birth to a healthy child, and probably so traumatised by her recent experience, that she was willing to convince herself that this was a fact.

In the midst of this, María had other pressures. Her elder brother Juan had come to England on business and to visit his sister. They hadn't seen each other in nine years, or even corresponded much. In 1507 she had written sarcastically, 'I hope that you will give me six years of patience to repay me all in one; Lord, you were willing to write to me at length.'[33] By 1510, things had apparently improved. Juan travelled first to Tours, was in Bruges by November, and warned their brother-in-law from there that he thought his business in England would keep him longer than originally intended.[34] Some of this business may have included María; the family had been dealing with various inheritance disputes for a number of years. By 6 February Juan had reached the royal court, then at Richmond. Awed, he described the white and gold turreted palace as 'a pleasure place of this king's'. He was, he said, 'feted' with many celebrations at his sister's behest, and was impressed by the esteem in which she was held, even as he was wary of spies reading his letters.[35] For her part, María was an accomplished actress. Juan wrote nothing of the queen or her situation because he clearly knew nothing to tell. María kept her mistress's secret even from her brother.

Nobody knew until May, when it became clear that Queen Catherine was not still pregnant and clear, therefore, that the storm must break. Even the Spanish ambassador – not Fuensalida any longer but Luis Caroz de Villaragut, who had arrived in the summer of 1509 – had not heard. He waxed scornful in a long letter to King Ferdinand's secretary. How Queen Catherine presumed herself still pregnant when her monthly bleeding had resumed was a mystery to him. Why on earth she had been made to go through the formal process of withdrawing into confinement to await the birth he could not fathom. What would happen now was anybody's guess. Royal councillors were directing their anger and frustration at 'the bedchamber women who gave the queen to understand that she was pregnant whilst she was not', rather than the queen herself or her male physicians, and perhaps Caroz was not surprised, having contemptuously described both the English and Spanish women in the queen's household as 'rather simple'.[36]

Much of Caroz's anger stemmed from his own feeling of impotence in the face of the all-powerful Fray Diego, the queen's conniving confessor, who was still in England by her side. Caroz had struggled since his arrival to get accurate information about what was going on in the palace, or to advise the queen or get her help for Spanish concerns, and he blamed the friar for this. It was a feeling shared by many. Francisca de Cáceres, having married financier Francesco Grimaldi and been summarily dismissed, had not regained her position. She remained in London, but without her husband, who was on his way back to Granada. Caroz knew all about Francisca's former situation as a Crown agent, but he didn't see this as a division of loyalties. He wrote that she was not only 'the most devoted' to the queen, but 'the most skillful for whatever suits the Queen or the King our Lord'. 'The friar', he noted grimly, 'fears her more than can be said.' Caroz wanted Francisca back in the palace, whether in the queen's service or not, for 'as soon as she is in the palace, she herself will recover her place, and even if she does not recover it, she will render the greatest services'. Without Francisca, he said plaintively, 'I do not know, as I ought to know, what passes there.'[37]

Queen Catherine, though, was an expert at holding a grudge. Even three years later, when Francisca was still in London and still seeking to regain her position in royal service, she would not have her back, and she would not help her former friend to enter anybody else's service either. In 1510 Caroz had wondered whether perhaps Francisca could serve King Henry's younger sister, Princess Mary. In 1513 this was still a possibility; Princess Mary, betrothed to Charles, Prince of Castile, would need to learn Spanish. Alternatively Francisca could perhaps go to Margaret, Duchess of Savoy. King Ferdinand thought either of these a good idea, no doubt because he wanted Francisca's skills as a loyal courtier.[38] But Queen Catherine refused to give Francisca a recommendation. She did not trust her, writing that 'she is so perilous a woman that it shall be dangerous to put her in a strange house'.[39] Queen Catherine expected complete fidelity from her ladies-in-waiting and nothing less would do, even if it was for the ultimate service of the Spanish Crown. In the end, Francisca's husband returned to England and took her and their son home to Granada.[40] Queen Catherine did not want her devotion.

1510 was a year of many lessons of loyalty, if the queen's women chose to learn them. The new regime of King Henry VIII took time to settle, and even without Francisca gossip spilled out beyond the palace. In May 1510 Caroz had more to report. Among Queen Catherine's ladies were two sisters of royal ancestry: Elizabeth Stafford, Lady Fitzwalter and Anne Stafford, Lady Hastings, first cousins of the late Queen Elizabeth of York, both in their twenties. Elizabeth was a courtier of long standing and she took her role seriously. She had been at Queen Elizabeth Woodville's funeral in 1492, had served Elizabeth of York and her daughter Princess Mary, and had moved seamlessly into Queen Catherine's household, leading the rest of the women through the coronation ceremony in 1509.[41] Her sister Anne was less experienced, having married early and lived away from the royal court. By 1510 she had been widowed and married again to a man with stronger court connections, so she joined the queen's household as a visiting peeress in 'extraordinary' (as opposed to 'ordinary') service. Where Elizabeth was serious, Anne was light-hearted and took her fun where she could find it. King Henry thought this an excellent idea. Elizabeth was not so sure. The spring seemed to have got into Anne's blood; she was behaving in a way that did not befit a married woman. What, Elizabeth wondered, did one do when the king, a married man with a pregnant wife, was illicitly courting one's sister, a married woman?[42]

Elizabeth's loyalty to her family won out. She spoke to their brother, Edward, Duke of Buckingham. It's often assumed that the families of women who caught the king's eye were flattered, or gleefully anticipating material gain. Not so the Staffords. The duke was not pleased. Stafford girls were not whores, even for the king of England. If the honour of the family was not to be dragged through the mud, this must be stopped.

It was decided that the duke would go and talk to Anne and find out the truth of the matter. But while he was in Anne's rooms, they were interrupted: William Compton, the king's most intimate attendant, arrived to speak to Anne in his capacity as go-between for the king. The duke erupted, and the quarrel between the two men was vicious, the duke reproaching Compton 'in many and very hard words'.[43] Inevitably, the king heard of this, and the duke was severely reprimanded. Unwilling to simply accept the situation, the duke played his trump card: Anne's husband George, Lord Hastings was informed. The very same night, Hastings removed his wife from court and placed her in a convent sixty miles away, the early modern equivalent of being told to go and stand in the corner and think about what you had done.

Henry was, predictably, incandescent with rage. That rage was directed at Elizabeth Stafford, whom he saw as a self-righteous, interfering gossip. A day later he turned her and her husband out of the palace. Had Elizabeth told the queen what she suspected, and did she also act out of loyalty to her mistress? For the queen's rage matched Henry's. Caroz didn't specify whether Catherine was angry about the dismissal of one of her favourites, or at her discovery that her husband was being unfaithful, but it may well have been both. For Henry it was all about the perceived power of women's eyes and tongues. He was angry at the brouhaha caused, as he saw it, by Elizabeth, but he was also paranoid. 'Believing that there were other women in the employment of the favourite,' Caroz wrote astutely, 'that is to say, such as go about the palace insidiously spying out every unwatched moment, in order to tell the Queen [stories], the king would have liked to turn all of them out, only that it has appeared to him too great a scandal.'[44]

Elizabeth's Stafford's ban was not permanent. She returned to court for various events in later years.[45] But she probably didn't serve the queen in 'ordinary', daily service again, and nor did her fun-loving sister Anne. We don't know whether Anne and Henry ever did carry their affair to its logical conclusion, but in either case she gained more by it than the king's fancy alone. Over a decade later in 1527 it transpired that she and William Compton, the king's go-between in this affair, had developed a close relationship as a result, so much so that Cardinal Wolsey denounced the pair of them for adultery.[46] When Compton died a year later, he left money in his will specifically to pray for Anne's soul as well as those of the king and queen, and he also left her the income from certain manors, which would have given her a small amount of financial independence.[47]

All women knew that this was worth having. Even Queen Catherine had suffered long and hard for lack of money, a pawn in the hands of men. If she felt bitter about her many years of misery under the late King Henry VII, former lady-in-waiting Jane Vaux, Lady Guildford was no whit behind her. Her late husband Richard Guildford had been one of Henry VII's most loyal and trusted supporters. He'd suffered attainder for him; been in exile with him; invaded England, fought many battles, kept the nation safe with his networks of spies. But he was a poor financial manager, and this was the one thing that Henry VII refused to overlook.[48] Jane had raised the royal children, taught them right from wrong, taken them to their marriages, mourned Prince Arthur's death along with his family, but such loyalty was worth nothing now. Richard Guildford, disgraced and removed from office, had embarked on a pilgrimage to Jerusalem and died there, far from home, in 1506. Jane had been left to deal with the fallout.

Four years later, in 1510, things were a little less desperate. Her connections with the king's mother Lady Margaret Beaufort had meant she'd been able to borrow money, and she'd inherited a substantial sum from that lady after her death the previous year.[49] Like Anne Stafford, Jane had been wise in making friends wherever she could find them, and one of those she found was the king's master of the horse, Sir Thomas Brandon. Sir Thomas's court service and royally sanctioned marriages with two wealthy widows had made him rich. His favourite house in Southwark was set back from the road amid private orchards and parkland on the major route into the south of the city of London, and he had plenty of time to enjoy it when he fell sick in 1509.⁵⁰ Jane did not care that he already had a wife. She sent her own servants to nurse him. As María tried to comfort the terrified, labouring queen on that freezing January night, Jane mourned: Sir Thomas had died.

But his death had also set her free. Sir Thomas didn't appear to care that he already had a wife either. His will provided for her dutifully, but, that out of the way, he focused his attention on Jane. She inherited all of his plate not otherwise bequeathed. She was to have the revenues of his estates in Norfolk and Suffolk, and others in Kent. Her servants were rewarded, her priest forgiven his debts, and the crowning glory: the beautiful house at Southwark was hers, with all of its priceless hangings, beds and carpets.⁵¹ If Sir Thomas's will raised any eyebrows, Jane ignored them; she had learned to take any advantage offered to her. Jane planned carefully. Sir Thomas's heir was his nephew Charles Brandon, a close friend of the new king's, and it would not do to alienate him. He wanted to live in the family house, and she decided to let him – for a costly rent.⁵² That would keep the wolf reliably from her door.

Still, like many others, she could not have thought of the late king's financial rapacity without anger. Two men in particular had been the king's instruments in enacting the kinds of policies that had brought Jane's family low, and at the height of a scorching summer they were finally to be brought to justice. Chancellor Richard Empson and royal attorney Edmund Dudley were so viscerally hated by Londoners that Dudley had taken the precaution of laying in a stock of weapons and employing extra men-at-arms at his opulent house in Candlewick Street.⁵³ It had availed him nothing. Before the old king's death had even been announced, both men had been quietly arrested and imprisoned in the Tower on charges of treason. There they had festered for over a year, scapegoats for an unpopular regime, protesting their loyalty, frantically insisting that they had only been following royal orders. Goaded by the continual demands for justice while on his summer progress, the king at last gave the order for their deaths.

In the early morning heat-haze of a bright August day, crowds of jeering Londoners watched as, one after the other, the last symbols of the old punitive regime were excised in a spray of blood. The savage satisfaction felt by one widow was mirrored by the grim resignation of another. Edmund Dudley's wife was now left, like Jane had been, to raise their children alone under the spectre of her husband's conviction for treason. Could this new reign really be different? Might royal service provide security once more? Or would loyalty, for women, always lead eventually to loss?

3

My Lord, My Husband

It was Shrovetide in the year 1512, and there was a new face at the Duke of Buckingham's dinner table. Lord Thomas Howard had travelled all the way from London to visit the family at Thornbury Castle in Gloucestershire, and he was here because he wanted to marry Elizabeth Stafford, the duke's eldest daughter.

The Howards were a family firmly on the rise again. In 1485 they had made a poor choice by fighting for the doomed King Richard III and had been stripped of their dukedom of Norfolk by the victorious Henry VII. Since then they had been doggedly clawing back royal favour until now the Earl of Surrey, this man's father, was lord treasurer of the realm, and Thomas and his brothers were among Henry VIII's closest companions.[1] It would not be a poor match. Thomas Howard was not particularly handsome, being small, more wiry than square, but he had an air of powerful determination. He looked out at the world from shrewd black eyes, and his peers were learning that it did not do to underestimate him. But Elizabeth was already betrothed. She and young Ralph, the future Earl of Westmorland, had grown close in the two years that he had been her father's ward, and she looked forward to marrying him later that year.[2]

Marriage, though, was not about emotions. The early modern aristocracy would have found our obsession with 'the one' unfathomable. Romantic love was even frowned upon and considered a dangerous obstruction to the things that really mattered. Girls like Elizabeth were raised to value the things that would give them the best future life and the most stability: wealth, property and position. Marriage was a business contract between two families, with financial terms quite literally drawn up in writing and signed by those who held the purse strings. Though Elizabeth's consent to the marriage was nominally required according to Church law, her signature on the secular agreement was not. Things were arranged for women, not by them.[3]

Twenty years later Elizabeth's letters reveal a forthright woman of strong character, uncompromising and sometimes fiery-tempered. In 1512, though, it was her father's opinion that was important, and Thomas Howard would brook no opposition to his suit for Elizabeth's hand. Immediately after his first wife's death in the winter of 1511 he had sent word to the duke's household, and now he was here to press his suit; 'he would have none of my sisters', Elizabeth later recalled, 'but only me'.[4] Howard was almost forty. Elizabeth was in her late teens.[5]

They may well have met before. Elizabeth's aunts, Elizabeth and Anne, were both ladies-in-waiting to Queen Catherine of Aragon, and the duke himself was regularly at court. Though there is no evidence that Elizabeth herself was yet in service with the queen, she will have visited and could easily have been introduced to Howard on such an occasion. This might explain why his mind turned to her when he was widowed. For teenaged Elizabeth, Howard's possessiveness was a sign of true love. Twenty years later she continued to insist that 'he chose me for love', proven by his refusal of her younger sisters.[6] Perhaps this was the only way in which she could come to terms with losing Ralph, her original betrothed. Howard, though, was almost certainly operating from a more practical, less romantic, standpoint. The legacy of his first marriage was a row of small graves and he had no surviving children.[7] He had seen first-hand the effect that this could have on a dynasty: King Henry VIII had just lost his own first son and heir, Prince Henry, after only fifty-two days, and the pressure on him and Queen Catherine was intense.[8] At forty years old, Thomas Howard needed a young wife to give him a healthy male heir as quickly as possible. Elizabeth was one of the most eligible brides in England, and she came with a dowry of 2,000 marks.[9] Of course he would not tell her any of this: any sensible girl would have known it already.

Howard's forceful approach was successful. By the end of the year they were married. Since it wasn't yet a legal requirement for churches to record marriages, we don't know exactly when the wedding took place, only that by mid-December 1512 she was referred to as 'Lady Howard' in a contemporary source.[10] The deed was probably done as soon as possible, because Howard knew that he was about to risk his life in the service of the realm. The king had been champing at the bit to make war on France since the moment of his accession, and finally he had what he wanted. Spain, Venice and the Pope had created an alliance, a Holy League, to put a stop to King Louis XII of France's intrusions into Italy, and Henry had joined that League in 1511. Alongside this, he had signed a treaty with King Ferdinand of Aragon to jointly invade Gascony.[11] Howard, an experienced military leader, was appointed second-in-command of the entire army. By early June of 1512 he was in San Sebastian in the north of Spain, not to return until November.[12]

No sooner wedded than abandoned by her new husband, Elizabeth's introduction to married life must have been disorienting in the extreme. At least she was not alone. She later wrote that she had served Queen Catherine of Aragon for sixteen years, off and on, and this is probably when her service began.[13] Though Elizabeth hadn't yet spent much time at the royal court, it was a logical place for her to be while her husband was away fighting. Stafford women had a history of royal service. Various women from her new marital family, the Howards, were also there to keep an eye on her. Many of the queen's women were in the same situation as Elizabeth: their courtier husbands had turned soldier with alacrity. War turned out to involve nearly as much waiting around as court service. The Holy League allies could not agree on an objective for the English army after their initial victory at Bayonne, and they were not given the food supplies or transportation promised by King Ferdinand. Forced to camp through a miserably wet summer, it was soon clear to them that the campaign was not conspicuously successful. Elizabeth's husband, writing to the king's advisors, warned of plague, and even mutiny.[14] The wives waiting at court feared widowhood.

Those fears were not unfounded. Elizabeth's new sister-in-law Muriel Howard, Viscountess Lisle, a courtier of many years' standing, had already been widowed once and was now married to Sir Thomas Knyvett, one of the king's jousting companions. Knyvett had been given command of the king's largest ship, *The Regent*, under the admiralship of his friend and brother-in-law Sir Edward Howard in the naval campaign designed to distract the French from the land assault in the south. In early August 1512 he was killed in action during a skirmish near the port of Brest. One hopes that Muriel never learned just how he died. Grappling with a French ship, somehow one of the powder magazines was set alight, causing an explosion so violent that 1,600 men burned to death or drowned. Admiral Sir Edward Howard was so distressed by his friend's death that he vowed to avenge it before he saw the king again.[15] But women had no scope for such violent retaliation. Pregnant, with small children to raise, all that Muriel could do was mourn.

Four months later on a cold winter's night, Muriel went into labour at the family's London home, Norfolk House in Lambeth, across the river from Westminster Palace. This time something went wrong. Amid the blood and the pain, she urgently dictated her last will, all her thought for her children: she bequeathed her three sons to the king and her two daughters to the queen, 'beseeching her grace to be a good lady to them'.[16] At the funeral ten days later, the procession took a deliberate detour so that the queen and her women might pay their respects to their colleague from the windows of Greenwich Palace, which overlooked the churchyard of Muriel's final resting place, the Greyfriars Monastery.[17] For Elizabeth, dressed in black and walking in the procession as one of the chief mourners, it must have been a sobering reminder that her new married life was by no means risk-free.

If Elizabeth had hoped that her own husband's part in the conflict was over, she was soon disappointed. The king intended to reinvigorate the campaign by joining it in person, and Thomas Howard was made Admiral in his dead brother Edward's place. Keen to prove himself worthy of a naval command, he chafed at restrictions laid on him and protested that he could think of no better service he could offer, unless the Scots or the Danes invaded.[18] Only a few months later he must have rued his apparent talent for prophecy. By June 1513 Henry VIII was in France, and he had left Queen Catherine as regent in England in his stead. On 12 August a Scottish herald delivered a formal 'defiance' to Henry VIII: King James was going to invade.[19]

Elizabeth will have known that it was a woman's task to defend her husband's property in times of conflict, but she may not have seen this first-hand. Now she had her chance. Though many months pregnant once again, Queen Catherine barely broke a sweat. Rather than let the Privy Council take the lead, she immediately took stock of supplies and signed warrants for armour, weapons and ordnance.[20] Thomas Howard sailed with part of the fleet to join his father on the Scottish border. Queen Catherine and – presumably – some of her female attendants prepared to journey northwards, but had only made it as far as Buckingham when news reached them of the decisive battle at Flodden.[21] Elizabeth's husband was covered in glory: according to some sources, it was he who had proposed the strategy to outflank the Scottish king, and it was certainly he who led the vanguard.[22] As was often the case for women, Elizabeth benefited from her husband's heroism. The queen had been careful to attribute the victory at Flodden to God, aware that the king had expected to be at the centre of any military glory and would not enjoy ceding that place to his wife. Inevitably, though, there was no getting away from the fact that she and the Howards had won a far bigger victory than the army in France. With the Scottish king dead and only his baby son on the throne, the threat from the north was effectively neutralised for a generation.

By February 1514 the survivors from both fronts were home. On Candlemas Day, in the Archbishop of Canterbury's red-brick palace at Lambeth, the leaders had their reward. Amid a crowd of nobles in their scarlet robes of estate, the queen and her ladies looking on, Elizabeth's father-in-law was elevated from the earldom of Surrey to the dukedom of Norfolk, the title that the family had lost back at Bosworth in 1485. In an attempt to equalise the two conflicts, the king made his friend and commander in France, Charles Brandon, Duke of Suffolk. To date, Elizabeth's own father, the Duke of Buckingham, had been the only duke in England: now there were three, and the balance of power would shift accordingly.

The ceremony wasn't finished. Elizabeth's own husband, Thomas Howard, stepped up and knelt in front of the king in his turn, to be created Earl of Surrey.[23] The glory was his, but Elizabeth was affected too. No longer Lady Howard, she was now the Countess of Surrey, and consequently higher in every procession, every list, every banquet. Elizabeth's star was firmly on the rise.

Wars and treaties were not only for boys with toys. Jane Vaux, Lady Guildford had seen their impact on women too, many times, for Jane was now past fifty. She had watched her own French mother flee into exile with Queen Margaret of Anjou, wife of Henry VI, as a direct result of war.[24] A trusted royal confidante and chaperone in her turn, she had escorted Princess Margaret to Scotland to marry King James IV in 1503. Beset by financial troubles after the death of her husband in 1506, Jane had retired from court service, and the generous bequests of her late friend – perhaps lover – Sir Thomas Brandon in 1510 had meant she could live quietly at Blackfriars.[25] She had raised her children and stepchildren to become courtiers in their turn: her son Henry and stepson Edward had just been at the king's side on the battlefield in France.

Jane might have thought that her days of formal service were over, but fate and the king decreed otherwise. This war had shifted Europe's diplomatic landscape. By 1514 ties to Spain had weakened and Charles, Prince of Castile had broken his betrothal to Jane's former charge, the king's younger sister Mary. This wasn't as inconvenient for England as it appeared, though, since now the peace treaty with France could be sealed in the most time-honoured fashion: eighteen-year-old Mary would marry the ageing French king, Louis XII. Princesses crossing borders to marry always took a complement of ladies-in-waiting with them, and it was usual for this to include an older woman, a mother-figure in the guise of governess. Jane was half French, and probably spoke the language. Either Mary asked, or the king had the thought by himself: Jane, Mary's 'mother Guildford', was told to leave her peaceful retirement and return to service.

Naturally, Mary already had her own household as a princess of England, and one might assume that sending her existing attendants to France with her was the easiest and most obvious course of action. This, though, was rarely what happened. A queen's household should reflect her new status, not her former position; it should include those of appropriate rank and experience, since this was one way in which the value placed on a diplomatic marriage was communicated. The nature of the surviving records makes it difficult to be sure who had been in Mary's service between 1509 and 1514, since there aren't any accounts for Mary's own establishment, but other records do provide some insight. Many of the women in Mary's service in 1509 had previously been her mother's ladies-in-waiting, and a number of them had continued to receive regular wage payments from Henry VIII: Elizabeth Catesby, Elizabeth Burton and Elizabeth Saxby, for instance.[26] It has sometimes been assumed that these women were Queen Catherine of Aragon's 'maids of honour' – young, adolescent women at court to finish their education and gain a degree of social polish – largely because the payments they received were the same as the salary of a maid of honour later on in the reign.[27] But the position of maid of honour doesn't seem to have existed in any formal sense yet, and even if it had they would have been paid by the queen, not the king, so these women must have belonged to Mary and not to the queen.[28] Most of them were also too old and too married to have been maids of honour in any case.[29] Their age and status is probably why they were not considered suitable to accompany Mary to France. In September 1514, a month before Mary's departure, the king granted them annuities – pensioned them off – 'for service to the late Queen Elizabeth of York, and to Mary Tudor'.[30] It was time for a changing of the guard.

It must have been stressful for Mary to start this new phase of her life with a new complement of ladies around her, particularly since she was not permitted to keep everybody that she wanted. The final choice was probably made collectively. While the king had the power of veto, it's reasonable to think that he was guided by Mary herself, perhaps also by the queen, and by those of the delegation seeking to place their own relatives in influential positions. A number of Mary's new companions were relatives of the Grey family, Marquesses of Dorset, who were prominent in her escort, and young Mistress Boleyn – probably Mary – was the daughter of the king's favourite diplomat, Sir Thomas Boleyn.[31] Mary's fiancé the French king also made his views felt. There was particularly heated debate about the inclusion – or rather, exclusion – of one of Mary's existing women: Jeanne Popincourt, a Frenchwoman, who had been in service with the English royal household since 1498, hired to teach the princesses French. From 1504 she was with Princess Mary exclusively, and from 1509 was paid her wages by the king along with the rest of Mary's women.[32] As a native speaker Jeanne was a natural choice for the trip to France, and Mary evidently wanted her there, since the Earl of Worcester wrote that Mary 'loved and trusted her above all the gentlewomen that she had about her'.[33] In 1513, though, Jeanne had begun a romantic affair with the Duke of Longueville while he was awaiting ransom in England as a result of the French war. The French king was horrified at the thought of a woman of such 'evil life' serving his new wife and reportedly said that he 'would she were burnt' rather than allow it. Mary had no choice but to give in.[34]

At least she had 'mother Guildford', who spent September sorting out the princess's wardrobe ahead of the journey.[35] The two surviving lists suggest that Mary also kept two of her chamberers, Anne Jerningham and either Alice Denys or Jane Barnes.[36] After elaborate preparations on both sides of the Channel, Mary and her party crossed to France at the unholy hour of four in the morning on 2 October 1514. They were formally received by King Louis in

Abbeville on 8 October, and the marriage took place there the next day. That night it was, allegedly, consummated, despite the ill-health of the groom.[37]

The next morning, shock, for both Mary and Lady Jane. Without warning, King Louis peremptorily dismissed all of his new wife's male English household, plus Jane and some of the other women, without discussion or explanation. This was highly irregular. Louis himself had approved the list of household staff intended to remain in France with Mary, and it was not a vast number by comparison with other queens. Why put everybody through those delicate negotiations if he intended to dismiss them immediately anyway?

The dispute quickly became focused on Jane. Mary was distraught at the loss of her 'mother Guildford', but in response to the English ambassador's entreaties King Louis claimed that Jane was interfering: 'She began to take upon her not only to rule the Queen, but also that she [Mary] should not come to him but she [Jane] should be with her; nor that no lady nor lord should speak with her [Mary] but she should hear it and begin to set a murmur and banding among ladies of the court.' If Mary needed counsel, he retorted, he could give it to her himself. He would not have either of them ruled by a woman.[38]

Louis' declaration says more about the political situation in his court and the perceived power of ladies-in-waiting to affect that than it does about Jane's behaviour. If Jane had been continually at Mary's side, she was simply doing her job. Everybody knew that Mary faced opposition at the French court. The dauphin Francis, heir to the throne, was the king's son-in-law and would therefore be supplanted if the king had his own son with Mary. His faction was so anxious over the prospect that they set women to spy; Francis' wife Claude was to remain outside Mary's chamber during the day, and Madame d'Aumont, a lady-in-waiting, was to sleep there at night.[39] Small wonder that Mary wanted the advice of someone like Jane who knew the French court, who spoke the language and who had English interests at heart, and small wonder that King Henry and his advisors had wanted her to have it.

Ironically, it was in King Louis' best interests for Mary to withstand the plotting of the dauphin's faction, but his fears about English interference were greater. Diplomatic marriages were as much about suspicion and distrust as they were about union. This was true on the English side as well. King Henry had begun his reign with a council made up of many of his father's advisors. By 1514 some of these were still on the roster, but other, newer ministers had since come to the fore, and among these was Thomas Wolsey. Now in his mid-forties, Wolsey was a large, meaty man with a keen eye, considerable administrative ability and a gift for networking. He'd risen through the ranks of the clergy to become royal chaplain, almoner and now cardinal, and this was matched by secular promotion as diplomat, royal councillor and, effectively, chief minister. There were no pies in which Wolsey did not have a finger, and few aristocrats who did not resent this. The son of a butcher, they felt, should never have risen so high.

Princess Mary fully understood these undercurrents and how to manipulate them. She wrote to both Cardinal Wolsey and to her brother King Henry asking them to secure 'mother Guildford's' return, and she blamed the Duke of Norfolk, the leader of the delegation to France, for allowing this to happen and for not acting in her interests: 'My lord of Norfolk hath neither dealt best with me nor yet with her at this time.'[40] She openly wished that Wolsey had been sent in his place. Wolsey and Norfolk were not on the best of terms and others there also saw this as a plot engineered by Norfolk to separate Mary from her political allegiances. If the match failed, Wolsey, as its architect, would be blamed, and this could serve Norfolk.[41] Such were the wheels within wheels of European court politics, all expressed through the treatment of one single lady-in-waiting: Lady Jane, 'mother Guildford'.

Wolsey immediately appreciated the gravity of the situation. He told Jane to stay where she was in Boulogne, and he wrote to the French king. He told Louis in no uncertain terms that 'you should for some time retain her in the queen's service and not so suddenly discharge her; for the king took her out of a solitary place, which she had meant never to leave, that she might go in the queen's service, and you will find her wise and discreet, whatsoever report may have been made to the contrary'.[42] It was rude, he implied, for the French king to so disregard the choice of the English king here, and discommode a woman who had come out of retirement to be of service. But Louis remained immovable. Jane was not permitted to return. Mary was forced to give way with as good grace as she could muster.

Missing from the sources are Jane's own feelings on the matter. We can't be sure that she had ever really wanted to re-enter royal service and go to France, but surely she cannot have been happy to be so summarily dismissed and to leave her charge alone to face the ravening she-wolves of the French court. The near-contemporary chronicler Edward Hall, indeed, tells us that some of the English women dismissed were so upset that 'some died by the way returning, and some fell mad'.[43] Jane was, at least, well rewarded. Mary had spent 600 French crowns on jewellery for the women that Louis had discharged, and she also asked Wolsey to 'be good lord' to Jane, which meant financial recompense.[44] Sure enough, on 21 November she was granted an annuity of £20, and in June the following year £40, 'for her services to the late King and Queen, and to Mary queen of the French and Margaret queen of Scots'.[45] She would not suffer for her service to the Tudors.

Jane's experience of suspicion, distrust and political faction in France was not unique to the French court. María de Salinas would have recognised it in England too, and not only from the English. Luis Caroz de Villaragut had been King Ferdinand of Aragon's ambassador in England since 1509, and he must have known María well. There were so few Spaniards left in the queen's house-hold that one would have thought they would naturally gravitate towards one another, and that Spanish ambassadors would have greeted their compatriots with pleasure. Not so. In December 1514, Caroz wrote to an Aragonese official complaining – not for the first time – that he couldn't get a decent foothold within Queen Catherine's household, that she wouldn't listen to him, and that she was therefore not aiding the Spanish cause. He was treated, he claimed, 'like a bull, at whom everyone throws darts'.[46]

One of the people he blamed for this was María. Hers was 'the worst influence on the Queen', and the queen loved her 'more than any other mortal'. This on its own would have been an issue if María blocked his access to the queen, but her connections made it worse; Caroz wrote that 'by means of Juan Adurza and Doña María de Salinas, Juan Manuel is able to dictate to the Queen of England how she must behave'.[47]

Spain, too, had its factions, and they had seeped beyond its borders. Like everybody else, Caroz understood that neither marriage nor distance lessened a woman's ties to her natal family, and the activities of certain of María's family members were not to the taste of the Spanish Crown. Her immediate family, the Salinas, were not the problem. They remained in service with Queen Juana of Castile and with King Ferdinand of Aragon. María's cousin Juan de Adurza, though, was a figure of suspicion.[48] The Adurza family also came from Vitoria, and were merchants and financiers like the Salinas. The relationship between the two families was well known; Juan Martínez de Adurza, a well-respected merchant and citizen, was in charge of managing María's own investments back home.[49] Around the same time as María left for England in 1501, her cousin Juan de Adurza had moved to the Low Countries, to operate as a financial reference point for Spanish merchant families running trading businesses.[50] While there he had fallen in with Juan Manuel, whom we have met before. The brother of Catherine of Aragon's former governess Doña Elvira Manuel and advisor first to Philip of Burgundy and after his death to his son Charles, Prince of Castile, he had long been on King Ferdinand's list of unwanted persons because he encouraged the Burgundian dukes in their aspirations for the Castilian crown.[51] Through his sister, Elvira, he had once manipulated Catherine of Aragon into declaring support for Philip of Burgundy against the interests of her father King Ferdinand, causing a diplomatic crisis and damaging her own situation in England.

Eight years on, times had changed, but Caroz was clearly

worried that this could happen again and that María was now Manuel's mouthpiece in Queen Catherine's household. In 1514 Prince Charles of Castile was fourteen years old and starting to choose his own advisors, and his own opinions. King Ferdinand naturally hoped to take the boy under his wing and inculcate a pro-Spanish, pro-Aragonese attitude, but there were others around Charles with a different agenda, and one of these was Juan Manuel. Now openly anti-Aragonese, Manuel was both hated and feared by King Ferdinand, who had spent much of 1513 and 1514 looking for legitimate ways to have him extradited to Castile and imprisoned.[52] It was Caroz's job in England to engender good relations between Henry VIII and King Ferdinand, but Henry's recent alliance with France was not good news for Spain. Naturally, he had an eye out for anybody who might be poisoning the English king against the Spanish.

There's no direct evidence that María was doing any such thing. If she were indeed in contact with her cousin Adurza, there is nothing to show that he and Manuel were explicitly or deliberately using her to influence the queen of England, nor that she was consciously complicit in such an enterprise. That Caroz thought it to be true, though, shows that this perception of the power of women to influence monarchs behind the scenes was a Europe-wide phenomenon: ladies-in-waiting were not considered mere decorative extras. Caroz was also worried that 'the few Spaniards who are still in her [Queen Catherine's] household prefer to be friends of the English, and neglect their duties as subjects of the King of Spain'.[53] But María's and the other Spaniards' survival in England depended on their relationships here. This was a loyalty tug-of-war that they were never going to be able to win.

Catherine of Aragon herself helped to cement the impression of María as someone of consequence when she wrote to her father at the end of 1515 asking him to aid María as one who had 'faithfully served her, and who has always comforted her in her hours of trial'.[54] Though she didn't say what María needed from him, later events make it fairly certain that this was to do with María's next adventure. She needed her legacy from the late Queen Isabella, her dowry money, because she was finally and belatedly going to get married.

We don't know why it hadn't happened sooner. María's surviving letters don't reach beyond 1509; there's no way to tell whether her family had continued to try to arrange a Spanish match for her after this time, or whether they and she had simply accepted that she would remain in England indefinitely. Marriages could certainly take time to enact. María's brother-in-law Ochoa de Landa had been trying to get her younger sister Inés married since at least 1508, and had only succeeded in 1513.[55] How had María felt, hearing about the endless negotiations and eventual success from a distance? By 1513 she was about thirty years old, well beyond the age at which most ladies-in-waiting were married. She must have watched most of her peers at court fret over the safety of their husbands in the conflicts with France and Scotland and felt both thankful and self-conscious about the stark void between their lives and hers. She must, too, have wondered what on earth her future might look like without a husband and children; there was not much scope for single noblewomen who were not widows.

The queen's letter, though, suggests that by the winter of 1515 the winds of change were blowing. Not much is known about María's intended husband. His name was William, Baron Willoughby of Eresby. He and María were of an age, but he had already been married and widowed once and had no surviving children. Like many nobles, he had fought in the war with France over the last couple of years, but he wasn't one of the king's especial friends, perhaps because he did not generally take part in jousts or other celebrations in London. His life revolved primarily around his estates and networks in Lincolnshire and East Anglia, where he seems to have been well liked and respected.[56] María, as we know, had her priorities firmly in order where marriage was concerned, and must have felt that this was a match of sufficient financial and social status to guarantee her the security and stability that she needed as a woman in the sixteenth century. In turn, her court networks would be useful to him.

Their marriage took a little time to arrange, perhaps because

Catherine of Aragon was pregnant once again and went into confinement in January 1516. Since that first terrifying experience of premature stillbirth in January 1510 – dreadful for both the queen and for María, who was almost certainly one of the three people to witness it – they and the rest of the queen's women had become unhappy experts in matters of early pregnancy and its loss. By this point Catherine had carried and lost at least five children, and the anxiety surrounding each pregnancy must have been almost intolerable.[57] Reaching the stage of confinement was itself a cause for celebration, but everybody was well aware that things could still go horribly awry. This birth, though, was blessedly straightforward. Queen and court were at Greenwich, and a healthy baby girl, Princess Mary, made her appearance at four in the morning on Monday, 18 February 1516.[58]

María was no doubt engaged in helping to care for the queen around this time, and this might have delayed her marriage, particularly if she needed Catherine to advocate with the Spanish royal treasury for her. There was, too, another equally pressing question about María's future. If she were going to marry an Englishman, it was tantamount to admitting that she was never going back home to Spain. This was not a small thing to come to terms with. Almost all of the other Spanish women who had come to England with them in 1501 had since returned home and married there. Even now, in late May 1516, French lady-in-waiting Jeanne Popincourt – she of 'evil life' whom King Louis had refused to allow in his wife's household – returned home with a handsome parting gift of £100.[59]

At some stage in early 1516, though, María paid a fee and swore an oath of allegiance, and on 29 May she received letters patent – signed by, or on behalf of, the king – declaring her official denization in England.[60] This was something akin to the status of permanent residency today, and it meant that she was not quite an English subject, and not considered naturalised English, but likewise no longer officially an 'alien' – a foreigner – in the eyes of the law. This was necessary in order for her to marry an Englishman. She now had rights that foreigners did not under English law, including the right to hold land, which she would need in order to survive if she were widowed.

This secured, the wedding could go ahead. The match was sponsored by the monarchs; Queen Catherine gave María a dowry of 1,100 marks, and Henry VIII granted the pair the manors of Grimsthorpe, Southorpe and Edenham in Lincolnshire.[61] The king himself attended their wedding on 5 June 1516, which makes it likely that the queen was there too.[62] Married at long last, María's whole identity underwent a nominal shift. No longer María de Salinas, Spaniard, she was now Mary, Lady Willoughby, English wife. María's future finally seemed secure.

4

Richly Beseen

The spring of 1517 was a hard one. It arrived in the wake of an unusually vicious winter; the court had been marooned at Greenwich for a month, trapped by the frozen River Thames.[1] It was some time before the queen's women were able to remove the fur linings from their gowns, exchanging heavy velvet for lighter-weight satins and silks, and the country was still in the grip of a long drought.[2] There were worries about the state of European diplomacy and, not unrelatedly, the lack of an English male heir, but the monarchs could not afford to appear openly anxious. Lavish celebrations were often used to project a sense of airy unconcern, as well as to give the court some much-needed levity. The king ordered a May Day joust.[3]

For young women like Elizabeth Blount, this was an opportunity. While only men would participate in the joust itself – women did not mount horses to hit one another with sticks – there was usually some sort of accompanying theatrical entertainment where the queen's women took the starring roles. In 1515 the May Day celebrations had taken the form of an adventure into 'the woods' with Robin Hood's outlaws, at Shooter's Hill in London. The queen's women had played character parts, 'Humility', 'Pleasance', and Lady May herself, riding on horseback and singing to the king as they carried him off to Greenwich in front of crowds of revellers.[4] These events must have been nerve-wracking. Elizabeth and her fellow maids must have shuddered at the thought of missing a step or a note in front of such an audience even while they hungered for the chance to be seen. For not all of the queen's women could be chosen for the plum parts, and the court must always put its best face forward. Only the prettiest, the most elegant dancers, those who could memorise lines and stage directions and not freeze with fright, would be given a part.

Fortunately, Elizabeth had all of these skills in abundance. Better known to us and to her contemporaries as 'Bessie', she had joined the court in 1513 and had dazzled in many revels since, even dancing with the king himself at New Year in 1515.[5] By now a reputed beauty, Bessie was also known for her particularly sweet singing voice and her literary interests, and was perfectly positioned to attract the attention of eligible court bachelors.[6] No doubt she hoped for another starring role in the May Day celebrations of 1517.

If she hoped, she hoped in vain. May Day revelry became violently twisted when habitual xenophobia escalated into a full-blown riot in the city of London. For some time, English merchants had been complaining that foreigners were replacing them in their jobs, their trades and their position in society, and then boasting about it. As the City authorities turned a blind eye, the Venetian ambassador rode to the king on 30 April with news of impending violence. But it was too late. On the eve of May Day, all hell broke loose. Stones were thrown, clubs swung and fires started at foreigners' lodgings in the east. Sir Thomas Parr, whose house was at Blackfriars, fled on horseback to warn the royal household, ten miles west at Richmond. A host of armed nobles was scrambled, but by the time it got there the riot had already fizzled out and hundreds of malcontents were on their way to prisons throughout the city.[7]

The May Day celebrations at court were cancelled. No doubt Bessie and her fellows were disappointed, but there were some in their midst who must have felt stronger emotions. María de Salinas, now Lady Willoughby, was almost certainly at court with the queen when the news arrived. María was married to an Englishman now, with an English title, anglicised name and English denization. But that did not make her less of a Spaniard, and as a Spaniard she had certainly experienced the 'envy of the English'.[8]

How did she feel, hearing that the Spanish ambassador's house had been attacked and that a Portuguese diplomat had barely escaped with his life?[9] Italian merchants, too, had been particularly singled out; if she had married Francesco Grimaldi as he had wanted a decade ago, she might have been an object for the mob's fury.[10]

The rioters were punished harshly, far more harshly than was usual. The king was frightened – evidence suggests he may have thought himself personally threatened by what he saw as an insurrection – and, therefore, he was furious. Foreign merchants were necessary to the English court as suppliers of luxury goods. More seriously, attacks on foreign merchants might be taken as attacks on the king's international allies, jeopardising diplomatic relations at a sensitive time. The rioters were thus indicted on this basis before being hanged, drawn and quartered all over the city.[11] What's not usually remembered is that the king's own wife was a foreigner, and so were a number of her household like María. The harsh reprisals could well have been intended as a statement about this too, the riots taken partly as an attack on the queen, and therefore on the king's honour. Perhaps the many executions were designed to reassure the queen and her court as well as the king's European allies.

Bessie Blount had hoped to be noticed at the May Day joust. In the event, María, instead, must have felt uncomfortably seen.

Bessie needed new clothes. Her outer gowns could be worn more loosely, the lacing adjusted as required, but her linen undergarments, her kirtle and her stomacher, would no longer stand the strain of her growing figure.[12] It was 1519, and Bessie was pregnant.

She wasn't the only one. The queen's last pregnancy had ended tragically in another stillbirth the previous November, but in a strange juxtaposition three of her ladies-in-waiting would give birth during 1519: Bessie, but also María de Salinas, Lady Willoughby and Elizabeth Stafford, Countess of Surrey.[13] Pregnancy was a source of joy and even of pride, and so pregnant women at court wore their gowns loose-laced, their condition emphasised by belts or jewelled chains.[14] Display – being seen – was the *raison d'être* of a lady-in-waiting, as fertility was for a married woman. But Bessie wasn't married. Her beauty and her skills as a courtier had attracted attention as planned, but her suitor was not an unmarried bachelor: it was the king of England himself.

Sleeping with the king wasn't as common for ladies-in-waiting as we tend to think it was. Henry is thought to have pursued his wife's women before – witness Anne Stafford, Lady Hastings, in 1510, whose brother had sent her away from court to prevent the scandal – but though in France the king's mistress held an official position (*maîtresse en titre*), in England such affairs were kept relatively private, which means that evidence is thin on the ground.[15] What we do know is that Henry liked to pursue, and to feel as if the lady had a choice. He liked to be chosen, not to force. In 1518 he was handsome, athletic and charming when he wanted to be – Europe's 'golden prince' – so, though we don't know how Bessie felt, there is no reason to assume that she was reluctant. Whether it was a good idea was another matter. Historically, royal mistresses might gain considerably, whether materially or in terms of political influence. Once their tenure ended and the king moved on, or – worse – once the king died, though, their position could be precarious in the extreme.[16] While sometimes the king might arrange a marriage for an ex-mistress that was better than she could have managed alone, this was by no means a guarantee, and if he did not, who would touch damaged goods? In 1518 Henry had not yet had any long-standing mistresses. Nobody knew what this might do to Bessie's future prospects.

In the short term she received very little. Any gifts were not recorded, and her male relatives were not rewarded in the way that mistresses' families were later on in the reign.[17] All that she had was the king's attention and his child in her belly. These affairs were usually open secrets at court. If it was awkward for Bessie and Queen Catherine to continue to work together, they didn't show it and nobody commented. But there were limits. Most pregnant courtiers continued to serve until it was time to withdraw into confinement and await the birth, usually four to six weeks before the baby was expected.[18] This is probably what María, Lady

Willoughby and Elizabeth, Countess of Surrey did. But Bessie's baby was born in June 1519 and her last recorded court appearance was in October 1518, which suggests it was not considered appropriate for her to stay at court while she carried the king's child.[19]

Bessie's world pivoted around her. As the king's mistress she had been extremely visible, but now she was hidden, treated as a shameful secret. Most likely she was sent to Blackmore Priory near Ingatestone in Essex, where she would later give birth.[20] It's possible that she, María and Elizabeth all retired into confinement in the general East Anglia area at roughly the same time, for we know that María went to Parham Hall in Suffolk, and Elizabeth's family home outside London was Tendring Hall on the Essex-Suffolk border.

It could have been difficult for the queen to lose three of her ladies at once, but the system of service was well oiled and their places would temporarily have been filled by ladies-in-waiting 'in extraordinary'. By 1519 the queen's women were still broadly set in three ranks: ladies, gentlewomen, and chamberers, plus the six maids of honour under the mother of the maids.[21] In fact, the royal household had been gradually expanding since the beginning of the reign. Like most large organisations, it was by nature a place of slight administrative chaos. Some people were paid wages, some had no salary but were entitled to 'bouche of court', i.e. food, lodging, fuel and light, some people had both, some neither, and some were merely 'hangers-on'.[22] In the 1510s ladies-in-waiting might belong to any of these categories. Bessie, as one of the maids of honour, was entitled to full bouche of court alongside her fellow maids. María, Lady Willoughby also received bouche of court in her own right, and those of her 'chamber' – her servants – too.[23] Elizabeth, Countess of Surrey's situation was less clear; though she served the queen, her husband was entitled to lodging on the king's side, so Elizabeth was accommodated with him, and her status as a peeress meant that she received no further salary.[24]

While the queen's 'side' of the royal household had been relatively stable since the start of the reign, the king's side had seen greater changes in the interests of keeping up with foreign rivals.

Royal households elsewhere, especially in France, were bigger, glossier, with more people and greater magnificence, and Henry needed to compete. Thus in 1519 he formalised the position of 'gentleman of the privy chamber' to match the French *gentilhomme de la chambre*, thereby conveniently creating a clear role for the young noblemen floating about the court known as the king's 'minions'. The queen had a privy chamber too, of course, but it seems to have functioned a little differently; while the king used his as a space for display and thus for politics, only the queen's women had access to hers without prior approval.[25]

Noblewomen experienced the same seclusion when they withdrew into confinement to await childbirth. María and Elizabeth would have spent considerable time and energy preparing the birthing chamber with appropriate furnishings and textiles, purchasing new linen and borrowing items from friends, as was customary. In the 1530s, Honor, Viscountess Lisle borrowed a bed from the Countess of Rutland, a counterpane, sheets and other textiles for it from the Countess of Sussex, and even sought to borrow an altar cloth from the royal wardrobe itself for the christening.[26] All three women would have arranged their own confinement in imitation of royal proceedings. The room would be made dark, warm and cosy with tapestries, carpets and curtains. Confinement was meant to be a time of rest, but it was also a time of fear. Childbirth did not discriminate, and women of all social statuses were well aware that they might not survive the experience.[27]

The best that María, Elizabeth and Bessie could do was to secure the services of an experienced midwife, and here again they borrowed from friends, or used recommendations. Once labour started, she became the centre of their world. Other married women would have arrived for emotional, religious and sometimes practical support – childbirth was a powerfully female experience – but for María, Elizabeth and Bessie the midwife was their crutch. Only she had the skill to change the baby's position, to ease the mother and coach her through the experience. They would each have been given caudle, a thick, hot drink of ale or wine mixed with spices and honey, thought to dull the pain and give strength, and the midwife might administer herbal remedies to help with lubrication, fatigue and pain management. At St Lawrence Priory, Tendring Hall and Parham, women prayed with and for Bessie, Elizabeth and María, calling on the Virgin Mary, St Anne and St Margaret. Our women might have clutched beads of coral, jet or amber, thought to speed labour and quell the pain of contractions. They might also have borrowed holy relics from local churches or abbeys: a birthing girdle or vellum, inscribed with prayers and images for visualisation, blessed by a priest and laid over the labouring woman's belly. Prayer cadences circled around the room: 'she shall hastily be delivered with joy without peril, the child to have Christendom and the mother purification of Holy Church'.[28]

Joy without peril. All three women came through their ordeal safely. Inside the rosy red-brick walls of Parham Hall, comfortably ensconced in the Suffolk countryside, María gave birth to a baby girl whom she named Katherine, for her mistress the queen.[29] The child would have been washed by the midwife and then wrapped securely in soft linen swaddling bands so that her limbs would grow straight. She would then have been handed to the wet nurse, whom María had chosen for her good character and robust physical health, traits that would, it was thought, be passed to the child through the milk. Noblewomen did not breastfeed. Their status, in fact, meant that all three of our women would have been given plenty of time to recover, much of it spent lying in bed in the birthing chamber while others handled the domestic and estate management. After forty days they were 'churched' at a service of thanksgiving for their safe delivery, and thus welcomed back into society as new mothers.[30]

Katherine may not have been María's first or only child. After three years of marriage, it's possible that there was an older sibling in the nursery or, if not, that her parents might have preferred her to have been a boy.[31] Elizabeth, Countess of Surrey was under less pressure. She had already had two, possibly three children, one of whom was the longed-for son and heir. Now, in 1519, she too gave birth to a baby daughter: Mary, perhaps named for the princess. Daughters of courtiers tended to become courtiers in their turn, as María, daughter of a lady-in-waiting, knew well. Perhaps Katherine and Mary would grow up to serve future queens.

Both María and Elizabeth could expect to return to court service. For Bessie Blount this was less certain. Royal mistresses were not automatically removed from their posts if they bore the king's children – a little later, Mary Boleyn may have done just this and returned to court – but all depended on the whim of the king. Henry did visit Bessie at Blackmore Priory during her pregnancy. One of his favourite country houses, the palace of New Hall, was only a few miles away, and this was probably not an accident.[32] No doubt he was pleased when Bessie gave birth to a healthy baby boy in early summer, more pleased than the prior, who had probably had to clear out of his house next door to the priory when it was commandeered for Bessie's confinement.[33] The child was immediately named Henry and given the traditional surname 'Fitzroy', a formal acknowledgement of his status as a royal bastard, but no public announcement was made and Bessie did not return to court.

Almost twenty years after her arrival on English soil, María was about to leave it for the first time. The court was at Dover, lodged in the castle, en route to France. The Treaty of London, signed by Henry VIII back in 1518, had stipulated that the French and English kings should meet in person, and finally this was going to happen. Before that, though, María was taking an arguably bigger step: she was selling her remaining property in Spain, her inheritance, to her younger sister Isabel. It made sense. There was no point in her keeping property she would never visit, or holding onto income that would be better reinvested in England. No doubt she felt a twinge of regret anyway. Spanish women inherited, owned and administered property in their own names, whether or not they were married, but in theory María couldn't do these things as a married woman in England.[34] Here she was under coverture, legally invisible, seen only as her husband's possession.

She had held onto her share of the family inheritance for four years since marrying William, Lord Willoughby, which suggests it held emotional as well as material resonance for her. Letting it go was tantamount to admitting not only that she was never going to return to Spain to live, but that she had now lost the agency that she would have had there.

What she was selling were her *juros* – akin to government bonds where the profit was the interest gained – inherited from her parents, to the value of 5,000 *maravedis*, plus 2,000 *maravedis* more in investments and property in their home city of Vitoria.[35] There were also household goods, furniture and even jewels. A surprising number of people were involved in the transaction. A Spanish notary had come to England expressly to handle the sale. On 30 May 1520, the document acknowledging the sale and María's receipt of the final amount, a respectable 330,000 *maravedis*, or c. 800 ducats, was witnessed by the queen's trusted Spanish servant Francisco Felipez.[36] A day later, the financial logistics of the sale were laid out and attested to in another document.[37] María's sister Isabel had paid the money to Martín Ibánez de Marquina in Vitoria, who was the uncle of Catherine of Aragon's physician, Fernán López de Escoriaza. Escoriaza had then paid the money to María, exchanging *maravedis* for English pounds along the way.[38] This document was witnessed by another of the queen's Spanish servants, Ochoa de Salzedo, plus the Windsor herald, and a man named Henry of Dover, servant of a Spanish courtier then in Dover.[39] Finances, clearly, were a man's business, but it would appear that the money María gained from this sale remained hers alone. In 1522 she was assessed for tax as an individual, as though she were operating as a *femme sole*, a sole woman, not subject to the rule of coverture that rendered most married women non-existent in the eyes of the law, and it's likely that this money was the reason for that; a small slice of financial power and visibility in a male-dominated world.[40]

As María signed away her Spanish past in Dover Castle, everybody who was anybody was in the town, waiting in the salt air and brisk spring breeze to cross the Channel. There was to be a seventeen-day orgy of feasting, dancing, sports and general one-upmanship between the English and the French courts near the city of Guînes, not far from Calais, a meeting that would become known as the Field of Cloth of Gold. María and the other women had probably had to overhaul their wardrobes. Queen Catherine naturally wanted her retinue to rival the French queen's, particularly since she was not at all in favour of a French alliance. In fact, she had engineered a brief meeting between her husband and her nephew Charles V, Holy Roman Emperor, on the Kent coast before the English court embarked for France, which was why there was a Spanish notary readily available to conduct María's property transaction.

The fleet mustered to take the English court and its accoutrements to France must have been the biggest that María had yet seen. Estimates made in advance suggest that the queen's retinue alone was comprised of some 1,175 people, a significant number of whom were women. Richard Wingfield, the ambassador in France, had written to reassure Henry that he could bring as many women as he could find. 'They which shall be meet for such an assembly may frankly come without any refuse,' he wrote, adding wryly, 'I never saw your Highness encumbered or find fault with over-great press of ladies.' On the other hand, though, he was also careful to tell Henry that the French intended to bring their best-looking women and urged Catherine of Aragon to do likewise, 'that the visage of England, which hath always had the praise, shall not at this time lose the same'.[41]

Many people there thought the French more richly dressed and thus finer-looking than the English, who were characterised by one commentator as 'well-dressed but ugly'.[42] Nevertheless, their presence was more than simply decorative. The women, as so often, were the focus for display and magnificence, there to be seen, a crucial feature of competition. María accompanied Queen Catherine to watch the jousts and to entertain King Francis I and his gentlemen at a banquet in the queen's hall, while Henry was likewise feted by Queen Claude of France and her women. Their job was to create an environment in which everybody could have fun, and perhaps allow diplomatic conversation to take place in a more relaxed, less formal way. They seem to have excelled, since it was noted that the Frenchmen were 'making merry' with the English women, and vice versa. Anne Browne, one of the English maids, danced with the French king and was described as 'an accomplished woman, and the handsomest in the company'.[43] After dinner, King Francis travelled the length of the hall on both sides 'and kissed the ladies and gentlewomen one after another . . . saving four or five that were old and not fair standing together', a lapse in chivalry that did not go unnoticed.[44]

While María was at Dover waiting to board a ship for France, Elizabeth Stafford, Countess of Surrey was on the other side of the country, eyeing the Irish Sea dubiously. A month previously her husband had been appointed the new Lieutenant of Ireland, and he had chosen to take his family with him to Dublin, meaning that Elizabeth temporarily left her position in the queen's household. While we don't know how she felt, it's hard to imagine that she was happy about this even without the prospect of missing the biggest party of her court career. The king's rule of Ireland existed more in theory than in practice, and Ireland, like most border regions at this time, was considered by the English to be a wild and barbaric realm, full of uncivilised peoples. Not only would the family be away from the centre of royal patronage and favour, opening the way for Surrey's enemies to talk him down, but no Lieutenant was ever given sufficient resources to properly subdue the country.[45]

Quite what Elizabeth thought, or how she and her several small children found Ireland, is not documented. It was certainly an adventure. She and her family would have lodged in Dublin Castle and would probably not have ventured outside the city, the safe 'Pale' of Dublin. Frighteningly, in August 1520 sickness was rife. Surrey wrote that 'There is marvellous death in all this country, which is so sore that all the people be fled out of their houses into the fields and woods, where they in like wise die wonderfully; so that the bodies lie dead, like swine, unburied.' He requested permission to send Elizabeth and the children into

Wales or Lancashire, where they could 'remain near the seaside until this death cease'.[46] It seems that the request was refused, since they were still in Dublin two months later.[47] The life of a lady-in-waiting, wife and mother was not always one of glitz and glamour.

Elizabeth was not the only Howard woman to miss out on the festivities in France, for England could not be left completely deserted. Her father-in-law, Thomas Howard, 2nd Duke of Norfolk, was made the king's deputy, head of the council, a position of trust and honour. His wife Agnes, Elizabeth's stepmother-in-law, had her own diplomatic role to play. With only a day's warning, three French ambassadors came to court to visit the Princess Mary, and Duchess Agnes had to scramble to produce enough noblewomen to attend her so that the appropriate impression of magnificence was maintained. She would have been justified in feeling annoyed. The French king was busy with their own monarch in France. Why send ambassadors now, unless to try to catch the English out with their court empty, their princess neglected? In the event, Agnes' presence saved the day; as the highest-ranking noblewoman below the royal family, three of her daughters by her side, nobody could say that the French, or indeed Princess Mary, had been slighted.[48]

In 1522, three years after the birth of her son – the king's son – Bessie Blount left their home in Essex to begin a new chapter. Her affair with the king was over. Her son Henry had his own nurseries and was as well cared for as any legitimate prince of the realm could be. There were rumours that Henry was on the cusp of beginning a new dalliance, and thus it was time for Bessie to be settled. She was to marry Gilbert Tailboys, who was part of Cardinal Wolsey's retinue, and it's likely that Wolsey was responsible for arranging the marriage on royal orders. Tailboys was only a few years older than Bessie, and apparently perfectly happy to marry the king's former mistress. Indeed, the two probably already knew one another. The Tailboys family were from Lincolnshire, of greater status and wealth than Bessie's own, and the couple were given land by the king.[49] Her position as a royal mistress had not damaged Bessie's prospects. If anything, she had gained by it.

It's not often noticed that Bessie had achieved the goal of most young women who came to court: to make a good marriage. Families went to great and sometimes impolitic lengths to secure this. Even royal women weren't above a clandestine wedding. King Henry's sister Mary, who had married the French king, Louis XII, in 1514, had been widowed only a few months later. Mary had carefully plotted her own future before she had even left England, extracting a promise from her brother that after Louis she might marry whom she chose. In fact she had already selected the king's close friend Charles Brandon, Duke of Suffolk, as her next husband, and both Wolsey and the king were aware of this. Politically astute, she played a strong game: knowing that neither would want her to marry a Frenchman, she stirred up their anxiety, so that Brandon might be seen as the better alternative. He led the embassy sent to bring her home. When he arrived, Mary dismissed her French attendants and re-engaged those English who remained in France, that she might be sure of their loyalty, and then she persuaded Brandon to do the one thing that Henry had explicitly said they were not permitted to do: they married in secret before returning to England.[50]

It's likely that Mary's English women knew about this. Among them was Lady Anne Grey, a young courtier who had come to France with Mary and married a younger son of the Earl of Dorset who was also part of the retinue. Anne returned to England with the newlyweds, and watched them ride the wave of King Henry's anger. Royals were not allowed to marry without the king's permission, because their marriages could affect the succession of the throne. Suffolk had to grovel mightily to allay Henry's suspicions that his best friend might be making a bid for royal inheritance; collectively they seem to have decided it was safer to place the blame on Mary, who might more easily be forgiven.[51]

And so it came to pass. By 1517, the couple were back in such favour that Queen Catherine came to visit them in Suffolk in March. Lady Anne Grey was still in Mary's service, but she was now a widow. The queen's visit was an opportunity for her to see her stepmother, Mary Scrope, Mistress Jerningham, who was one of the queen's ladies. But they had more on their minds than a simple social call. Mistress Jerningham used the trip to enact an illicit betrothal between Lady Anne and royal ward John Berkeley, then in Suffolk's household.[52] Perhaps, having seen her mistress successfully marry whom she chose, Lady Anne and her stepmother thought it worth risking the king's anger. Suffolk himself was horrified, writing to Wolsey that he would rather have lost £1,000 than that this should have happened in his house when the king trusted him with young Berkeley; but the damage was done, the ladies had won and the betrothal stood.[53]

Ordinarily, the king had no objection to attending and even sponsoring the weddings of ladies-in-waiting. In the spring of 1520 maid of honour Mary Boleyn, daughter of the king's favourite diplomat Sir Thomas, was married to one of the king's own gentlemen of the privy chamber, William Carey, with the king himself in attendance.[54] At the Field of Cloth of Gold that summer, Mary and her sister Anne had both been present, but on opposite 'sides'. Sir Thomas Boleyn's diplomatic contacts had secured for Anne a place in Margaret of Austria's court and then in the household of the French queen, Claude.[55] By 1522, both Boleyn sisters were among Queen Catherine's maids in England. Kinship relations within the royal household and even across European courts were common, and Anne Boleyn had been brought back to England because it looked like she might be married to the heir to the earldom of Ormond in Ireland. This came to nothing, and in the meantime she joined the queen's household, probably thanks to her mother's position there.[56]

Anne became one of several girls trying to make their mark at court during the 1520s. With King Henry around, this was not notably difficult. In March 1522 ambassadors from Flanders were in town, and Cardinal Wolsey asked the queen to help him provide entertainment for them. Together they concocted a pageant called the *Château Vert*, green castle, whereby eight 'good' feminine virtues would defend the castle, literally a castle built at the chamber's end, against eight 'bad' characteristics, played by boy choristers from the chapel royal, and eight lords. Competition for the parts must have been intense, but the Boleyn sisters were equal to it. Beauty, Honour, Perseverance, Kindness, Constancy, Bounty, Mercy and Pity were played by Mary, the queen dowager of France, Gertrude Blount, Countess of Devonshire, Anne Browne, Elizabeth Danet, Jane Parker – daughter of diplomat and translator Henry, Lord Morley – both Boleyn sisters and one more unnamed, though we can't be sure who played which role.[57]

The pageant was to happen at the cardinal's palace of York Place on the night of 4 March, Shrove Tuesday. A few days earlier the king had taken the motto 'she has wounded my heart' at the joust.[58] Whoever this referred to – and we can't now be sure – gossip must have been running through the court like fire through a forest, fuelling the atmosphere of the evening's entertainment. The chamber was hung with tapestries and lit by wax torches, grouped together like branches of a tree. The women were dressed in gowns of white satin with their names embroidered in gold and positioned themselves in the castle, while the eight 'vices', 'dressed like to women of Inde' – sixteenth-century western racism commonly denoted 'badness' by darkness of skin – prepared to attack. Eight masked lords, led by the king as 'Ardent Desire', marched in and the eight ladies immediately folded, offering the castle to these fine knights. 'Ardent Desire' decided that the women ought to be 'won' instead, and a sticky battle of rose water, comfits, dates and oranges began.[59]

It must have been fun and exciting, perhaps trying to hit the man you most liked, and trying to keep out of the way of over-excited choristers. The 'masked' element of the thing was useless where the king was concerned – his costume and his height alone set him clearly apart – but the women may well have been harder to identify, perhaps emboldened by their hidden faces. Masques like the *Château Vert* exemplify the way that we're used to thinking of ladies-in-waiting, as a sea of nameless faces and figures on display and yet hidden. If that were the case, there would have been little need for masques at all. In fact, ladies-in-waiting were experts at negotiating being seen and unseen, but the fiction of a masque allowed them to be both at the same time. Who had wounded the king's heart? Perhaps this was a chance to find out.

5

Stout Resolution

The table groaned under its bounty. Capons, beef, mutton, venison, all freshly slaughtered and then roasted or boiled; 'conies', chicken, pigeon, even a heron: a carnivore's paradise. There would be tarts and custards to follow, the whole washed down with weak beer or ale and rich wines.[1] Elizabeth, Countess of Surrey was hosting a family feast, and everything needed to be perfect.

Ordinarily, she would have had her husband there with her. But the earl was many miles away to the north leading the defence against the Scots, who were once again threatening the border.[2] In his absence, Elizabeth did as any noblewoman would do. She took a leave of absence from her position at court and resumed her place at home as chatelaine of the estate. This was such a complex role that there were 'how to' books in circulation explaining how best to be 'wise and sound administrators'.[3] Mostly, Elizabeth needed to manage those beneath her. She needed to know the laws relating to land, tax and inheritance; be aware of the agricultural calendar so that the right tasks were done at the right times; and make sure that her workers were not lazy. There were estate officials to handle the minutiae and to keep records and accounts. Elizabeth would have perused these and made sure she was satisfied before signing them.

She also needed to offer hospitality on a grand scale. She and her household were at the family's main home, Tendring Hall on the Suffolk-Essex border. Elizabeth's kitchen accounts show that on 5 August 1523, a multitude of in-laws descended for a family celebration, possibly marking the betrothal of Elizabeth's young sister-in-law to Henry Radcliffe, the future earl of Sussex.[4] Her parents-in-law the Duke and Duchess of Norfolk, their children Anne, Countess of Oxford, Elizabeth, Dorothy and Thomas, along with her aunt-in-law Lady Wyndham, all came to dinner and stayed until the next day, so Elizabeth also had to provide overnight accommodation for them and for their servants.

Hence the groaning tables. Meat was expensive and consuming it a sign of status. The family dined in Elizabeth's own private chamber, separately from the rest of the household in the hall.[5] While this was probably quieter, and the comparative privacy a mark of rank and exclusivity, it may also have made things more difficult for Elizabeth herself. Two years previously Elizabeth's father the Duke of Buckingham had been summarily executed for high treason. Her father-in-law and her husband had sat on the jury that convicted him, and her father-in-law, the man now dining at her table, had pronounced the death sentence.[6] Her father's crime had been one of attitude. It was no secret that he expected to be regent if anything happened to Henry VIII, and it did not take a genius to spin ill-judged remarks into a design on the throne.[7] Bonds of kinship created by marriage were supposed to help guard against such things – Elizabeth's husband should in theory have supported his father-in-law against any accusations – but the usual unwritten rules of loyalty often went out of the window as soon as the word 'treason' was uttered. For Elizabeth, though, it remained complicated. Women's family identities aren't often considered in the general narrative of Tudor history, but Elizabeth hadn't stopped being a Stafford when she became a Howard. Part of her role was to foster relations between the two families. Now, though, the Staffords were traitors, their descendants tainted. Her marital family preferred to ignore the kinship tie, and none of Elizabeth's relatives visited during these years. Instead, she hosted Howard family celebrations and sent venison pasties to her father-in-law's London house.[8]

Elizabeth's father's execution had sent shockwaves through the nobility. If the premier peer of the realm could be killed for appearing over-mighty, nobody was safe. And yet by May 1524

Elizabeth might have been forgiven for wondering what had become of that lesson. At the age of eighty, her father-in-law the old Duke of Norfolk had finally passed on. Elizabeth was now Duchess of Norfolk, her hook-nosed husband the new duke. It was usual for a peer to have a funeral commensurate with his or her rank, but the old duke's made no concessions to royal anxieties. The whole county turned out. Nine hundred people wore nine hundred and fifty marks' worth of black cloth. Three hundred priests were rounded up to pray for his soul. The procession from Framlingham, where he'd died, to his final resting place at Thetford Priory lasted several days, but even the funeral service itself was a marathon. An hour-long sermon on the lion of the tribe of Judah – the lion being the 'badge', the symbol, of the Howard family – so frightened some of the common folk that they fled from the church.[9]

Elizabeth and her husband now had significant shoes to fill. A close relationship to the royal court was becoming increasingly important for nobles as King Henry's reign progressed; the court was the place where connections were made, loyalties assured, news gathered and reported. It was part of Elizabeth's role as a noble-woman to achieve these things, not only at home in East Anglia but also at court as a lady-in-waiting. Combining the two was the tricky part. Elizabeth later wrote that she had served at court for sixteen years, but her surviving household accounts show that this wasn't one single consecutive period of time.[10] Like noblemen who held court office, ladies-in-waiting with husbands, children and homes to manage tended to divide their time between locations. But this divide wasn't always even or clear-cut. The time that they spent at court or elsewhere fluctuated according to the needs of all concerned, and while it's possible that there was some sort of rota system of service – we know that this was the case for the king's privy chamber servants – either it wasn't as stringent, or it didn't apply to peeresses.[11] Elizabeth was comparatively lucky. Her estates in East Anglia weren't insurmountably far from London, and her accounts show that she was able to visit fairly regularly.

Her friends visited her too. Towards the end of 1523 Ladies Parr and Bryan came to dinner, and on another occasion Lady Morley brought her daughter Mistress Parker and 'another of the Queen's maids'.[12] Parr and Bryan were courtiers like Elizabeth; Maud Green, Lady Parr had served Catherine of Aragon for almost as long.[13] Alice, Lady Morley was a neighbour, but her daughter Jane Parker was one of the queen's maids of honour, and had clearly travelled with a friend.[14] Relationships formed at court did not stop existing outside that bubble.

These and other court visitors would have had much to discuss at Elizabeth's table during the mid-1520s. Perhaps they brought her the news that the king's latest mistress, Mary Boleyn, Lady Carey had had a baby daughter, and though the king hadn't acknowledged the child like he had Bessie Blount's son Henry, the chances were reasonable that she was his.[15] Perhaps one royal bastard was enough, though in the summer of 1525 the king added to the speculation over the succession by making Henry lord admiral and Duke of Richmond and Somerset, and then sent him north to act as a semblance of royal presence in a troubled region.[16] In a show of even-handedness – or to placate her mother the queen – Princess Mary was also sent away in the same year to Ludlow, Princess of Wales in all but name.[17]

The king's focus on his children was part of a general drive for domestic reform. In January 1526 a new set of court ordinances was published: the Eltham Ordinances, devised largely by the plump and pompous Cardinal Wolsey.[18] They were needed. Controlling the number of people who entered the palace precincts was virtually impossible, and even keeping track of those who claimed food, lodging and salaries was a task too great for the manpower allotted to it. The kitchen might in theory be providing for a household of 500 or so, but in practice over three times that number were dining at the king's expense.[19] These, the latest in a long line of court ordinances, were designed for retrenchment. The problem was that ordinances were always more theory than practice, and often a futile remonstration against habits that were difficult to police. Courtiers must not, the Eltham Ordinances scolded, 'cast, leave, or lay any manner of dishes, platters, saucers, or broken meat, either in the said galleries, or at their chamber doors', but have their own servants take them straight to the scullery.[20] Clearly, nobles expected some sort of palace 'room service'. Twenty years later, behaviour in the public areas of the palace was still a problem; a proclamation begged courtiers not to 'make water' within the precinct of the court.[21]

Since the queen's household mirrored the king's, there wasn't much that was relevant to ladies-in-waiting. The only part that Elizabeth and her friends might have been concerned about was the allowances for bouche of court – food, drink, light and fuel, the amount allotted according to social rank. As a duchess, Elizabeth was entitled to two loaves of bread and a gallon of ale in the morning, one loaf and another gallon of ale in the afternoon and two loaves, one gallon of ale and a pitcher of wine at supper, to be shared between herself and her servants. From November to April she could have one torch, one prickett (candle), two sises (small candles), one pound of white lights, ten talshides (timbers for fuel) and eight faggots of wood, and for the other half of the year as much wax, white lights, wood and coal as she could get for £39 13s 3d, an attempt at rationing supply, though this sum was roughly three and a half years' wages to a tradesman. Jane Parker, as one of the queen's maids, had the same food allowance to be shared between her and the five other maids, but less light and fuel.[22] Again, this was probably hard to enforce. Reining in entitled courtiers was not an enviable task, and palaces were not always pleasant environments for Elizabeth and the other ladies.

María de Salinas, Lady Willoughby was one of only a few women to be mentioned by name in drafts of the Eltham Ordinances, receiving lodging and bouche of court as part of the queen's household.[23] This was probably because of her status as one of the queen's closest ladies-in-waiting, and the fact that her husband did not hold office at court with her. In October 1526, though, she was almost certainly not there. William, her husband of ten years, was dying. He had summoned his estate and household officers to his bedside in Orford Friary in Suffolk, along with the prior and as many of the friars as could be spared, so that his will might be read and witnessed in their presence. It was four in the afternoon, and daylight was giving way to the dancing flames of many candles. The room in which William lay was too small to fit all of the people who had turned up. They spilled out into the adjoining great chamber, clustering by the doorway. Thomas Russhe, receiver of William's lands, began to read the will loudly enough for everybody to hear.[24]

The first half was unremarkable: religious bequests to churches and friaries, and reiteration of the property set aside for María, her 'jointure' that would support her during her widowhood.[25] But then Russhe reached the part stating that the residue of all the rest of the estate was also to go to María for the term of her life, and then to their daughter, seven-year-old Katherine. María and William had no male children. His male heir was his next-oldest brother, Sir Christopher, who had had designs on the estate for years. So far as William and María were concerned, Sir Christopher had already had all that he was entitled to. For María particularly this must have seemed obvious. In Castile, daughters inherited alongside sons as a matter of course, and a mere uncle would not have had any legal recourse.[26] In England, though, things were less clear-cut. Some of the lands now gifted to María had earlier been set aside for Sir Christopher, and it wasn't certain that a will could trump a previous agreement. This was why William had called witnesses: 'All you that be here, for the love of God I pray you that you will testify that the same is my testament and last will and full mind.'[27] Later that night he died, and María was left to deal with the fallout.[28]

María's marriage had evidently been a strong one. William wanted their daughter Katherine to marry only according to María's advice and that of her godmother, Queen Catherine, and though he'd been married once before, he was having a tomb made for himself and María, choosing to lie beside her, not his first wife, in perpetuity. His decision to leave her almost all of his property shows that he trusted her above anybody else, not only to manage it properly but to negotiate the legal fight that he knew he was creating. Finally, and most significantly, he made her his chief executrix, in charge of carrying out the will itself: he placed his immortal soul in her hands.[29]

In the months after William's death María must frequently have cursed the English legal system. A proverb from her homeland claimed, 'Better to be a widow than to be a married woman', and in Castile this was true. There she would have been entitled to the property that she had brought to the marriage as dowry, plus half of her and her husband's joint estate.[30] In England things were lamentably different. Some women did retain control of their dowries by agreement with their husbands, but the law would not uphold this for them. They were only entitled to a third of their husband's wealth after his death, or however much property he had assured to them in jointure at the time of their marriage, and this was never usually as much as half of the estate.[31] William, however, had left María most of his land. The problem now was actively claiming this inheritance. Her brother-in-law Sir Christopher insisted that some of the lands had been entailed upon him at an earlier date and that this trumped anything William had said or done later on. María argued vociferously that this was not true.[32] In theory, it was for the law to decide whose claim was stronger. But the law wasn't an abstract monolith, and legal right and precedent were only one part of the game. Nepotism and legal patronage, the vested interests of powerful men and the fact that María was a woman and Sir Christopher a man were equally significant.

Lawsuits in early modern England were a game of reputational damage. People of María's standing sued one another readily, but the aim was generally to force the other party to settle out of court to avoid a stain on their honour, not to seek an actual resolution. Slander was therefore an important part of litigation. María and Sir Christopher's petitions used standard, but inflammatory, phrases: the charges were 'outrageous', brought only to put each other to 'great delay, charge, cost and hindrance', to his or her 'utter undoing'. Sir Christopher was using 'crafty means' to get what he wanted, and María was obstinate, taking 'sinister counsel', bearing 'cruel mind' towards her brother-in-law.[33]

María used every tool at her disposal to win the dispute, and she wasn't afraid to play dirty. She continued to administer the estate and collect the revenues, even though theoretically the lands belonged to the Crown until the legal process had run its course.[34] Sir Christopher tried to stop her. At one point he claimed that she sent her men to cut down the corn on thirty acres of land belonging to him near Orford, even though it wasn't ripe. Apparently she had said that she 'would rather it should rot on the ground' than that he should have it. Her servants, when questioned, replied blandly that the land was María's, and they were merely peaceably carrying out their standard duties; Sir Christopher was the one who had entered unlawfully.[35]

María knew exactly what she was doing. Delaying the formal settlement of the estates bought her time to manoeuvre. Her daughter Katherine was still a child. In England, the guardianship of minor heirs and heiresses automatically belonged to the Crown in a system known as 'wardship'. The Crown gained the right to administer the property that the heir was due to inherit and to skim the profits, as well as the gift of the heir's marriage. These rights were usually sold on to the highest bidder. María knew she couldn't afford to buy her daughter's wardship.[36] No doubt this pained her. In Castile she would have been Katherine's guardian automatically, exactly as her own mother Inés had been the guardian of María and her siblings after their father's death.[37] Now María would lose control over Katherine's environment, her upbringing and her future.

The best-case scenario, then, was somebody with whom María saw eye to eye. Naturally she will have hoped for a guardian who would treat Katherine well and teach her what she needed to know to succeed in this world. But ideally this would also be a person of high status, with political pull that might translate into legal patronage and influence with the king. One can imagine her casting a mental eye over the English nobility and making delicate inquiries in the course of her normal duties at court. Whatever she did, it paid off: Katherine's wardship was bought by Charles Brandon, Duke of Suffolk, and he was the perfect candidate.

María knew the affable duke well already. She was godmother to his daughter, had served at court with his wife, and probably socialised with him at home. The Brandon and Willoughby estates bordered one another, which was the main reason for Suffolk's interest. If he could in due course marry young Katherine to his own son and heir Henry, the two patrimonies would be united in an extremely pleasing and profitable manner. More immediately important for María, Suffolk was a royal councillor, the king's brother-in-law, a man of rank and influence. If he threw his weight behind her in the matter of the estate dispute, Sir Christopher might well back down.

The wardship was officially agreed on 20 November 1527. Suffolk was to pay the exorbitant sum of 4,000 marks into the royal treasury, in yearly instalments of 500 marks. He also had to put up his Oxfordshire lands as collateral, because his credit was such that Wolsey and the king did not trust him to stick to the payment schedule. In return, he would receive forty marks per year for young Katherine's expenses.[38] That he agreed to these terms shows how valuable her lands and marriage were, and how cannily María had worked the system to her own and her daughter's advantage. Seven-year-old Katherine would not even need to move very far. The duke's home at Westhorpe in Suffolk was only twenty miles from the Willoughby seat at Parham. His wife Mary, the queen dowager of France, was warm and kind, a woman of strong opinion but a realist who could teach Katherine how to navigate royal politics. Katherine would grow up with Suffolk's own daughters Frances and Eleanor, who were almost the same age.

At stalemate, Sir Christopher clamoured for Wolsey's attention, trying to force the legal issues. María wouldn't bring the evidences, she wouldn't abide by his decree, she was still delaying the process.[39] The great cardinal, though, was otherwise engaged. That summer, the king, driven by fears of dynastic extinction and – perhaps – the lure of Mistress Boleyn's seductive eyes, had publicly expressed doubts about the validity of his marriage to Queen Catherine. The whole of Europe was in shock. Why, Henry demanded, had they not had a son? Why so many dead babies? Was God angry with him? Poring over his Bible, in Leviticus he found an answer: a man should not marry his brother's wife. It is an unclean thing, and he will be childless. Princess Mary, as a girl, did not count. Too well Henry knew that even one male heir would not be sufficient. Catherine, now aged forty-two and possibly menopausal, had not been pregnant since 1517. Should he – could he – do anything to change his desperate situation? Naturally he turned to his chief advisor, facilitator of all his desires, the cardinal. Marriage was governed by the Church. It wasn't unprecedented for kings to get out of marriages that had become problematic, and the Pope was the man to ask.

On 17 May 1527 a tribunal met secretly in York Place, Wolsey's London home. Clerics and lawyers must have eyed one another with astonishment as they realised why they had been called: the king was placing himself on trial for having lived almost twenty years in unlawful matrimony.[40] Unfortunately, it was clear fairly quickly that this was not going to be as straightforward as Henry hoped. Because Catherine had indeed been married to Henry's brother Arthur, she and Henry had had a dispensation from the Pope to allow them to marry. To ask the Holy Father to now pronounce the marriage invalid and permit an annulment meant that he would also have to declare that that dispensation should not have been granted: tantamount to admitting fault in one's predecessor, something that no Pope was keen to do. Moreover, there were rumours that Henry's desires were not purely conscientious in nature. He continued to spend a lot of time with maid of honour Anne Boleyn. On Shrove Tuesday 1526 he had jousted under the motto 'Declare, I dare not!', which many took to be a reference to his love for her.[41] Then, nobody had batted an eyelid. By 1527, though, it was clear that this was more than a passing fancy. The Pope was not going to countenance an annulment simply to legitimise adultery.

Nor was he physically able to do so. In May 1527 renegade troops belonging to Charles V had sacked Rome and the Vatican and taken the Pope captive. Charles V was Queen Catherine's nephew, and though he pronounced himself horrified at his troops' action he now had the Pope effectively at his mercy. This was not good news for the king of England. In the summer of 1527, therefore, Wolsey himself was sent to France to broker a peace and shore up support for Henry's cause with diplomatic representatives from across western Europe, as well as to attempt to negotiate the release of the Pope – or to set himself up as a papal vice-regent in the interim, able to pronounce on Henry's marriage.[42] Before he left he saw María and Sir Christopher, heard their complaints, and apparently washed his hands of them, telling them firmly to go back to the law courts.[43] Clearly, such things were not his priority just now. He may have been growing afraid for his own position. By July King Henry was 'at all times' with the Dukes of Norfolk and Suffolk and Anne Boleyn's father, none of whom were friendly to Wolsey. Even after the cardinal returned home, he found that it was made difficult for him to see the king alone.[44]

María and the Duke of Suffolk might have been content to wait for the cardinal to return to domestic affairs, but Sir Christopher was not. Impatient, in the spring of 1528 he began doing what noblemen often did in land disputes: breaking and entering. On a cold February afternoon he came to the manor house at Eresby in Lincolnshire with a few servants, one of whom climbed the gate and broke the lock so that the rest could enter. They were not a large group, and they were not armed for conflict. What they had come for were the evidences, the paperwork that might help Sir Christopher to claim ownership. He sent his man up to the evidence house, which was not locked, but the door was blocked from the inside with 'two great sand stones'. Thomas, his carver, was able to crawl under the door, remove the stones and let the men in. They took away some of the evidences and, after a few days playing lord of the manor, departed. News travelled quickly and a lawsuit was soon begun in young Lady Katherine's name. María termed it unlawful entry; Sir Christopher said he had every right to be there.[45] The Duke of Suffolk was sufficiently concerned about the potential impact on his ward's inheritance to write to Wolsey asking that 'remedies may be had herein' and that Wolsey let him know what he planned to do about it.[46]

The answer was not a lot. The lawsuits continued, but the attention of many of the key players was elsewhere. It was a year of gathering storm clouds, and of girding loins for the mysterious something just out of sight on the horizon. We tend to think that events at court existed in a bubble, but this was far from the case. María's legal battle was reliant on the patronage of court figures, but she was also giving support in turn to her mistress the queen. It was a tense time to be in the queen's household. Catherine had known for over a year that something was going on. She had found out about the secret May tribunal in York Place within twenty-four hours, and almost immediately despatched two of her most trusted servants, her physician Fernán López de Escoriaza and Francisco Felipez, to Spain to her nephew the emperor, begging for his assistance.[47] They made it there safely, though King Henry had explicitly ordered that they be preventatively arrested and held up in France.[48] Cardinal Wolsey spent much of 1528 trying to infiltrate the queen's chambers. Some reports suggest that this was already standard practice. There was much contemporary anxiety about the 'doubleness' of servants, and biblical translator William Tyndale accused Wolsey in print of having bribed certain of the queen's servants into reporting her deeds and words. Indeed her almoner Robert Shorton did so, albeit through protestations of loyalty.[49] Wolsey and the king were keen to get at least one of Queen Catherine's Spanish servants on side, which speaks for their continued close relationship to her. The attempted arrest of Francisco Felipez in France in the summer of 1527 was supposed to be staged so that the king could pay his ransom and thus bring him 'in more firm confidence', because he was 'privy unto the Queen's affairs and secrets'.[50] When this failed, they probably looked elsewhere. As Francis Bacon would later darkly remark, 'Spanish women spy well'; no doubt Catherine knew this as well as Henry.[51] At least one woman was said to have left court 'for no other cause, but for that she would no longer betray her mistress'.[52] Women, as well as men, were part of this deadly game. By the end of 1528, the stage was set for the greatest play in Christendom; but who was to direct?

Part Two: 1529–1536

6

Faithful to Her

The queen's women sat in attitudes of relaxation in the privy chamber at Bridewell Palace, fanning themselves languidly. As the Bishop of Carlisle had earlier remarked, mopping the sweat from his face, it was a very hot day, and it had not been made any cooler by the egos on display at Blackfriars that morning.[1] María de Salinas, Lady Willoughby and the rest of Queen Catherine's ladies-in-waiting had listened in grim horror as a papal court of law, presided over by the Pope's representative Cardinal Campeggio, continued to place the royal marriage on trial. Legal counsel from both sides had been debating the matter for weeks already. The court had come to Bridewell Palace, next door to the friary, so that the king and queen might both make their appearances on the allotted day. Queen Catherine had already protested the legality of the court once; now, magnificent in her righteousness, she simply refused to engage. She declared the judges too biased to rule on her case and then she went on her knees before her husband, asking him gently how she had offended him. As King Henry, red in the face and looking everywhere but at his wife, took refuge in silence, Queen Catherine rose, summoned her attendants and swept out of the hall, ignoring calls for her return.[2]

Now María and the others took solace in embroidery, every window set open to its widest. They must all have been acutely aware of the king's glowering presence a floor below.[3] Perhaps they had even heard him haranguing Cardinal Wolsey a few hours earlier. If so, nobody can have been particularly surprised when the gentleman usher keeping the door of the queen's chamber came to announce the arrival of Wolsey and his colleague, Cardinal Campeggio.[4] Queen Catherine stood, but as her ladies came to remove the skeins of embroidery silks she had draped around her neck she stopped them. She and a companion left the privy chamber to speak to the cardinals amid the crowds in her presence chamber. When told that the cardinals had come to ask her what she intended to do regarding the trial and to give her counsel, she gestured to the white sewing thread and protested her femininity: 'to make answer to your request I cannot so suddenly, for I was set among my maidens at work, thinking full little of any such matter'. Playing to the audience, she bewailed her lack of impartial counsel, before taking the cardinals into the privy chamber and berating them soundly.[5] One can imagine María and the other women gravely pretending to pay no attention.

In the months after the trial, the atmosphere at court grew steadily more oppressive. Cardinal Campeggio ultimately refused to rule on the matter, proroguing the court instead. Few people ever told King Henry 'no'. Having failed conspicuously to produce the annulment the king required, Cardinal Wolsey was deprived of his office as lord chancellor and banished to his manor at Esher. By the end of November 1529 the tension was such that one felt anything might happen, and at a banquet in celebration of St Andrew's Day it finally did. A sudden hush fell over the room as one voice rose above the hubbub of courtiers dining. Queen Catherine of Aragon was speaking to her husband. She told him forcefully that his treatment of her was akin to the pains of purgatory on earth, because he refused to visit her or dine with her in her apartments any more. She cared 'not a straw' for the opinion of his almoner – Wolsey – or anybody other than the Pope; for every doctor or lawyer he found to decide their divorce case in his favour, she would find a thousand to declare their marriage valid and indissoluble.[6] These were bold words, born of desperation. Though the legatine court at Blackfriars had been formally adjourned, the Pope had not yet agreed to have the case tried in Rome, and she was losing hope that he ever would.

Ever sensitive to the ebb and flow of royal favour, courtiers knew that this was an unprecedented situation. Their shifting alliances became heightened, the stakes ratcheted ever higher, and this did not make for peace. Anne Boleyn remained at court with the king and queen in an awkward *ménage à trois*. Though Henry began renovations specifically for Anne at the soon-to-be-renamed York Place almost the moment he seized it from the cardinal in November 1529, these would not be ready for some time. The evidence suggests that she continued to occupy a different set of apartments within the same palace as the royal couple. Thus, after his emotionally charged dinner with Catherine on St Andrew's Eve, the king retired for supper with Anne in her own chambers – at which he was told waspishly that he should never have stooped to discuss the divorce with his wife. Anne snapped that Catherine would inevitably best him in verbal sparring and one of these days he would simply give in.[7]

The king went to some effort to reassure her and other observers. Just over a week later he bestowed the earldom of Wiltshire on Anne's father Thomas, and the next day threw a huge celebratory banquet at which Anne was treated as though she were the queen, and not the absent Catherine.[8] Her extended family turned out en masse, including the two Duchesses of Norfolk: Elizabeth Stafford, the 'younger' Duchess, wife to Thomas Howard, 3rd and current Duke of Norfolk, and her stepmother-in-law Agnes, the dowager duchess. Elizabeth, as we know, had served Queen Catherine for many years. Agnes, too, was no stranger to court occasions. Their status as duchesses meant that they were both frequently in attendance at banquets, revels and ceremonies. But mother and daughter-in-law relationships could be fraught then as now; their shared connection to the royal court did not make them friends. In fact they had a history of sniping at one another. In the summer of 1528, the deadly sweating sickness had rampaged through the country with more virulence than usual. Anne Boleyn caught it; her sister's husband died of it.[9] The Duke of Norfolk also caught it at his home in Suffolk and several of his servants died. Dowager Duchess Agnes, hearing of this, mentioned it in a letter to Cardinal Wolsey and offered her own allegedly infallible remedy against the

illness. She added snidely that her stepson's illness had occurred
'as I think through default of keeping'.[10] By this she meant house-
keeping, Elizabeth's job as Norfolk's wife. Her words have been
read as a dig at her daughter-in-law. For a minor remark, this had
major implications. To criticise a woman's household management
was to imply that she wasn't fit to be an aristocratic wife and to
carry out the public, political responsibilities that came with it.
Agnes was suggesting to the king's chief advisor that Elizabeth
wasn't up to the task of being Duchess of Norfolk. This was hardly
the act of a supportive matriarch.

Resentment was still simmering between the two duchesses the
following year. On one occasion Elizabeth was, in her eyes, slighted
at court, and she was furious about it; her beloved mistress the
queen told her to give way and allow Agnes, the dowager duchess, to walk in front of her in the position of greater precedence.
Elizabeth felt brushed aside, dismissed and relegated. Elizabeth
and her husband spoke 'angry words' to Queen Catherine, who,
according to the Imperial ambassador Eustace Chapuys, was still
offended by the incident some time later.[11] Chapuys had only been
in England for a few months when he reported this in December
1529, but already he had a keen sense of the personal politics gov-
erning Henry's court. A Savoyard, Chapuys' native language was
French, and he was used to a court full of schemers on the make.
A small man with an openness of expression that led people to
confide in him, his dark eyes were nevertheless shrewd and he
was extremely quick on the uptake, grasping the likely political
implications of an event before others had fully understood what
had even occurred.[12] He was committed to aiding the queen in her
troubles with the king, and he knew whose support would make
his job easier. This incident, he noted, would make it much more
difficult to recruit Elizabeth's husband to the queen's cause.

This spat over who should go in front of whom sounds trivial,
even childish, but it had implications that contemporaries took
seriously. As Duchess of Norfolk, Elizabeth was the premier peeress of the realm. All the aristocratic titles of England were ordered
first by rank – duchess, marchioness, countess, viscountess,

baroness – and then by antiquity within those ranks. The older
the title, the more senior its holder. The dukedom of Norfolk was
the oldest of its kind, second only to the royal dukedoms, and this
routinely put Elizabeth and her husband at the head of every procession, every list, every hierarchy. Rank determined the lodgings
allocated, the offices held, the fabrics and colours worn, the very
food on one's plate; it mattered, and so the order of precedence
in a court procession was indeed worth a quarrel. But, for men,
rank was simple. There could be only one Duke of Norfolk at a
time. For women it was more complex. Elizabeth, as the wife of
Thomas Howard, 3rd Duke of Norfolk, held the title of Duchess
of Norfolk. But Agnes, as the widow of the previous duke, also
held the courtesy title of Duchess of Norfolk. It was all very well
to differentiate by calling the widow the 'dowager', or simply by
referring to the two as the 'older' and 'younger' duchesses. Was
it the older or the younger, though, who took precedence? This
was a knotty point, and the answer was not the same everywhere.
Nonetheless Elizabeth would undoubtedly have known that in
England it was the older, dowager duchess who was placed ahead
of her younger counterpart.[13] The widowed Agnes, therefore, took
precedence over Elizabeth, the younger duchess. When Elizabeth
attempted to interrupt this custom the queen had intervened
to uphold it, exerting control and insisting on peace within her
household.

We don't know exactly when or where this happened, but it
was public enough for Chapuys to hear about it. Both Elizabeth
and her husband Norfolk had been 'much offended', he wrote,
'especially the Duchess, who belongs to the House of Lancaster'.[14]
Therein lay a clue. Elizabeth, born into the Stafford family, had
royal blood; her paternal grandmother was Catherine Woodville,
sister of Edward IV's queen, and among her great-grandmothers
was Margaret Beaufort, grandmother of Henry VIII. Agnes, the
dowager duchess, came from the Tylney family, who were of
Lincolnshire gentry stock. Elizabeth felt that this ought to make a
difference even after marriage had nominally levelled the playing
field, and she might also have felt that her lengthy service as one

of Queen Catherine's ladies-in-waiting meant that she deserved
the higher place.

Agnes, the dowager duchess, had never served Queen Catherine 'in ordinary', but she too had lengthy experience of the royal
court and had known the queen since she had arrived in England,
far longer than her daughter-in-law had. Agnes had escorted the
king's older sister Princess Margaret to Scotland for her wedding
with James IV in 1503, and reprised the role for his younger sister
Princess Mary's marriage to Louis XII of France in 1514. She was
one of the godmothers to the queen's daughter, Princess Mary, in
1516.[15] But she was also the grandmother, by marriage, of Anne
Boleyn. The prospect of having kin on the throne of England was
one that most courtiers would jump at, and Agnes was probably
not averse to the idea.

By now a widow in her early fifties, Agnes' long career had suddenly become useful to the king because she had been present on
Catherine and Prince Arthur's wedding night back in 1501. She was
one of a number of people called in the summer of 1529 to give a
statement about what she had seen. Like everybody else, she knew
only that they had been put to bed together, but this was inevitably
used to argue that sexual intercourse had occurred. Prince Arthur,
she remembered, was 'about the same stature that the young Earl
of Derby is now at'. She had seen them placed together 'in one bed
the same night' and, with the rest of the court, had left them to
it.[16] The other English women asked responded in the same way.
Jane, Lady Guildford, now sixty, said that she'd left the couple
in bed that night 'in mind and intent as she believeth to have
carnal cognition together as man and wife' and had found them
still there together the next morning.[17] The fact that they gave
these statements did not mean that either woman was 'against'
the queen in the matter of the royal divorce. It would not have
been politic to refuse. Duchess Agnes perhaps resisted as far as
she dared by insisting that they come to her in Suffolk to record
it. Perhaps, though, ladies-in-waiting like her daughter-in-law
Elizabeth thought that those asked should have refused to give any
testimony at all. In fact, surviving records suggest that hardly any

women were asked to give statements about Queen Catherine and Prince Arthur. This was partly because women's testimony was generally considered less valuable and less reliable than men's, but it was also an indictment of the process. Ladies-in-waiting were party to secrets about their mistress's marriage bed and everybody knew it. Why else had King Louis XII of France, for example, been so averse to the presence of Jane, 'mother Guildford', in his wife's household? If the king were so certain that Catherine was lying, that she had in fact slept with Arthur, who better to prove it than her women?

Instead, the Crown commissioners asked all the male aristocrats they could find who had been there that night. Their nobility itself was regarded as a sign of their trustworthiness, even though they had surely seen far less than the queen's women. Beyond that, royal officials simply avoided approaching those they knew would not give the evidence required. María de Salinas, Lady Willoughby, for example, was never asked to tell what she knew, even though – or, more likely, because – she was one of only a very few prime candidates in England to know the truth of the matter. As one of Queen Catherine's Spanish women, she had had access to the queen's chamber in the days immediately following the marriage. She had heard Francisca de Cáceres mocking Arthur's alleged inability to perform; she had seen Catherine's sad face. But she was still in Catherine's service. She wasn't likely to lie to please the king.

The English were not the only ones collecting testimonies of that night. The Spanish court, too, began to search for those who had been present, and their lists of those to ask contained many more women than those of the English.[18] Familiar names appear; María de Rojas, now the wife of Don Alvaro de Mendoza, living close to Nájera: 'she used to sleep in the Queen's own bed after the death of her first husband, Arthur'. Catalina Fortes, who had left in 1509 to become a nun, and was indeed now living in the convent of Madre de Dios in Toledo: 'she was much in her [Catherine's] confidence'. The wife of Juan de Cuero, who had 'acted up' as Catherine's chamberlain after the departure of the Manriques. Even Catalina of Motril, 'once the Queen's slave, who used to make her bed and attend to other services of the chamber', who had married a Morisco crossbow-maker named Oviedo and recently returned as a widow to her home town of Motril in Granada. We can't be sure that all of these people were successfully located and questioned, but some certainly were; there were more specific instructions and interrogatories made for Catalina Fortes, for one, and there are many references in diplomatic correspondence to sending these depositions to the court in England. As late as 1532, the Spanish court was still searching for women who knew the truth. Catalina de Guevara, somebody noted, had sworn on oath that the queen was a virgin when she married Henry.[19] There is no record of Francisca de Cáceres being sought for testimony, though we know that she was still alive and living in Granada.[20] There's no record of María de Salinas being approached by the Spanish either, and this was probably because it was impossible to send envoys to take her deposition so far away in England. By the end of 1529 the matter was at stalemate, and nobody knew quite where it might go next.

The new year brought heartbreak for Elizabeth, Duchess of Norfolk. In 1529 her husband the duke had purchased the last year of the young Earl of Derby's wardship from the king. Early in 1530, in a move of questionable legality – he did not have royal permission – he married the young earl to his and Elizabeth's eldest daughter, Catherine. So far, so good; this was a political, social and economic coup. But London was not a safe place. Sickness abounded. Cardinal Campeggio himself had complained about the 'inconstant weather' and counted himself fortunate if he was not lying on his bed groaning.[21] Plagues like the sweat did not always spare the young, and Catherine had been staying at Norfolk House in Lambeth. Just a few short weeks into this next chapter of her life, on 15 March 1530, Elizabeth's daughter died of plague. Her death was described as 'one of the greatest blows the Duke has ever received', but nothing was mentioned about Elizabeth's undoubted grief.[22] High mortality rates did not inure anybody to the loss of a child.

The marriage with the Earl of Derby was nevertheless too valuable to lose. Elizabeth and Norfolk had another daughter, Mary, and Elizabeth understandably thought the obvious solution was for Mary to marry Derby instead. But Norfolk had been discussing Mary's potential marriage to the king's illegitimate son (Bessie Blount's Henry Fitzroy), and both he and Anne Boleyn were keen for that to go ahead. Anne, eager to secure a formal connection to the royal family to bolster her own intentions in that direction, was vocal about it, using 'high words' to Elizabeth. Not seeing why an upstart Boleyn should dictate the marriages of her children, Elizabeth responded in kind, and was almost dismissed from court.[23] At this point, dowager Duchess Agnes involved herself in the dispute by suggesting her own youngest daughter, Norfolk's much younger half-sister, for the Derby match. Norfolk jumped at the solution. The paperwork was drawn up with both his and Agnes' signatures, but Elizabeth was not part of the formal arrangements.[24] Wracked with grief, one daughter lost and the other married against her will, Elizabeth must have felt pushed aside, resentful of the influence that Agnes still held within the family, and furious with her niece Anne Boleyn.

The Howard dynasty was hedging its bets. The Duke of Norfolk was Anne's maternal uncle. Ambassador Chapuys, ear to the ground and quick to see faction everywhere, thought that Norfolk was at the head of Anne's 'party'. There are some grounds for his assertions even if the 'party' was not as clearly defined as he would have it. While Norfolk was probably not responsible for Anne's rise – he spent most of his time away from court between 1525 and 1528 – he undoubtedly benefited from his position as the patriarch of her family once the king began seriously to doubt his marriage. Contemporary sources show him at the forefront of many state matters from 1529, often alongside Anne's father and brother, and the Venetian ambassador thought that after Wolsey's disgrace and death in November 1530, 'every employment devolves to him'.[25] Did he do this for Anne? As so often for this period, their relationship is difficult to see in the surviving material and it's likely that it was not a close or personal one. Arguably there is more evidence for

antagonism than affection, but much of this dates from her tenure
as queen when she was under an enormous amount of pressure.
Whatever Norfolk's level of support for his niece, it probably had
more to do with dynastic ambition than familial love, and his later
actions reveal that he was never prepared to stand by her if she
failed. A loyal servant to his core, for Norfolk obedience to his
king and his king's desires would always come first.

Historians often assume that where a patriarch led, his family
followed. There is something very satisfying in imagining scenes
of family counsel around a long table in a panelled room, where
the family patriarch planned the moves of individual family
members like pawns on a chessboard. Clearly, the reality was less
straightforward. Thomas Howard himself would later rehearse a
long list of disagreements with family members going back twenty
years.[26] Usually, when we think of a family group like this, we are
thinking of men. Any women in the picture are often depicted as
pawns, ordered around by those men for the greater good of the
family. It is true that early modern gender relations did support
the superiority of men over women, and also emphasised the
household hierarchy of husband over wife and father over children. It was often in women's own interests to support the broader
goals of the family, since what was good for the family was good
for those belonging to it. Norfolk's wife Elizabeth, though, had
spent over fifteen years in service with the queen. Left alone at
court for lengthy periods while her husband dealt with military
issues far away, she'd had ample opportunity to develop strong
ties to the queen and the rest of the royal household. Was she now
to throw away those long-held loyalties and follow her husband in
supporting their niece's bid for the throne?

Though in service with the queen, Elizabeth lodged with her
husband at court, as most wives did.[27] It must have been obvious
when their rooms were empty of Norfolk's explosive personality.
It's likely that he did most of his paperwork in this space and that
there were letters from relatives, clients, absent friends, councillors
and foreign intelligencers stored in chests or littering the table. In

the autumn of 1530 this included letters from Gregorio Casali, the king's ambassador and advocate at the Vatican, the court of the Pope, on whom the decision regarding the validity of the king and queen's marriage currently depended. Casali had been tasked with collating scholarly opinions of the marriage, in addition to his usual work of reporting back events, gossip and the general mood in Rome. While ambassadors reported officially to the monarch who employed them, they often corresponded with other courtiers as well. Casali and Norfolk had been keeping each other up to date for years.[28] The queen had little access to this kind of information. Her visitors were restricted and her letters were watched, opened and read. She would not know Casali's latest news.

Unless, of course, somebody told her – or better yet, forwarded the letter. But Elizabeth's movements might be noted if she attempted to see her mistress alone at an odd time of day or night, and there would be little opportunity to pass it on otherwise. She must send a gift. A gift that could contain a paper missive, one that would naturally be taken apart and its secret found. Elizabeth must have given some thought to this puzzle, or else it was not her first foray into espionage, for she chose an orange, an expensive, imported fruit bought by nobles to convey their wealth, status and taste. What better gift for a Spaniard? The pith of the orange would keep the letter dry, and she could use ribbon to hide where the peel had been lifted. Sent in a basket with other food items, it would be perfect.

On 27 November, ambassador Chapuys reported to Emperor Charles V that the Duchess of Norfolk had sent the queen a present of poultry and an orange, inside which was the letter from Casali, which he now forwarded.[29] Casali was not personally in touch with Elizabeth, which suggests that she had happened upon the letter opportunistically rather than acting as a link in an established chain of communication. Since Casali was indeed in contact with her husband Norfolk, and the couple shared lodgings on the king's side of the royal court, it is reasonable to suppose that this was where she found it. Chapuys seems to have thought so; he feared that she was being used as a cat's paw by

Norfolk trying to pass false information to the queen. Nowhere, unfortunately, did he divulge the contents of the letter itself, and there is no way for us to know exactly what it contained. He did admit that 'at all events this seems to open a way for the Queen to communicate more freely [with her friends] and disclose her plans to the Duchess, for which purpose it has been deemed expedient to dissemble better in future'.[30] This was espionage as it was routinely practised in most royal courts. There was, as yet, no formal, centralised, bureaucratic intelligence organisation in Tudor England, though certainly established networks of spies were routinely used in military contexts.[31] Otherwise, intelligence networks, news networks and espionage blurred; all were a central feature of early modern diplomacy, and women were equally as involved as men. It was not surprising that the queen was so cheered by Elizabeth's communication, nor that an experienced diplomat like Chapuys immediately saw her as a potential route for future intelligence and plans.

By the end of the year the king had been summoned to Rome, and begun an angry exchange of letters with the Pope trying to circumvent this. Christmas was spent with the queen at Greenwich in an uneasy atmosphere, though Christmas traditions and revels were conducted as usual. Anne Boleyn's temper was no sweeter. On New Year's Day she reportedly told one of the queen's ladies that she wished all Spaniards were at the bottom of the sea. When the lady remonstrated, Anne replied that she 'cared not for the Queen or any of her family, and that she would rather see her hanged than have to confess that she was her queen and mistress'.[32] At about the same time, she put her servants in livery emblazoned with the popular continental motto *ainsi sera, groigne qui groigne* – 'let them grumble, this is how it's going to be'. Was she trying to convince others, or herself? For the new year had not started auspiciously. Anne's quarrels with the king were reported by several ambassadors; some said this was to do with the king's continuing affection for his daughter Princess Mary, that Anne feared this happy family tableau. One Imperial ambassador wrote that Henry had summoned some of Anne's relatives and begged them 'with tears in his eyes' to mediate between them, though this news was third-hand by the time it reached him and should perhaps be taken with a pinch of salt.[33]

At the end of the month, Elizabeth sent another message to the queen. Chapuys' initial caution about her motives and her husband's involvement was understandable, but needless. Her message said that the queen's opponents were trying to draw her, Elizabeth, over to their 'party', but that they would never succeed. Moreover, the queen should be 'of good courage', because said opponents were at their wits' end, 'being as much amazed and bewildered in this affair as the first day it began'.[34] The unequivocal support was one thing. The information about those around Anne Boleyn was another altogether. Only somebody as close to Anne's family, indeed part of that family, could have imparted this with any authority. Only Elizabeth could have provided this intelligence. Self-evidently, her husband the duke would not have wanted the queen to know this. One assumes that he was unaware, or else he might at the very least have rethought the security of his filing system. Though Elizabeth's general opinions and loyalty to the queen were known, she wisely kept her more questionable activities secret.

Elizabeth's words reflect the speed with which the king's 'great matter', his divorce, was finally moving. Parliament had been in session since 1529. It had so far passed several Acts restricting the power of the clergy, and thus, by extension, of the Pope in Rome. On 11 February 1531, the Convocation of Canterbury – the ecclesiastical equivalent of a parliament – granted Henry the title of 'singular protector, supreme lord, and even, so far as the law of Christ allows, supreme head of the English church and clergy'.[35] Though caveated to allow those still convinced of the Pope's headship to agree, and requiring passage through the secular Parliament, this was a significant step on the road to allowing the king to decide the validity of his own marriage and thus, in due course, to remarry as he chose.

All concerned were under severe stress. In April the queen was reported ill with 'hysteria', and Anne quarrelled violently with the king over his continued relationship with his daughter, Princess Mary. After the storm, the king complained to Anne's uncle Norfolk of her language and bearing, saying plaintively that she was not like the queen, who had never in her life used such words to him.[36] The report comes from Chapuys, but he had it from Elizabeth. On this occasion, she may have given the queen her information in person rather than sending a written or verbal message. She told the queen about the king's complaint, adding that her husband Norfolk was in 'marvellous sorrow and tribulation'. Confidently, Elizabeth declared that Anne would be 'the ruin of all her family, and that if God wished that she should continue in her fantasy it would be a very good thing for the Queen'.[37] Though this sounds at odds with the legal strides being taken in Parliament and with the Church, it is evident that on the ground at court things felt far less clear-cut and the future remained uncertain.

Elizabeth's espionage is often written about with a raised eyebrow or in a tone of slight amusement, as though she was a bizarre eccentric, or should have known better than to choose the 'losing' side against her own family. But in the early 1530s there were good reasons for Elizabeth to have made the choices she did. Her relationship with dowager Duchess Agnes, the family's matriarch, was, as we have seen, increasingly fraught. Elizabeth could not hope to occupy what she felt was her rightful position within the dynasty while Agnes, with her wealth, experience and contacts, remained alive, and the two continually got across each other. Nor was her relationship with her husband Norfolk much solace. She had borne him five children before 1521, of whom three still lived. Five or so years later, in 1526 or 1527, he had taken a mistress. Elizabeth 'Bess' Holland was employed within their household, allegedly as a laundress, and was probably related to Norfolk's treasurer, John Holland.[38] It wasn't unusual for noblemen to take mistresses. The king himself had done so on several occasions. Wives were expected to put up and shut up, and Queen Catherine had set an exemplary example of precisely this, turning a blind eye when Henry begat children first with Bessie Blount and then with Mary Boleyn, Lady Carey. Elizabeth may have done likewise initially.

Evidence of her displeasure comes from letters that she wrote later on in the 1530s. These letters suggest that gradually Bess's star rose, and her place by Norfolk's side became both permanent and accepted by the rest of the household. Elizabeth would later allege that Norfolk had instructed her own servants to beat her because she would not accept Bess's presence.[39] Small wonder that Elizabeth felt sidelined by the Howards. Small wonder, too, that in the depths of grief over her daughter's death in the spring of 1530, she was horrified to find that any control she had expected to exercise over her remaining daughter's marriage had been undermined by her niece Anne Boleyn, another upstart mistress.

She must have felt, in short, that she and her mistress Queen Catherine were fighting the same battle in much the same war. Elizabeth, too, tried for many years to persuade her husband to give up his mistress and return to her. She, too, would argue that theirs had been a loving marriage, that she had borne him children, that she did not deserve this treatment. This fellow-feeling, perhaps even a need to help the queen in order to uphold the sacrament of marriage as a lifelong commitment, is entirely understandable.

In May 1531 the Duke of Albany sent a letter to the king to tell him that the divorce case was 'in good trim at Rome'. Elizabeth, Chapuys reported, saw this letter and 'went immediately and told the Queen'.[40] Clearly, she continued to have access to confidential information of this kind, presumably still through her husband Norfolk, and she used her access on both the king's and queen's sides of the court to her full advantage. The queen, on hearing this news, was visibly distressed. Chapuys was able to calm her down by telling her that the Duke of Albany was actually about to leave his position in Rome and so could write more boldly than he had done before, since it would no longer matter to him if he were proved wrong. The Duke of Norfolk, indeed, had been heard to say that 'the Devil and no other must have been the originator and promoter of this wretched scheme'.[41]

Elizabeth's calm, and presumably also the queen's, was short-lived. By the end of the month Elizabeth had been dismissed from court, 'owing to her speaking too freely, and having declared in favour of the Queen much more openly than these people like her to do'.[42] Had her espionage activities been discovered? Perhaps. Even if her specific messages had not been revealed, Chapuys' report suggests that she had been careless in what she said in the general space of the royal court. Anne was allegedly behind her dismissal, which must have been galling for Elizabeth. She had to return to comparative isolation in East Anglia to stew over her husband's infidelities. The queen was left to fight on without her spy.

7

On the Queen's Side

It was a big moment. Mary Howard, cousin to Anne Boleyn, was making her court debut, and they could hardly have chosen an occasion with higher stakes or more pressure. The Lady Anne was about to be created Marquess of Pembroke: not marchioness, the wife of a marquess, but marquess, the male title, in her own right. It was an unprecedented move for a woman in her situation and it made the king's marital intentions all the clearer. Mary had been chosen to bear Anne's new regalia, the mantel and coronet of a peeress, even though at thirteen she was very young for such a visible and responsible role.[1] But there were good reasons for this and they were not lost on any of those watching. Mary was the daughter of the Duke of Norfolk, and the betrothed of the king's illegitimate son Henry Fitzroy. She was a visual reminder of the close relationship between the Howards and the Tudors. Her presence made it evident that the powerful Howard dynasty saw Anne's bid for the throne as a family matter, and had thrown its weight behind her.[2]

Perhaps the more senior women helped her to get ready, their experience settling her nerves. She made sure she had Anne's red mantel securely across her left arm, its heavy velvet folds held tightly against her bodice so that it couldn't fall, gripping the coronet in her right hand, and praying that she would not trip, or drop something, or – heaven forbid – faint. The court was at Windsor, and the route they had to walk was probably not a long one. We don't know precisely where Anne was lodged but by this point the king rarely kept her far from his own rooms, and the investiture almost certainly happened in his presence chamber.[3] The little cavalcade entered the room and processed up its length, where Anne, dressed in red, her long, dark hair loosed like a blanket around her shoulders, kneeled before the king. The Bishop of Winchester read out the patent of her creation, and then Mary had to hand the mantel up to the king so he could place it around Anne's shoulders, and then the coronet, which he placed upon her gleaming head. It was done, and Mary's sore left arm, no doubt aching from the weight of the mantel, had been worth it: she had made no mistakes.

This was a strange time to be a woman in service at court. The story of Anne's rise, of Queen Catherine's diminishment, of the political machinations and religious changes that made this possible is well known, but it isn't usually seen from the perspective of the women beside them who witnessed it. The past year had been one of deepening divides and developing strategies, moves upon counter-moves, diplomacy and subtext and household micro-aggressions that echoed louder than Henry and Anne's stormiest argument. On 14 July 1531 Henry and Catherine saw one another for the last time. They, plus Anne, had been at Windsor. On that day, Henry and Anne rode off to start the customary summer progress, leaving Catherine behind and neglecting even to inform her of the fact. Her messages were received with poor grace; Henry told her not to send any more.[4]

Instead, the queen and her ladies were sent to The More in Hertfordshire.[5] This house had belonged to Cardinal Wolsey, an ill-omen, perhaps, if they chose to see it that way; Wolsey, disgraced after his failure to secure the king an annulment, had died on his way south to London to stand trial for treason in November 1530. Queen Catherine initially continued to live and to be treated in the style that befitted her status. A Venetian visitor to The More in August 1531 reported that she had a household of about 200, with thirty 'maids of honour' – that ubiquitous and useful term – standing around the table and about fifty 'doing its service'.[6] By September, though, Imperial ambassador Chapuys was warning that some of her maids had been dismissed.[7] Even earlier than this, the queen herself was anxious about the future, more so than she admitted in her spirited replies to the weary relay of royal councillors sent to her by the king. At Easter she countermanded a new gentleman usher's recruitment and wrote to him herself to apologise, saying that she preferred to take no more servants until she was 'more in quiet than currently'.[8] She would not repeat the poverty-stricken years of her widowhood where she struggled to support her household.

By this point in 1531 the king had given up on his attempts to wrangle an annulment out of the Vatican, and even for papal permission to have the case tried in England.[9] Henry had, in fact, been threatening papal jurisdiction in England for some time. Finally, in February 1531, he had himself declared Supreme Head of the English Church. His ministers inveigled the clergy into accepting this 'so far as the law of Christ allows', a feat of semantic gymnastics that saved both Henry's face and everybody else's consciences, but left questions as to how or even whether this authority could be upheld in a legal court.[10] Less than a month later a new diplomatic alliance, the Schmalkaldic League, was formed among northern European states who were sympathetic to Martin Luther's 'new learning'. Though Henry was not, and never would be, Lutheran he was undeniably interested in their anti-papal stance and the potential advantages of an alliance. The feeling, apparently, was mutual; 1531 saw no fewer than five English embassies sent north to explore this.[11]

Henry may, too, have been interested in some of their less revolutionary ideas. Anne Boleyn certainly was, and so were some of her women. Books of questionable legality had been making their way into England for some years, and among these was William Tyndale's *The Obedience of a Christian Man*. Anne managed to get her hands on this text shortly after its publication in Antwerp in 1528.[12] She had recently been given her own lodgings separate from the rest of the queen's maids, and probably increased her own number of ladies.[13] Having read Tyndale's book, she lent it to one of her women, young Anne Gainsford. Gainsford was being courted by equerry George Zouche and, in the time-honoured inexplicable way of young men seeking attention, he thought it would be funny to steal the book from her. He was sufficiently dense to be caught reading it by the dean of the chapel royal, who immediately confiscated the book and reported him to the cardinal. Mistress Gainsford then had to admit this to Lady Anne, who was not angry but went straight to the king and asked for her book back. This granted, she then presented it to him and entreated him to read it, which he did, and 'delighted in it'. Thus new ideas were slowly but surely trickling through the royal household.

From Rome, English policy looked confused, adrift. In September 1531 Imperial ambassador Miguel Mai was contemptuous, telling Emperor Charles V that he had always thought that the English had 'recourse to evasions and villanies' and that he 'thanked God they did not know what to ask for, as they are now asking for what has been refused thirty times'.[14] This, though, was deliberate. The English were now pursuing a Janus-faced policy: nominally seeking remedy from Rome but deliberately creating delay, while they also began the creation of an internal framework by which this and other cases might be dealt with in England, subject only to English jurisdiction.[15] This took time. The king might want to break with Rome altogether, but many of his nobles and the common people of England were some way behind him. Personnel, too, had been tricky. After Wolsey's fall in 1529, the Duke of Norfolk had shouldered much of the administrative burden of the 'great matter', but, as his wife Duchess Elizabeth no doubt could have told us, he was not a man of sufficient subtlety of mind to even begin to step into the cardinal's shoes.[16] Somebody else, however, was. Those in service at court began more and more to notice that the king favoured a short man, heading towards stoutness, dark-haired, keen-eyed, blunt in speech and manner and quietly, alarmingly efficient. Though he didn't begin to gain significant office until early in 1533, those with their eyes and ears open did well to befriend Thomas Cromwell at the beginning of his meteoric rise.

If things were in flux politically and diplomatically, so were they in the royal court. Anne Boleyn didn't yet have a household commensurate with the status of a queen even as she behaved like one, living at court with the king while Queen Catherine remained elsewhere. The trappings of queenship did not belong to the individual but to the office. Anne might now be a marquess, but she was not yet a queen. Tracking the development of her household, and the group of women who served her, is no easy task. Like all noblewomen in court service, Anne would have had a few female servants even before she caught the eye of the king. The first time that women are explicitly described in a written source as being 'with the Lady Anne' is the New Year gift list for 1532, where the king gave gifts to five women so described.[17] Listed at the end of the rest of the women, under the status of 'gentlewomen', several of them are identifiable. At the top of the list was Anne Savage, the daughter of Sir John Savage of Rocksavage in Cheshire, whose family had a history of Crown service and links to the Brereton family, also courtiers at this time. Savage was later described by a family servant as 'a lady of masculine spirit, over-powerful with her husband, seldom at rest with herself', and, if true, one can see how she and Anne Boleyn might have enjoyed one another's company.[18] Anne Joscelyn is trickier to pin down, but was one of the Joscelyns of Hyde Hall in Sawbridgeworth, Essex, either by birth or by marriage, and thus likewise had connections to the royal court.[19] 'Margery', listed without surname, may be Margery Horsman, who continued in Anne's service even after her later marriage to Michael Lister; Jane Ashley went on to marry Peter Mewtas. Mistress Wriothesley, given no forename, may have been Jane Cheney, who married Thomas Wriothesley, later Earl of Southampton, at some point before 1533. Service with the king's wife-in-waiting was an oddly liminal position for anybody to be in, and it's not surprising that those listed here were relatives of men in lower-level court service but were not yet themselves of significant status. That several went on to make impressive marriages and careers that outlasted that of their mistress, however, shows how far service with the queen could carry girls like these.

Christmas 1531 was a time of 'no mirth' without the queen and her ladies.[20] Though Anne herself was gradually gaining the accoutrements of queenship – income, clothing and property – clearly her household wasn't yet a satisfactory replacement for Queen Catherine's. It's easy to think of Anne and Queen Catherine, and the women around them, in competition. But Anne had just as much reason as Catherine to be anxious about her future, hanging on the whims and feuds of men. While Catherine may have begun to feel like she was reliving the nightmare of her early years in England, Anne's bad dream was just beginning. Around this time Anne Gainsford (she who was responsible for the loss of Anne's copy of Tyndale) was horrified when her mistress beckoned to her and showed her a piece of hate mail she had received: a poison pen drawing of herself beheaded, 'pronouncing certain destruction if she married the king'. Gainsford, unnerved, told her friend, 'If I thought it true, though he were an emperor, I would not myself marry him with that condition.' Anne, perhaps joking, perhaps grimly, responded that she was resolved to have him 'whatsoever might become of me'.[21]

Not everybody was happy to see Anne's star rise. The king's sister Mary, Duchess of Suffolk and queen dowager of France, was initially loath to speak up, but by the early 1530s was clear in her disapproval and not too shy to say so. She knew Anne. Anne had been part of Mary's retinue in France when she had first gone to marry the French king in 1514, and they had danced together in masques in London. But she knew and loved Queen Catherine more, and she remembered how infatuated her brother had been in 1509.[22] In June 1531 Chapuys, the Imperial ambassador, reported shrewdly that 'the said Duke of Suffolk and his wife would, if they dared, oppose this second marriage of the king with all their force'.[23] Anne knew this. Suffolk had allegedly had the temerity to question her honour. A month later she hit back, accusing Suffolk of having slept with his own daughter; by this she meant his young ward Katherine Willoughby, daughter of María de Salinas, Lady Willoughby, who remained by Queen Catherine's side.[24] Katherine was only twelve, and destined for Suffolk's son Henry. The idea that she could tempt Suffolk away from Mary, his wife, was a crude insult to both of them.

Tensions and tempers continued to escalate. Mary used 'oppro-brious language' against Anne, and their feud was taken up by their menfolk: in 1532 Suffolk's man Sir William Pennington duelled at Westminster with the Duke of Norfolk's adherent Richard Southwell, a clash that ended in Pennington's death. His body was found inside the Westminster sanctuary, and the incident was swiftly cast as murder by Pennington's supporters.[25] The official legal write-up ignored these allegiances, laying the cause of the brawl at the feet of a lawsuit between the pair. But their fight was a microcosm of bigger political alignments. 'The whole Court was in uproar,' Venetian ambassador Carlo Capello wrote, with Suffolk himself ready to march into Westminster and forcibly drag out Southwell and his followers.[26] Small wonder that this was not repeated in the legal documents and that the affair was generally hushed up by Thomas Cromwell; the king did not want his future wife's sexual honour debated in a court of law, particularly not when his sister had levied the unpleasant accusa-tion. While popular conduct books might airily dismiss women's words as unworthy of male attention, here they had set the whole court aflame and even caused a man's death.

A great blast of gunfire rent the air. The ladies, their ears protected by the hoods they customarily wore, must nevertheless have been half deafened even streets away in the Exchequer palace. Only in Calais would such a display occur; only in Calais was there a garrison of soldiers ready and waiting to fire a salute 'with guns and all other instruments' to mark the return of the kings to the city. If she had looked out of the window, Jane Parker, Viscountess Rochford, might have seen the rows of soldiers in blue and red uniforms lining one side of the narrow street, serving-men in tawny on the other, an honour guard for King Henry to return to his lodging.[27]

The ladies had been kicking their heels in Calais while the king went to Boulogne for a formal meeting with the French king, Francis I. This was not ideal, and it hadn't been the original intention. Henry had wanted to meet Francis to gain his support for his annulment and remarriage, and to reaffirm their alliance against Holy Roman Emperor Charles V. Wives often accompanied men on diplomatic assignments, but Henry wanted to take Anne Boleyn with him. In October 1532, however, Anne wasn't his wife, and she wasn't a queen. How could Queen Eleanor of France, herself a niece of Queen Catherine of England, behave as though Anne was remotely her equal? Sensibly, nobody seems to have suggested that she do so. Marguerite of Angoulême, a princess of France and Queen of Navarre, was proposed instead; but at the last minute she pleaded ill-health.[28]

It was a humiliating blow, for now Anne could only tag along like a spare part. Jane knew that Anne had been waiting for this trip since the summer. Beset by women 'hooting and hissing' at her wherever she and the king went on their summer progress, she had even turned back early, preferring to sink her energy into her preparations to wow the French.[29] Some thought that Anne and the king planned to marry while in France. Ambassador Chapuys reported in cipher that 'she considers herself so sure of success that not later than a week ago she wrote a letter to her principal friend and favourite here, whom she holds as sister and companion, bidding her get ready against this journey and interview, where, she says, that which she has been so long wishing for will be accomplished'.[30]

Perhaps this 'principal friend', as close as a sister, was Jane. Jane was in fact Anne's sister-in-law. The two had been maids of honour together since the early 1520s, and no doubt Jane had known her future husband, Anne's brother George, now Viscount Rochford, well too. Their families were neighbours on the borders of East Anglia. George was ambitious, well educated, a poet, and likely to grow closer to the king. He was also a son and heir set to inherit his father's estate. Jane's family, the Parkers, Barons Morley, were courtiers too and people of culture; her parents had been in the service of the king's grandmother Lady Margaret Beaufort, and her father Henry was a well-known translator. While it probably wasn't a love match, their union served both sides, and so Jane and George had married sometime in 1525.[31] Both had continued to serve at court, and as Anne rose, Jane – a Boleyn, now – rose with her. At some stage Jane must have been quietly transferred from the queen's household to Anne's service. Her star was firmly yoked to the Boleyns, and Jane was too much a courtier not to play the hand she had been dealt. Thus in October 1532 she was in Calais, with Anne and several more of their relations, smelling gunpowder and awaiting the king's return.

·No fuss was openly made about France's lack of enthusiasm for meeting with Anne herself, but the lack of a formal audience may have meant she could not take as large a retinue as she had apparently intended.[32] Jane was one of only a handful of noblewomen to travel with Anne, and she must have known what was planned. On the evening of Sunday, 27 October, a little over two weeks after their arrival in France, Henry hosted the French king at a banquet. No expense was spared. The room itself glittered, the light of a hundred candles catching on the cloth of silver, goldsmith's work, jewels and pearls with which the walls were hung. At one end was a cupboard 'seven stages high' full of gold plate; the candelabra branches were silver and silver gilt. Plate was routinely used to magnify the effect of candles, the only source of light on an October evening, but this was quite literally dazzling, and the food was yet to come. The French king was served French-style, King Henry 'after the English fashion': three courses, each with upwards of forty different dishes.[33] While the kings consumed their bodyweight in meat, Jane and the rest of the women were busy dressing. They had costumes of cloth of gold and silver and crimson tinsel satin, panels of cloth loosely tied together with gold laces, and masks upon their faces. Following Anne, Jane and the six others slipped into the chamber. They selected dancing companions from among the men by prior arrangement, perhaps deliberately cultivating the jealousy of those left unchosen, for there were no other women present. Jane and the others were literally showing King Francis what he had missed by excluding Anne from the summit. After a little dancing, King Henry went further; he removed their masks 'so that the ladies' beauties were showed'.[34]

Their looks, though, were only part of their charm. Of the six women present, four were Anne's own relations: Jane, of course, but also her sister Mary Boleyn, Lady Carey and two cousins, themselves sisters, Elizabeth Howard, Lady Fitzwalter and Dorothy Howard, Countess of Derby.[35] Jane, of course, was a courtier, and had more or less grown up at the royal court, as had Mary Boleyn. The others, though, weren't career courtiers in the same way. How could they be? Queen Catherine still had a household full of ladies-in-waiting; Anne could not yet benefit from their expertise. During the summer the Venetian ambassador had reported that the Duchess of Norfolk and the king's own sister Mary, the queen dowager of France, would be part of Anne's train, but this was almost certainly wishful thinking since Mary, at least, flatly disobeyed her brother's order that his nobles bring their wives and 'adamantly refused to go'.[36] In the event, Anne once again fell back on her own family, the Howards, and once again was left without any noblewoman higher than the rank of countess to attend her. It was true that neither of the Howard sisters had a particular connection to Queen Catherine. Their presence might indeed have been meant to show that that the Howard dynasty, the Duke of Norfolk himself – historically a friend of the French – supported Anne. To anyone who knew the English aristocracy, though, it must have been clear that they were something of a let-down, a 'making do' in the face of opposition.

Nevertheless, the banquet was a success. King Francis had spent some time talking with Anne after the dancing and she had surely impressed him. It was time to go home, but the weather had other ideas. Violent storms blew up all along the coast. Ships were blown back into Calais harbour 'in great jeopardy'. In Holland the tide breached the coastal defences; in Antwerp the water rose three feet above the wharf.[37] The English party were storm-stayed. Amid the wind and the rain they could not stir out of doors, and Jane and the rest of the royal party were trapped in the Exchequer. No doubt they amused themselves as best they could with singing, dancing, gambling and conversation. For Anne and Henry it must have been more serendipitous than otherwise. They could spend time together amid a much-reduced establishment. Jane must have wondered whether they were discussing marriage. She and her husband George had not managed to have any children, and surely Jane could sympathise with the royal anxiety regarding the succession. But there was no point in Anne birthing a bastard, and evidence suggests she and Henry had not yet consummated their five-year relationship.[38]

Tucked up safe from the raging storm in Calais, they decided now was the moment to change this. But they needed some formal sign. Edward Hall's *Chronicle* tells us that 'The king, after his return, married privily the lady Anne Boleyn, on St Erkenwald's day, which marriage was kept so secret, that very few knew it.'[39] St Erkenwald's day was 14 November, the day that they arrived back at Dover. If there was some sort of secret marriage, or more likely a binding pre-contract ceremony, this would explain Princess Elizabeth's arrival the following September. Now the family relationship between Anne and the women attending her in Calais served its purpose: kin kept secrets. If Jane knew what had happened, she did not tell.

A pre-contract ceremony in November 1532 was sufficient to allow Anne and Henry to commence sleeping together, but it was not enough for them to declare themselves fully wed. On 25 January 1533, therefore, Anne Savage, now Lady Berkeley, found herself standing demurely behind her mistress Anne Boleyn in a small chapel closet in the newly refurbished Palace of Whitehall. Whitehall had previously been called York Place, owned by Wolsey as Archbishop of York, but had come to the king's hands in 1529 and been swiftly renamed. Not only was it conveniently centrally located, but as a former bishop's palace it had no queen's apartments, and thus Anne and Henry could stay there without Queen Catherine. Almost immediately they began to plan a grand refurbishment.[40] Anne and Henry had walked through the unfinished rooms, poring over plans and consulting craftsmen together, and maybe Anne Savage had watched them do this, close enough to Anne to count as chaperone, far enough away that the couple could feel alone.

Now she watched them promise themselves to one another.[41]

The marriage was so secret that it took a little time for anybody to report it. Even Chapuys, who invariably heard everything sooner or later, did not know about it for another month.[42] By this time there were rumours that Anne was pregnant, and it was becoming clearer by the day that the divorce would be settled somehow.[43] There had not yet been any mass movement of ladies-in-waiting from Queen Catherine to Anne, but there were signs that this might yet occur. On Holy Saturday, the day before Easter Sunday, Mary Howard, having proven herself at the ceremony for Anne's creation as marquess the previous September, took her place behind Anne once again. This time they were to process publicly to mass in the chapel royal at Greenwich as the king and queen always did on this day: it was an official usurpation of Queen Catherine's position, replacing her with Anne, and everybody understood that this was a sign of an impending change in her status.[44] She wore 'a gorgeous suit of tissue', 'loaded with diamonds and other precious stones'. This time Mary bore Anne's train. Her fair colouring, chestnut hair just glimpsed underneath her velvet hood, and demure, downcast eyes made a striking contrast with Anne's olive skin and dramatic, black-eyed gaze. Other women followed them in procession, and Chapuys thought that they were treated with 'the same or perhaps greater' ceremonies than those ordinarily used for a queen.[45] Sure enough, he also reported around the same time that Anne's household was formally appointed, which meant that her ladies-in-waiting were chosen and given lodging and bouche of court if they were not already in receipt of these.[46] Frustratingly, no complete list survives from this time to tell us who they were, but both Jane, Viscountess Rochford and Mary Howard must have been among them. On this Holy Saturday, the preacher in the chapel royal not only included Anne in his prayers but formally prayed for her as queen of England. The shift had occurred. According to Chapuys, 'even those who support her party do not know whether to laugh or cry at it'.[47]

They did not have long to decide. Coronation rumours already abounded, and Mary surely knew that if such a thing came to pass she would be given a prominent role in Anne's immediate entourage. Yet her burgeoning court career placed her in a difficult position. Her mother Elizabeth, Duchess of Norfolk was openly, vocally and immovably loyal to Queen Catherine. She was not likely to approve of her daughter entering Anne's household, and yet they both knew that it was not Mary's own choice to make. She was only fifteen; it was for her parents to decide where she should live, and her betrothal to the king's son made the new queen's household the most obvious place. No doubt her father the Duke of Norfolk did not want her with her mother, imbibing the duchess's stubborn loyalties and implacable defiance against the inevitable. If Mary were to survive in this world, she must learn to be politically flexible.

Celebratory gun salutes had not stopped firing since Queen Anne and her ladies took to the queen's barge at Greenwich to travel by water to the Tower, ready for the procession the next morning.[48] Mary Howard was one of these ladies, heading out on the water in the bright sunshine. For months Mary would have heard that Anne was unpopular in the city and with ordinary people, that she could not go abroad for fear of being mobbed, that she was cat-called and insulted. One would not have known it from the throng of boats on the river and spectators on the banks. Every guild in the city had launched a barge, banners flying in the fresh breeze, the ordinary river traffic quite unable to find a clear route through the ships decked out in gold cloth, sparkling in the sunshine reflected off the murky waters of the Thames. It was late May 1533, and Anne was finally to be crowned queen.

Mary must have begun to feel like a veteran of large royal ceremonies; there had been so many since she began her court career. This, though, was the biggest yet. Coronations happened rarely, perhaps only once a generation, and this one had a particularly interesting flavour. The king's annulment had been hastily pronounced by Thomas Cranmer, the new Archbishop of Canterbury, only six days previously, and there had not yet been any reaction from Rome.[49] Catherine of Aragon was no longer queen but 'princess dowager', a title that so enraged her that she tore her pen through the page in a single furious stroke whenever it was used in letters addressed to her. Anne's coronation, though, had not depended on the annulment, just as her marriage had not. One could not plan a coronation in six days. Stages were built, cloth ordered, appointments chosen and guild pageants planned and rehearsed far in advance of the planned date of 1 June. Henry, clearly, was going to marry a new wife and have her crowned whether the Church was in agreement or no.[50]

Like all royal ceremony, coronations were governed by ordinance based on precedent, and there were rarely any surprises. It was important that it be so. Any deviation might be read as de-legitimising Anne and Henry's marriage and the succession of their future heirs. She and her ladies, therefore, travelled in Catherine of Aragon's royal barge and followed the precise ceremonies that she had done at her coronation in 1509, dressed in the same crimson velvet trimmed with ermine.[51] Mary Howard was too young to have witnessed Catherine's coronation and would only have understood Anne's on its own terms. Her grandmother Agnes, dowager Duchess of Norfolk, though, a widow in her fifties, must have watched with cynical interest even as she played her own part, carrying Anne's train.[52] For all the meticulous adherence to precedence, there was a strained quality to the familiar ceremonies.

Anne's coronation is often read with hindsight as a herald of the mood of religious reform that would shortly envelop England, but to do this is to misunderstand the thrust of the ceremony. People found it jarring not because it was a sign of religious change but because it was self-consciously otherwise. The choice of Whitsunday, the second-most important festival of the Church calendar after Easter, was an attempt to entwine Anne's elevation with the descent of the Holy Spirit upon the Apostles, associated with the foundation of the first Catholic Church and 'true' faith, ramming home the legitimacy of her queenship. Anne's coronation can therefore be read not as an attempt to showcase a new religion but a means of emphasising Henry's recently declared supremacy over the old one, and this must have felt uncomfortable to many of those who felt that Anne's queenship was a divine ill and not a divine right.[53]

Was Mary aware of this, walking behind Anne's litter on the gravelled streets, too warm in velvet and ermine, trying to remember to smile and laugh and pay attention to the pageants? Did she notice, as one writer claimed to, an ominous silence in pockets of the watching crowds, a mocking of the monarchs' initials, 'HA', set up on every street corner?[54] A coronation ceremony was supposed to reinforce a sense of spiritual destiny, a sense that Anne was chosen by God to be queen: a body royal, as well as a body natural. How did that sit with the women who had lived with her, shared a bed with her, helped her lace up her gowns, watched as the king singled her out to flirt with – a girl no better than themselves?

Some did not even try to get past this. Mary's mother Elizabeth, Duchess of Norfolk, was no more reconciled to her niece's position and utterly refused to attend the coronation at all, 'from the love she bore to the previous Queen'.[55] The Duke of Suffolk was there, his six-foot frame impossible to miss, but his wife, the king's sister Mary, queen dowager of France, was not, and nor was María de Salinas, Lady Willoughby, Queen Catherine's loyal Spanish friend. Mary had some excuse. She was dangerously ill. She had had several bouts of a recurring sickness since 1518, and on 25 June 1533, between seven and eight of the clock in the morning in Suffolk's house at Westhorpe, she died, aged only thirty-seven.[56] Her death was framed by some as a reaction to Anne's coronation; one chronicler thought that she died from grief, 'the sorrow caused by the sight of her brother leaving his wife'.[57]

It must have been tempting to see the two events in juxtaposition, the old giving way to the new. The national mourning at Mary's passing was widespread, more so than any joy at Anne's coronation. The French, in view of Mary's position as queen dowager of France, sent a sizeable delegation to her funeral at Bury St Edmund's, and she was described as 'beloved in the country and by the common people of this town'.[58] The king ordered requiem masses to be sung in Westminster on 9 and 10 July, but did not order the court to appear in mourning, which might have been

construed by some as a sign of disfavour.[59] María, Lady Willoughby
had not attended Queen Anne's coronation, but she made no
demur at travelling to Bury St Edmunds for Mary's funeral. Her
own daughter Katherine, now fourteen years old – the same age as
Mary Howard – had been raised by the dowager queen of France
at Westhorpe. Mother and daughter dressed in black alongside the
rest of the Brandon women to perform the elaborate processional
ceremonies and offerings as mourners.[60] Both, though, must have
been anxious. With no woman at the head of the Suffolk household, with Queen Catherine diminished and Queen Anne on the
throne, what would happen to Katherine now?

8

Fragility and Brittleness

The hammering and sawing had lasted most of the previous day, echoing through the cold air, a jarring note at odds with the sweeter tones of the cathedral bells of St Paul's above. Now the people of London saw the tall wooden scaffold and began to gather, knowing that something unusual was about to take place. Before long, a small cavalcade arrived: led by guards in royal livery, two Observant friars, two monks, two priests, two laymen, and in the middle of these men a nun, were placed on the wooden platform where everybody could see them. John Salcot, Bishop of Bangor, mounted the stairs to the open-air pulpit known as St Paul's Cross and began a lengthy sermon, recounting and embellishing their crimes. The sole woman, the nun, was at the centre of his wrath: she had, by her 'feigned superstition', the bishop declared, prevented sentence being reached on the royal divorce, and she and her accomplices had used 'subtle, crafty and superstitious' means to draw others to their cause, 'to the intent to sow a secret murmur and grudge in the hearts of the king's subjects against the majesty of our sovereign lord and all his proceedings'.[1] Her 'visions' were nothing but malicious inventions, a sin against God and the king, and nobody who valued their lives and their faith should give her any credence. After this, the nun and the others were forced one by one to 'confess' to their crimes. That done, the guards stepped forward, and all of them were returned to the Tower. Everybody watching knew that it was unlikely they would leave it alive.

Thirty miles to the west amid the rolling Surrey hills, another woman heard the news and dread must have settled around her heart. Ambassador Chapuys might write scornfully of this 'comedy', 'for it hardly deserves any other name', but too well. Gertrude Blount, Marchioness of Exeter knew that the affair of the nun was no laughing matter.[2] The nun's name was Elizabeth Barton. It was not only Gertrude who had thought she was a visionary, a mystic whose prophesies strongly defended traditional Catholic doctrine.[3] Back in 1526, an ecclesiastical commission led by the late Archbishop of Canterbury, William Warham, had pronounced Barton's revelations genuine. Her authority made sense within the Christian tradition of influential female mystics, which is perhaps why so many people were ready to accept her.[4] After 1528, though, her visions became increasingly political, and she met three times with the king, eventually warning him against divorcing Catherine of Aragon and predicting his death within a month of doing so. From that moment she became a marked woman, a dangerously powerful opponent of Henry VIII's Church sovereignty.

Like everyone else, Gertrude knew that any association with the nun was risky. A courtier by blood, she had joined her father William Blount, Lord Mountjoy in Queen Catherine of Aragon's service in the early 1520s not long after her marriage to Henry Courtenay, then Earl of Devon and since Marquess of Exeter.[5] She knew how quickly things could change and how dangerous it could be to be found on the wrong side of the divide, not least because she and her husband lived in continual negotiation of their royal blood. Henry Courtenay was King Henry's first cousin. They'd grown up together, and Courtenay had always – so far – enjoyed royal favour. But his earliest memories were of his father in disgrace, executed as a traitor in 1502 for conspiring against King Henry VII from within his own privy chamber, and only a couple of years ago men from his affinity in Devon had made much of his lineage, calling him heir apparent to the throne. His claim to King Henry's crown remained like an unquiet ghost in the back of the closet.[6] Both Henry and Gertrude knew that they had to watch their step.

And yet both were deeply uneasy at the king's divorce, and more so about the threat of new religion that Anne represented in many people's minds. Gertrude was not prepared to parrot the party line as another colleague, Eleanor, Countess of Rutland would do: the case of the nun, Eleanor had written to her father, was one of 'the most abominablest matters that I ever heard of in my life'.[7] But nor would she throw caution entirely to the winds as her colleague Elizabeth, Duchess of Norfolk had done, declaring her views to anyone who would listen and getting herself dismissed from court. Gertrude was wilier than that. If she was to be of any use to the queen or to those who supported her she needed to stay at court, and that meant she needed to walk a careful path, to balance on a tightrope while appearing unconcerned. So she had attended Anne Boleyn's coronation in June earlier that year, but she'd also stayed in close touch with Queen Catherine throughout 1532 and 1533.[8] That September she had been made one of the godparents of Princess Elizabeth.[9] Her position as one of the country's highest-ranking peeresses made her an understandable choice, but godparenthood meant more than spiritual guidance for a child; it was designed to bind the natural and spiritual parents together too.[10] For a royal baby, it was a chance for the king to signal royal favour and trust, or to attempt to solidify bonds of loyalty and service, to draw people to his cause. A sign of favour, perhaps; or was it a warning to the Courtenays that Henry would accept nothing less than complete submission to his will?

If the latter, it was one that Gertrude set quietly to one side. Only ten days after the christening she sent a message to Imperial ambassador Chapuys, Catherine of Aragon's chief supporter, informing him of the movements of key court figures and the reasons behind certain recent council meetings. Relaying this to Emperor Charles V, Chapuys described Gertrude as 'the sole consolation of the Queen and Princess'.[11] Gertrude might publicly toe the line, but behind the scenes she was Chapuys' chief informant.

This was risky, but not actively dangerous. Women could get away with all sorts of clandestine activity if it remained just that: clandestine, quiet, covert. Involvement with Elizabeth Barton, though, was a different proposition. Gertrude had been introduced to the nun through her association with the Observant friars, and must have been aware that she was not the only person of rank within the nun's circle of influence. The Archbishop of Canterbury himself had said her theology was sound; initially at least, Barton must have seemed safe enough. But this would count for nothing now if the king had decided otherwise. Too well Gertrude knew what would happen. Now that Barton was under arrest, she'd be questioned for the names of her associates, and Gertrude had good reason to fear every messenger who arrived at her house in West Horsley.

The Friday after midsummer's day in 1533, Gertrude had sent two of her servants to Barton, who was then lodged at Syon Abbey, asking her to come to her home in Surrey. They passed a gift to Barton: 'a little book in form of a pair of tables with blank leaves', which was a portable writing tablet, perhaps intended as encouragement to continue to write down her revelations.[12] The abbess advised Barton to go, describing Gertrude as 'an honourable woman', and so she did, and she and Gertrude spoke privately the next morning. According to Barton's testimony, Gertrude's reasons for wanting to speak with her were nothing to do with national politics but were personal, and explicitly female. Gertrude thought that she might be pregnant, and she was afraid because she had had pregnancies end in stillbirth or miscarriage before. She asked Barton to pray to Our Lady 'that she might have issue that would live'. During the conversation Barton mentioned the possibility of war, and Gertrude likewise asked her to pray for her husband that he would come through safely. He had been so sick at the time of the queen's coronation that she was still worried for him, and said touchingly that 'though her person was there, her heart was at home'.[13]

These are the concerns of a woman worried for the people she loved and for the child she bore, not a woman seeking maliciously to destroy the king's sovereignty over the Church, or his recent marriage. And yet could the two be separated? By June 1533 Barton had already made several public, damning revelations about the future of Henry's throne and even his life. She had, she claimed, seen the seat ready for him in hell should he go through with his marriage to Anne Boleyn. For Gertrude to seek out her advice in any context was to see, and choose to ignore, this fact; or even, considering the gift of the writing tablet, to encourage it. Catherine of Aragon herself knew that any contact with Barton was unwise because of the way in which it would be perceived by the king and his council. She refused point-blank to meet with or have any dealings at all with the nun. Chapuys therefore reported that though Catherine had no fear for herself, she did fear for Gertrude, and for others who had been 'familiar' with Barton.[14]

Gertrude might not have explicitly consulted Barton about anything other than personal issues, but she was in good company. The list of people who had contact with Barton is striking in terms of those who would, a little later, be clearly understood as pro-Catherine, and in many cases religiously conservative. And many of them were also women. Margaret Pole, Countess of Salisbury, Lady Hussey, the dowager Countess of Derby; all had heard of the nun's revelations.[15] So far as the king was concerned, if you were pro-Catherine you were not only anti-Anne but anti-Henry, and that was a dangerous opinion indeed. On 25 November, a mere two days after Barton's public penance, Gertrude received a letter. It would have arrived borne by a royal messenger, and this alone would have made her catch her breath. Sure enough, the letter was from the king, and it laid out her 'abuse, lightness, and indiscreet offences' committed in seeking the company of 'that most unworthy subtle and deceptable woman called the holy maid of Kent'. However, it also contained a royal pardon.[16]

She sent for her secretary. She wrote to Thomas Cromwell, by this point the king's official secretary, acknowledging receipt of the pardon, and her letter makes it clear that she had been waiting on tenterhooks for the sword of Damocles to fall since Barton's arrest, if not before. She had been sick, she explained, 'caused by my conceit that the king had been heavy lord to me'.[17] She then composed a reply to the king himself, and sent a draft to Cromwell.[18] It remains a masterclass in abject grovelling. She prostrated herself at his feet – a strong visual – asking him to 'first and chiefly consider that I am a woman whose fragility and brittleness is such as most facilely, easily and lightly seduced and brought into abuse and light belief'. She had never given true credence to the nun's prophecies; she simply hadn't known any better. Her husband was furious with her, and she feared she might have lost his love forever. She was the 'most sorrowful and heavy creature alive' and she would never do such a thing again.[19]

She was following a cultural script. In theory, women were, and were understood to be, the weaker sex. They could not be considered responsible for their actions and impulses, nor held to the same high standards as men. As Spanish humanist Juan Luis Vives wrote in 1520, 'a Woman is a frail thing, and of weak discretion, and that may lightly be deceived'.[20] Vives' text, though, was a conduct book: a wish list of virtues to be inculcated into young girls, itself a tacit admission that these were not inherent characteristics. Letters like Gertrude's show that women were well aware of this and weaponised their lesser status, writing themselves as objects of pity when it was in their interest to do so. A little later, Elizabethan noblewoman Mary Throckmorton even described this very process, explaining that she had answered a man's letter 'like a woman, very submissively'.[21] Letters like these had a recognised format and conventions of politeness that must be followed. Using a secretary, rather than writing in one's own hand, was a sign of respect towards one's social betters. Gertrude wrote only her signature in her own hand, and this was placed deferentially to one side, a few lines below the rest of the writing.[22] Petitionary letters demanded an appropriately obsequious salutation and sign-off: Gertrude finished by praying for 'the prosperous conservation of the most noble and royal estate to your highness's succession and posterity long to endure, which I shall not fail to do, my poor life enduring'.[23]

Gertrude was fortunate. Her sex, her rank and probably the fact that her husband was the king's cousin meant that her life was not realistically in danger, else Henry would not have sent a pardon along with his upbraiding letter. She understood that written subservience was exactly what he wanted in return, and she gave him a stellar performance of feminine compliance. A warning, this time; but would it stem the swelling tide of female resistance?

The life of a lady-in-waiting was ever a balance between court service and country magnate, and for María de Salinas, Lady Willoughby these things became increasingly entwined during the 1530s. María was still ostensibly in Queen Catherine's service, but records show that she was also busy elsewhere. While Gertrude wrote letters to ambassador Chapuys, in September 1533 María attended a wedding. Her only daughter Katherine was to marry her long-standing friend Charles Brandon, Duke of Suffolk. This marriage caused many raised eyebrows. Katherine was fourteen to Suffolk's forty-nine, and he had been *in loco parentis* as the owner of her wardship. There had, perhaps, been signs; Anne Boleyn's 1531 jibe about him having slept 'with his own daughter' might have been an exaggeration, but there was rarely smoke without fire.[24] While it wasn't uncommon for young women to marry older men, and fourteen was an acceptable age for a noble girl to contract marriage, a thirty-five-year age gap was on the large side. Chapuys described Suffolk and Katherine's marriage as 'singular and strange', not least because it occurred with such unseemly haste after the death of Suffolk's previous wife.[25] Katherine had grown up in their household. Originally, the plan had been for her to marry Suffolk's eldest son Henry. Now, though, that plan was abandoned: now she was stepping straight into the still-warm shoes of her quasi-mother.

María, as Katherine's mother, seems to have approved of the match, and perhaps had even encouraged it. Suffolk would be a good protector for Katherine's estates. She may have been the more willing to push Katherine into Suffolk's arms because the legal battle over those very estates had come to the fore once again. Wolsey's fall at the end of 1529 had meant that no resolution had ever been reached on the Willoughby lands, and the new Chancellor, Sir Thomas More, took a little while to take stock of the situation. He seems to have asked for more information from both María and her obstreperous brother-in-law Sir Christopher Willoughby. She was only too happy to oblige, and entered the fray once more with a lengthy explanation of the dispute. María did not write in English herself, or at least there's no surviving example of her doing so. But she could speak fluently now, and her feisty, sarcastic tone found its way through the drier phrases used by her lawyer as he took down her dictation. Sir Christopher had inveigled her husband out of extra money, she claimed, and then paid back a bond with that money. He might well, she said acerbically, 'pay my lord with a feather of his own goose'; 'but it is an old proverb, one beateth the bush and another taketh the bird'.[26]

Sir Thomas More tried to be fair. He felt that Sir Christopher did deserve more than Willoughby's will had allowed. But More's decrees, handed down with the full force of the law three times between 1529 and 1532, were not sufficient for either party.[27] Soon there were additional lawsuits over detention of deeds and failure to deliver money when ordered.[28] In Orford, the town in which Lord Willoughby had died, Sir Christopher even caused a riot among the locals when he turned up to mass on a February Sunday and insisted on keeping the people there for over an hour afterwards, trying to get them to acknowledge his title to the manor, 'sometimes by flattery, sometimes harshness'. Eventually, local constable Richard Hunt told him wearily, 'Sir, you say you do love us. Wherefore, if you do so as you say, we desire you not to hinder our liberties, for in so much as in time coming after my lady's death this town shall be your inheritance.'[29] María must have been wickedly pleased at this show of support from her tenants.

Managing this dispute took a considerable amount of her time. Nor could she count on her new son-in-law to be available to fight her corner when she needed him, for he had his own tightrope to walk. Suffolk was uneasy about the king's divorce, but clearly felt that he had no choice but to do as the king asked him. He and María probably discussed the issue, for this was politics close to María's heart too. In December 1533 he was instructed to go with some other councillors to Queen Catherine at Buckden in

Huntingdonshire and to move her to another bishop's palace at
Somersham, just the other side of Huntingdon itself. They were
also to inform her of her change in title from queen to princess
dowager, and to get her servants to swear to a new oath naming
her as such.[30] Suffolk was not at all keen to do this, and he told
María so: he 'wished some mischief might happen to him to excuse
himself from this journey'. He even 'confessed on the sacrament'
before he left, worried about the danger to his soul from the task
ahead. María, remaining at home with her daughter, Suffolk's
new wife Katherine, sent a message to ambassador Chapuys to tell
him what was about to happen and about Suffolk's unwillingness;
perhaps she did not want Queen Catherine's 'party' to see him as
an enemy.[31]

Undoubtedly, Suffolk knew what sort of reception he could
expect. In the great chamber, before all of her household, he told
Catherine what was to happen and bore the brunt of her anger. She
would rather be 'hewn in pieces' than be called princess dowager.
She refused to move to Somersham, and she refused the service of
anybody sworn to her as anything other than queen of England.
Many of her servants, too, refused to take a new oath, claiming
that since they were sworn to her as queen, 'the second oath would
be perjury'.[32] This was a problem unique to the royal household.
Usually servants took an oath only to one master or mistress. But
the queen's servants were explicitly sworn to the king as well, and
now this was a problem: when the king and queen were openly at
variance, which part of the oath should stand?

Chamberlain Lord Mountjoy – the father of Gertrude, Marchioness of Exeter – soon wrote that the women in particular
were loath to stop calling her queen.[33] A list was made, probably at
this time, of those who refused to take the new oath. Many were
indeed women. Some, like Blanche Twyford and Margery Otwell,
had been in Catherine's service for over fifteen years. The list gives
a sense of the reduced status of Catherine's household, for those
left in her service were distinctly un-aristocratic; the daughters
of knights at best, and many not even that.[34] Noblewomen who
would willingly have served Catherine were not permitted to do

so – the king would hardly want to promote the concept of a rival royal household – and those on the make were well aware that service with the new Queen Anne was a far more likely route to favour and promotion.

These women's refusal to swear may not immediately have cost them their positions, for five months later, in May 1534, Chapuys was still reporting that 'certain maids in waiting of the Queen's, having refused to take the said oath, had been arrested and locked up in a room'.[35] In June the king once again sent messengers 'to make the ladies about her swear', with instructions to remove those who would not; this was not carried out, as Chapuys observed wryly, because of 'the difficulty of causing so many ladies to come to this capital against their will and by force'.[36] Her household, it was reported, 'regard less the King's commandment' than their mistress's own wishes, a touching display of loyalty based more on a relationship built over decades of service than any particular oath.[37] As was so often the case, royal servants had become an extension of royal will – just not the king's royal will.

Suffolk, for his part, was frustrated, embarrassed and wished himself anywhere else on earth. No doubt María heard all about it when he got home. 'We find this woman more obstinate than we can express,' he wrote to Cromwell.[38] On the day that Queen Catherine was due to move to Somersham she locked herself in her privy chamber and told them that if they wanted her to move, they would have to move her by force, something that the councillors, not surprisingly, baulked at. Princess Mary, too, was causing trouble. While Suffolk dealt with Catherine, the Duke of Norfolk had been sent to Mary to tell her that she was no longer a princess, and to remove her into her sister Princess Elizabeth's service, neither of which Mary took well.[39] Women might in theory be the weaker sex, but 'this unbridled Spanish blood', as Anne Boleyn put it in March 1534, had created formidable opponents.[40] The divide between Anne and Catherine was becoming clearer and clearer. Balancing loyalties was harder and harder: María and the other ladies-in-waiting were finding that choices must be made.

By the end of 1533, Mary Howard was fully settled at court as one of her cousin Queen Anne Boleyn's ladies-in-waiting. Mary's marriage to Henry Fitzroy, the king's illegitimate son, had gone ahead in November and so Mary was now the Duchess of Richmond at the age of only fourteen.[41] She was, though, a married woman in name only. The couple were not to cohabit just yet. Fitzroy, too, was only fourteen, and the death of his uncle Prince Arthur back in 1502 had done nothing to allay royal fears about the potential ill-effects of too much 'chamber work' too soon. Fitzroy remained in London and Mary with the royal household, enjoying all that court culture had to offer.[42]

Both had had choices made for them. They were part of the new regime. Mary served Queen Anne along with many other Howard and Boleyn relatives. It was to be expected that a new queen would pack her household with family, her natural supporters in this world where patronage and kinship so often entwined. The king's own mother, Elizabeth of York, had done just the same. Thus Queen Anne's mother Elizabeth, Lady Boleyn, her sister Mary, the widowed Lady Carey, sister-in-law Jane, Viscountess Rochford, cousins Mary and Margaret Shelton and aunt Elizabeth, another Lady Boleyn, were all part of her regular household along with Mary Howard.[43] Mary's mother Elizabeth, Duchess of Norfolk, though, did not return to court and was never seen in Anne's service. Her loyalties remained with Catherine of Aragon. In fact, few women are known to have served both queens, and those that did tended to be either Boleyn relations who had jumped ship or the wives of male household officers who stayed on between queens. Isabel, Lady Baynton, for example, was the wife of Edward Baynton, who served as vice-chamberlain to five of the six queens, and Margaret, Lady Coffin was the wife of Queen Anne's master of the horse. While the ladies-in-waiting belonged to the queen's privy chamber, her most personal service, the rest of the apparatus of the queen's household – the cooks, stable boys, councillors and all of those whose job it was to keep the establishment running – remained largely intact, ready for a new queen to simply step neatly into her place in an already functioning machine. For a

domestic-born consort like Anne Boleyn, who had not been raised
to be queen, both this and her ready bulwark of support in the
form of kin were godsends.

Mary and the other women were there to make Queen Anne
look good, and they soon succeeded. Anne's court was a place of
dazzling beauty and sparkling wit, and her women were its lifeblood. After her coronation there was, perhaps, a sense that years
of struggle had paid off, and the tension was released in a gush of
high spirits. As Queen Anne's vice-chamberlain Edward Baynton
wrote to the queen's brother only a week after the ceremony, 'as for
pastime in the queen's chamber, [there] was never more. If any of
you that be now departed have any ladies that ye thought favoured
you and somewhat would mourn at parting of their servants,
I can no whit perceive the same by their dancing and pastime
they do use here.'[44] For Mary and her friends, witty banter in the
form of verse was a favourite amusement. In was not unusual for
young men at court to profess to die for the love of one or other
of the queen's maids, and though Mary was now married she still
joined in the delicious game of courtly love. Poetry was one of
the more harmless ways in which to participate, and she regularly
passed a blank manuscript notebook around her circle of friends,
encouraging them to copy their favourite poems, make up new
ones and write banter and riddles to one another in the margins.
One can imagine Mary and her friends Mary Shelton and Lady
Margaret Douglas, the king's niece, poking fun as young courtier
striplings tried to write their own original verse, sighing for love
of a particular girl, pleading in rhyme for her to 'ease me of my
pain', claiming to be 'suffering in sorrow' and 'desiring in fear'. No
need to guess, either, who was the object of affection in this poem;
the first letter of each of the seven embarrassing stanzas spelled
out 'Sheltun'.[45]

The quarto-sized manuscript volume in which these lines
appear was originally owned by Mary – her initials, MF, Mary
Fitzroy, are stamped into the binding – and was passed to Margaret Douglas at some stage in the later 1530s or early 1540s. Through
her family it ended up at Chatsworth House, the seat of the Earls

of Devonshire, from whom it gained the name 'the Devonshire Manuscript'. It now resides in the British Library as one of the only surviving examples of women's involvement in the composition and circulation of poetry at the Tudor court.[46] Though historically valued more for its many unique verses by poets Thomas Wyatt and Henry Howard, Earl of Surrey, these three women – Mary Fitzroy, Margaret Douglas and Mary Shelton – were the core of its life as a working text in the 1530s, a fact that tells us a lot about the atmosphere of Queen Anne Boleyn's court. Most of the poems had a distinctly cynical air. Next to the 'Sheltun' acrostic Margaret Douglas has written scornfully 'forget this'; Mary Shelton's own hand contradicts, adding 'it is worthy' underneath. Perhaps the lad's suit was not so hopeless after all.

Love as a meaningless exercise, and the faithlessness of lovers, were central themes in poetry at this time, though used as a device to express a general mood of frustration with courtly life. Thomas Wyatt was a particular master of the jaded hack pose. No doubt they had a point – Anne's court was not a calm place – but it was also clearly fashionable to be a cynic. Misogyny, too, was all the rage. A common parlour game at this time was to use verses to play a provocative game of attack and defence of women, and there are parts of this manuscript that suggest it was used to compile ammunition for such a purpose. The women, though, fought back: culturally aware, they copied stanzas from old masters like Chaucer and Hoccleve that indignantly defended the female perspective and pointed the finger instead at the ease with which men could 'bring a woman to slanderous name'.[47] They even repurposed lines to create their own original poems.

Poetry no doubt helped them to hone the skill of exchanging banter without going too far. While women like Gertrude, Marchioness of Exeter were in the midst of a political balancing act, younger female courtiers like Mary Howard had an additional sort of tightrope to walk. Contemporaries outside the royal court routinely underappreciated the difficulty of a courtier's job, but Mary and the others would have had to work hard to develop the necessary diverse skill set, and to reach the standard required by

a Renaissance court. Mary needed to be able to converse appropriately with a wide variety of people; to dance, sing and ideally
play musical instruments; to ride and hunt; and to be able to stay
up late and get up early repeatedly without flagging. As the Italian
Baldesar Castiglione's *The Book of the Courtier*, written in 1528,
explained, the female courtier also had to walk a continuous and
precarious path of minute behavioural adjustments. She was there
to entertain, to be witty and vivacious, but without crossing the
line into indiscretion or perceptible loss of virtue.[48] This was a
consistently difficult judgement call.

Outside the court, noblewomen fell over themselves to compete
for Queen Anne's favour. This wasn't because she personally was a
source of attraction or cult of personality, but because she was the
queen of England and patronage was part of her job. One of the
most enthusiastic of these was Honor Grenville, Viscountess Lisle.
By the 1530s Honor was the second wife of Arthur Plantagenet,
Viscount Lisle, an illegitimate son of King Edward IV, and the
couple lived in Calais by reason of Lisle's position as Lord Deputy
there.[49] A woman of determined character and decided opinions,
Honor was not about to let physical distance prevent her from
being known at court. This was the only way in which she could
realistically further the careers of her husband and children, and
she set about it with gusto. Gifts of live animals seem to have been
a particular specialism. In May 1534 she sent Anne a present of
quails – to be eaten – and 'your linnet that hung in your chamber'
– a songbird, not to be eaten.[50]

Sometimes the gift was unintentional. At the end of 1533 the king
himself heard talk of a spaniel that the Lisles had given a friend,
and took the dog for himself.[51] Clearly their spaniels were popular.
The next year chief minister Thomas Cromwell, on being offered
a hawk, requested a spaniel instead.[52] Alas, they had none left save
Honor's own pet, called Pourquoi, on account of the quizzical tilt
of his head. At least Pourquoi, or 'Purkoy' as he was anglicised,
did some good: Honor eventually gave him to courtier Sir Francis
Bryan as a New Year's gift, and the queen was so enamoured with
him that she took him for herself, much as her husband had done

earlier.[53] By the end of 1534, though, he had met a calamitous end, having fallen out of a high window, and the queen had loved him so much that nobody dared to tell her until the king did so.[54] No doubt Honor sympathised. She set her mind to evolving a new gift, a different pet for the queen. Catherine of Aragon had owned a pet monkey. Would Anne like one? Emphatically, Anne would not: 'of a truth, Madam, the Queen loveth no such beasts nor can scant abide the sight of them'.[55] Exotic and high-status monkeys might be, but Honor would have to think of another way to get the queen's attention.

Queen Anne's court was becoming a centre of culture, new learning and sparkling wit. It was also a place of intense pressure and accompanying anxiety, for all these things were empty frivolities unless she could also produce a son and heir. Her women knew the score as well as she did, and some of them at least would have been in her confidence as she tried to conceive, every month a rollercoaster of hope and disappointment. By April 1534 Queen Anne was visibly and publicly pregnant; in early July Henry postponed a face-to-face meeting with Francis I in France because she was afraid to cross the sea in her condition.[56] And yet no baby appeared. This has sometimes been construed as a miscarriage, but medical historians suspect that she experienced pseudocyesis, a 'phantom pregnancy', where her body produced the signs and symptoms of pregnancy out of sheer psychological desperation.[57]

No doubt Anne's women, too, thought that she was pregnant during 1534, and helped to care for her and to encourage and reassure her. Female companions could be a comfort to a queen in Anne's position; but they were also a danger. As it often did towards the end of a wife's pregnancy, the king's eye went roving. Chapuys, ear to the ground as always, reported that Henry had 'renewed and increased the love which he formerly bore to another very handsome young lady of this court'. Said young lady had, it was said, shown an attachment to Princess Mary, and the fickle court followed her lead.[58] We don't know who this 'young lady' was. Though Chapuys mentioned her several times, he never gave her name. But her attachment to Princess Mary, if true, suggests that in any case she was not someone with whom Queen Anne saw eye to eye.

As those around Queen Catherine had known, queens could do little when faced with a rival. Queen Anne's sister-in-law Jane Parker, Viscountess Rochford knew this better than most. She had watched as Queen Catherine was supplanted by Anne herself. Perhaps she now determined that she could not let her cousin suffer the same fate; or perhaps Queen Anne demanded her sister's help. Jane had been married to George Boleyn since 1526 but had no surviving children, and we do not know whether she had ever been pregnant at all. If anyone could understand Anne's crushing anxiety in a society that valued women only for their reproductive ability, it was Jane. But she had to be careful. Queen Anne had already tried once to have her rival dismissed; the king had told her firmly to 'consider where she came from'.[59] The queen and her women knew all too well that another might tread in Queen Anne's footsteps and supplant her in turn. In October 1534, Jane 'joined in a conspiracy' to find a way to remove the offending maid, 'through quarrelling or otherwise'.[60] The plot, however, went awry. Jane herself was temporarily rusticated by the king, and was still in exile two months later in December with no knowledge of when – or whether – she might be permitted to return.[61] No matter how carefully ladies-in-waiting balanced their loyalties, nobody's position was incontestable.

9

Extreme Handling

On the night of Tuesday, 31 March 1534, Elizabeth Stafford, Duchess of Norfolk, was in her chambers at Kenninghall Palace in Suffolk when she heard a commotion downstairs.[1] Her husband Thomas, Duke of Norfolk had unexpectedly arrived home from the court. Parliament had been prorogued the previous day, but to cover the hundred miles he had allegedly been 'riding all night'.[2] He was not in a good mood. For all that he was a small, spare man, Elizabeth must have heard him stamp up the stairs – his chambers were below hers, in the innermost part of the 'H'-shaped house – and then not stop but keep going, up the next flight and into her own outer chamber.[3] Was she frightened, hearing his approach? Did they exchange any conversation at all? Or did he simply do as she later reported: lock her into a chamber and refuse to let her out?

Maybe she shouted. Elizabeth was not a person to accept things in silence. Maybe she paced back and forth as she listened to him in the rooms beyond, banging open chests and presses, issuing terse orders to the household staff who had been rudely wakened from sleep. We don't know how long he kept Elizabeth confined, but we know that he took her richest jewels and clothing and then ordered her removal to a much smaller house in the village of Redbourn, Hertfordshire, not far from Dunstable on the great road north.[4]

In the years leading up to this moment, Elizabeth's life had been uncertain and, at times, traumatic. Some of what follows makes for difficult reading, not least because much of it was relayed in her own words. Following her removal to the house at Redbourn, Elizabeth spent the rest of the 1530s writing long letters to Thomas Cromwell in which she detailed several earlier episodes of domestic violence at the hands of her husband and household. Her protestations about her husband's behaviour were received first with impatience and then with weariness and even embarrassment by her family and friends, in what can feel like an uneasy echo of some present-day reactions to survivors of domestic abuse. In sixteenth-century England, though, a certain amount of violence was considered socially acceptable in particular contexts, and a wife's refusal to reconcile with her elite husband was both politically and socially shameful.[5]

How had things reached this pitch? We don't know what 'last-straw' event caused Norfolk to ride pell-mell from London to Kenninghall expressly to deal with Elizabeth in 1534, but we do know that their relationship was already on the rocks. Elizabeth had chosen a different path from the rest of her marital relations in the late 1520s and early 1530s when she quarrelled with Anne Boleyn, passed sensitive information to her mistress Catherine of Aragon, and was eventually expelled from court in 1531 for speaking too openly about her support for the queen. In September 1533 Imperial ambassador Chapuys reported that Elizabeth's brother-in-law George Neville, Lord Bergavenny, had been summoned to court in order to mediate between husband and wife; Elizabeth 'would not see or listen to' Norfolk, 'on account of his being in love with a maid of honour to the Royal concubine [Anne Boleyn] known by the name of Holland. For this reason the duke of Norfolk, since his return from France, dared not go and see his duchess until after Bergavenny's mission, who, as above stated, went thither, and promised that the duke would in future lead a conjugal life with her.'[6] Norfolk, then, had taken a mistress, and Elizabeth objected.

In the early 1530s she evidently did so loudly, vociferously and publicly, since Chapuys knew of it, but her own words on the matter come to us from a little later, in the letters that she wrote to Thomas Cromwell from Redbourn after her removal there.[7] Cromwell might seem like an odd choice of confidant. He was a man, for a start. He was also the king's chief minister, known for his ruthlessness, bound to serve Henry before anybody else; he would not keep her secrets if it wasn't worth his while, and he was unlikely to take her side. But Elizabeth wasn't looking for sympathy for its own sake, or not from Thomas Cromwell. She needed his legal expertise. She needed his influence with the king and the nobility even more, for there was no other recourse for women of her status in her position. Nobody but the king could force Thomas Howard to do anything Thomas Howard didn't want to do. More women than Elizabeth understood this. In the 1530s alone several others wrote to Cromwell with similar marital complaints, seeking his mediation, and some were desperate. Lady Hungerford, for instance, had been imprisoned in a turret of her husband's castle and feared for her very survival unless Cromwell could intervene and grant her a separation.[8] Elizabeth's own half-sister-in-law Katherine Howard, Lady Daubeney wrote likewise, asking him for help with her divorce in 1535.[9] Another Howard sister, Anne, Countess of Oxford, had written to Cromwell's predecessor Cardinal Wolsey in much the same vein in the 1520s, suggesting that 'marital counsellor to the nobility' was something of a known side role for royal ministers.[10] It may even have been a broader practice than the sources suggest. The seizure of Wolsey's and Cromwell's papers after their deaths mean that their in-trays are disproportionately represented among our surviving material.

Letter-writing was not an especial gift of Elizabeth's. Most of her letters were, thankfully, written by a secretary to her dictation; her own handwriting is unusually bad even by the standards of her sex at this time. Even when dictated, she did not always follow a traditional petitionary structure, and she and her secretaries filled every available part of the paper, squeezing postscripts into impossible corners and making them difficult to decipher. The style, though, remained the same regardless of the scribe.[11] In writing, she ranted. She explained the same things over and over, even using the same phrases, as though repetition might help to hammer home her point. One can imagine Cromwell wincing when he saw her seal on a letter in his in-tray.

Her choicest phrases were reserved for her husband's mistress, Bess Holland. She called Bess 'harlot', 'that queen', 'washer of my nursery', 'the causer of all my trouble'. She made it clear that the affair had begun long before Bergavenny's mediation of 1533: as early as 1527, in fact.[12] Bess was the daughter of John Holland, Norfolk's secretary, a relation of the Barons Hussey of Sleaford in Lincolnshire, and she had, apparently, been in Elizabeth's service when she caught Norfolk's eye. It wasn't unusual for elite men to venture outside the marriage bed, whether as a one-off or a longer-term liaison. Charles Brandon, Duke of Suffolk fathered at least three illegitimate children; Edward Howard, Norfolk's own brother, sired two.[13] Norfolk was not behaving particularly unusually when he lewdly informed Cromwell in 1537 that there was 'a young woman with pretty proper tetins' – literally, 'tits' – in a particular lodging house at York.[14] If women did object, they were at least supposed to do so privately.

Ordinarily, a woman's birth family were her first resort in a troubled marriage. They might give her shelter, protect her, mediate with her husband or seek higher redress. Unluckily for Elizabeth, her parents were dead, and her brother Henry, now the family's patriarch, lived under the stain of their father's attainder for high treason. He could not inherit the dukedom of Buckingham, and as Baron Stafford he was considerably below Elizabeth's husband in status. The last thing that he wanted to do was to cause a ruckus with a senior noble of unpleasant character. By the time Norfolk moved Elizabeth to Redbourn, Stafford had been asked more than once to take Elizabeth into his house. His letters in reply, both to Norfolk and to Cromwell separately, are a model of epistolary deference: the scribe's hand is neat and professional, the margins respectfully wide.[15] If his words were not what they wanted to hear, at least they could not fault his courtesy. Regretfully, he could not help, and he wished they would stop asking. He reminded Norfolk of Elizabeth's 'accustomed wild language, which lieth not in my power to stop'. Norfolk should know 'by long experience' that Stafford could do nothing to moderate his sister's behaviour, and he was worried about the impact that it might have on his own and his family's reputation.[16] To Cromwell he was even more explicit: 'be assured that I would not only receive her into my house but I would fetch her on my feet at London . . . but the redress of this standeth not in the advertisement of her kin'. They had explained to her many times that to disagree with her husband like this was a shameful thing, but nothing could 'break her sensual and wilful mind'.[17] He was ashamed to be her brother.

This, unfortunately, wasn't an unusual response. Elizabeth's aunt Anne, Countess of Huntingdon also advised her to take back her objections (a bit rich, coming from a woman who had been accused of adultery with both the king and his groom of the stool); Cromwell also advised her to try a softer approach with her husband; and even the king intervened.[18] Elizabeth did have some sympathy from an interesting, albeit unhelpful quarter. In July 1533 one Mistress Amadas was hauled before the king's council for having said, among other things, that 'there was never a good wedded woman in England but Prince Arthur's dowager, the Duchess of Norfolk, and herself'.[19] Clearly, this was a deliberate conflation of their situations as faithful wives to adulterous husbands, and no doubt Amadas wasn't the only one to note the similarities between the Norfolks' situation and the king's 'great matter'. Both Elizabeth and Queen Catherine saw themselves, and were seen by others, as long-suffering, wronged wives of terrible husbands. Moreover, Bess Holland, Norfolk's mistress and Elizabeth's rival, was in service with Anne Boleyn: could there have been a more nightmarish parallel?[20] Small wonder that Elizabeth felt so strongly about the queen's situation; there is no better illustration of the way in which the political was inextricably personal for women in service at court.

The Norfolks' marriage may have been problematic even before Bess. At some point during the 1530s, Elizabeth accused her husband of violent abuse dating back to 1519. Norfolk repeated the slander in a letter to Cromwell. Elizabeth was going around saying that 'when she had been in childbed with my daughter of Richmond two nights and a day, I [Norfolk] should draw her out of her bed by the hair of the head about the house and with my dagger give her a wound in the head'.[21] Norfolk, though, denied this absolutely: 'my good lord, if I prove not by witness . . . that she had the scar in her head forty months before she was delivered of my said daughter, and that the same was cut by a surgeon of London for a swelling she had in her head . . . never trust my word after . . . there is no man alive that would handle a woman in a childbed after that sort, nor for my part would not have done for all that I am worth'.[22] From a man who in 1536 would threaten to bash Princess Mary's head against the wall 'until it was as soft as a boiled apple', this is quite a statement.[23] Nor, if true, did he really need to deny his actions with such vehemence. Violence from husband towards wives was acceptable in early modern society provided that it was done as a form of behavioural correction, and that it did not proceed to extremes.[24] Norfolk could simply have justified himself along these lines.

Violence during childbirth, though, was likely to be considered 'extreme' by anyone who heard it. It's possible that this was part of the point. While nobody is seeking to disbelieve a woman who claimed domestic violence at any point in history, it's also true that early modern women might say that the violence had occurred during pregnancy because it made the case look worse and generated more sympathy. Narratives given in these circumstances were consciously designed to strike familiar and emotive chords with a reader or listener, and Elizabeth certainly saw herself as a victim to whom redress was owed.[25] If she did exaggerate, or alter the circumstances, it was an effective strategy, as Norfolk's appalled and panicked missive reveals.

This is not to say that she was lying, or that he was not an abusive husband. Her own letters describe another violent episode repeatedly in words that elicit a visceral reaction even 500 years later. The women at Kenninghall, she wrote, had 'bound me and pinaculled me and sat on my breast until I spat blood'.[26] They had done this because she had spoken out against Bess Holland. Even worse, in a different letter she said that Norfolk was directly responsible, that he had 'set his women' to do this 'and never punished them'.[27] Ever since, she had been sick 'at the fall of the

leaf and in the spring of the year'.[28] The image of Elizabeth treated
in this way would have been equally shocking in its day for the
strong sense of social hierarchy overturned. This, indeed, was one
of Elizabeth's biggest problems with Bess. Many of the insults that
she used were ones relating to social status: 'drab', 'queen', 'washer
of my nursery' are terms that mix contempt for a lower-ranking
woman with suggestions of prostitution. Poignantly, it becomes
clear that she had thought her marriage with Norfolk was a love
match. Even if it hadn't been, she was the daughter of a duke, she
had brought a dowry of 2,000 marks, she had always behaved
herself well and she had given him five children: what more could
he possibly want?[29] What on earth did Bess have that she didn't?

It's unlikely that she ever got a satisfactory answer to this question. At least living at Redbourn meant that she no longer had to
deal with Bess under her own roof, though whether it was worse
or better to know that the couple were together at Kenninghall
in her absence is a matter for conjecture. Elizabeth's removal had
clearly been a shock to her. Inventories made later on show that
she had been in the middle of some complex embroidery work that
she had had to leave behind. Tellingly, one of these was 'a great
pomegranate of gold' that remained unfinished: the pomegranate was Catherine of Aragon's badge.[30] Needlework was a sharp,
pointed and unanswerable form of resistance for women who had
no other outlet.

Elizabeth's life at Redbourn was substantially different. She
was given an allowance of £50 a year and a household of only
twenty people, a much smaller establishment that hardly befitted
a duchess.[31] The isolation was perhaps the hardest thing. Her earliest letters focused on this. In the summer of 1534, she wrote to
Cromwell asking him to send her some venison. Venison was the
preserve of the elite, who possessed deer parks in which to hunt,
and it was a common gift between nobles, a sign of esteem. This
year, though, she had none: 'there be many of my friends that sent
me venison the last year that dare not send me none this year for
my lord's displeasure'.[32] She also said repeatedly that she was kept
in 'prisonment', that she longed to go abroad and see her friends,

and that no one came to see her except 'such as my lord appoints to know my mind and to counsel me after his fashion'.[33]

At least, though, it was a quiet life. There was no more 'breaking and fighting'.[34] Initially, she seems to have hoped that Cromwell's intervention might have taken her out of Redbourn, removed Bess from Kenninghall and reunited her with her husband, but this proved overly idealistic. Cromwell was not the man to take a woman's side against an adulterous husband. It was in his interests to maintain a reasonable relationship with Norfolk, and he did so.[35] The onus was on Elizabeth to reconcile, but once it became apparent that Norfolk was never going to give up Bess, she utterly refused to do so. Over time, then, her letters became more defiant, and her aims changed. She no longer sought his return to her. In fact she abused him roundly but probably truthfully, calling him 'a great player', someone who 'can speak fair as well to his enemies as to his friends'.[36]

For his part, Norfolk wanted a divorce. It's not difficult to imagine where he'd got that idea.[37] Unlike the king, though, Norfolk had no real grounds that would have been accepted in a court of law. The way that the word 'divorce' was used as a catch-all phrase at this time makes it hard to know quite what he envisaged, though he was clearly enthusiastic, promising Elizabeth the return of her jewels, clothes and household goods if she would agree.[38] Did Norfolk want to marry Bess? If so he needed an annulment, not a divorce, just like the king. But this would only be granted on grounds of 'consanguinity' – too close a kinship tie between husband and wife, which wasn't the case for Norfolk and Elizabeth – and he could not claim childlessness, since they had had two sons. A 'divorce' in the strict sense of the word could only be granted by a Church court on grounds of adultery (the wife's), cruelty (the husband's), or heresy (either party). Norfolk could not claim any of these things either. Elizabeth refused unequivocally to consider any sort of divorce, with an implacability that echoed Queen Catherine's. Duchess of Norfolk she was and would remain, and she wrote with smug satisfaction that Norfolk 'had rather than £1000 he could have brought me to have been divorced'.[39] Elizabeth clearly suffered much at Norfolk's hands, but contemporary standards held her to be in the wrong. She had little agency, and less recourse. All she could do was accept the stalemate between them and try to build a new life at Redbourn.

Elizabeth's isolation echoed Catherine of Aragon's. From Enfield, to Ampthill, to Buckden, to Somersham and then, in the spring of 1534, to Kimbolton Castle in Cambridgeshire, Catherine and the few ladies-in-waiting remaining to her had spent years on an involuntary scenic tour of the fens, far from London, the court and the king. Kimbolton was a moated courtyard-style house typical of the late fifteenth century, owned and recently remodelled by a branch of the Wingfield family. It was less damp and better situated than some of her previous habitations, even if all there was to look at was the reflection of the flat, monotonous landscape in the still water of the moat.[40] The improvement in lodging was the only bright spot on the horizon for Catherine's household. Everything else that the former queen stood for had been torn down in law. In March 1534 a new Act of Succession was passed: Princess Mary was declared illegitimate, and was replaced in the succession by her baby sister Princess Elizabeth. Almost immediately, royal commissions were set up to force subjects to swear an oath to uphold this new state of affairs, and in November Parliament passed an official Act requiring such an oath by law. The king's royal supremacy over the Church was also enshrined in parliamentary law in the same year, and likewise required an oath to be sworn. Support for Catherine had therefore been spun, in law, as opposition to the king.

Recalcitrant souls were persuaded to swear these oaths by a new Act expanding the definition of treason. The crime of treason had previously rested on overt action. Any attempt to harm the king, his family or his royal lineage was treasonable. Now, actual action was no longer required to return a guilty verdict. Refusing to swear either of these oaths was treasonable. Even more frightening, simply speaking words against the king or his new marriage, or words in favour of the Pope, Catherine, Mary or anything that might be construed as a verbal attempt to deprive the king of any of his titles by any means was sufficient to have you strung up. Even knowing of somebody else's treason and failing to reveal it was made into an offence: misprision of treason, the ultimate crime of inaction. The king and his ministers had found that they must rewrite the law in order to silence opposition to his supremacy over the Church and to the 'great matter'. The violent ripping and rearranging of the fabric of religion and society was the reason why Henry passed more treason legislation than any other king before him.[41]

England no longer felt like a safe place. Royal commissioners were sent around the country to receive oaths – not those of women, obviously, since, as Bishop Stephen Gardiner complained in May, the process already took too long and would be worse if they were to be included.[42] Wives had no legal identity anyway. Their opinions were surely of no importance. Lists of men who refused to swear, or those who were reported for speech that was now treasonable, arrived with increasing regularity on Thomas Cromwell's desk throughout the year of 1535. Ironically, some of these were the sayings of women, who conveniently regained legal significance when their words were deemed unacceptable. In February 1535, Margaret Chanseler was famously hauled up for calling Anne Boleyn 'a goggle-eyed whore'.[43] Anne, Lady Shelton, who had custody of Princess Elizabeth and her sister the Lady Mary, was accused of treating Mary too kindly, and told firmly that she must not be allowed to use the title of 'princess'. One of Mary's maids refused to swear the Oath of Succession; she was locked up in her chamber and threatened with prison if she did not give in. Even after swearing, the same maid was shortly sent away on suspicion of encouraging Mary in her pretensions.[44]

Nor was it only those in royal service. When Mary left Greenwich in October she was surrounded by a 'great troup' of London wives, 'unknown to their husbands', who wept and cried that she was still a princess. Some of those women were taken to the Tower, and it was feared that Mary would follow them, though Imperial ambassador Chapuys thought this would not necessarily be a bad

thing. There were plans afoot to spirit her out of England if necessary, and this would be easier from the Tower, where the constable
– Sir William Kingston – was, allegedly, their 'good servant'.[45]

Cromwell and the rest of the king's advisors were fighting a
battle on two fronts. Opposition to the king's marriage and to the
succession was one thing. Opposition to the royal supremacy was
another, and it was considered the more serious crime. Priests
were required to preach the king's headship over the Church, but
it was difficult to ensure that they did so. As the Archbishop of
York patiently explained to Cromwell, 'I cannot be in all places;
nor, perhaps, shall I hear of all faults; nor can I put learning and
cunning to preach in the heads of those that have it not already.'[46]
Many clerics were unhappy about the king's divorce, but they were
even more concerned about his supremacy over the Church and
the implications of the loss of papal authority. Appeals to Rome
were forbidden. Taxes and tithes formerly paid there must now
be sent to the royal treasury. Nobody was allowed in or out of
monastic precincts, a state of affairs that caused much woe for
women like Jane Vaux, Lady Guildford, once lady-in-waiting to
many royal women. In the long tradition of elderly noblewomen
she had retired to live out her old age within the precinct of
'Gaunt's Chapel' in Bristol, and now found she was not permitted
to come and go through the church as she chose.[47]

Worse still, 1535 saw the beginning of a royal visitation of all
monastic institutions, orchestrated and administered by Thomas
Cromwell. The reason, ostensibly, was to make sure that all monks
and nuns swore the Oath of Supremacy in person, but it soon
became clear that there was more to it than this. Commissioners
were keen to ferret out where monastic standards were low, where
there was corruption, where there were dark deeds and sordid
tales. They also inquired minutely into the finances of each insti-
tution, making notes and keeping record for a grand totting up
of the value of monastic England: the *Valor Ecclesiasticus*. It must
have been difficult not to think this sinister. The king had already
taken the money due to Rome: why else would he be keen to know
what his own monasteries were worth unless he intended to take

that too? But though this was whispered up and down the country, few really considered that they might be witnessing the end of monasticism in England. It was fair to seek reform of moral condition. It might even be fair to close down the smaller, run-down, poorer houses. If reform was to occur, now was instead the time for redress of grievances: some, like William Fordham, a monk at Worcester, wrote to Cromwell asking for personal advancement, in Fordham's case for restoration to the position of cellarer.[48]

Nevertheless, 1535 was a bleak year for the great and the good as well as for ordinary people. Sir Thomas More had resigned the chancellorship of the exchequer back in 1532 because he did not feel that he could serve the king in that office and yet oppose royal policy. Now he refused to take the Oath of Supremacy and was arrested for treason. John Fisher, Bishop of Rochester – Catherine of Aragon's former confessor – did likewise. Both men were imprisoned in the Tower in April 1534. Repeatedly questioned over the course of a whole year, they could not be brought to swear. On 22 June 1535, Fisher was beheaded for treason. On 6 July More was brought to the scaffold in his turn: 'I die the King's good servant', he declared, 'and God's first.'[49] As if in response, the weather worsened. It rained continually through the summer and a fearful people muttered about the vengeance of God. The harvest failed and plague followed. Thomas Broke wrote to Cromwell that 'death and penury of wholesome bread are very prevalent in the city', and sent a list of the dead.[50]

And yet some things remained refreshingly constant. María de Salinas, Lady Willoughby was still in touch with her former mistress, Catherine of Aragon. Catherine had been haemorrhaging servants all through 1534 and 1535. In July 1534 Chapuys wrote indignantly that the king had sent away one of Catherine's Spanish women 'who has all her life been in attendance'.[51] Could this have been María? There can have been few other Spanish women left in Catherine's service. If it was María who was sent away and forbidden to return, at least she might have been able to be present to help her daughter Katherine give birth to her first grandchild, a boy named Henry, in September 1535.[52]

Not long after this, bad news arrived. Catherine of Aragon was sick. It had been kept quiet. Chapuys did not hear of it until early December, and only then because he had happened to pay a visit to Cromwell, who had just sent someone to inform the king.[53] Chapuys, alarmed, asked permission to visit her, or to send a servant there. Cromwell was amenable to the latter, but said he could not allow Chapuys to go himself unless the king agreed. While waiting for the answer, Catherine apparently recovered, as her physician wrote that 'there was no fear for the present'.[54] Rumours, though, had already spread abroad even before Chapuys himself wrote to the emperor on 13 December, and, as ever, women were involved in the exchange of information. On that same date the papal nuncio at the French court wrote home to the Pope's secretary to report that Sir John Wallop, the English ambassador in France, had heard that Catherine could not live more than six months 'or a little longer'. Wallop knew this from his wife, Lady Wallop, who was Catherine's 'creature' and had heard it herself directly from Catherine's physician.[55]

This pessimism was, unfortunately, well placed. On Wednesday, 29 December Chapuys received a letter from the queen's physician informing him that Catherine had had a relapse and that this time it was worse than before. Could he get leave to visit her? He could, and did, the very next day; but on his way out of Eltham Palace he was overtaken by the Duke of Suffolk, who had been sent to tell him that news had just arrived that Catherine was 'in extremis' and that Chapuys was unlikely to reach her in time. Chapuys was sceptical. He even went back to his lodging and wrote a long letter to his master the emperor before he finally set off.[56] Somebody else, though, received the same news and took it wholly seriously. On the same day – Thursday, 30 December – María, Lady Willoughby also sat down at her London home, the Barbican in the north of the city, and dictated a letter to her secretary for Thomas Cromwell.[57] She was polite, but haste made her brief: a quick line of customary salutation was ended with an impatient 'etc' before she launched straight into her suit. She knew that it was not the first time that she had asked him for permission to visit Catherine, but this time 'need driveth me to put you to pain'. She had heard that Catherine, 'my mistress' – María was careful not to call her queen, yet avoided having to use the objectionable 'princess dowager' – was ill once again. 'You did promise me to labour the king's grace to get me licence to go to her grace afore God send for her', she reminded him, 'for as I am informed it is no other likelihood but it shall be shortly.' She needed a letter from Cromwell or from the king explaining that she had permission, otherwise the guards would not let her in. Nobody could help her but him: 'Mr Secretary, under God and the king all my trust is in you. I pray you, remember me now at this time.'

The clock was ticking. She must have waited in an agony of impatience for an answer. Since María evidently had her own channels of communication with Catherine's household, she was probably as regularly updated as Cromwell himself. Her son-in-law the Duke of Suffolk may also have passed information to her. None of it was good news. Catherine got worse every hour, reported her apothecary; 'these two days and nights she has been able to take nothing, either to eat or to drink, that would remain in her stomach, and she has not slept more than an hour and a half for the pain in her stomach'.[58]

María made up her mind. Perhaps she had never intended to wait for licence from the king or a response from Cromwell, but had simply written as an empty gesture towards correct protocol, should questions be asked later on. At some point either late on 30 December or the next day, she rode the sixty-five miles almost due north to Kimbolton. It would have been an uncomfortable journey in the January cold. Most likely she and her servants would have had to pause overnight. The light would fade early, and risking the horses' footing on England's rutted roads in the dark was perilous, as indeed she discovered. Arriving at Kimbolton on New Year's Day at six in the evening, she was wet, cold and muddy; she had, she said, taken a fall from her horse only a mile away. She was emotionally overwrought as well, upset by the fall and yet relieved that Catherine still lived, saying that 'she thought never to have seen the Princess again'. The household officers asked for her licence to visit. Certainly, she told them, it was 'ready to be showed'; she 'would not otherwise presume' to visit, but just now she needed to recover herself. If they didn't want her to die of a chill, they had better let her into Catherine's chamber so that she could 'repair to the fire'.[59] She would show them all the documentation they desired in the morning. Discomfited, no doubt, by her distressed state, they let her go. Catherine was glad to see her, and María had not left her chamber since; five days later, and they reported to Cromwell that they had yet to see either her or her paperwork. One cannot imagine that he was much surprised.

Did María genuinely fall from her horse near the end of her journey, or was it a ruse to gain her entry into the house? The historian and biographer John Strype, reading the officers' letter 150 years later, was firmly convinced that she had faked it, adding the words 'as she pretended' to the description of her fall.[60] It was certainly effective, and María undoubtedly had sufficient chutzpah to have carried it off with aplomb. And yet she clearly had shown up looking plausibly as though she had fallen into the wet and the mud. Even if she had deliberately lain down in it to create that impression, she must have arrived close to freezing. In either case, her need for warmth and dry clothes was no lie.

Catherine's chambers were in the south range of the courtyard, overlooking the gardens. What did María and Catherine say to one another during those days, sat together in the winter sunlight? That María still described Catherine as her 'mistress' is touching, and shows that the bond of service and friendship remained unbroken despite their time apart. Catherine's conversations with Chapuys, once he arrived, were all about the need to keep up the fight against the king's marriage, the succession and his supremacy for the sake of Princess Mary, but also for the English people, who were suffering 'great danger to their souls'. She was worried that 'the divorce affair' had caused 'the evils and heresies of this country', and Chapuys reassured her that sometimes God allowed these things to occur 'for the greater exaltation of the good and confusion of the bad', and that it would soon be reversed when those who had swerved from the faith returned.[61]

Though both Catherine and María had said that they thought that this was the end, in fact Catherine rallied. She began to keep food down; she could sleep again. Her physician thought her out of danger, and so she sent Chapuys home to London. On the afternoon of the Epiphany, 6 January, she even combed and tied her hair 'without any help from any of her maids'.[62] On the morning of 7 January, though, her condition worsened. At ten in the morning she was given extreme unction. By two of the afternoon she was gone.[63] María, in all probability, was at her side as she died, though the enduring tale that Catherine died in her arms is, alas, a later invention with no basis in contemporary evidence. There may have been many people from the household by the bedside, praying for her soul as it departed. For the Spaniards in particular – María, confessor Jorge de Athequa, physician Miguel de la Sa, apothecary John de la Soto, and likely more unnamed – it must have been an unbearably sad day. Some, like María, had come to England with Catherine over thirty years previously, and owed their present lives to her patronage. They had served her in better and worse times, both richer and poorer, in sickness and in health, and they had sworn oaths to serve her with loyalty until death parted them. Now it had, and nothing would ever be the same again.

10

Inconstant and Mutable Fortune

Within hours of Catherine of Aragon's death, the king and council had been informed. Steps were taken to begin the preparations for burial and for permanently disbanding the household. None of these things were as straightforward as they would normally have been, had Catherine died the king's full wife and queen of England. Where, for instance, should a princess dowager be buried, and with what honour? The king had absolutely no intention of allowing her to be commemorated as a queen, no matter the Imperial ambassador's protestations or the risk of diplomatic consequences with Spain; Chapuys was left to write ominously to the emperor, 'Your Majesty will consider to what state things have come.'[1] Nor could she be buried in an Observant friary as she had asked, since, as Cromwell explained, there were now none left.[2] A new burial place must be chosen, mourners and attendees appointed, black cloth sourced, distributed and made into clothing. There were goods to requisition and a will to enact.

The indomitable María de Salinas, Lady Willoughby remained at Kimbolton through the month of January 1536, listening to these debates unfold and watching the king's officers trying to maintain a semblance of order while they waited for firm directions from London.[3] Only eight hours after Catherine's death, her body was secretly 'opened' for disembowelling by a few of her servants – not, apparently, ones with any experience or right thereof, since they consisted of a candlemaker and two others. If María heard the servants' confidential report that Catherine's heart was 'black and hideous', and that they feared poison, no doubt she was appalled.[4] Nothing was proceeding as she and the others felt that it should. Catherine's body was not encased in a lead coffin until 15 January, eight days after her death, by which time keeping vigil over it must have been a singularly unpleasant task despite the deep winter cold.[5] The women were not even able to get their black mourning clothes made in a timely manner. They were forced to make do with 'kerchiefs on their heads and old robes' for almost three weeks after Catherine's death.[6] At least there *were* mourners. As January progressed, a trickle of noblewomen joined María at Kimbolton, including her own daughter, Katherine, Duchess of Suffolk, to perform the role of chief mourner for the masses that must be held in the following days.[7]

Gradually, arrangements were made. Catherine was to be interred in the church of Peterborough Abbey, as the nearest religious house befitting the status of a princess dowager, but she was not to be buried with the honour that would be due to a queen, and she was not to be buried in London.[8] The king wanted to seize all of her goods, but others were not comfortable with this. Even the famously grasping Sir Richard Rich, solicitor-general, wrote that 'it would not be honourable to take the things given in her lifetime'.[9] He explained to the king that Catherine, as a royal woman, had in fact been a *femme sole*, not subject to coverture, which meant that the will she had made should be allowed to stand.

We don't know whether the king allowed all of Catherine's bequests to be enacted, but her will is a testament to the bond between the former queen and her ladies-in-waiting. Those mentioned were most likely in her service at her death – and had therefore not, after all, been dismissed the previous year. They were the first individuals listed.[10] Most were given money, even life-changing sums. For Elizabeth Darrell, orphaned daughter of a knight, the £200 'for her marriage' was as much again as she might expect to receive from her father's estate.[11] Mistress Blanche – Blanche Twyford, who had served Catherine among her chamberers for many years – was given £100, over fifteen times her yearly salary; Margery Otwell, also a chamberer, and Dorothea Wheler had £40 each. Mary, the wife of Catherine's Spanish physician Fernán López de Escoriaza, was also given £40, as was Isabel Otwell, daughter of Margery above.[12] The 'little maidens' – unfortunately unnamed – had £10 each. Near the end was the only Spanish woman named as an individual rather than as somebody's wife: 'Isabel of Vergas', who received £20. This is almost certainly the 'Elizabeth Vergus, Gentlewoman of the Queen, native of Spain' who received English denization in 1517, and this suggests either that she had stayed in Catherine's service or that she had at least remained in England and in contact with her mistress.[13] María de Salinas, Lady Willoughby was not mentioned in Catherine's will. This doesn't mean that she had been forgotten. Noble and royal women often used their wills to help those who needed it most; María, a widowed baroness with a sizeable estate in Lincolnshire, needed no financial assistance.

The corpse remained at Kimbolton for another twelve days, lying in state in the chapel ringed with candles and torches, servants standing vigil at all hours of the day and night. Banners of crimson and gold were brought, showing the arms of Spain and England, and the symbols of the holy Trinity, of the Virgin Mary, St Katherine and St George. The whole house was hung with black fabric, and in the winter darkness María must have felt as though she and the rest of the queen's servants had some-how been entombed alongside her. On Thursday, 27 January the coffin was carried from the chapel to a wagon outside, covered in black velvet. Priests, gentlemen, household officers and heralds rode ahead of it, and María and the other women came behind it on horseback, themselves and their horses likewise dressed in black. In sombre silence they rode nine miles to Sawtry Abbey to rest overnight, and the next day on to Peterborough Abbey. Once there, the coffin was conducted to the abbey church and placed onto 'eight pillars of beautiful fashion and roundness' under a canopy of estate. Catherine's crimson and gold banners were set about the chapel, and the whole was illuminated by the light of a thousand candles.[14]

On 29 January the funeral itself began. María, dressed in black and standing with the rest of the ladies, could read Catherine's motto emblazoned in large gold letters all around the chapel: *humble et loyale*. She might have been forgiven for thinking that this had hardly served her mistress well. During the Bishop of Rochester's sermon indignation must have risen in almost tangible waves from all of those listening; not only did he preach against the Pope and against Catherine's marriage with the king, but he invented a new and cruel twist. He alleged that on her deathbed Catherine had acknowledged that she had not been queen of England.[15] One can imagine the ripple of surprise and anger that must have gone around the church. The bishop had not been at Catherine's deathbed; he could not have known what she said or didn't say. This was pure invention, a rewriting of Catherine's life and death, in the face of those who had been there and who knew better. But there was nothing they could do except go on with the service and weep with fury as much as with grief. The heralds present made offerings of gold cloth on behalf of María and the other mourners, to be made into vestments for the church, and then Catherine's coffin was lowered into its resting place 'at the lowest step of the high altar', the place covered with a cloth of black velvet.[16] She was gone, and now they must move forward in this new world without her.

While Catherine's erstwhile ladies-in-waiting saw their mistress into the ground, Queen Anne's fluttered about her in concern. Within days of Catherine's burial – possibly even the very same day – Anne had a miscarriage.[17] She claimed that it was the result of stress undergone some days previously, when her uncle the Duke of Norfolk had come to tell her that the king had taken a bad fall from his horse while tilting at the ring. If the king died, would Queen Anne still be secure, with only a daughter living and a baby in her belly?

Much has been made of these events. Henry's fall was indeed serious. He was 'two hours without speaking' – probably unconscious – during which time his council must have undergone considerable stress.[18] Prior to this, the king's death had not been much thought about, or at least not much written about. He was forty-four – no longer young, perhaps, but hardly old, and in good health. Such an accident could not help but create concerns for the future, in both his own and others' minds. It also spelled the end of his jousting career, and appears to have re-inflamed, or perhaps burst, an existing ulcer on his leg that now stubbornly refused to heal, causing him continual and often severe pain. He became increasingly irritable, his behaviour more irrational, and for the queen and her household the royal court became an environment of extreme stress.[19]

Queen Anne's women, like Catherine's, had shared her sorrow over her miscarriage. Anne herself had allegedly consoled them when they wept and told them that 'it was for the best, because she would be the sooner with child again', and this time there could be no doubt about its legitimacy.[20] The king said bitterly that he saw God would not grant him male children, and that he would speak to Anne when she was up. Grieving and fearful, she snapped that it had happened not only because she had been made so anxious by his fall, but because her heart had been broken when she saw he loved others.[21]

By this she probably meant Jane Seymour, one of her own maids, for by March 1536 Jane was firmly on the king's mind. The eldest daughter of Sir John Seymour and Margery Wentworth of Wolf Hall in Wiltshire, Jane's eldest brother Edward was already climbing the greasy pole of royal service. Jane's own career is difficult to pin down. Chronicler Charles Wriothesley later wrote that she had been in Catherine of Aragon's service before Anne Boleyn's, and she was definitely at court by 1534 when she is mentioned on a New Year gift list.[22] It's likely that her transfer to Queen Anne happened in 1533 when Catherine's household was reduced, perhaps because the king had already noticed her from afar, or even because Queen Anne herself selected Jane. If the latter, Anne must soon have regretted this. In many ways Jane appeared to be the queen's opposite. She was fair-skinned, with light hair and eyes, a direct contrast to Anne's brunette colouring. Where Anne's dark eyes mesmerised many an ambassador, Jane kept her gaze modestly downturned, her pale, thin lips closed tight. It was easy to think her meek and mild, a sweet and gentle antidote to Anne's sharp-tongued charisma, but Jane was no innocent young girl; she was over twenty-five, and it soon became clear that her wits and determination matched her queen's.[23]

Keeping a close eye on these events was the wily Gertrude Blount, Marchioness of Exeter. Gertrude remained in close proximity to the royal court, and though she was not in 'ordinary', daily service with Queen Anne she was certainly there frequently in 'extraordinary' by dint of her husband's position close to the king. Gertrude's views had not changed with the death of Catherine of Aragon, and she was no more reconciled to the reign of Queen Anne. She was one of several courtiers and nobles who wanted to see the return of Princess Mary to the succession. They assumed that the way to achieve this was to remove Queen Anne and bastardise her daughter Princess Elizabeth, and they thought that the king's preference for Jane Seymour might be a means to this end. Thus Gertrude kept her ear to the ground and reported all the rumours that she could garner to Imperial ambassador Chapuys, for now that Catherine of Aragon was dead he was Princess Mary's greatest champion.

King Henry showered Jane with gifts as he would a potential mistress; she returned them unopened, as might a future wife. In March 1536 Gertrude heard that Jane had refused a gift of money from the king, claiming that such attention was inappropriate to an unmarried woman of her station, that all she had was her honour, 'which she would not injure for a thousand deaths'.[24] If the court had thought Anne Boleyn prone to drama, Jane proved that she could match her. As Gertrude reported cynically, Jane had been 'well taught' by her kin to accept nothing less than marriage from the king, a remark that suggests that such machinations on the part of a courtier family were thought eminently plausible. In response, the king declared he loved her all the more, but that he would show his love by only speaking to Jane in the presence of her family as chaperones. To make this easier, and more difficult for anybody to police, he promptly turfed Thomas Cromwell out of his rooms at Greenwich Palace so that he might install Jane there along with her brother and sister-in-law. These rooms communicated secretly with the king's own chambers, and thus he could visit Jane in privacy, yet – theoretically – without judgement.

Gertrude passed all of this information to Chapuys, and asked him to 'assist in the matter' – presumably to try to encourage the king to favour Jane at the expense of Queen Anne.[25] Whether Gertrude was really part of a coherent 'faction' plotting to overthrow Queen Anne is a matter of conjecture. While there certainly were people who wanted to see Anne brought low, there's little evidence of cohesive political action. Gertrude and her friends might hope that Queen Anne would fall and Jane step into her place, restoring Princess Mary to the succession, but they could do little to actively bring this about.[26]

Something that Gertrude had not heard was that it was not only the king who was rumoured to 'love others'. Around the beginning of 1536, Thomas Cromwell, the king's chief minister, was told a story. In the French king's court, he was informed, rumours about Queen Anne's sexual fidelity were flying: letters had been obtained in which she was accused of adultery. This story reached England by means of Stephen Gardiner, Bishop of Winchester, who had been Henry VIII's resident ambassador at the French court since the previous September. Gardiner had written to his man Thomas Wriothesley, who then passed it to Cromwell. Such talk had been treasonous in England since the passing of the Treason Act in 1534. In France, though, they could say and write what they liked about the English queen. Somehow, the story reached the king. Perhaps Cromwell thought it safer to share it personally rather than wait for it to break via another source; Gardiner was not known for his discretion or, indeed, for his love for the queen. The king was furious, but, as ever, well able to dissemble his rage, and a discreet investigation was ordered. Of course, he could not publicly announce that he doubted his wife after he had rearranged the religious and political framework of Europe in order to marry her. Even while her behaviour was under investigation he continued to push for European recognition of his annulment and remarriage, and for Anne's status as Queen of England. Politics was ever thus.

The source for the January investigation into Queen Anne's fidelity is Alexander Ales, a Scottish theologian who was in London around this time. He later recounted these events in a letter to Queen Anne's daughter Elizabeth I in September 1559.[27] Ales had close relations with a number of English bishops and courtiers, including Thomas Cromwell. An evangelical and later Protestant, he had travelled through many European courts and was used to sifting the dross of rumour to pick out the gold. Above all, he was an eyewitness to the events he narrates.[28] Ales tells us that Cromwell, Wriothesley and others who 'hated' the queen were set to finding the truth of the matter. Her chambers were watched day and night; they bribed her porter and her servants; and, crucially, 'there is nothing which they do not promise the ladies of her bedchamber'.[29] They told those they questioned that the king 'hated' the queen because she had not borne him an heir, and that 'nor was there any prospect of her doing so', a remark that most likely places this investigation after Queen Anne's miscarriage in January 1536.[30] If information about the queen's sexual behaviour was required, what better source than her female attendants, who were with her every moment of the day, even on the close stool, even as she slept at night?

On some level, then, Gertrude, Marchioness of Exeter was right to wonder whether the king was seeking more than a mistress in Jane Seymour. It does indeed look as though the king was contemplating ways to end his marriage to Queen Anne in the early months of 1536, and that examining rumours about her sexual behaviour was part of this. Such an investigation presented difficulties for the investigators. If secrecy was important, care had to be taken. They needed to know who would be safe to question without giving the game away to others, or to the queen herself; they needed to be sufficiently sure about existing loyalties and networks before they began asking questions. That probably ruled out women like Mary Howard, Duchess of Richmond, Jane Parker, Viscountess Rochford or the Shelton sisters, all of whom were Anne's close relations. There were, though, those whose connections to certain of the investigators were perhaps stronger than their loyalty to the queen. At least one Wriothesley woman was in Queen Anne's service, and Thomas Wriothesley was part of the investigation.[31] Margery Horsman, one of the queen's gentlewomen, came from a family with strong connections to Thomas Cromwell, and was noted as behaving strangely at this time. Queen Anne's vice-chamberlain Sir Edward Baynton wrote that he had 'mused much at the conduct of Mrs Margery, who hath used herself strangely towards me of late, being her friend as I have been'.[32] Perhaps Mistress Horsman sought to distance herself from anybody too close to Queen Anne.

Nothing immediately came of this investigation. Nothing was made public; no records survive. But this does not mean that it did not occur. Thomas Cromwell's papers were later deliberately 'thinned' over the period covering Anne's arrest and execution. Any evidence provided in writing or taken at dictation from Anne's women would no doubt have been among the papers that were culled. Somebody was asking questions about Queen Anne's fidelity as early as January 1536, and her ladies-in-waiting needed to be on their guard.

The Countess of Worcester was in a tight spot. Her brother had pulled her into a secluded corner and demanded to know the truth of rumours he had heard: had she been showing undue favour to men who were not her husband? Had she – God forbid – committed adultery? Was the baby in her womb the fruit of another man's seed? Had she no care to her own and her family's honour? Perhaps she winced. Perhaps she protested and tried to turn his questions. What she did not do, apparently, was deny the accusations outright. Instead – out of panic? – she responded defensively. Her own fault was small, she claimed, in the light of one far larger; for real infamy he should look to the queen. And he needn't take her word for it. 'Mark' could tell the whole tale.[33]

This is the story told by Lancelot de Carle, then in London as secretary to the French ambassador. He doesn't tell us when, or where, this occurred; he does not even give the names of those involved. But, placed alongside other sources, he helps us to unravel the events of spring 1536 and he reveals the centrality of the queen's women to the story. De Carle, a budding poet, was an eyewitness to the events of May 1536 and wrote them out, probably soon afterwards, as a lengthy poem. His lady with questionable morals has indeed been plausibly identified as Elizabeth Browne, Countess of Worcester.[34] Elizabeth came from a family of courtiers. Her older half-sister Anne Browne had served Elizabeth of York until her somewhat scandalous marriage to Charles Brandon, Duke of Suffolk.[35] Her mother, Lucy Montague, is probably the 'Lady Lucy' mentioned frequently in court records throughout the 1520s and early 1530s until her death in 1534.[36] Elizabeth had married Henry Somerset, 2nd Earl of Worcester, in 1527, as his second wife, and was known at the royal court from at least 1530, when the nurse and midwife of her recently delivered child were rewarded by the king.[37] By 1533 she was in Anne Boleyn's service, taking a position of honour next to the queen at her coronation banquet.[38] That she borrowed £100 from Anne early in 1536 without her husband's knowledge suggests that the two may have had a close relationship; Elizabeth, pregnant during the spring, named her baby Anne.[39]

Elizabeth had two brothers who were 'close advisors' to the king, as de Carle describes. Sir Anthony Browne was one of the gentlemen of the privy chamber, and her half-brother William Fitzwilliam, later Earl of Southampton, was treasurer of the royal household. Either could have been responsible for questioning Elizabeth; either could have been involved along with Cromwell and Wriothesley in the general investigation of the queen's behaviour, the more so since both held a general distaste for Queen Anne and her followers.[40] Many contemporary sources tell us that it was a lady-in-waiting who first revealed Queen Anne's indiscretions; that it was Elizabeth specifically is corroborated by several.[41] In May 1536 she was described twice as Anne's first accuser by John Husee, London agent of the Lisle family, who was in town throughout and reported events back to his employers in Calais.[42]

De Carle's poem and Ales's letter are not usually set alongside one another as sources for Anne's fall, but in fact their respective narratives reinforce one another. Ales tells us that an investigation into the queen's behaviour had been quietly ongoing since January. The conversation that de Carle describes between the Countess of Worcester and her brother makes sense in the context of that investigation. The countess was one of Queen Anne's women, and it was natural for her brother to ask her quietly if there was anything amiss, perhaps even to ask about her own conduct and to warn her to steer clear of trouble. The brother in question was left with a conundrum, as de Carle himself explained. If he did not share his sister's revelations he was failing in his duty to the king, and could expect to suffer if they later became known. On the other hand, if he reported his sister's shocking words to the king and they were disbelieved or proven to be false, he would 'open himself up to the serious penalties promised / To the queen's detractors, as provided by the law'.[43]

He decided – perhaps in light of the existing investigation – that the former risk was the greater and that he must disclose his sister's words, but that he did not want to do it alone. He approached two others close to the king, and between them they informed Henry, probably around the middle of April while the court was at Greenwich, the king's favourite palace.[44] Much as Ales related, the king allegedly changed colour, and ordered a full, though still covert, investigation. Plans for the court's imminent trip to Dover to view the coastal defences continued, but on 24 April two special commissions of oyer and terminer, juries charged with considering the most serious of crimes, were called. From the 25th, Cromwell began spending an undue amount of time with various bishops who were former canon lawyers, at least one of whom was asked how one might go about getting rid of Anne.[45]

The atmosphere in Queen Anne's household must have been tense, as it had no doubt been since January. The strain under which the queen and her ladies-in-waiting were operating became particularly evident over the emotionally charged weekend of 29 and 30 April. By this point, Anne and those around her were most

likely aware that something was very wrong. Poignantly, around
Wednesday 26th, Anne had made her chaplain Matthew Parker
promise to look after her daughter Elizabeth for the future.[46]

The queen's apartments at Greenwich were spacious and
fashionable, like the palace itself. Built of red brick with large mul-
lioned windows, it overlooked the River Thames to the front and
parkland to the rear, and was built around a central courtyard, the
royal lodgings mirroring one another on the first floor for the best
views. Queen Anne, always with an eye to trends, had her ceilings
decorated in the latest 'antique' fashion, with gold bullions set on
white painted battens. Her presence chamber contained a vast
cupboard built specifically to house the expensive, shining plate
that she did not need to use and a great bed of state that she did
not need to sleep in, all marks of her status as queen of England.[47]
Most did not need the reminder. On Saturday, 29 April, however,
Anne found one of her musicians, Mark Smeaton – the 'Mark' of
the Countess of Worcester's story – 'standing in the round window
[in] my chamber of presence'. She asked why he looked so sad, and
he replied that it was 'no matter'. Affronted by his abrupt shutting
down of a social superior's inquiry, she told him haughtily, 'You
may not look to have me speak to you as I should do to a noble
man, because you be an inferior person.' 'No no, madam,' he
replied, 'a look sufficed me, and thus fare you well.'[48] This was
doubly rude: it was not for him to dismiss her. At the least, this
was overstepping the boundaries of social hierarchy, whether or
not anything inappropriate had ever passed between them.

Queen Anne's exchange with Smeaton must have been over-
heard. Within hours Smeaton had been apprehended and was
undergoing questioning at Thomas Cromwell's house in Stepney.
On Sunday 30th the court's Dover visit was postponed, and Anne
had another strange altercation with a different man: Henry
Norris, the king's groom of the stool. She had asked him why he
hadn't yet gone through with his marriage, and he told her that
'he would tarry a time'. She – jokingly? Flirtatiously? Warningly?
We do not know – told him, 'You look for dead men's shoes, for
if ought came to the king but good, you would look to have me.'

Immediately they both knew she had gone too far. To suggest that anything might happen to the king was, by law, as good as threatening to accomplish his demise. Norris, alarmed, replied immediately that if he were to have any such thought, 'he would his head were off'. Anne warned him that she could undo him, and they 'fell out'. At some point after this she marched him to her almoner, John Skip, and insisted that he swear on the holy Bible that she was 'a good woman', a virtuous woman.[49]

None of these conversations could have happened privately. The queen would at least have had another woman there as chaperone, and this may be how the king heard of her conversation with Norris. And yet the May Day jousts went ahead as usual. Greenwich, the 'pleasure palace', boasted its own tiltyard complete with towers from which the entertainment could be viewed. Queen Anne's brother George, Viscount Rochford, led the challengers and Henry Norris the defenders. Norris, ready to go, found that his horse would not run; the king offered his own, a gesture of friendship to a comrade-in-arms.[50] But partway through the king abruptly stood and left, departing shortly for Whitehall Palace on horseback with only six attendants, a move that everybody, including the queen, thought was odd.[51] At roughly the same time, Jane Seymour also left – a fact that Anne surely noticed – and went to Sir Nicholas Carew's house at Beddington in Surrey, some miles to the south of the city.[52]

Anne and her women retired to her chambers at Greenwich. It must have been a terrible night. It was impossible not to know that something was gravely wrong, but equally impossible to know what would happen next. On the morning of 2 May, Smeaton was taken from Cromwell's house at Stepney to the Tower and placed in chains. He had confessed to having slept with Anne on three separate occasions. Anne's brother George, Viscount Rochford followed the king to Whitehall, and was taken to the Tower in the afternoon. Norris was also arrested.

They did not come for the queen until the afternoon. For Anne herself and at least some of her women, it must have been an agony of waiting for something, anything, to happen. Queen

Anne's chambers at Greenwich were set at the back of the palace, across the courtyard from the king's, which overlooked the river.[53] All morning they could see the tiltyard, the scene of yesterday's strange departure; all morning they must have wondered what was happening on the river, at the front of the palace, straining to hear any sound of arrival. Greenwich, being a pleasure palace, had no moat. Such things were considered out of date, old-fashioned, unnecessary in this golden age of peace. Queen Anne had never thought to need defence in her own palace, but now she must have been frighteningly aware that there was no escape and no way to prevent whatever was going to happen.

Some of the queen's women may already have had an idea of what that was going to be. The queen was arrested in the after- noon by several of the king's leading councillors, and held in her chambers until the tide turned to allow the river journey to the Tower.[54] It was a journey of some two or three hours. A queen went nowhere without ladies-in-waiting, even to prison, and Queen Anne was to be accompanied by five women. Wives of her own and the king's officers, these women probably lived at court, may nominally have been in Queen Anne's service and may, therefore, have been briefed; they may have known about the arrest before it occurred and have had to dissemble that fact all morning. Two hours was a long time to sit in a river barge in silence, but there is no record of any words passed between those on board.

It was still 'full daylight' when they arrived.[55] Ascending the Queen's Stairs, she and her ladies entered through the Court Gate into what was then known as the Tower by the Gate – the Byward Tower, close to the constable's lodging. There Anne fell to her knees. She called on God to help her 'as she was not guilty of her accusement', asking the councillors to beseech the king for mercy.[56] The servants of a queen, even a queen under arrest, were not usually supposed to be physically higher than she was. Did the women with her sink to the ground as well, a startled beat behind?

On the wharf, the cannons boomed for the fourth time that day, and the city knew that another prisoner had been committed.

11

Such about Me as I Never Loved

As the noise of the cannons faded Queen Anne rose, and the little cavalcade of women and councillors entered the Tower of London. Anne and her women were conducted to a room in which to rest and gather themselves while the councillors withdrew to talk with the constable, Sir William Kingston, and to pass on the king's instructions. Once the men had departed, Kingston returned to the queen and her ladies. 'Shall I go into a dungeon?' Anne asked him. 'No, Madam,' he replied, 'you shall go into the lodging you lay in at your coronation.'[1] Though the queen fell to her knees again and wept that it was too good for her, no doubt her ladies-in-waiting were relieved to hear that they would at least be physically comfortable. It was usual for elite prisoners to be housed according to their status and so the queen of England was unlikely to be thrown into a dungeon, but these days one never knew which way the king's mood might swing – or his anger.

Kingston led them back out of the Byward Tower and to the right, along a walkway bordered by high walls on both sides. Everywhere there were reminders of others who had entered and never left. Did the women look up at the Bell Tower, where Thomas More and John Fisher had been imprisoned until their deaths the year before? A little further and Kingston directed them left through the gates of the Garden Tower. A burst of colour from the lieutenant's garden in full spring bloom on the left, and then the sudden chill of thick stone walls as they turned to enter Coldharbour Tower, where Anne's maids of honour had been lodged in 1533.[2] The White Tower loomed behind them as

Anne and her women crossed the courtyard to enter the great hall. This was familiar ground. The royal apartments had been remodelled in time for Anne's coronation in June 1533. It had taken a year, but the results had been worth it. Domes had been added on all four corners of the White Tower's roof, topped with gilded weathervanes that glinted brightly even on dark days. On all sides of the courtyard there were whitewashed buildings with timber framing picked out in yellow ochre, a sunshiny effect that had been of a piece with the joy of the coronation but now seemed jarringly optimistic.[3]

The Tower had not been much used as a palace in the intervening years. As the women followed Kingston into the great hall, they couldn't have missed the racks of bowstaves that had been stored there in place of the usual trestle tables and wooden forms.[4] Walking the length of the hall in its silent, empty state was a far cry from the coronation feast, when the room had been full of courtiers, the smell of roasted meat issuing from the service doors at one end, the king atop his chair of estate on the dais at the other. Behind his chair was the flight of stone steps that led upwards to the royal lodgings. Climbing these, they entered the outermost room of the king's suite, and at the far end Kingston produced the key that unlocked the door to the queen's watching chamber. Here the women turned left to walk through the series of rooms that made up the queen's apartments, from watching chamber to 'great' or 'presence' chamber, to dining chamber, to privy chamber, with access increasingly restricted as one moved through the suite. To the right, her windows overlooked the privy garden; to the left, the inner ward in front of the White Tower.

The rooms were large, and the women's voices must have sounded abnormally loud as Kingston escorted them through the complex. The bright yellow-ochre timbers continued inside as well as out. The rooms were likely wood-panelled and adorned with 'antique-work', a decorative style referencing the classical art of ancient Rome, often fantastical beasts and figures painted or sculpted in wood or plaster relief.[5] There might also have been costly hangings on the walls – the king's collection of tapestries was worth more than anything else he owned – or luxury fabric, like cloth of gold or silver. Monarchs usually took their furniture and textiles with them when they travelled, but there had hardly been time for Queen Anne's staff to arrange for this. The rooms must have felt oddly empty, left only with the odds and ends of the sumptuous hangings, cushions, chairs and beds that would normally have filled the space.

Neither the women nor Queen Anne herself, nor, indeed, the constable knew how long they would be there. Imprisonment at this time wasn't a sentence in and of itself. Prisons were used as holding pens for those waiting to be charged, and there was no time limit on how long that could take. It wasn't unusual for imprisonment to be deliberately dragged out and for prisoners to be repeatedly, exhaustingly questioned in the hope that they would trip up and incriminate themselves.[6] While it was unlikely that Anne would simply be left there indefinitely – the king could neither marry a new wife, nor conceive a legitimate heir while she was imprisoned – there was no way to know how long she might have to hold out. A queen's chambers were usually filled with people, not only her own servants but musicians, visitors, dignitaries and often members of the king's household. Now, as Kingston shut the door behind him, there were only five women and Anne.

Who were they, these women who were confined with their queen? Four of the five are revealed to us in the letters that Kingston wrote to the king or to Thomas Cromwell each day. This, indeed, was why the women were there. Their job was not only to attend to Queen Anne's daily needs but to relay her words, her behaviour and her demeanour back to Kingston for him to report to the authorities. They weren't there to comfort her but to spy on her, and both she and they knew it. Perhaps the most important of the five was Kingston's own wife, Mary Scrope, Lady Kingston. Lady Kingston had a long history of court service. She'd served the king's sister Mary Tudor in the early 1500s before moving to Queen Catherine of Aragon's household.[7] She'd been married and widowed, raised her children at court, and we have met her once already at the Duke of Suffolk's house in 1517, trying to covertly engineer a wedding between her stepdaughter and the duke's wealthy ward. If there was advantage to be had, Lady Kingston sought it. In 1536 she was in her early fifties.[8] Experienced, self-assured and pious, she no doubt had her own opinions about what was and was not appropriate behaviour for women at the royal court, and Queen Anne does not seem to have considered her a friend. The king, perhaps for this reason, thought her trustworthy; a safe pair of hands in which to place his own interests. She was not a Howard or a Boleyn client. In fact, both she and her husband had close links to, and sympathy for, the Lady Mary, as Chapuys had noted back in 1535, and when in London they were neighbours of Thomas Cromwell at Blackfriars.[9] Likely, the king thought that she and Kingston would be reliable informants and would not treat Anne with overmuch kindness.

The rest were all linked to the king's own household through their husbands. Margaret Dymoke, Mistress Coffin, was the wife of William Coffin, who was the queen's master of the horse but had previously served in Henry's privy chamber.[10] 'Lady Boleyn' was most likely Anne's aunt Elizabeth Wood, wife of Sir James Boleyn, who was chancellor of Anne's household but also a knight of the body to the king.[11] The fourth woman mentioned by Kingston, 'Mrs Stonor', was most likely Isabel Agard, wife of John Stonor, one of the king's sergeants-at-arms; she served as mother-of-the-maids to successive queens.[12] The fifth, unfortunately, was never named.[13]

They were not the queen's friends. She herself made this clear when she told Kingston that if she'd had the choice, 'I would have had [those] of my own privy chamber which I favour most.'[14] While no doubt all of the five women had spent time at court during Queen Anne's tenure and may have been nominally attached to her household, they may not have had access to her privy chamber, and were probably not her regular daily attendants. This made sense. It was no good choosing the queen's friends, who might already know her secrets and protect them. Queen Anne also thought, probably correctly, that her five attendants were specifically selected by the king. She said plaintively, 'I think much unkindness in the King to put such about me as I never loved', and later commented bitterly that 'the King wist [knew] what he did' when he put Lady Boleyn and Mistress Coffin with her, 'for they could tell her nothing'.[15] Kingston's letters show that the queen was deliberately kept in the dark as events unfolded, for he would not tell her why she was imprisoned, and told her only lies about the whereabouts of her brother, who was also in the Tower. It would not have been out of character for Henry to deliberately choose women whom he could trust to keep silence, and whom he knew his wife did not like.

It's likely that age and reputation also fed into his choice. Kingston told Anne that the king 'took them to be honest and good women', and there is an echo here of the 'juries of matrons' selected by law courts to physically examine women who claimed pregnancy as a reason to postpone a death sentence.[16] Those 'matrons' were typically married or widowed, mature women of good community standing and spotless sexual reputation who could be trusted to uphold standards of moral judgement and behaviour on behalf of the state.[17] Rather grimly, the same logic applied here. Each of the five women was well into middle age, married and experienced; each might be expected to react with horror to the queen's alleged infidelities.

Immediately, they were put to work. Lady Kingston was their leader; Kingston had been ordered to tell the women that 'they should have no communication with her [Anne] unless my wife were present'.[18] This, though, was impossible to maintain through the night, as he pointed out to Thomas Cromwell. Only Lady Boleyn and Mistress Coffin slept in the queen's bedchamber. He and his wife slept in the next room along, and the two other gentlewomen one more room beyond.[19] He wrote as though this were not only normal, but absolutely immutable. Perhaps it was standard practice for only two women ever to sleep in the same room as the queen; perhaps even now Kingston did not feel as though he could override the queen's wishes in this regard. Kingston reassured Cromwell that Mistress Coffin nevertheless told him 'everything she thinks meet for you to know'.[20] The trust placed in Coffin's judgement is extraordinary in such unprecedented circumstances and her agency to withhold information, to protect the queen or to misrepresent her was considerable. It may be that the women operated in pairs for this reason, so that there might always be another individual to hear what Anne said. Perhaps it was simply too risky for them to misreport her or each other.

The queen's women were not ordinarily permitted to leave the court without her permission. Now, though, the tables were turned: it was Queen Anne who could not leave, and her women were her guards. They were supposed to get her to talk, and she needed little encouragement. From the beginning, the queen spoke of the men imprisoned alongside her, of the strange encounters she had had with the musician Mark Smeaton and groom of the stool Henry Norris only the weekend before, and relayed old conversations in a way that suggests she was trying to work out what accusations she faced, what gossip might come to light and how it might be spun. Her ladies asked leading questions. When Queen Anne told of how she had made Norris swear to her virtue, Mistress Coffin asked, 'Madam, why should there be any such matters spoken of?' Without any more prompting, the queen described the conversation that had led to the secret oath before her almoner: how she had teased Norris about putting off his marriage, and then told him that if the king died and the queen were widowed, Norris would look to have her, a statement so close to treasonous speech that it was no wonder that Anne had had him swear that nothing untoward had taken place between them.[21] Mistress Coffin duly relayed the story to Kingston, who reported it to Cromwell: fuel for the fire with which they hoped to burn her.

If Queen Anne knew that the women around her in the Tower were spies, why did she tell them things like this, things that were potentially so incriminating? Perhaps she thought that the stories she related were already known because of the arrests that had already occurred. More likely, her mental state made her careless about what she revealed. Kingston reported that the queen, a woman on a knife edge, ricocheted from weeping to laughter many times. At points, she was prepared to die; at other times, she was desperate to prove herself innocent and to survive.[22] She engaged in the same kind of 'magical thinking' that anyone might under such circumstances. Soon after her arrival, she told Kingston that if she should die, 'you shall see the greatest punishment for me within this seven years, that ever came to England', and a little later she predicted that the country would see no rain until she was freed.[23] One can imagine her desperately seeking signs and omens in the smallest happenings, or silently asking the yellow-ochred walls or the trees outside her window whether things would be all right.

To spend time incarcerated with a person facing the spectre of their own death was to walk a knife edge of a different kind. Lady Kingston and the other ladies-in-waiting had to give Queen Anne personal service – help her to get dressed, brush her hair, sleep next to her – and yet spy on her, report her words and keep some sort of mental distance between themselves and the queen. This must have been incredibly difficult. Though Kingston didn't write about anyone's mental state but the queen's, the five women waiting upon her must have been just as drained. How were they to serve a woman in such straits without developing sympathy for her, even if they had been previously briefed against this? No doubt they were worried that any show of compassion might implicate them alongside her, and perhaps they were even concerned about appearing complicit in front of one another, afraid that a fellow lady-in-waiting might take it upon herself to report her colleagues for overfamiliarity.

Only Lady Boleyn was actively unkind. When the queen complained that neither Lady Boleyn nor Mistress Coffin could tell her anything of what was happening outside her apartments, Lady Boleyn commented tartly, 'Such desire as you have had for such tales hath brought you to this.'[24] Perhaps the long days were wearing Boleyn's patience thin, or perhaps she was genuinely appalled by the stories Queen Anne had revealed. Nonetheless there was hardly any need for such a caustic remark. The others seem to have refrained from making unhelpful observations but, not surprisingly, they were not recorded as being particularly compassionate or comforting either. There was no sense in Kingston relaying kindnesses between the queen and her five attendants. Not only would such acts of care be poorly received by Cromwell and the king, but they weren't relevant to the investigation.

Though the queen complained that she received no news, the Tower was not a hermetically sealed entity for all the women who attended her – or at least not in terms of getting information out. One of the five women was reporting to Imperial ambassador Chapuys. He referred to this woman only as 'the lady who had charge of her [Anne]', and said that this lady had sent to tell him 'in great secrecy' how Queen Anne had affirmed both before and after taking the sacrament that she had never been unfaithful to the king.[25] He was confident that his informant had not concealed anything from him, and indeed she seems to have kept a weather eye out for danger to Chapuys himself, rushing to warn him that Queen Anne had blamed the ambassador for poisoning the king against her, because from the moment of his arrival at court 'the King no longer looked on her with the same eyes as before'.[26] Chapuys never identified his source, but Lady Kingston appears the most likely. A few years previously, when considering plans to spirit the Lady Mary out of the country, Chapuys had noted that it would be easy to do so from the Tower because Constable Kingston appeared to be a supporter of the emperor and to Mary.[27] Lady Kingston was also a friend to Mary, and therefore known to Chapuys, which was not the case with any of the other women there.

Lady Kingston may not have been the only woman sharing titbits of information with outsiders. The account of Queen Anne's imprisonment given in poetic form by the French ambassador's secretary Lancelot de Carle bears a strong similarity to William Kingston's descriptions in his letters to Cromwell. Perhaps the French ambassador was also party to confidential information. One wonders whether the women were ever explicitly warned to report only to Kingston. Surely neither the king nor Thomas Cromwell would have wanted foreign ambassadors to know that Anne had sworn to her innocence on the Eucharist itself. That her women were never called to account for this, though, suggests that their actions were understood in the context of the usual currency of information that was the lifeblood of any court.

While Queen Anne and her five ladies languished in the Tower, much was going on outside. By the end of 4 May, two days after the queen's imprisonment, courtiers Sir Francis Weston, Sir William Brereton, Sir Henry Norris, musician Mark Smeaton and the queen's brother George, Viscount Rochford were also under arrest in the Tower. This put Rochford's wife Jane Parker in a particularly difficult position. On 4 May, Jane sent a message to her husband in the Tower to ask how he did, and to tell him that she would 'humbly suit unto the King's highness' for him.[28] This was the duty of a wife, the least that was expected of any noblewoman. George, though, seems to have had little hope of her success. Though he sent her his thanks, he then asked Kingston when he would be brought before the council, and wept as he spoke of his judgment.[29]

By 12 May, ten days after the queen's arrest, the investigation was largely complete. Four of the men in the Tower alongside the queen were brought to trial: Smeaton, Norris, Weston and Brereton. They were accused of adulterous liaisons with the queen that were spun as treason.[30] Adultery itself was a matter for the Church courts, not the secular law, but it gained a new dimension when it involved a queen. For her to conceive a child by a man who was not the king was to endanger his royal lineage, the 'body politic' itself, and it could therefore be made to count, at a stretch, as 'compassing or imagining the death of the king' under treason law.[31] All were found guilty and sentenced to death.

Events continued to snowball, and there is a strong sense of pieces being moved into place for a final denouement. On 13 May the queen's household was formally broken up.[32] This meant that her women at court were dismissed, to return to their husbands and families at home, and it would have been understood as a sign that Anne was not expected to remain queen regardless of the result of the legal process. On the next day, Thomas Cromwell wrote to the various English ambassadors stationed abroad:

'the Queen's abomination both in incontinent living, and other offences towards the King's highness was so rank and common, that her ladies of her privy chamber and her chamberers could not contain it within their breasts'.[33] He went on to say that 'it came so plainly to the ears of some of his grace's council that with their duty to his Majesty they could not conceal it from him'.[34] This is precisely the sequence of events given by de Carle in his poem, describing the Countess of Worcester's unguarded speech with her brother about the queen's behaviour. De Carle, employed by the French embassy in London, evidently repeated the official line given out by Cromwell.

Women's words had their uses. Cromwell's, though, imply that the Countess of Worcester was not the only woman who had provided evidence against the queen. He noted that 'certain persons of the privy chamber and others of her side were examined' and that this had made the whole matter so evident that they could not do otherwise than proceed.[35] No depositions relating to any of these trials have survived, but there is little doubt that Queen Anne's ladies-in-waiting were among those who were questioned and, willingly or otherwise, gave information. Only they could have witnessed the 'frail and carnal lust', 'base conversations and kisses' and 'vile provocations' that the queen was alleged to have shared with the men now condemned.[36] If she was guilty, her women knew it. If this was a conspiracy fabricated against her, it could not have been executed without their connivance. In either case, their testimony could not but carry weight.

On Monday, 15 May, Lady Kingston and the other four women dressed Queen Anne with care. A knock on the door revealed Constable Kingston and his lieutenant, Edmund Walsingham; they had come to take the queen to her trial in the great hall. Lady Kingston and Lady Boleyn, her two highest-status attendants, were to accompany her.[37] Even if they were prepared for the sight, the changes wrought in the hall over the past week must have been a shock. Gone were the racks of bowstaves. A great wooden 'scaffold' had been made to function as the 'bar' in a courtroom, with benches and seats for the jurors and spectators.[38] The queen's uncle the Duke of Norfolk was in the chair of estate on the dais, his son, Queen Anne's cousin Henry, Earl of Surrey at his feet. The queen was conducted to a seat at the bar. We don't know where Ladies Kingston and Boleyn sat while the trial took place, but it may have been close to the queen in case she needed anything, in an odd distortion of her coronation banquet when two countesses had sat at her feet ready to proffer water to wash her hands, or a napkin.

The trial began. The indictment that was read accused the queen of seducing five men, including her brother, and of 'entertaining malice' against the king.[39] The official records of the queen's trial are no longer extant. What we do know is that the most noteworthy pieces of evidence – the snippets thought worthy of comment by contemporary chroniclers – were those provided by women, and this is a fact often overlooked. Sir John Spelman, one of the judges present, wrote briefly that 'all the evidence was of bawdery and lechery', and then noted specifically that 'this matter' had been disclosed by 'a woman called Lady Wingfield, who had been a servant to the said queen and of the same qualities'.[40] Wingfield had become sick, and before she died had told of the queen's behaviour.

Lady Wingfield's evidence is a tantalising glimpse into the fruits of Cromwell's investigation in the early months of 1536. Lady Wingfield was Bridget Wiltshire, known by her first and highest-status marriage to Sir Richard Wingfield, though she had since been married twice more. Bridget had attended Queen Catherine of Aragon at the Field of Cloth of Gold in 1520, and had apparently become close to Anne Boleyn in the decade after this.[41] Sometime between 1525 and 1529 Bridget left court, and then received a letter from Anne. In it Anne apologised for not having 'showed the love that I bear you as much as it was in deed' and made reference to some 'indiscreet trouble' that had befallen Bridget.[42] Was this salacious, or could it simply have been an exhortation to Bridget to school herself to acceptance of her recent widowhood? Perhaps it was effective; in 1530 Chapuys noted that Bridget had married Sir Nicholas Harvey, a diplomat like her first husband, and had entered Anne's service at court.[43]

That the queen's letter to Bridget is preserved among Cromwell's papers strongly suggests that it was seized as part of the investigation against Queen Anne in 1536. It's usually assumed that Bridget's testimony against the queen and her death shortly after occurred in 1534, because the New Year gift list of 1534 is the last known reference to her at court.[44] This, though, is not a reason to assume her death in the same year. There are no more surviving lists of New Year gifts or rewards until 1538, and no other comprehensive lists of women in court service until Jane Seymour's funeral in November 1537, so it's hardly surprising that there are no references to Bridget after 1534.[45] It's eminently plausible that she was questioned as part of Cromwell's investigation in the early months of 1536, and had then died before Queen Anne's arrest in May, meaning that she could not be brought to the trial as a witness. In fact, no witnesses were called at all; but this was not unusual in a Tudor treason trial, which operated by written testimony and not live questioning.[46] Arguably Lady Wingfield's death was extremely convenient for the prosecution. She could not be harmed by any evidence attached to her name, and nor could such evidence be disputed.[47]

So it proved. Queen Anne defended herself well – chronicler Wriothesley wrote that she 'made so wise and discreet answers to all things laid against her, excusing herself with her words so clearly as though she had never been faulty to the same', and even her arch-enemy ambassador Chapuys allowed that she had answered the charges 'satisfactorily enough'.[48] Yet, one by one, the jury of peers declared the queen guilty, and sentence was pronounced. Queen Anne, her uncle Norfolk declared, was to die a traitor's death. Lady Kingston and Lady Boleyn had to stand and escort Anne back to her lodging, and somehow help her prepare herself for her death.

There was a short break, and then Queen Anne's brother George, Viscount Rochford was brought to the hall for his own trial. The same format was followed, and George likewise defended himself well, with particular rhetorical flair and eloquence. It was thought that he would be acquitted.[49] Nothing in his indictment was sufficient to secure a conviction. Again, we have no official record of the evidence presented; again, what made it into contemporary accounts was female testimony. One of the jurors handed George a folded note. Its contents made it clear that George's wife Jane had given evidence against him. Not only that, but what she had said was enough to condemn him.

So much for suing to the king on his behalf, he must have thought. Though he was told not to read it aloud, defying the courtroom, he did so. The note related how George and the queen had laughed together about the king's poor sexual prowess, and that the queen had told her that the king 'was not skilful in copulating with a woman, and had neither virtue nor potency'. Jane also said that George had questioned the paternity of Queen Anne's daughter Princess Elizabeth.[50] Of course King Henry did not want this picked over by the courtroom. Early modern Europe held that if a wife looked elsewhere for sex, her husband bore the blame for failing to satisfy her at home.[51] This may even have been part of the reason why Queen Anne was accused of straying with so many men. Just one liaison, and people would ask why the king had failed. Five, and attention turned to the queen's insatiable appetite, her carnal sickness, and the king became a victim of a wicked woman, not an example of failed masculinity. Jane's testimony ruined this tidy picture. Not only had the queen and her ladies-in-waiting been discussing Henry's abilities in the bedroom – something to make any man wince – but, far worse, they had been laughing at him, and now everybody knew it.

Jane was judged harshly for what was read as a wife's betrayal, both in her own time and by us since.[52] It has been suggested that when Jane told her husband that she would sue to the king for him, she tried to do so. The king, though, was seeing nobody but Thomas Cromwell and his immediate body servants, and so she had to go to Cromwell instead. At that point, very likely, she was interrogated herself, and gave up what she knew.[53] Many of Queen Anne's later apologists claimed that Jane's accusations were false, that she made them up out of spite or jealousy.[54] If Jane had truly, actively sought the deaths of her husband and sister-in-law at this time, it would have been far easier to follow the path of least resistance and agree that the queen had, indeed, slept with the men imprisoned in the Tower alongside her, rather than create the story about the king's impotence. Some sources claimed that Jane was in fact the origin of the charge of incest between Queen Anne and George, but this cannot now be substantiated.[55]

We will never know just what happened to Jane during this time. The fear factor of an interrogation by Thomas Cromwell should not be underestimated, and it's likely that she knew the rumours flying around and that she thought George and Anne were already condemned regardless of what she said or didn't say. Few people left the Tower alive in 1530s England. Jane also had her own position to consider. Traitors lost their goods, lands and titles to the Crown. While the widows of traitors were sometimes allowed to claim their jointure and goods, this was at the king's discretion. If George was to die a traitor, there was nothing in the law to help Jane.[56] It would have been a smart move on Thomas Cromwell's part to promise her his assistance for the future if she would tell him what she knew – and Thomas Cromwell was always smart.

It was only at the introduction of Jane's evidence that George's trial began to unravel. Like his sister, he was condemned to death. Jane's testimony had been crucial. Queen Anne's fall could not have happened without the co-operation of her ladies-in-waiting, and their evidence suggests that there had indeed been some suspect exchanges going on in the queen's household during these years, even if those events did not wholly amount to the five charges of adultery that were presented at the trials in the Tower's great hall. Over two thousand people attended these.[57] Every man who heard Lady Wingfield's evidence, Jane's evidence and the evidence presented from other ladies-in-waiting must have thought of the women in his own life and feared anew the danger and ubiquity of female gossip.

Two days later, on Wednesday, 17 May, Lady Kingston and the

others in attendance on the queen would listen from her chambers next to the White Tower as the roar of a distant crowd rose and fell five times, marking the deaths of the five men accused of adultery with the queen. They would have heard the sound of hammering and sawing that would mean that the queen's scaffold was being built. Queen Anne's mood continued to veer wildly. One evening, Constable Kingston reported that she had said she would go to a nunnery, and was 'in hope of life'.[58] By the evening of 17 May, though, the day that her brother and friends died, she had confessed and received absolution and was said to be resigned to her death, having been told that this would happen the next day. The allotted hour came and went, and Anne's fragile calm was cruelly upset: the execution had, apparently, been put off until the next day.[59]

The five women with her must also have been emotionally and mentally at the end of their endurance. Now, French poet de Carle wrote, they too were 'plagued by great anguish', and the queen had to console them, exhorting them not to lament her death.[60] De Carle may simply have been following a trope of grieving attendants here, but it's equally possible that the five women who were not Anne's friends had come to feel grief for her after seventeen days of close, tense confinement.

The scaffold was erected not on the public site of Tower Hill but within the Tower complex itself, to the north-east of the White Tower. The queen was called at eight in the morning on 19 May. She – and therefore no doubt some of her women – had been awake since two, when her almoner had arrived to pray with her, and together they waited the long hours until dawn.[61] Constable Kingston arrived to escort her to the scaffold, and sources agree that four of the five women accompanied her.[62] These must have been four of the same women who had attended her throughout her imprisonment. Though one source describes them as 'young' women, it made no sense for four different women to have been drafted in for this occasion, and one did not send teenagers to accompany a queen to her death. Nor was the king likely to have sought to honour his condemned wife by providing higher-status attendants on her scaffold.

Queen Anne made a short, traditional speech in which she acknowledged her fault and asked for prayers, and then the women took off her furred cape and she passed her hood to one of them. Another handed her a linen cap to hold her hair free of her neck. She knelt upright before the block, and one of the women – perhaps Lady Kingston – bandaged her eyes; de Carle wrote shortly afterwards that this woman was 'pouring forth continuous tears'.[63] This last duty done, the four women withdrew from the scaffold and knelt, presumably still clutching Anne's clothing, 'bewailing bitterly and shedding many tears'.[64] Anne remained kneeling upright, and was killed with one stroke of the executioner's sword. Her women then returned to the scaffold and collected her head and her body, wrapping them in white cloth and carrying them to a chapel within the Tower nearby.[65]

Such accounts of open grief may well be exaggerated. De Carle himself did not watch the execution. The site within the Tower was deliberately chosen as a means to limit the audience, and foreigners were not permitted. There are, however, several accounts that tell us that the queen's four attendants were in tears as they watched her die, and one can well imagine it. They had spent seventeen days incarcerated with the queen. They had watched her fall apart and put some semblance of herself back together over and over. They had seen her in grief and in terror. Like any lady-in-waiting, their loyalties and emotions could not always align, and we need not assume that political allegiance had removed their capacity for empathy.

Queen Anne was buried in St Peter ad Vincula, the public church within the Tower grounds. The five women – Ladies Kingston and Boleyn, Mistress Coffin, Mistress Stonor and the final, unnamed woman – were free to go.

There was no time to draw breath after Queen Anne's execution. The king married Jane Seymour almost immediately, and many of Anne's former servants were drafted into her household, including Mistress Coffin and Mistress Stonor, and the newly widowed Jane Parker, Viscountess Rochford. Jane, as she had no doubt expected, found life financially difficult. Her jointure, the settlement assured to her by George's family when they had married, allowed her only 100 marks a year, or £66 13s 4d. Though this was as much as six years' wages to a skilled tradesman, it wasn't much for a lady-in-waiting. Elizabeth, Duchess of Norfolk had been married with a dowry of 2,000 marks, just as Jane had, but her jointure was set to be five times Jane's.[66] The dowager Duchess of Norfolk had £308; her daughter Lady Daubeney had £196 from her first marriage.[67] Crown officers had ransacked and inventoried every room in every house that George Boleyn owned, for the goods of a convicted traitor belonged to the Crown. The biggest and best of Jane's homes was Beaulieu Palace in Essex, and it may have been there, in the chamber over the kitchen, that a chest of Jane's possessions was emptied and listed, the contents bundled up and taken away. Old clothes from court masques; white silk hose wrought with gold, ten pairs of sleeves in velvet, satin, damask and tinsel, broken beads of gold and pearl. Even if Jane no longer wore them, there was value in the fabric and the gold. Two books – clearly Jane enjoyed reading – and a prayer book, a primer 'boarded with silver and gilt'.[68] These, and other things, Jane wanted back.

Thus she wrote to Thomas Cromwell, and played the part of the 'poor desolate widow' in full. She asked him to speak to the king for 'such poor stuff and plate as my husband had, that of his gracious liberality I might have it to help me'. She laid out her financial situation and complained that it was 'very hard for me to shift the world withal'.[69] Sure enough, both Cromwell and the king wrote to her father-in-law, Thomas Boleyn, Earl of Wiltshire, asking him to allow Jane more money – a concession, perhaps, to her co-operation with the trial process. Wiltshire was not at all willing to do this, but after grumbling that he and his own wife had lived on far less in their day, he allowed Jane fifty marks more per year, insisting that he did this only 'to satisfy the King's desire and pleasure'.[70] Jane was also allowed to reclaim some of her husband's goods.[71]

As he had with Queen Catherine of Aragon, King Henry

soon ordered his craftsmen to obliterate any material sign of his second queen. Anne's memory was not supposed to be preserved. Her arms, mottoes, badges and colours were physically removed from wood, stone, plaster and brick and replaced with those of Queen Jane. Some women, though, quietly kept her memory alive regardless of the royal will. A book of hours once belonging to Anne survives at Hever Castle, and has been found by Kate McCaffrey to contain the vestiges of inscriptions: a list of names, three out of four of which are female, linked by kinship and locality to Anne, and with connections to the royal court.[72] Two of the names, Elizabeth Shirley and Philippa Gage, were sisters. Both had court connections: they were daughters of Sir Richard Guildford, who had been one of Henry VII's councillors. Philippa had been at court while her husband, Sir John Gage, was lord chamberlain of the royal household in the late 1520s, and her children also had court careers.[73] The third name in the book was Mary West, who was the Guildford sisters' greatniece. This suggests that the book of hours was passed quietly between female relations as the sixteenth century wore on, a dangerous thing to do at a time when to deliberately preserve Queen Anne's memory in this way was to subvert the thrust of royal policy.

But how did the book reach the Guildford sisters' custody in the first place? There is a long oral tradition that on the scaffold Anne passed her prayer book to one of the ladies with her there. None of those women were connected to the Guildfords or their close relations. The Guildford women did, though, have family members at court at that time. It's been suggested that at some stage Queen Anne herself passed it to Elizabeth Shirley's daughter, another Elizabeth, who was married to the king's sergeant of the cellar, Richard Hill. However, the Guildford sisters also had connections even closer to the queen, and to the investigation against her. Philippa Gage's daughter Alice Gage was married to Sir Anthony Browne, the king's master of the horse. She was therefore the sister-in-law of the Countess of Worcester, who had been Queen Anne's first accuser. Did Alice's husband tell her what he feared, before he dared share it with the king? Alice's marriage gave her a higher status than her cousin Elizabeth Hill enjoyed, and Alice was therefore a fixture in more elevated court circles.[74] It's entirely possible that Queen Anne had in fact given Alice her book of hours, and that Alice had sent it home to her mother and aunt. Certainly it was safer there. Alice continued to live and serve at court until her death in 1540, and could not have risked such a book being found in her possession.[75] Regardless of the precise route into these Kent families, the book's existence shows that loyalties for women were complicated, and not always binary. Philippa Gage had served Catherine of Aragon, and yet inscribed her name in Anne Boleyn's book. While some branches of these families took up reformist religion in the vein of Anne Boleyn herself, others would later be classed as Catholic recusants, enemies of the Crown. No matter their religious opinions, some ladies-in-waiting thought of this as separate to their loyalty to their late queen. Without these women, Queen Anne's memory would not have been preserved for us to find.

While the Guildford women took steps to preserve Queen Anne's memory, and Jane, Viscountess Rochford begged Cromwell for financial assistance, life in Queen Jane Seymour's new household went on. Among those living at court was the king's niece, Lady Margaret Douglas. One of Lady Margaret's closest friends was Mary Howard, Duchess of Richmond, who was the daughter of the Duke of Norfolk, wife of the king's illegitimate son Henry Fitzroy, and cousin to the late Queen Anne. Mary was undoubtedly involved in the investigation around Queen Anne's morals, but there's no evidence she had had anything to add to the explosive evidence of the trial. In any case, she had something else on her mind. Around Easter of 1536, before Anne's execution, Lady Margaret had confided a secret to Mary. Mary's kinsman Lord Thomas Howard, youngest half-brother of the Duke of Norfolk, had been making eyes at Margaret for some months, with Mary's connivance. Finally, he had asked Lady Margaret to marry him, and she had agreed.[76]

A clandestine marriage was risky indeed. Lady Margaret was royal. She could not marry without the king's permission, and he was hardly likely to allow her to marry a younger son of no title or fortune, even if Lord Thomas was related to the queen. Mary knew this, and yet she supported her friend. She helped them to meet, waiting for Lady Boleyn to leave the room and sneaking Lord Thomas in with one of his servants.[77] It must have seemed a little like a game. Or perhaps Mary reasoned that she was serving her own family's interest, for though she was young she was intelligent and politically aware. A marriage made could not easily be undone. Longer-term, it could be no bad thing for the Howards to have made another marriage into royalty, and surely Queen Anne herself would support the match.

Quite what plans were ever made to reveal it and to go ahead with the marriage is not clear. The secret was kept through April and into May, and it stayed a secret even as the court and the queen's household crumbled around them. The ladies-in-waiting were formally dismissed from service on 13 May, Queen Anne died on the 19th, Queen Jane stepped into her shoes, and still nobody knew that the king's niece had agreed to marry a Howard boy. But the house of cards was too precarious. How the matter came to light remains a mystery, but come to light it did in early July. Predictably, the king was absolutely furious. Parliament had just passed the Second Act of Succession, which made both of his daughters illegitimate, and Lady Margaret's position in the succession had correspondingly risen.[78] To find that she had thrown herself away on a nobody was yet another stunning blow in this year of terrible happenings.

On 14 July, Lord Thomas and several male servants of his were hauled in for questioning. The couple had been careful. All that the servants knew was that for a quarter of a year there had been 'love betwixt them'.[79] One of the servants did, however, incriminate Mary, Duchess of Richmond beyond all doubt. Thomas Smyth, one of Lord Thomas's men, reported that he had seen the couple meet in Mary's chamber.[80] Panicked over the succession and enraged at this calm disregarding of royal protocol under his very nose, the king sent both Lord Thomas and Lady Margaret to the Tower and had Lord Thomas attainted for high treason, claiming – preposterously – that seeking to marry Lady Margaret had constituted an attempt on the throne itself.[81] The king was unlikely to execute his own niece, given her new significance to the succession, and in the event he did not execute Lord Thomas either, simply leaving him to languish in the Tower.[82] Perhaps it was too soon for more traitors' deaths.

Mary, Duchess of Richmond, as their accomplice, must nevertheless have been frightened. In theory, Lord Thomas's attainder for treason opened Mary to a charge of misprision of treason, a crime introduced in 1534: knowing of treasonous activity but keeping it secret. If the Crown chose to see her behaviour in this light, she would be facing lifetime imprisonment and confiscation of goods and property. The all-important matter of the succession, however, saved her, even as it condemned her friends. Mary's husband was Henry Fitzroy, Duke of Richmond, the king's illegitimate and only son. As Queen Anne fell, wily commentators kept an eye on Richmond: now that both princesses were illegitimate, they wondered aloud whether the king might make his bastard son his heir, to inherit the crown of England.[83] It was not beyond the bounds. The Act of Succession rendering Princess Elizabeth illegitimate included a clause that allowed the king to appoint his own heir, and it was widely rumoured that this was specifically for Richmond's benefit.[84] It would have been extremely inconvenient to attaint Richmond's wife for misprision of treason at the same time as effectively naming her queen-in-waiting, and this is probably the reason why she walked free.

Such a glittering future, though, was not to be. Richmond had been in London during Anne's fall and had attended her execution, but in early July he fell suddenly ill. By 8 July the illness had become serious, and Chapuys was reporting that he did not have long left to live.[85] On 23 July he died at St James's Palace, and Mary was a widow at the age of sixteen. Rather poignantly, Richmond had just been granted Baynard's Castle to use as a London home, a move that suggests that their married life was set to begin as both turned seventeen.[86] Now, Mary's future disappeared amid the funereal incense and prayers for the dead, and her best friend was under house arrest and unavailable for succour; 1536 was a dark year indeed.

Part Three: 1536–1547

12

Too Wise for a Woman

Lady Hussey dipped the quill in the ink and carefully inscribed her name underneath the answers she had given to their questions. Her three interrogators signed in their turn: Sir Edmund Walsingham, lieutenant of the Tower of London; Thomas Wriothesley, royal administrator and secretary to Thomas Cromwell; and William Petre, another of Cromwell's men.[1] No doubt the paper would go straight to Cromwell's desk; she knew he held her fate in his hand. Please God this would be the end of it and they would let her go.

Anne Grey, Lady Hussey was no shrinking violet. Now in her early forties, she had decided opinions and was not usually afraid to express them.[2] The summer of 1536, though, had not been a good time to exercise her usual loquacity. In early June her husband John, Lord Hussey had travelled south from their home in Lincolnshire to attend the opening of the new Parliament in London. Anne had gone with him, not for Parliament – women, even peeresses, played no role there – but to stop at Hunsdon in Hertfordshire to visit her friend and erstwhile mistress the Lady Mary, the king's eldest daughter.[3]

The summer of 1536 was an uncertain time for royal women and for those in their service. Queen Anne Boleyn had been attainted and executed for treason only a few weeks previously, and it wasn't yet clear what all the consequences of this would be. Queen Anne's daughter Elizabeth would no doubt lose the title of 'princess' and her place in the succession – the Act to ensure this was already in draft.[4] The as yet unborn children of the new

Queen Jane would take precedence. But what would happen to Mary, Elizabeth's half-sister? As the daughter of the late Queen Catherine of Aragon, Mary's position had been below Elizabeth's for some time already.[5] The annulment of her parents' marriage had made her illegitimate in the eyes of the English Crown. In 1533 her household had been amalgamated with, and subjugated within, Elizabeth's, and Mary's women had faced repeated threats of dismissal.[6] Mary herself had steadfastly refused to accept the invalidity of her parents' marriage or her own illegitimacy, and there had been resultant fears for her safety.[7] Now, though, Queen Anne, the causer of this rift, was dead. Surely the king would set aside all former differences and welcome Mary back into the fold?

Lady Mary herself was not the only one who thought this. Former friends and associates began to flock to her house at Hunsdon, and Lady Hussey's visit took place in this context. Her husband had been Mary's chamberlain, and she herself among the ladies-in-waiting before the household reduction at the end of 1533, and Lady Hussey hadn't seen Mary since then.[8] In such an atmosphere, old habits died hard, or recent events produced over-confidence. On one Monday, Lady Hussey called for drink 'for the Princess'. The next day she answered an inquiry as to Mary's whereabouts with the information that 'the Princess' had gone walking.[9] Mary was not, of course, a princess any longer and it was illegal to call her that. By the beginning of July, Lady Hussey had been arrested and taken to the Tower of London.[10]

She was held there for at least a month and questioned at least twice. She fell sick; it made no difference.[11] The questions she was asked open a window onto the king's anxieties. Why had Lady Hussey called Mary 'princess'? Had anybody else done so? Who had been there? What were they saying about the king's first marriage and about Mary's legitimacy? Had she been in touch with Mary before or since?[12]

Henry knew that the behaviour of royal personnel was part of the negotiation of royal status, and he had long used his daughters' households to advertise his views on the succession.[13] If Mary's servants and friends treated her as a princess, not only would this encourage Mary herself in her pretensions, but it implied that it did not matter whether she had agreed to the royal supremacy or the Act of Succession, and thus that these things themselves did not matter. This he could not have. Nor could he imagine that Mary had arrived at such obstinacy all on her own, and he had had quite enough of disobedient women of late. He sent Thomas Cromwell to 'visit' the women who had recently been with Mary, to bring them before the council and compel them to swear to the statutes.[14] This is probably how Lady Hussey's incautious words were discovered and taken as encouragement of Mary's disobedience.

It may well have been a genuine slip of the tongue. Mary had been the de facto heir to the throne for nearly fifteen years, and Lady Hussey's dismissal from her service at the end of 1533 meant that she had never had time to get used to calling Mary anything else. There is no evidence that Lady Hussey refused to sign either the Oath of Supremacy or of Succession. Even so, it was intensely thoughtless at such a politically charged hour. All that Lady Hussey could do now was perform the submissive behaviour and abject apologies required of her and attempt to reassure her interrogators. She had only called Mary 'princess' out of old custom, she explained. She had not heard anybody else do so; neither she nor anybody else had said that the king's first marriage was lawful, and nobody had spoken of Mary as the king's legitimate daughter. She'd had no further messages or tokens from Mary. If she had offended the king, 'she most humbly beseecheth his Highness of mercy and forgiveness, as one that is repentant for that she hath so offended, and purposeth never hereafter to fall in to semblable danger'.[15]

By the time Lady Hussey signed this on 3 August, Mary herself had finally capitulated. This was partly thanks to another lady-in-waiting: Mary Scrope, Lady Kingston, who had been with Queen Anne Boleyn in the Tower. The king evidently considered Lady Kingston to be a safe pair of hands, for she went almost straight from the Tower to Mary at Hunsdon explicitly to help convince her to submit to her father. How Lady Kingston persuaded Mary to do this no source is able to tell us. Convince her she did, with the help of both Thomas Cromwell and the new Queen Jane Seymour. Lady Kingston even helped Mary to draft the letter to her father.[16] Mary acknowledged the annulment of her parents' marriage, her own illegitimacy, and her father's position as head of the English Church. It was a tremendous coup for the king, and Lady Kingston was his instrument. This was a task for 'a very confidential lady', as Chapuys wrote, and this gives Lady Kingston the air of a Crown agent: someone who was trusted to corral royal women into obeying the king.[17] Within weeks, Mary was rewarded with seniority within the household she shared with her sister and was visited by the king and queen. The return of some of her favourite ladies-in-waiting was another carrot to soften the threat of the stick.[18]

That Lady Hussey was not immediately released shows how disturbed the king remained by the spectre of disobedient women. And yet he could hardly pardon his daughter while punishing her adherents indefinitely. As the days began to shorten and farmers began to think about the harvest, Lady Hussey was freed to return to her home and her husband in Lincolnshire. But had the king's drastic treatment of her unguarded words frightened her into genuine submission or merely its semblance?

Lady Hussey must often have longed for the safety of Sleaford Castle and the company of her children during her frightening ordeal. No doubt she needed time to recover and regroup. But the mood of unease and uncertainty was broader than the royal households, the court or the aristocracy, and it was waiting for her when she reached home. Back in March 1536 Parliament had passed an Act for the dissolution of monasteries with an income of less than £200 per year, and commissions were now at work evicting nuns and monks, sequestrating valuables and dismantling centuries-old buildings.[19] Lincolnshire stifled under a cloud of fear and increasing indignation. Wild rumours circled. It was said that all the jewels and plate were going to be taken away from parish churches. There were going to be taxes on all christenings, marriages and burials. Taxes would even be levied on horned cattle.[20]

In some areas, these tales landed amid long-standing exploitation by landlords or, indeed, landladies. Among Lady Hussey's Lincolnshire neighbours was a fellow lady-in-waiting of some standing: our friend María de Salinas, Lady Willoughby, who lived thirty miles east of Lincoln at Eresby Place. María was strongly attached to her Lincolnshire home. She had known the county since her marriage to William, Lord Willoughby in 1516, and they had spent time there when not required to be with the king and queen at court.

María's legal settlement with her brother-in-law Sir Christopher Willoughby meant that she could continue to live at Eresby and to manage the lands there. Her management style was what we might call hands-on. She clearly knew her estate inside out, well aware that its profit lay in farms that had not been kept in good repair during the years of legal dispute. 'Except it be well looked to,' she wrote, 'it will decay sore shortly . . . I fear me that 500 marks will not bring it in due repair again.'[21] Custodians of land, whether widows or other guardians, were not permitted to milk the land's finite resources for profit at the expense of the future heir. But lawsuits were expensive. María still had to pay the Crown £100 a year as per the estate settlement.[22] She needed to effect the repairs that had not been done during previous years while maintaining her own noble lifestyle in order to be taken seriously, and exercise due magnificence towards those below her in social standing. For this, she had to find ways to make money from her lands and tenants.

She couldn't ruin the land itself. But there were many ways to extort money out of tenants, and María squeezed hers financially until all the goodwill had run dry.[23] The dirty work was done by a triumvirate of estate officers acting on her orders: her surveyor, local priest Sir Francis Stoner; Thomas Gildon, her receiver-general, responsible for collecting and collating rents and other monies; and Anthony Missenden, her steward of manorial courts, which dealt with matters such as fines, debts and so forth.

Together they worked the manorial legal system, hauling tenants up for matters that were usually allowed to slide. Her council reprimanded her tenants for failure to keep their tenements in repair, binding them on pain of a fine to do the repairs and then declaring them unsatisfactory and levying the fine in any case. Brewing without licence, harbouring vagabonds, using common land, keeping 'meretricious' women, failing to control destructive farm animals – all were used as a vast money-spinning exercise. Other landlords saw their profits fall during these years; María's rose.

Resentment smouldered. On Monday, 2 October, Dr Raynes, the Bishop of Lincoln's chancellor, arrived at Louth, to the north of the Willoughby lands, to carry out a visitation of the clergy there. He was expected. A group of townsmen had been guarding the treasure house of the church through the night, believing in the rumours that said that the jewels and plate would be seized. Armed and angry, they forced the chancellor and the priests there to swear an oath to be true to the people, and burned the chancellor's papers.[24] News of their actions spread like wildfire and sparked off similar altercations in the towns and villages nearby. Commissioners were thrown out of monasteries. There were many threats of violence to people and property, and many houses were ransacked. Within days, those from the professional classes and even some members of the gentry had begun taking leadership roles. The rebels made banners, took up slogans, wrote ballads and marched towards Lincoln. And inevitably, they began settling other, more personal scores.

María seems not to have been at home at Eresby Place, which was fortunate, since as soon as the next-door town of Spilsby rose her house was broken into and ransacked. Several of her senior officials had been riding around the estate trying to prevent the tenantry from joining the rebels. Discovered three miles from home, the bailiff of Eresby was promptly fined for his efforts and was forced to give local rebels all the 'harness', i.e. armour, that was in the house.[25] At West Keal they broke down the doors of the parsonage 'so to have killed Mr Gildon' – Thomas Gildon, María's receiver-general.[26] Anthony Missenden, her steward of courts, fled.[27]

María's surveyor and priest Sir Francis Stoner encountered particular danger. Like the bailiff of Eresby, he tried to 'stay' the rebels. He took the sum of £100 and, allegedly, 500 men and rode towards Lincoln to help suppress the rebellion. Inevitably, he was seized. Stoner was threatened, accused of having prevented 300 people from joining the rebellion – his mission had apparently had some success – and called 'traitor to the commons'. He was forced to give up his money, and Spilsby men Robert Bawding, the late Lord Willoughby's cook, mercer Thomas Smyth and Alexander Dolman demanded Stoner's death. Bawding exclaimed, 'Mr Surveyor, you have been many times hard against me', and indeed this was true.[28] The records of the Willoughby courts show that Bawding and the rest had been continually fined for many small, inconsequential offences and might legitimately feel 'very sore' against María's officers.[29] In the event, Stoner was lucky; the gentlemen there connected to the Willoughby affinity spoke up for him and saved his life.

There was no one single cause of the uprising. Five different rebels could have given five different reasons. But in many areas, extortion from local landlords was a significant factor, and we often forget that women as well as men were responsible for corruption on their estates. Government policies that had encouraged such rapacity were another cause, though with classic rebel rhetoric the malcontents did not blame the king for this but his advisors, specifically Thomas Cromwell and Sir Richard Rich. Some remained angry about the king's second marriage to Anne Boleyn and demanded the restoration of Princess Mary to the succession. Many, bolstered by the clergy, were dismayed not only by the dissolution of the smaller monasteries, but by rumours of religious change in general. This was why the rebellion became known as 'our pilgrimage of grace', a march for the grace of God.

As the rebellion progressed, women remained in the thick of it. Lady Hussey, incautious supporter of the king's daughter Mary, had no sooner returned home to Sleaford Castle after her sojourn in the Tower when rebellion broke out on her doorstep. Sleaford was only thirty-five miles from Louth, and the Husseys heard about the rising almost immediately. Lord Hussey was in a difficult position. His sympathies lay with those who opposed religious change, but to openly set himself against the king was to court death, and like most nobles he had little time for rebellious nobodies. He organised musters and tried to gather the gentry, but he also knew that his tenantry would not rise to fight for him. Instead on 7 October he fled, disguised as a priest, leaving Lady Hussey behind.[30] The next day a party of rebels came to Sleaford to 'take' him. When they found him gone, they threatened Lady Hussey and put her 'in fear for her life'. They would burn the place, they said. They would 'destroy' her children. They forced her to swear that she would go after her husband and bring him back, and 'like a fool' – her husband's words – she did.[31]

Beyond this, though, Lady Hussey also gave the rebels food and drink, and even offered them money.[32] For this reason she is usually thought to have been in sympathy with them, even actively working on their behalf. She was not the only one. As the rebellion moved northwards in October, Lady Elizabeth Stapleton, wife of Sir Christopher Stapleton, was with her husband and family at the Grey Friars in Beverley, Yorkshire. Her brother-in-law joined the rising. Though she'd been told to stay inside, Lady Stapleton went out to watch the commons pass by, and when asked why her husband and son had not joined, she replied that they were inside the house; 'Go pull them out by the heads!'[33]

Like the rebels as a whole, the women who involved themselves in the Pilgrimage of Grace were motivated by a variety of factors. Some, like Lady Stapleton, saw it as a fight for traditional religion. It was 'God's quarrel', she said.[34] Queen Jane Seymour herself reputedly went on her knees before the king to ask him to stay the dissolution; she was told 'not to meddle with his affairs'.[35] Others had personal scores to settle. Katherine Howard, Lady Daubeney was one of these. The half-sister of the Duke of Norfolk, her first husband Sir Rhys ap Gruffudd had been executed by the government for high treason in what amounted to a show trial in December 1531, because the couple's actions against the king's officers in south-west Wales and their snide remarks about Queen Anne Boleyn had made the government nervous. In November 1536 it was reported that Katherine had gone to the rebels with 3,000 men and half a cartload of plate which was now being minted for coin.[36] Court politics, like ladies-in-waiting, was rarely confined to court.

In London, María de Salinas, Lady Willoughby must have been alarmed when she heard about the rising. The news travelled quickly. The disturbance in Louth began on the morning of 2 October, and a day later local nobles were writing to the king to tell him that 'a great multitude of people' had risen and the number was still growing.[37] As news trickled south through October and into November, María would no doubt have been afraid for her home, her estates and her loyal officers. Worse: her son-in-law, the Duke of Suffolk, was appointed to lead the force northwards to suppress the Lincolnshire revolt. Worse still: he took his wife Katherine, María's daughter, with him.[38]

Initially, nobles seem to have assumed that the pilgrimage would be easily put down. Thomas, Lord Borough wrote that he had sent word to his neighbours to be in readiness 'to make them a breakfast' – a grimly delicious turn of phrase.[39] But the rebellion grew. Leaders were elected. Lawyers drafted proclamations and articles; the gentry joined or were press-ganged. The king himself cloaked his fear in righteous indignation, absolutely refusing to countenance any of the rebels' demands. York fell. Hull capitulated.

The Duke of Suffolk was sent north because of his wife Katherine's lands in Lincolnshire, but he had hardly spent any time at all in the region.[40] Perhaps he asked for his mother-in-law María's advice, and she surely prayed for their safety. Suffolk probably left Katherine at Grimsthorpe Castle in the south of the county, which would have been a little safer than the strongholds further north.[41] It was a big ask for a seventeen-year-old to stay alone in such a dangerous location. Like her mother, though, Katherine was a brave woman. In place by 10 October, only eight days after the first rising at Louth, she immediately began finding out and reporting the local rumours to her husband by letter, that he might have a clearer idea of the situation on the ground as it unfolded. At times this must have been extremely nerve-wracking. On 10 October itself the rumour was that Suffolk had lost a field and 20,000 men, and she must have been afraid for him.[42]

By December she had evidently been of such use that Suffolk decided to leave her at Grimsthorpe to keep an eye on things while he spent Christmas at court debriefing with the king.[43] This was necessary if he wanted to remain in favour. Those marshalling defence on the ground were compelled to compromise by the sheer size of the rebel force, to the rage of the king, who could not see why a single inch must be given. Over Christmas 1536 a truce held; Robert Aske, the lawyer who had become the rebels' major leader, was invited to court, feted and feasted on false promises.

Aske soon realised he'd been had. Come January he recalled his men, expecting further confrontation. Sir Francis Bigod, a knight from north Yorkshire who shared Cromwell's evangelical beliefs and had so far opposed the rebellion on these grounds, distrusted the king's good faith. His dislike of royal interference in the Church gave him common ground with the rebels, and on 15 January 1537 he launched another revolt, accusing Aske of betraying the rebel cause. Once more the rising spread, and again women were in its midst. Lady Dorothy Darcy wrote to her husband Sir George from Gateforth in Yorkshire begging him to return.[44] Catherine, Countess of Westmorland, also left alone as her husband travelled south to handle other urgent business, found herself unexpectedly called on: Sir Thomas Tempest reported that she had stayed the country, and 'rather playeth the part of a knight than of a lady'.[45]

Not all of the queen's women were so directly affected by the Pilgrimage of Grace. Some were busy with other concerns. Mary Howard, the newly widowed Duchess of Richmond, was one of these. After the unexpected death of her husband Henry, the king's illegitimate son, in July 1536 Mary had returned to her father the Duke of Norfolk's house at Kenninghall on the border between

Norfolk and Suffolk.[46] Quite how she felt about this is not known. Not all widows went back to their family, but Mary was only seventeen years of age and still a minor. Nobody was going to allow her to make her own life choices unless it was absolutely necessary.

She might have preferred to stay at court with her friends. Her experience as lady-in-waiting to Anne Boleyn might even have made her a helpful asset to Queen Jane Seymour's household, but it might also have made her unwelcome. Mary was Anne Boleyn's cousin. She'd been at the centre of her court, woven indelibly into the fabric of Anne's queenship and of the monarchy, married as she was to the king's illegitimate son. The deaths of Anne and of the Duke of Richmond had broken those threads, and perhaps the king and the new Queen Jane preferred them to remain that way. Howard women were not wanted at court just now.

Mary, then, lived at Kenninghall with her father when he was home, with her brothers, sisters-in-law and their children, and with Bess Holland, her father's mistress and her own erstwhile colleague at court. Her mother Elizabeth Stafford remained under house arrest in Hertfordshire at the duke's behest. Mary and Bess may have been friends. Yet there were still visual reminders of Mary's mother everywhere: Stafford knots entwined with the Howard lion, her mother's arms stamped onto plate. Many of Elizabeth's clothes and jewels remained in coffers in the nursery, taken from her at her removal. If Mary had peeked into these she would have found the unfinished counterpoint that Elizabeth had been making when she left, for her own and her husband's bed. Over a hundred of the letters T and E – Thomas and Elizabeth – were still waiting to be sewn into place, a visual sign of unity now morphed into a chilling reminder of what happened to unruly women in this household.[47]

Mary's rooms were below the duke's, on the first floor above the chapel. She had an outer chamber, a bedchamber, an inner chamber and a chamber for her maidservants. All were hung with costly tapestries to keep the cold at bay and provide colour and decoration. She had cupboards and coffers to store clothes, papers and embroidery silks, and a long table with two benches for herself and her maids to sit at if she chose not to eat in the dining chamber along the corridor.[48] Kenninghall was sometimes called Kenninghall Palace, and with good reason; built only a decade ago it was not only large but luxurious and well appointed. Mary could have gone out riding. She had horses in the stables cared for by the duke's staff. She could visit Bess, her father's mistress, at her house at Mendham nearby, where she had her own room.[49] She could and did embroider with her maids, tend the numerous gardens, and if women had played tennis she could have done that too – perhaps she watched her brothers do so. Kenninghall might not be the royal court, but it was no isolated hovel.

She probably hoped not to be there long. Now that Mary was widowed, there were two pressing issues facing her and her father. The first was her jointure. Mary had been married to the king's son, and – allegedly – had not brought any dowry to the marriage, because Queen Anne had secured the alliance for the family and had persuaded the king to waive the usual financial arrange-ments.[50] He had, however, granted Mary a jointure of 1,000 marks, or £700 per year – the equivalent of a lifetime's wages for a skilled tradesman.[51] This was income from estates that would support her in the event of her widowhood.

Nobody, least of all the king, had expected this to occur so soon. Richmond was only just seventeen when he died and Mary likewise. In theory, the king now owed Mary her jointure estates and income. Henry, though, was never one to willingly give out cash if he could find a way to avoid it, and he certainly didn't want to have to finance his daughter-in-law for the rest of her life. Almost immediately, he pointed out that the marriage had not been consummated and that Mary had not fully been Richmond's wife: he owed her nothing.[52]

This was not legally correct and no doubt Henry knew this. He was simply hoping that enough people would support it to enable him to bully Mary and her father into agreement. In this he misjudged. The matter was referred to the country's judges and the king's 'council learned' of lawyers.[53] Mary's natural champion was her father Norfolk; it was usual for men to act for and alongside their female relatives in such matters, and a father was particularly bound to do so for his daughter. It was in both their interests. If the king did not want to finance Mary for the rest of her life, no more did her father want to.

Moreover, Norfolk expected Mary to remarry. She was young, had not yet borne children, and therefore her duty to her family was not yet complete. In fact, with all the trouble this was causing, Norfolk wished aloud that her original match with the heir to the earldom of Oxford had gone ahead. Like most nobles he kept tabs on his peers' families, and he knew that 'at this time there is neither lord nor lord's son nor other good inheritor in this realm that I can remember of convenient age to marry her'.[54] Not only this, but without her jointure her value on the marriage market was less in any case, as he also observed: 'if she should marry and her children not to inherit some good portion they were undone'.[55] She might be the king's daughter-in-law and the daughter of the Duke of Norfolk; but without the money this wasn't worth much.

The king's judges dragged their feet. Then, news of the rebellion in Lincolnshire reached London. Immediately Norfolk returned to Kenninghall to muster troops in preparation to march north. He had not been in the king's good graces since the fall of his niece in the spring, but he was the king's best general, above all a military man. It was unthinkable that such a crisis could be resolved without him, and a victory would restore him and his family to royal favour.[56]

Though initially told to sit tight at home – his conservative sympathies and dislike for the dissolution of the monasteries made the king doubt his trustworthiness – on 11 October Norfolk departed. Mary, meanwhile, remained at Kenninghall and on her father's mind. Having treated once with Aske and the rebels, Norfolk returned south in early November and was then ordered to go northwards again. As he did so, he wrote anxiously to Thomas Cromwell about Mary's situation. Could Cromwell speed the judges along so that it might be concluded in this legal term? He was, it transpired, worried about Mary's singledom: 'I am somewhat jealous of her that being out of my company she might bestow herself otherwise than I would she should.'[57]

This is an extraordinary thing for Norfolk to have written about his daughter. Did Mary have her eye on somebody? It would make sense for her to wait for her father to leave so that she might make a new marriage without his interference. Norfolk's letter amounted to an admission that he could not control his own daughter. Perhaps realising this, he hastily backtracked, adding that 'notwithstanding that unto this time it is not possible for a young woman to handle herself more discreetly than she hath done since her husband's death'.[58] It would not do for Cromwell to think her ungovernable, or him incapable.

Whether or not Mary had given Norfolk any reason to suspect her is lost to us. We only know that she remained single through that winter. Norfolk was back at court by 15 December and spent Christmas there, returning to Kenninghall in early January 1537.[59] On his way home he was met by a messenger bearing a letter from Mary. It was not the first she had sent. Mary may have remained chaste while her father was away, but she had not been idle. She had consulted not only her own council but taken further legal advice and was in no doubt of her right to her jointure. Impatient, she wanted resolution and apparently did not think that the Pilgrimage of Grace was adequate excuse for delay. She knew that, at this stage, her father remained her best option as mediator with the king, but she clearly did not trust him to keep up the pressure. Her letter was designed to touch nerves, and to bounce him into further action.

If she didn't know that her father was such a good intercessor, she wrote, she would speak to the king herself. She might yet do so, because 'as yet proceedeth no effect but words, which makes me think the King's highness is not ascertained of my whole right therein, for if he were, he is so just a prince that I am sure he would never suffer the justice of his laws to be denied to me, the unworthy desolate widow of his late son'. If she were to come to London and sue to the king for herself, she did not doubt that 'his highness should be moved to have compassion on me'.[60] It was an unsubtle threat, manipulation couched in the most respectful

TOO WISE FOR A WOMAN   199

of terms. Mary thought that her father was doing a poor job and
she could do better herself. Nobody could do epistolary passive
aggression like an aggrieved Tudor noblewoman.

Norfolk forwarded her letter to Cromwell with his own. He
was unabashedly appalled. 'My lord,' he blustered, 'in all my life
I never communed with her in any serious cause and would not
have thought she would be such as I find her, which as I think
is but too wise for a woman.'[61] Was it not enough that his wife
remained obtuse and recalcitrant, shut away in Hertfordshire and
yet still spreading rumours all over London; must he now subdue
his truculent daughter as well?

For now all that either of them could do was to remit the
matter to Cromwell's judgement. Norfolk had barely reached
home before news arrived that the north had risen afresh. By the
end of January 1537, he had entrusted his will and Mary's future
to Cromwell and was in Doncaster by 2 February.[62] This second
rising gave the king the excuse he needed to use further violence
against the rebels, with Norfolk as his instrument. The putdown
was brutal. Declaring martial law, Norfolk moved through the
northern counties enacting mass executions of men, women and
children.[63] The dissolution of the monasteries did not stop; the
Lady Mary was not restored to the succession; Thomas Cromwell's
ascendancy was not halted. But, like most popular revolts, success
and failure were not clear binaries. María, Lady Willoughby, the
rapacious landlady, had to settle for less profit from her estates in
the future. Her daughter Katherine gained a new home whether
she would or no; she and her husband the duke were ordered by
the king to make their home permanently at Grimsthorpe, and
the shape of Lincolnshire politics was thereby changed forever.[64]

Almost all of the noblewomen who had involved themselves in
the Pilgrimage of Grace escaped without personal repercussion.
Some, indeed, were irrepressible under even harsher fortunes.
Lady Hussey, supporter of the Lady Mary, suffered yet another
blow when her husband was arrested for his hesitancy during
the rebellion. Like a good wife, Lady Hussey visited her husband
in the Tower.[65] It was a tense time. Likely neither yet knew what

the charge would be and were desperately trying to work out the odds of his survival. Lord Darcy, too, was imprisoned for the same reason, and Lord Hussey had been present at Darcy's questioning. Perhaps reasoning that the questions asked might shed light on the line of legal inquiry, Lord Hussey told his wife everything that he had heard. What he had heard was inflammatory – Darcy had openly blamed Cromwell for the entirety of the rebellion – and when asked by her maid Catherine Cresswell about the welfare of the two lords, Lady Hussey repeated it.[66]

Cresswell was hardly likely to keep such juicy gossip to herself. She told her husband. He told others. Soon the story was all over town, and being investigated in its own right. Lord Hussey was executed in June 1537 for conspiracy against the king and raising a rebellion against him, having failed to convince the jury of his loyalty. Lady Hussey, now widowed, walked free. The king and his councillors might not like the rebellious behaviour of the country's noblewomen, they might fear what they saw as women's gossiping tongues, but it seemed that they could not do much to stop it.

13

Sworn the Queen's Maid

Anne Basset had done it. As the family's business agent would shortly write to her mother Lady Lisle, 'Mistress Anne your daughter is sworn the Queen's maid on Saturday last past.'[1] There were many more details to add, specifics of money, clothing and lodging, but they must all have sat back for a moment and basked in the glow of success. To obtain a position in the queen's household was not a task for the easily discouraged. This was why Anne's older sister Katharine had been sent alongside her: it was never likely that there would be room for both as maids of honour, but Lady Lisle rightly thought that the more options presented to the queen, the more likely one would succeed.

For all that Anne was the younger sister, there never seems to have been much doubt that she would be the more successful. She was widely considered to be the 'fairer' out of herself and Katharine, and looks were an important qualification.[2] Katharine was quiet, gentle and kind. She was very soon beloved by those who spent time with her, but she was not one to push herself forward, and her more reserved, sweeter nature was lost on the royal court. Anne was bolder, brighter, sparklier; her surviving letters show that she could be assertive, even selfish, but like her mother she was also quick-witted and determined. In 1536 she wrote apologetically to her mother to say that 'I know well that I am very costly unto you, but it is not possible to do otherwise . . . one must do as others do.'[3] Less obviously affectionate in writing than her sisters, sharply aware of what was needed in order to get on, Anne shone where it mattered. Once she had set her sights on something, she didn't stop until she had achieved it.

The goal of court service had been a long time in the making. Anne's mother – Honor Grenville, Viscountess Lisle, but always known as Lady Lisle – had been seeking court positions for Anne and Katharine, two of her daughters from her first marriage, since at least June 1536.[4] Living in Calais had meant she was entirely reliant on others to send word of vacant positions, and then to seek out and make interest with courtiers who might put in a good word for her daughters. Much of this work had fallen on John Husee, who was employed as the Lisles' business agent in London.

The family's very geographical distance was part of the reason they were so keen to get the children into court positions. Governance was personal in Tudor England. The personality of the monarch, his likes and dislikes, his fancies and foibles, affected the patronage that was offered and the decisions that were made. To be near to him, therefore, was to be one step closer to your goals; to be out of sight was not only to be out of mind, but to open yourself to 'back friends', as the Duke of Norfolk frequently put it, people who might poison the king's mind against you.[5] Arthur, Lord Lisle was the king's cousin and lord deputy of Calais, but neither of these things would save him if – God forbid – he found himself in a political crisis, and his conservative religious beliefs made him increasingly out of step with royal policy.[6] That very fact may have made it more difficult for the Basset girls to enter Queen Jane's household. In any case, though, recent events meant that female royal service probably felt less secure than it used to. Two queens consort had now been removed from office. Pledges of loyalty to a new mistress probably felt much less finite, since she might not last, and yet also more dangerous, for service might place women in danger by association. Not only this, but the once-distant prospect of becoming the next queen was now a threatening possibility, for this, too, had now happened twice. Yet for the moment Queen Jane was beloved by the king, and more to the point, she was pregnant with – she hoped – his son. The court was still the centre of politics, and service there was still a route to royal patronage, with the potential for influence and power. Competition for places in the queen's service therefore remained fierce.

Things had not changed much since Queen Catherine of Aragon's day. There was still a finite number of positions for women to serve the queen 'in ordinary', and that number was still between twenty and twenty-five. Teenage girls like Anne and Katharine Basset were competing for an even smaller number of places, because there were only ever six maids of honour at any given time. The key was to keep abreast of upcoming vacancies. Unless you could find out in advance who was leaving (usually to be married) and speak to the right people in time, the vacancy would have come and gone before it was even publicly known.[7] Finding out who the 'right people' were was an undertaking in itself, but it was one to which John Husee was equal. It helped that the Lisles were well connected, specifically Lady Lisle. For it was not Lord Lisle's contacts who mattered here; as Husee wrote to his mistress, 'it is no meet suit for any man to move such matters, but only for such ladies and women as be your friends'.[8] The best way to get a daughter into the queen's household was to know those who were already there.

Lady Lisle's niece Mary Arundell, who became the Countess of Sussex in January 1537, was one of the queen's women, and that relationship provided a route to the patronage of other noblewomen in the queen's household. Lady Lisle was able to cultivate the formidable Margaret Pole, Countess of Salisbury and kind, capable Eleanor Paston, Countess of Rutland.[9] The Lisles had long been on friendly terms with Margery Horsman, who had moved seamlessly from Anne Boleyn to Jane Seymour's service, and they were also in touch with William Coffin, the queen's master of the horse, and his wife Margaret, who had been one of the women in the Tower with Queen Anne Boleyn and now served among Queen Jane's gentlewomen.[10] Husee used these existing links to make new contacts. Mr Coffin, for instance, told him that if labour were made to Gertrude, Marchioness of Exeter, the cause 'might there be sped'.[11] In June 1536, though, Lady Lisle's friends in

England all thought Anne too young, at fifteen, to be one of the queen's maids.[12] Husee reported that 'the Queen hath her whole determined number appointed' already; he advised Lady Lisle to wait.[13]

In January 1537 Lady Lisle began to press Anne's preferment with renewed energy, and not only Anne's but her sister Katharine's too. The game was one of complex strategy, with multiple routes espied, pursued and discarded bewilderingly swiftly. Ultimately she needed to find a way to place the girls in front of the queen, that they might be seen, judged and, with luck, selected for the next vacant space in the household. But one did not simply walk into the privy chamber. Husee himself could not enter that room unless bidden by the queen. What they needed, Husee reported, was to enter the service of a noblewoman who herself served the queen, so that they might be taken into the privy chamber in the course of that duty.[14]

Anne was settled quickly with Eleanor, Countess of Rutland.[15] Katharine's placement was more difficult. The queen's sister-in-law Lady Beauchamp was suggested, but this came to nothing.[16] Lady Lisle's niece, the Countess of Sussex, was the obvious choice, but she would not take Katharine; 'she saith that she hath three women already, which is one more than she is allowed'.[17] It was true that numbers of servants were theoretically fixed according to social rank. The Eltham Ordinances of 1526 stated that a countess whose husband was also lodged in the court was permitted two beds for servants, increased to three if she were a widow or her husband did not lodge at court.[18] This, though, was difficult to police, and Lady Sussex's response to the Lisles suggests that one might get away with one extra servant, but that was the limit of the lord chamberlain's goodwill.

Margery Horsman, now Margery Lister, promised that if her husband would agree, she would take Katharine into her own chamber, or put her with 'young Mrs Norris', and 'bring her into the Queen's chamber every day'.[19] Then, though, a better option: Mr Coffin had spoken to the Duchess of Suffolk – Katherine Willoughby, she of the strong nerves and brave spirit who had gone north with her husband during the Pilgrimage of Grace rebellion less than a year ago – and the duchess had agreed to take Katharine into her household when she came to court again, which would not be until all fear of plague was past. John Husee wrote to Lady Lisle in March 1537 with detailed instructions as to the letter of thanks she should send, only to be brought up short. Lady Lisle was not convinced that the duchess was the best guardian for Katharine. Husee went to some lengths to show Lady Lisle that everybody concerned thought that Katharine could 'be nowhere better'.[20] The root of Lady Lisle's concern may have been the duchess's increasingly reformist religious beliefs, set against Lady Lisle's own conservatism, or it may simply have been that she was loath to trust her daughters to a woman only a few years older than they. Tantalisingly, on 25 April Husee reassured her that 'the matter that your ladyship doth write of is not so much to be doubted; for the Duchess is both virtuous, wise and discreet'.[21] No more information is forthcoming.

This was April 1537. Lady Rutland would not take Anne until after the summer progress, 'when all heats and dangers of sicknesses be past'. In the meantime, they must have the correct clothes – Katharine would need 'double gowns and kirtles of silk, and good attirements for her head and neck' – and Lady Lisle should continue in her quest to secure the queen's goodwill.[22] Thus began the summer of the quails. Queen Jane was pregnant, and developed a craving for the small, plump gamebirds, which were considered a delicacy. The Lisles had lots of quails. The Calais countryside abounded with them. The king knew this, and wrote to Lord Lisle asking for some for the queen. Lady Lisle jumped at the opportunity, and soon baskets of fat quails were wending their way over the Channel to the queen's dinner table along with prettily worded notes about Lady Lisle's daughters and their desire to serve in the queen's household.[23] Gifts and tokens likewise flew back and forth between Lady Lisle and the many noblewomen whose influence she hoped might in turn inspire the queen. Husee's letters began to sound like chequerolls of those she ought to thank, remember and reward.

The summer of 1537 was a particularly difficult time to seek such patronage. The queen's pregnancy meant that she did not accompany the king on his usual summer progress. He was under orders never to be more than sixty miles away from her – though what anybody imagined he could have done had there been an emergency remains unclear – but this nevertheless meant that they spent more time apart than usual, and so it would have been harder to secure his consent for household appointments.[24] Lady Lisle was herself pregnant, and took her chamber at some stage in June, a fact that may well have made her less attentive to business than usual.[25] Plague, too, was still rife. Queen Jane was even more afraid of the sickness than the king, and he was rarely calm about any serious outbreak. Access to the court was forbidden for any-body who had been where there was sickness, which again made it more difficult to transact business as usual.[26]

Nevertheless, the wheel continued to turn. One July dinner time, Queen Jane, eating Lady Lisle's quails, spoke to her two immediate attendants – the Countesses of Rutland and Sussex – about Lady Lisle, and was told about the two daughters seeking court positions. The countesses must have sung their praises despite never having met either of the girls, or else Queen Jane was in a magnanimous, quail-sated mood, because she agreed to take one of them into her household. Both must be sent: 'her Grace will first see them and know their manners, fashions and conditions, and take which of them shall like her Grace best' – i.e. which she liked better. The Countesses of Rutland and Sussex would each be temporarily responsible for a Basset girl, and then later, once the queen had taken her favourite, the other would go to the Duchess of Suffolk as planned.[27]

Months of machinations had paid off. Lady Lisle must have been thrilled, and the girls were surely excited. Now there were clothes to be bought, for though Husee said that 'your ladyship shall not need to do much cost on them till time you know which of them her Grace will have', both nevertheless needed 'two honest changes . . . the one of satin, the other of damask'. The last page of his letter also took a tone calculated to strike sobriety into the most excited heart. For Husee did not like the royal court; it was, he reminded Lady Lisle, 'full of pride, envy, indignation and mocking, scorning and derision', and she must exhort the girls to be 'sober, sad, wise and discreet and lowly above all things, and to be obedient . . . and to serve God and to be virtuous, for that is much regarded, to serve God well and to be sober of tongue'. It was a strong admonition to behave themselves, and though he hastened to add that they probably needed no such warning, he clearly felt it necessary to inject a note of caution.[28]

In July the queen had said to send the girls in six weeks. Her Majesty wanted to make the choice before she withdrew to her chamber to await the birth of her child. It was thought that that would be about Michaelmas, but the sooner they arrived the better because, Husee reported, there would shortly be a vacancy on account of Mistress Parr's marriage: 'it were good to have them in areadiness'.[29] By 1 September he was urging Lady Lisle to send them as soon as possible, within fifteen days, because the queen intended to withdraw within twenty days. If the choice were not made before she did so, both girls would remain at Lady Lisle's expense until the queen came out of confinement.[30]

They were duly sent, and received and feted by Lady Lisle's friends – Lady Dudley, Husee told her, had been particularly kind to them.[31] The Countesses of Sussex and Rutland, in whose retinues they were to be for the time being, immediately set about improving the girls' wardrobes that they might appear to their best advantage before the queen. The two countesses lent, altered and gave away their own clothes freely, demonstrating how seriously they took their duty of care. Neither wanted the girls to embarrass their sponsors or their mother when they entered court society, and both appeared genuinely anxious that Anne and Katharine should do well.[32]

The queen was at Hampton Court, where she intended to take her chamber for the birth of her child. There, a fine new set of apartments were under construction for the queen, with views overlooking the river front and a chamber adjoining the king's, so that he could enter his wife's rooms without anybody knowing that he'd left his own apartments. Originally made for Queen Anne Boleyn, in 1537 the king decided he was not satisfied, and began building work there anew. By the autumn they still weren't ready. Instead, Queen Jane occupied the old stacked lodgings in the middle of the palace, a courtyard to either side, her rooms on the floor above the king's own.[33] At least this meant that she and her ladies were somewhat lifted above the noise of the builders, and further away from the smell of the brick kilns in the park. They could also see who was coming or going. As Anne and Katharine Basset made their way through the gatehouse, perhaps the two countesses with them pointed out the windows of the queen's chambers above. Attired in a mixture of their own and borrowed clothing – Anne wore a new velvet gable hood lent by the Countess of Sussex – the girls followed their sponsors up the stairs, through the watching chamber and presence chamber, and were waved into the queen's privy chamber. There they were introduced to Her Majesty.[34] It must have been a moment of tense excitement. Though the exact process is hidden from us, the outcome was unanimous. Anne, the younger, fairer, livelier Basset girl, was the successful candidate. She would enter the queen's service as a maid of honour, while Katharine would remain with the Countess of Rutland until such time as the Duchess of Suffolk returned to the south.

Anne was probably sworn in there and then, either in the privy chamber itself or elsewhere in front of the queen's chamberlain or vice-chamberlain. A customary fee was paid, and she would have been taken through the oath orally. Though the exact oath sworn by the queen's women is not extant, enough survives to know that she would have sworn loyalty to both the queen and king, pledging to be 'good' and 'true' and 'faithful' and to be retained by no other, a part of the oath that was designed to protect against multiple allegiances.[35] Anne was now part of the royal household.

Husee, businesslike as always, informed Lady Lisle that Anne 'furnisheth the room of a yeoman-usher', which meant that her position was equivalent to that of a yeoman usher in the king's service, a nod, perhaps, to the somewhat confused reality of female service in the queen's household.[36] For all that there had been several ordinances relating to household service over the previous fifty years, none had said more than that the queen's service should be 'nigh like unto the King's', an impossibility where her female servants were concerned.[37] For Anne, though, the matter was comparatively simple. As one of the six maids of honour, she received £10 a year, lodging, some basic clothing as livery and an allowance of food, fuel and light. She must have her own servant, and she would be nominally under the protection and management of the mother of the maids, who was there to supervise the six girls.[38]

In a manner reminiscent of boarding schools, Lady Lisle was promptly sent a list of things that Anne would need, as listed in 'Mrs Pole's book of reckoning' – it's possible that Mrs Pole was the mother of the maids at this time.[39] Bedding was not supplied, and most of the list was clothing. The royal court was the place where fashion arrived first in the country. Since the role of the queen's women was to be on display, it was important for them to keep abreast of the latest fashions, though English women held a reputation internationally for dowdy dress. France, where Anne Basset had spent most of her life so far, was usually the trendsetter where fashion was concerned, as indeed Queen Anne Boleyn had known.[40] Now Queen Jane sought to make a change: Anne was to wear out her French clothing first, but then she would need new, English gowns. She needed a gable hood of velvet regardless. These were so named for the pointed arch at the front, like a gabled roof, the heavy, somewhat awkward structure made with wire and the hair covered by two wide 'tubes' of fabric hanging down the back. Though Husee thought 'it became her nothing so well as the French hood' – a smaller, lighter, rounder headpiece set further back so that the hair, combed flat and centre-parted, could be seen – gable hoods were the queen's preference, and 'the Queen's pleasure must needs be fulfilled'.[41]

Hoods were only the finishing touch to an outfit in 1530s England. Winter was coming, and staying warm was a priority. Layers, then, were the key. Anne wore a linen smock or shift next to her skin, the collars and cuffs probably embroidered with 'blackwork', the style of embroidery brought from Spain by Queen Catherine of Aragon and her women and still all the rage in England. Over this she wore a bodice designed to flatten the chest and push her breasts up, creating a smooth silhouette for her kirtle, a dress designed to function as an under-gown. At court, this was usually worn with another gown on top so that only the front triangular panel of the kirtle was visible, elaborately decorated. Anne's gowns would have been cut with a low, square neckline and a V-shaped neck at the back, sometimes filled in with another layer of fabric called a 'partlet'. Her sleeves were attached separately, and she might also have worn a stomacher, an extra piece of decorative fabric for the front of her gown. Hose or stockings, made of finely woven woollen cloth and held up with garters, kept legs warm; flat-heeled slippers made of various fabrics went on her feet. Her gowns and sleeves would be lined with fur during the winter, and the whole was comparatively warm.[42]

Within weeks, the queen's pleasure had taken a turn and Anne was no longer to wear her French-style gowns either. Now she needed 'a bonnet or two, with frontlets and an edge of pearl, and a gown of black satin, and another of velvet . . . And further, she must have cloth for smocks and sleeves, for there is fault founded that their smocks are too coarse.' Anne had already had made a new gown of russet worsted and black velvet, and Lady Sussex planned to turn her old gowns into kirtles.[43] Though Anne wasn't of high enough status to be wearing cloth of gold or silver, or the colour purple, nobody was going to waste perfectly good velvet if it could be reused elsewhere.[44] Anne's clothes were individually tailored, and would have fitted as perfectly as possible. Velvets and damasks, though, were heavy, and these clothes were not designed to mould to or move with the body. Women at court did not move with speed, and they needed help to get dressed and undressed. Their peripheral vision was restricted by the gable hood in particular, and the many layers of fabric over their ears might also have made it more difficult to hear.

Though Anne was destined to join the other maids of honour,

Husee's letters make it clear that she couldn't do so immediately. Jane Ashley, whose place she was taking, had first to marry and depart. For the first few weeks Anne remained with the Countess of Sussex in her lodgings, which may have been a slightly gentler introduction to court life.[45] Lady Lisle could rest awhile; it was up to Anne now to make her appointment bear fruit for her family.

Queen Jane, too, laboured to bring forth fruit, for her family, for her husband and for England. It had been a straightforward pregnancy and everybody hoped that it would be a boy. The pressure for Jane was unimaginable. What if she produced a girl, yet another useless princess in a country that so desperately needed an heir? Queens Catherine and Anne had not survived their lack of male progeny; would Jane?

On Sunday, 16 September, only a day after Anne Basset was sworn in as the new maid of honour, Queen Jane 'took her chamber', withdrawing from court to the sanctuary of her own apartments to await the birth of her child.[46] Following tradition, the room in which the baby would arrive must be hung with rich tapestries on every wall, leaving only one window bare for light. There must be layers of carpets on the floor, a royal bed and a pallet bed on which the queen would actually give birth. The overall impression was one of softness, warmth, dark and muffled sound: a womb enclosing a womb.[47] It was an odd time for sixteen-year-old Anne to begin court service. For the duration of the queen's confinement, her world became exclusively female as her ladies-in-waiting took on the roles normally held by male officers. Her chambers would have been far quieter than usual, with none of the usual visits from the king and his gentlemen. Perhaps Anne had been inside her mother's rooms during her lyings-in when she gave birth to Anne's younger sister Mary, but she would only have been a small child. Now she saw how things were done among royalty.

Almost a month later, the queen went into labour. Hours passed and still the baby wouldn't come. The birthing chamber was stifling. The thick hangings on the walls and ceiling let no heat escape, and the fire was kept stoked. Miles away in the city, friars, priests and city men processed solemnly to St Paul's to pray for a safe delivery.[48] Anne Basset, as a young and unmarried woman, would not have been with the queen in her chamber; no doubt she too spent much time in prayer. For the rest of the queen's women at Hampton Court the world had narrowed to a single room, a bed, an exhausted woman's blood and pain. Queen Jane laboured for two days and three long nights, her women watching over her in that hot, airless room. Finally, the baby was wrest from her exhausted body, and – joy! – it was a prince, a 'man child' born on the eve of St Edward the Confessor's day.

There was national euphoria. Fires were lit all over the city of London, prayers of thanksgiving offered in every church.[49] Three days later the baby was christened Edward in the chapel at Hampton Court, carried by Gertrude, Marchioness of Exeter along a route marked out with barriers to keep back the crowds, all the way from his rooms on the first floor through the king's chambers and the great hall, down the stairs, across the courtyard and into the chapel. Rich carpets marked the way to the font, raised on a dais to give the audience of courtiers and nobles the best possible view. After the ceremony the court retired to the queen's chambers for wine and light refreshments, and to congratulate the king and queen on their achievement.[50] Anne Basset, the queen's newest maid of honour, attended the christening and the celebrations with wide eyes and a new gown of black velvet turned up with yellow satin.[51] Plans were already afoot for the queen's churching ceremony, in which she would be purified and welcomed back into society. Anne's mother Lady Lisle was told that Anne would need yet another new gown.[52] But within two days, Queen Jane was no longer sitting up in bed. She was feverish and had 'an unnatural laxe'; the last rites were administered.[53] Soon she was delirious. The prayers of her women, still watching over her, went unanswered. Just before midnight on 24 October 1537, Queen Jane died of child-bed fever. She was not yet thirty.

The nation's joy turned to sorrow. None took it heavier than the king, who retired to Westminster 'and kept himself close and secret a great while'.[54] Plans for the queen's churching became plans for her funeral. Anne Basset's gown of tawny velvet was changed for one of black.[55] Early in the morning on Monday, 12 November, the corpse began its final journey. The queen was to be buried in St George's Chapel in Windsor Castle. For several days already her body had lain in the chapel at Hampton Court while formal masses were said for her soul. At each of these a senior noblewoman acted as chief mourner, but even the newest and least of Jane's women had a role to play: on Tuesday, 6 November the chief mourner had been the Countess of Rutland, and Anne Basset bore her train.[56]

It was a long, slow ride to Windsor. Forty-nine noblewomen followed the hearse in chariots and on horseback, and more had ridden ahead in advance. Anne Basset was lucky. She had a place in the last chariot, and was likely warmer than those on horseback. In the pre-dawn darkness, the long, winding procession must have looked sinister, shapeless black figures illumined here and there by torches held aloft by footmen. After the days of mourning and the solemnity of the journey, the burial itself was comparatively brief. Offerings were made at the high altar by the highest-status mourners, and then the women respectfully withdrew and were given refreshments while the burial took place. Queen Jane was no more. Officially, the nation plunged into mourning. In London a death knell of bells was rung in every parish church from noon till six in the evening, with a 'solemn dirige' – part of the liturgy from the Office of the Dead – likewise sung in every church.[57] The queen's women, as part of the royal household, were part of the ritual of mourning; Anne Basset, her mother was informed, would need no more clothing 'until her mourning gear be cast off'.[58] The outward appearance, though, may not have been matched by inward grief. Anne had barely known her mistress. She had served her for only forty days. If there was no queen, there was no need of a queen's household. Anne was out of a job.

The noblewomen of Queen Jane's household went home to husbands and children, or to their dower estates, and the younger

women to their parents or guardians. For Anne Basset, this presented a problem. Her family were in Calais. Nobody thought it
would be very long until there was another queen, but she could
not stay at court, and there was little time to make arrangements.
Fortunately, kinship carried a strong sense of obligation, and
Anne was taken in by her mother's cousin the Countess of Sussex,
in whose chambers she had been lodging at court. Lady Lisle's
response to this shows that it was done in something of a scramble. Only two days after Queen Jane's burial she wrote to thank
the countess for having Anne, assuring her that if Anne could not
get a place in the next queen's household 'I shall not fail to send
for her, and to recompense your charges, for I did not send them
for that I would put you or any of my kin or friends to charge.'[59]

Anne, it seems, was not as grateful as her elders felt she ought
to have been. When Husee wrote to Lady Lisle a month later, it
was to reassure her that 'by my lady Sussex's report Mistress Anne
is clearly altered, and in manner no fault can be found in her. So
that I doubt not but that the worst is past, and from henceforth
she will use herself as demurely and discreetly as the best of her
fellows.'[60] This sounds as though Anne had thrown her weight
around in the countess's household and had been told to learn her
place. Perhaps she struggled to adapt to her new situation, feeling
as though she'd been on the cusp of a glittering career only for it
to be snatched away, leaving her languishing in the countryside,
on sufferance in somebody else's household.

No doubt she wasn't the only one to feel this way. It was the
beginning of a strange time. England had not been without a
queen since 1509. Distraught though the king might be at Queen
Jane's death, he still had only one male heir and he of all people
knew how important it was to produce a second – a 'spare' – as
he himself had been. His duty was to marry again, and so within
days his councillors were urging him – 'peradventure not wisely,
yet after mine accustomed manner plainly', as the Duke of Norfolk
wrote – to seek a new wife.[61] The choice of a royal bride was not
only an issue of domestic peace but of diplomacy, and religion was
now an inextricable part of international relations. Such a decision

could not be made without the input of the king's council and of his ambassadors, and – indeed – of other sovereigns. Should the king marry 'at home', another domestic subject, a woman of his own nobility? Or should he marry abroad, perhaps a French duchess, a Spanish infanta or a Scandinavian princess? Everybody had an opinion. It was tantamount to throwing open a door to political faction and inviting it to make itself at home.

Some thought it likely that the king would continue what had become his usual pattern and take a former lady-in-waiting as his next bride. He may have had his eye on the possibilities, for in January 1538 John Husee reported that 'the election lieth between Mistress Mary Shelton and Mistress Mary Skipwith'.[62] Mary Shelton had been at court for some time. She was a cousin of the late Queen Anne Boleyn, and was good friends with the king's niece Margaret Douglas and Mary Howard, Duchess of Richmond.[63] Mary Skipwith was in fact Margaret, niece to one of the king's gentlemen of the privy chamber, Sir Thomas Heneage. This piece of gossip is not repeated in any other surviving source, but that may simply mean that it was known only to those with inside access to the royal court; Husee warned Lord Lisle to 'keep silence until the matter be surely known'.[64] Mary Shelton was certainly on people's minds during this time, which might be a symptom of the king's own thoughts towards her. In December 1537 the recently widowed Christina, Princess of Denmark and Duchess of Milan, was described by ambassador John Hutton as resembling Mary Shelton, a comparison clearly meant to be flattering.[65]

Most people thought an alliance abroad would be preferable. Thomas Cromwell, still the king's chief minister, certainly did not want another noble family raised up to the heights of the Seymours, who now stood closest to the throne as relatives of Prince Edward. Cromwell had recently yoked himself to their fortunes by marrying his son Gregory to the late queen's sister Elizabeth, the widowed Lady Oughtrede, and the rise of another subject-queen would weaken the value of that alliance.[66] The Duke of Norfolk would have loved to see yet another Howard girl on the throne, but he too thought it unlikely. He preferred the prospect of a French princess, partly because he was in receipt of a sizeable pension from the French king, and partly because the French were, naturally, friends of the Pope and would not promote further religious reform in England. Cromwell, conversely, favoured the Hapsburgs.[67] King Henry himself appeared to agree that a foreign marriage was preferable. He was worried about France and Spain getting increasingly close to an alliance, which had long been something that England sought to disrupt and was now more dangerous than ever because of its potential to unite all of Catholic Europe. Nothing came of the rumour about Mistresses Mary Shelton and Margaret Skipwith. In fact, in the summer of 1538 the latter married George Tailboys, son of the king's former mistress Bessie Blount, with some degree of haste and a special Act of Parliament to allow Tailboys – then a ward of the Crown – access to his inheritance before the age of majority, to allow the couple to begin married life at once. Perhaps it was convenient to have Mistress Skipwith safely bestowed elsewhere.[68]

1538 saw Henry attempting to play the French and the Spanish against each other at home and abroad. This ended in some embarrassment when, having thought the French princess Mary of Guise free for his taking, it was found that she had quietly and swiftly been married to Henry's rival King James V of Scotland in the spring of 1538. Happily there remained Christina of Denmark, about whom Henry was enthusiastic; she was a good choice as bride even if she had not resembled Mary Shelton. But the negotiations proved complex. Henry wanted impossible things from Charles V, such as inclusion in any future peace treaty with France and a refusal to support the upcoming papal General Council, neither of which were remotely in Charles's interests. Christina herself was worried about the prospect of becoming Henry's fourth wife, 'for her Council suspecteth that her great aunt was poisoned, that the second was put to death and the third lost for lack of keeping her child-bed'.[69] Aside from his effect on his wives, Henry's own life was not assured. In May it was reported that one of the old wounds on his leg had closed up, poisoning his blood, 'so that he was sometime without speaking, black in the face, and in great danger'.[70]

In the meantime, the court was not entirely devoid of women. There was no queen, but the king had daughters, and the Lady Mary, though no longer princess, at least was of an age, at twenty-two, to take on some of the more female-oriented royal roles, in the same way as the king's own younger sister had done after the death of their mother back in 1503. Lady Mary spent much of 1538 at court. Though she kept her usual attendants and does not seem to have augmented her salaried household, her surviving privy purse expenses and jewel inventory for these years do suggest that the country's noblewomen used Mary's court presence as something of a base for their own. The list of jewels that she gave away over these years reads as a roll call of elite women: the Countesses of Hertford, Sussex and Rutland, the Duchess of Suffolk, Lady Dudley. She acted as godmother to endless noble babies.[71] At least one woman who had previously been in Queen Jane's household was now paid for boat journeys by Lady Mary, suggesting that temporarily, at least, she had become part of Lady Mary's establishment.[72]

All that young Anne Basset could do was to wait. The king had promised that she would 'have her place whensoever the time shall come'.[73] In February 1538, when it was thought that time might be soon, Anne asked her mother for an 'edge of pearl' to wear on her French hood, because she had had to return the one she had borrowed from the Countess of Sussex.[74] In April the pearls arrived: but, John Husee wrote on her behalf, 'six score is not enough, nor indeed they are not to be worn in the Queen's service unless they might be set full'.[75] Anne, desperate to be ready whenever the call to court should come, was impatient. Her mind on her own needs, as ever, she raged to her mother's friend Thomas Warley, calling the pearls that Lady Lisle had sent 'all rags'.[76] Lady Lisle was furious. Children did not speak thus to their parents. Ambitious Anne might be, and like many teenagers desperate to keep up with her peers, but that did not mean that she could treat her mother with disrespect. It fell to Husee to make this clear, and he wrote that he had been 'meetly plain' with her; 'I doubt not that ever she shall offend your ladyship in like case.' He hoped that Lady Lisle would now forget it, 'for she taketh the matter very heavily'.[77] It was several letters, however, before Lady Lisle could be brought to forgive her impetuous daughter.

Mary Howard, dowager Duchess of Richmond, only a few years older than Anne Basset, also tried her parents' patience during 1538. Her father-in-law the king still had not agreed to give her possession of her jointure estates now that his son Henry Fitzroy, her husband, was dead, and she consequently had no income. Living on her father the Duke of Norfolk's charity, under his roof, was not what independent Mary had had in mind for her widowhood, and for all that she was only nineteen she was not prepared to let the matter rest in his hands any longer. On 2 January 1538 she wrote to Thomas Cromwell, not for the first time, but in insistent tones. Her husband had died a year and a half ago, she told him, and though her father had 'many times' promised to sue to the king for her nothing had come of this. She had asked him for permission to come to London and speak to the king herself, but 'he hath made me so short an answer that I am more than half in despair'. Would Cromwell please help?[78]

Her letter did not divulge the means by which she sought to persuade her father to bring her to London, but his own letter to Cromwell a few months later in April made it clear that she was making his life a misery. 'My daughter of Richmond', he wrote, 'doth continually with weeping and wailing cry out on me to have me give her licence to ride to London to sue for her cause, thinking that I have not effectually followed the same.'[79] Norfolk was not a man with whom one could reason, and he had already disapprovingly labelled her 'too wise for a woman' for having consulted her own legal counsel about her situation. Perhaps emotional blackmail was a better weapon; or perhaps it was all she had left in her arsenal. Norfolk's reluctance was, as ever, his fear of the king's reaction. He asked Cromwell to 'feel his Grace's mind'.[80] Cromwell replied that the king was content that Norfolk should bring Mary to court, and Mary herself wrote in 'as hearty thanks as my poor heart can think'.[81] Around Whitsuntide the journey was made, and thus began a complex negotiation between the men in Mary's life. It was a delicate situation. The king did not want to pay Mary the money that he owed her; Norfolk did not want to pay for Mary either, and he did not want to annoy the king. Thus while he did indeed ask the king about her jointure, he also asked about a possible second marriage for her. It was a tidy solution to a difficult problem. If Mary remarried, the fact of her first marriage to the king's son could be conveniently forgotten, and the question of her jointure with it. The king could simply settle a dowry upon her, a one-time payment, rather than having to hand over estates and lose that yearly income. He might then look more kindly upon Norfolk and the rest of the family.[82]

There were only two men that Norfolk thought suitable for his daughter, and the one he thought best was Sir Thomas Seymour, brother of the late Queen Jane and uncle to Prince Edward. He claimed that this was because Seymour was 'so honestly admired by the King's majesty', and because he did not think it a good idea to marry Mary in 'high blood or degree'.[83] While it was true that the Seymours could not yet lay claim to the noble heritage of the Howards, as the family of the heir to the throne they were hardly nobodies, and the Howards were in any case parvenus themselves only a couple of generations back. Norfolk's willingness to ally with the Seymour family shows how precarious he felt his own position in the king's favour to be. The match, though, had advantages for the Seymours too, for Thomas Seymour would gain a bride of far higher status than he could otherwise look for. The king thought it an excellent idea, joking somewhat bawdily that Mary needed 'one of such lust and youth as should be able to please her well at all points'.[84] Seymour himself wanted Cromwell's approval, and probably his business-minded approach to the financial negotiations. It was decided that Cromwell and Seymour would have a conversation within the next few days, because Mary was due to return to the country shortly and the king wanted the matter concluded before that time.[85]

Perhaps that conversation took place, and perhaps it did not. Nobody, it seems, had thought to consult Mary herself. Mary, intelligent, politically aware and decisive, was not at all willing to acquiesce. Within a fortnight her father Norfolk was on his way back to his estates in Suffolk. By August he was once again asking Cromwell to seek resolution of Mary's jointure situation.[86] Mary wrote to Cromwell herself, asking him the same thing.[87] The marriage with Seymour died a quiet death, and since it is clear that all parties bar Mary had agreed to it, it's highly likely that Mary herself placed a spanner in the works. That she, a girl of nineteen, dared to defy her father, Thomas Cromwell and the king in this way is extraordinary. Perhaps these great men began to feel like Anne Basset, whose court career was snatched away, or indeed like much of the rest of the English population, struggling in the midst of religious reform: nothing in this world could be relied upon any more.

14

Juggling

Elizabeth Stafford, Duchess of Norfolk was anxious. She was worried about the behaviour of one of her chaplains, Sir William.[1] She had recently asked Sir William whether he planned to fast this Lent, as was customary. He said 'he had fasted this Lent ever since he was fourteen years of age and now he would not fast this Lent till he did see a new world'. Elizabeth, shocked, had rebuked him and asked him what he meant; he had replied, 'another way'. She promptly had him locked in the bailey at St Albans and searched his possessions. Sure enough, a forbidden book came to light, 'a book of juggling' that her priest had kept for the past three years.[2]

Elizabeth had been appalled. Lenten fasting was not something that was officially up for debate amid the many religious wranglings of King Henry's reign so far. Sir William's words strongly suggest that he was of a reformist mind, perhaps feeling that change had not yet gone far enough. Sir William was threatening to break the law, and his book of 'juggling' was suspect too. 'Juggling' in an early modern context meant deception and trickery, deceitful argumentation that could lead people astray, and so the book was likely also of a reformist persuasion.[3] Elizabeth sent for the local justice of the peace to investigate further, and Sir William made 'but a small answer'. Advised to send him to Thomas Cromwell, Elizabeth had hastened inside to make the arrangements, and now dictated the letter that would go with her recalcitrant priest. The letter survives, and Elizabeth's anxiety is palpable throughout. She made it clear that she had acted swiftly, that she did not allow her servants to transgress in this way. She had dismissed another for his 'ill rule' only days before this episode. She had witnesses – the very bearers of this letter – and they would vouch for her words and actions, and the fact that the suspect book did indeed belong to the priest and not to Elizabeth herself. She begged Cromwell to 'take no displeasure with my rude writing for I have not counsel to put myself in the writing of my letter; I have written to you everything of this matter and so I pray your good lordship so to accept it'.[4]

Elizabeth's fear made some sense. It was March 1539, and religious and political conformity had started to feel more and more like walking a tightrope, or, indeed, like juggling. For the past year or so reform had continued apace. The smaller monasteries were mostly dissolved. Protestors against this were silenced with violence; in August 1537, for instance, Sir William Parr had had a man nailed to a pillory by the ear for saying that he trusted to God before he died 'to see or hear all such as were of counsel with plucking down the abbeys hanged'.[5] Maid of honour Anne Basset's family were finding things difficult in Calais because of their religiously conservative, even dangerously 'papistical' practices. In July 1537 Cromwell had written a stern letter to the Calais council condemning 'the prayers of women and their fond flickerings'.[6] Not unrelatedly, the family's loyal London agent John Husee warned Lady Lisle anxiously to 'leave part of such ceremonies as you do use, as long prayers and offering of candles, and at some time to refrain and not speak, though your ladyship have cause, when you hear things spoken that liketh you not', in the interests of conforming 'to the world as it goeth now'.[7]

And yet things were less crystal-clear than they appeared. Little changed at the royal court itself, as the Archbishop of Canterbury, Thomas Cranmer, himself pointed out in exasperation. In the summer of 1537 he wrote to Cromwell, 'if in the Court you do keep such holydays and fasting days as be abrogated, when shall we persuade the people to cease for keeping of them?'.[8] The Six Articles, a piece of legislation pushed through in June 1539, veered in a decidedly conservative direction. Some thought Thomas

Cromwell, often seen as the architect of religious reform, was losing his touch.[9]

For noblewomen this was a particularly fearful time. Elizabeth would have known that only a few months ago three noblemen had been executed for treason on grounds of conspiracy related to religion. Not only that, but one noblewoman, Elizabeth's erstwhile colleague Gertrude Blount, Marchioness of Exeter, remained imprisoned in the Tower for her part in the same alleged conspiracy. Probably Elizabeth knew that Gertrude had long been skirting the boundaries of dangerous behaviour. During the king's 'great matter', his divorce from Queen Catherine of Aragon, Gertrude had continued to serve at court while passing confidential information to Imperial ambassador Chapuys. Intelligent and wily, she had been very careful to stay just on the right side of royal favour; she was Princess Elizabeth's godmother, but also a supporter of the anti-royal, Roman Catholic 'nun of Kent'. Then she had slid out of trouble with a well-judged display of submission to King Henry's will. This time she was not so lucky.

The problem was that Gertrude and her husband Henry Courtenay, Marquess of Exeter were close friends with the Pole family – Henry Pole, Lord Montague, his brothers Reginald and Geoffrey and their mother Margaret, Countess of Salisbury. This was a dangerous friendship. Both the Poles and Gertrude's husband Henry were of the Yorkist bloodline, and their claim to the throne was arguably stronger than King Henry's own. Thus far this had not been a significant problem, for all had made it very clear that they did not want Henry's crown. But the second Pole son, Reginald, had dragged them into danger regardless. A strong adherent of Roman Catholicism, appalled by the king's divorce, he had taken himself into exile in 1532, risen to the rank of cardinal and had continued to stir up opposition to King Henry abroad. Publicly, the Poles had distanced themselves from Reginald's views and actions. Privately, they agreed with him.[10]

In the diplomatically strained atmosphere of 1538 – Emperor Charles V of Spain and King Francis I of France had made an alliance, always a dangerous thing for England – the king was especially concerned to root out any 'fifth column', particularly one based in the south-west of England, a traditional invasion route.[11] The Poles were watched and their conservations reported. Geoffrey Pole proved to be the weak link, and was certainly guilty of treason. He had been in contact with Reginald, and not only this but he had asked ambassador Chapuys to push Emperor Charles V to invade England.[12] Geoffrey was arrested in August 1538 and threatened with torture. While he could not give up physical evidence – it had all been burned, he said – he could and did recount many incriminating conversations between the Courtenays and the Poles. He was questioned over and over; he had a nervous breakdown and tried to commit suicide, and still they questioned him. He first mentioned Gertrude in his third examination on 3 November 1538. The king had sent assassins to kill Reginald, but Reginald had escaped because he had seen letters warning him, and Geoffrey thought that those letters were written by either Gertrude or by her lady-in-waiting, Bess Darrell, to his brother Henry Pole, Lord Montague.[13] In them she had reported confidential Privy Council conversations, gleaned from her husband, who had allegedly offered to be 'bound body for body' for Montague, a figurative hostage for good behaviour.[14]

Gertrude had been close to Montague. They had written frequently to one another, and he had great respect for her clear-sighted, shrewd understanding of people and events. She had been ill lately and Montague had been anxious, telling his brother Geoffrey that 'if the wisdom of my Lady were not, he would not be able to bear this world'.[15] But she had known that Geoffrey was a danger and had tried to distance herself and her husband from him, just as his mother Margaret, Countess of Salisbury had tried to do.[16] It was to no avail. Margaret was held under house arrest. Gertrude herself was arrested either late at night on 4 November or early in the morning on the 5th and taken straight to the Tower with her young son.[17] She was questioned three times but, merci-fully for herself, could add little to the investigation. She was asked about Sir Edward Neville, a family friend given to prophecy, who had sung politically suspect songs in her garden at West Horsley and railed against 'knaves' who stood in the way of 'lords'. She had heard about the assassins sent to kill Reginald Pole from him, and he was also now arrested.[18]

If it had ended there, she might have been released. But Gertrude's maidservant Constance Bontayn was questioned and Constance, in fear for her own life, spilled information of a different nature. In 1534 Gertrude had had communication with the nun of Kent, but it had not been of a political nature and she had been pardoned, the matter put to bed. Now Bontayn revealed that Gertrude's contact with the nun had been considerably more controversial than anybody had deposed at the time. Gertrude had ridden to see the nun at Canterbury before the latter had even moved to London, and she had done so in disguise, pretending to be her own maidservant. The nun had then come to Gertrude's house at West Horsley and 'lay there in a trance', though what she said Bontayn didn't know.[19] It was enough to prolong Gertrude's imprisonment. The Pole brothers had certainly committed treason and her husband Henry Courtenay was brought down by association, the paranoid king determined to do away with him. On 9 December, in the wind and the rain, he, Henry Pole and Sir Edward Neville lost their lives to the executioner's axe.[20] Geoffrey Pole, a broken man, was pardoned and released into exile in January 1539.[21] His mother Margaret remained under house arrest; she had answered her examination on 12 November with such clarity and decision that her questioner William Fitzwilliam had grudgingly accorded her respect, writing that 'there hath not been seen or heard of a woman so earnest in her countenance, manly in continuance, and so precise as well in gesture or in words, that wonder is to be'.[22]

Still it was not finished. In late December Gertrude had tried the old trick of supplication; one Thomas Phillips wrote with appalling understatement to Thomas Cromwell that Gertrude 'fears she stands in the King's displeasure' and so asked for Cromwell's favour, particularly since she had no 'raiment' and neither did her maids.[23] Whether she received more clothing is not recorded, but she certainly didn't get Cromwell's favour this time. Gertrude's belongings had been searched, a natural result of her arrest, and one 'little coffer' became the source of yet more sorrow. While her husband and the Poles had been careful to burn any incriminating letters, Gertrude, it seems, had not exercised her usual circumspection and had kept copies of letters between Exeter and Reginald Pole. As Chapuys put it in January 1539, 'their treason had been fully proved since their death', and this was enough to allow Cromwell to claim that Exeter and Gertrude had 'suborned the Princess, putting in her head various opinions and fancies and encouraging her to persist in her obstinacy against her father'.[24] Gertrude's coffer also yielded a letter in which Sir Nicholas Carew informed her of certain conversations in the king's privy chamber. On 31 December he too was arrested. Carew, a close friend of both the Poles and the Courtenays, had long been known to be a religious conservative, and this was sufficient to drag him into the investigation of this alleged conspiracy. That he had tried to intercede for Gertrude no doubt also brought him under suspicion. Carew would be executed on 8 March 1539.[25] Within two months, two of the greatest noble families in Henry's England had been destroyed, and Gertrude and her son yet remained in the Tower.

With this example before her, small wonder that Elizabeth, Duchess of Norfolk was concerned to stay on the right side of the regime. Gertrude was a person known for her shrewdness, her circumspection and her political acumen, and yet she had ended up in fear for her life. Elizabeth, the sort of person who saw life very much more in black and white and tended to put speech before thought, must have felt frightened indeed. It was a confusing and fearful time, trying to maintain a form of religious observance that would pass muster as being neither too 'popish' nor yet too reformist, and yet satisfy one's own conscience. This touched women as well as men, nobles as well as commoners, and former ladies-in-waiting as well as current courtiers. Elizabeth's letter about her 'juggling' priest shows that she had fully imbibed the message of caution, perhaps overly so. Thomas Cromwell, a reformer himself, was unlikely to come down particularly hard on a priest whose beliefs ran along the same lines as his own. We hear nothing more of Sir William, and Elizabeth herself suffered no repercussions for unwittingly harbouring him.

Elizabeth may have been the more nervous because her domestic situation remained precarious. She was still marooned in Redbourn in Hertfordshire, still separated from her husband the Duke of Norfolk, and even when afraid for her religious reputation she could not resist an opportunity to petition Cromwell in the selfsame letter about her living situation. She had now been in Redbourn for five years, and her aims had changed. She no longer sought her husband's return, perhaps recognising that he was never going to give up his mistress, and now asserted that her life 'would be but short' if they did reconcile. Instead, inspired by her daughter Mary Howard, Duchess of Richmond's situation – Mary finally received the first of several jointure grants from the king in the spring of 1539 – Elizabeth asked for 'a better living'.[26] What she wanted was more money, her jointure money, to allow her to live in a manner consistent with her status as a duchess. She did not want to stay with others on their charity as her husband now demanded she do. 'I am of age to rule myself', she wrote with great condescension, 'and keep my own house still and trouble no other body as I am sure I should do.'[27] Unfortunately for Elizabeth, her demands represented a different kind of 'juggling', a juggling of legal status that was never going to be acceptable. Jointure was for widows, not for wives, even separated wives. So long as her husband remained alive, Elizabeth would remain under his subjection, and there was nothing she could do about it.

The *Great Harry* was the largest ship that maid of honour Anne Basset and her colleagues had ever seen. It had recently been remodelled and refitted and the paintwork was bright and new, a broadside of bronze cannons gleaming in the August sunshine. The women were probably told about the changes that had been made – the height of her hull had been brought down so she was less top-heavy and would roll less in heavy seas, and she now had four masts with sails arranged in such a way as to give her greater manoeuvrability – but Anne, though she would have smiled composedly and feigned attention, was more likely looking about her and taking in the sights and sounds of Portsmouth harbour.[28] It was less impressive than it would have been earlier in 1539, when there was a genuine fear of invasion and the entire fleet had assembled here. Now only seven or eight ships remained, but the receding threat was why it was safe to visit; that, and the ongoing construction work to improve the defences.[29] The dockyard at Portsmouth was busy, like any port. The crews of ships like the *Great Harry* ran into the hundreds, not to mention the merchants and labourers going about their daily business. The Swane bakery nearby was doing a roaring trade, and the smell of fresh bread warred with the fumes from the four brewhouses.[30] Anne could probably hear several different languages, much as one could in London, but with the tang of salt in the air.

The ten women, all former ladies-in-waiting, were shown around the dockyard and then taken on board to admire the *Great Harry* itself. Afterwards they retired to their lodgings in the town – such a trip no doubt occasioned at least an overnight stay, perhaps in the old Domus Dei hospice – and had a secretary write an overblown letter of thanks to the king, which was then signed by each of them. The ships were 'things so goodly to behold, that in our lives we have not seen (excepting your royal person and my lord the prince your son) a more pleasant sight'. They sent their 'most humble and entire thanks' for the entertainment, which lacked only the king's own presence.[31]

It seems an odd occasion, but perhaps illustrative of the limbo in which female courtiers remained in the summer of 1539. There was still no queen, and thus no female household. There was ostensibly no reason for ladies-in-waiting to have been gathered in this way, particularly not if the king himself was not part of the fun. Of the group, Mabel Clifford, Countess of Southampton was the most senior, and since her husband the earl was then lord admiral it may well be that he had arranged and perhaps even led the tour himself. Several others were also connected to men in the king's service. Alice Gage, Lady Browne was the wife of Sir Anthony Browne, the king's master of the horse. Jane

Champernowne, Lady Denny, Jane Ashley, Lady Mewtas and Anne Pickering, Lady Knyvett were all wives of gentlemen of the privy chamber.[32] Since the king was on progress in the vicinity of Portsmouth, these women may well have been there by dint of their husbands' service. Perhaps the king, used to having a wife and ladies to entertain, had attempted to create some semblance of courtly normality by gathering them together in this way.

Anne Basset was one of the most junior women there. She had been in royal service only a month and a half before the death of Queen Jane had rendered her jobless. Nobody had thought that it would take so long for another queen to arrive, and so Anne, increasingly impatient, had been boarded by various friends and relatives for almost two years. After spending a year and a half with her cousin Mary Arundell, the young Countess of Sussex, Anne had recently moved on, but there were politics involved: Lady Sussex 'doth not take her departing in good part'.[33] Anne had little choice and probably did not care, for the moiety of her attention was always saved for her own concerns and her own career. The king had undertaken to provide for her in the absence of her immediate family, and though he had not done so up to this point – his promise did not always amount to his coin – from midsummer 1539 Anne was paid a wage of 50s a quarter and moved to the household of Sir Peter and Jane, Lady Mewtas in London.[34]

Anne already knew them. Jane Mewtas had been Jane Ashley before her marriage and Anne had taken her place as maid of honour to Queen Jane Seymour in the autumn of 1537.[35] This was how Anne had ended up on the trip to the *Great Harry*: as she told her mother shortly afterwards, she had to go where Mistress Mewtas went, though she was surely pleased to feel herself part of a courtly group again. After the Portsmouth trip they retired swiftly back to the Mewtas's house 'beside our Lady of Barking in Tower Street' in London, and Anne was not sure when they would next rejoin the court. To her mother's annoyance this meant that Anne was unable to speak to the king personally on behalf of a family client, and Anne felt the need to apologise fulsomely for

this in her next letter.[36] It was difficult to do as her family wanted
when she could not control her own whereabouts.

Not long after this, in early October, Anne moved again, to
distant cousins the Dennys – Sir Anthony and Jane. This time it
was for the sake of her health. While living at the Sussexes' Anne
had had an illness that she had evidently struggled to throw off.
The king, knowing this, sent her to the Dennys, 'for whereas
Mistress Mewtas doth lie in London there are no walks but a little
garden, wherefore it was the king's grace's pleasure that I should
be with my Cousin Denny; for where as she lieth there are fair
walks and a good open air; for the physician doth say that there
is nothing better for my disease than walking; and I thank God I
am a great deal better than I was'.[37] Was it also nearer at hand for
the royal court? Sir Anthony Denny's house was at Westminster,
the opposite side of the city to the Mewtas's, and therefore close to
Whitehall Palace. If this was a consideration, it was because things
were finally moving forward. While Anne wrote to her mother
on 5 October from Westminster, there were ambassadors with
the king at Hampton Court and a marriage contract was signed.
There was going to be a new queen named Anna, from a small
Rhineland principality named Cleves.

Negotiations had been ongoing for much of 1539.[38] Jülich-
Cleves-Berg was a collection of small states on the banks of the
Rhine close to the Dutch border ruled by Duke Wilhelm, Anna's
brother. Cleves was a good choice for Henry VIII as one of the few
places in Europe that was an almost precise religious match for
his own Church of England. Their alliance represented a classic
juggling of different sorts of interests. While Cleves had close links
to the Lutheran Schmalkaldic League of nearby Germanic states
it was not itself Lutheran, but neither was it Roman Catholic. In
fact, Anna's late father Duke John had created his own religious
settlement in the mid-1530s, just like Henry VIII.[39] The marriage
between Henry and Anna represented a way for Henry to acquire
a link with the Schmalkaldic League without having to become
Lutheran, and thereby gain diplomatic support in the face of the
recent Franco-Spanish alliance. For Cleves it was an opportunity

to gain an ally in its quest to regain the recently vacated Duchy of Guelders from Charles V.[40]

The betrothal was concluded with remarkable speed. This was partly because of the time of year. Winter was coming, and travelling sooner would be far pleasanter than later. Transporting a royal bride, though, was a complicated business. Should Anna go to England by land or by sea, and who was to pay for this? What would she need to bring, who would accompany her, who receive her, and what were the appropriate gifts and entertainments and lodgings and wages that must be provided at every stopping point along the route? Thomas Cromwell's 'remembrances' – to-do lists – show that he was in charge of much of this from the English side and he must frequently have felt like things would never be ready in time.[41] And yet the arrangements fell into place. Anna was due to arrive in December. She was to travel by land to Calais, then across the Channel by boat, and so to London.

One of the earliest choices made by the English was among the most interesting. Only a few days after the marriage contract was signed, a woman named Susanna was sent to Thomas Cromwell with a letter from Sir Anthony Denny informing him that 'the King has already signified his pleasure to the bearer, late Mistress Parker, now Mistress Gilmyn, how he will she use herself in this journey to our mistress that God willing shall be'.[42] Cromwell was to outfit her suitably for the journey. This was Susanna Horenbout, and she was to journey to Cleves to bring the king's new bride home. Noblewomen sometimes did journey to meet a new royal bride en route, but Susanna wasn't noble. In fact, she was an artist: not only the daughter of renowned painter Gerard Horenbout and sister of Lucas, but a skilled painter in her own right. The well-known German artist Albrecht Dürer had bought a painting from Susanna in 1521 and wrote, admittedly with stunning condescension, that 'it is very wonderful that a woman's picture should be so good'.[43] At some point during the 1520s Susanna had come to England with her father and brother, and there they had remained. Susanna had married first John Parker, keeper of Westminster Palace and yeoman of the wardrobe, and after his death in

1537 John Gilmyn, a vintner in the city of London and sergeant of the king's woodyard.[44] But it was not her artistic talent that King Henry needed in December 1539. He already had a portrait of his future bride. If he sought a spy he was a little late, having already signed the marriage contract. No, what Henry needed most was someone who could speak to Anna and prepare her for her new life. What he needed was Susanna's language. Born in Ghent, Susanna's mother tongue was Dutch, and it bore strong similarities to Anna's Low German. Susanna may even have spoken German itself.

Susanna was sent separately to the official welcoming party who would await Anna at Calais, and she was sent with five servants, not as part of a bigger group of noblewomen.[45] This was an interesting decision. No doubt there were others Henry could have chosen for this task, and we can't be sure that it was Henry's own idea to send anybody, never mind to choose Susanna specifically. Merchants of the Hanseatic League were commonly used as interpreters, and if Susanna could speak German, most likely her brother and father could too. But Susanna's gender was also useful. A woman would be able to spend far more time with Anna than a man could on such a trip, and she would have knowledge of and insights into the queen's household that were unique to the women who lived and served in it. Passing on customs, ceremonies, traditions and unwritten rules of court etiquette was part of the role of ladies-in-waiting all over Europe. This was the kind of task for which only a woman would do.

Unfortunately, no records survive to tell us of Susanna's reception, or what passed between them on their slow journey back to England. From Antwerp, English ambassador Henry Wotton wrote with details of Anna's retinue. Eighty-eight people of the 263 in her train expected to remain with her in England, and six of these were ladies-in-waiting: five young gentlewomen and their equivalent of mother of the maids.[46] They reached Calais on 11 December and were greeted by Lord Lisle as deputy of Calais and by the Earl of Southampton, resplendent in purple velvet. Anna was led into Calais through the Lantern Gate near the ships in the harbour, which she stopped to admire. They promptly fired their guns in salute, making 'such a smoke that not one of her train could see the other'.[47] She passed down a line of local soldiers and dignitaries to the king's Calais palace, the Exchequer, opposite St Nicholas's Church. Anna wasn't the first of Henry's queens to stay here, and she was probably given the same suite of rooms as Anne Boleyn had been on the monarchs' visit in 1532. The 'Chequer', as it was called by contemporaries, was a large and well-appointed house; it had stables, a tennis court, gardens.[48] There was plenty to amuse Anna and her retinue, Susanna included, and this was lucky, for – again like Anne Boleyn – they were storm-stayed. Anna did not leave Calais for twenty-five long days.

This gave her plenty of time to observe and to be observed. She used the time wisely, asking the Earl of Southampton to teach her the card games that the king enjoyed. She also asked him and the other nobles to supper with her, probably so that she could gain a sense of English dining customs and perhaps to hear more about the king and the people with whom she would be living.[49] No doubt Susanna was also a help here. Lady Lisle, as the wife of the deputy of Calais, was able to give her daughter Anne Basset a welcome insight into her new mistress. Anna was 'so good and gentle to serve and please' and Anne was relieved to hear it, writing that this was 'no little rejoicement' to the queen's servants, and 'most comfort' to the king.[50]

With the arrival of a foreign queen, the royal household had reverted back to the more normal custom of appointing Anna's servants on her behalf, in advance of her arrival. A foreign-born queen would take time to get to know the nobility and to form relationships in her new country, and while in due course she could make these decisions for herself (with the king's approval) she nevertheless required service in the meantime. Thomas Cromwell had been fielding requests for positions since at least November. In fact, he had also been busy with general household reform in yet another attempt to curtail its staff and expenses, and this means that Anna's household is particularly well preserved in lists made for this purpose.[51] So far as her ladies-in-waiting were concerned, little had changed except that there were more of them than there had been earlier in the reign. There were thirty women set to attend Anna 'in ordinary'. Many of the ten women who had visited the king's ships in Portsmouth in August were now employed in the queen's service, including the ambitious Anne Basset.[52] Mary Howard, Duchess of Richmond – now in possession of her jointure estates, and still not remarried – was appointed one of Anna's highest-status ladies. Jane Parker, Viscountess Rochford, who had served every queen thus far, was also on the list. Anne's ladies-in-waiting were poised for their new queen.

The court spent an impatient Christmas at Greenwich. After days of the wind that 'blew as if all would have gone asunder', on Saturday, 27 December Anna was finally able to make the crossing.[53] She was greeted by foul weather, a face full of hail and the Duke and Duchess of Suffolk.[54] Katherine Willoughby, Duchess of Suffolk was among England's highest-ranking peeresses, which was why she had been chosen for this task. She was a similar age to Anna, twenty to Anna's twenty-four, and a woman of brave spirit and sharp tongue; a male contemporary would later remark acerbically, 'it is a great pity that so goodly a wit wasteth upon so froward a will'.[55] Portraits show that she had the fair complexion considered so attractive, with chestnut hair and hazel eyes and a frank, uncompromising gaze. For Katherine, leading the party greeting Anna must have been a bittersweet moment. The last time that a foreign princess had stepped onto English soil to marry a Tudor prince, Katherine's own mother María de Salinas had been part of the overseas retinue.

Earlier in 1539 María had died, without ever seeing her home country again. For someone who had lived her life with such gusto and played such a large part in the reign of Henry VIII's first consort, extraordinarily little has survived to tell us about María's death. We do not even know for certain when or where it occurred. Musters taken in Woodbridge in Suffolk in April 1539 noted that María was in residence at Campsey Priory with her servants.[56] On 20 May of the same year, the Suffolks were granted her lands as a result of her death; but a surviving indenture dated July implies that she was still alive.[57] If María left a will – and as a widow it would be odd if she had not – it has not survived, and nor is there any record of her funeral or burial location. The most obvious place for María to lie was with her late husband at All Saints Church, Mettingham, in Suffolk, and this could indeed be where she was laid to rest if she had died at one of her Suffolk properties. More likely, though, she died at Eresby in Lincolnshire, her main family home, and was buried at St James Church in Spilsby.[58] Though there is a legend that she was buried with Queen Catherine of Aragon at Peterborough, this is pure invention; the queen's tomb, when opened in 1891, was found to contain only one lead coffin.[59] We do know that María's daughter Katherine had been unusually absent during the spring and summer months of 1539. John Husee many times bemoaned her lack of response to his letters, and it seems reasonable to assume that the death of her mother might have had something to do with this.[60]

Was Katherine thinking about her mother as she journeyed to Kent to greet the new queen? No doubt she was able to appreciate the way that Anna and her German ladies were feeling, coming to a strange country for the first time. Katherine was joined by several local noblewomen all part of the same kinship network, a convenient web of women who could be scrambled at short notice when Anna's departure was known or her ships sighted.[61] Anna landed in the dark at five in the evening and was solicitously conducted to Deal Castle to dry out. There the Duke and Duchess of Suffolk met her, with 'a great number of knights and esquires and ladies of Kent and other'.[62] The weather remained terrible, but Anna pushed on regardless and reached Rochester for New Year's Day. She and her retinue were likely lodged in the bishop's palace next door to the cathedral.[63] From her chamber window she could see a courtyard, and on New Year's Day there was a bull-baiting there which she watched from above. Suddenly there was a noise at the door, and six men entered dressed in coats patterned like marble, with hoods. One crossed the room and greeted Anna, embracing her and kissing her.

The man was, of course, the king, and accounts of this first meeting differ. Contemporary English chronicler Wriothesley took his lead from the story given out later on and wrote that the meeting had gone disastrously: Anna had not known who Henry was and had been almost rude, ignoring him in favour of the bull-baiting. Henry had reappeared dressed appropriately and dined with her but had immediately told some of his gentlemen there present that he did not like Anna, and thus the story became that the marriage was doomed before it had begun.[64] But other chroniclers did not paint such a drastic picture. Edward Hall – usually a Henrician mouthpiece – said only that she had been 'somewhat astonished' at his sudden coming, 'but after he had spoken and welcomed her, she with most gracious and loving countenance and behaviour received and welcomed on her knees, whom he gentle took up and kissed: and all that afternoon communed and devised with her, and that night supped with her'.[65] Only a few days after the meeting itself Anna's diplomatic envoy, chancellor Henry Olisleger, wrote an account that tallies with Hall's. Henry had indeed come to see Anna as 'a private person' in disguise, as was a common tradition for kings greeting new brides, but the occasion had passed off well. She had invited him to dine with her and he had given her a sumptuous golden cup as a New Year gift, and then reappeared the next morning for breakfast.[66]

Perhaps Anna was 'abashed' at the king's greeting. Back home contact between unmarried women and men was more strictly controlled and men did not simply burst into the *Frauenzimmer* in this way. Perhaps this made things awkward, and Henry was not quite sure how to react to anything other than obvious enthusiasm. Anna may not have been used to the thinly veiled deception of disguise used so frequently by Henry and his courtiers. But Anna was not the only woman in the room. It's unthinkable that the Duchess of Suffolk and the others – German-speaking Susanna Horenbout, Mrs Gilmyn, for one – would not have prepared her for the king's visit, and if he had been genuinely annoyed by her reaction it's reasonable to think that they might have received part of the blame.

Within a few days, Anna had reached London. At Blackheath she was introduced to the rest of the women who would serve her 'in ordinary', and then to yet more women, sixty-five in total. She thanked them for their attention 'and kissed them all' – a feat which must have taken some time – before retiring with them to golden tents containing 'fires and perfumes' to banish the January cold.[67] The official reception went without a hitch. Endless city officials lined a route which had been specially widened, and she rode down it with the king, smiling and waving. Behind her rode her German women, 'all richly apparelled with caps set with pearl, and great chains of divers fashions after the usage of their country, which were very fair of face'. As had been the case for Catherine of Aragon's city entry in 1501, these six women were paired with six English women, the rest following in chariots behind. The night was spent in banqueting at Greenwich, and the next day Anna and Henry were married.[68]

In many ways the royal household now settled back into its usual pattern when there was both a king and a queen. Most of Anna's German women returned home shortly after the wedding. Anna sent a message to her family via one of the departing baronesses, Lady Keteler: 'she gave most hearty thanks unto them, for that they had so well bestowed her and preferred her to such a marriage, as she could wish no better, nor none other could content her mind so well'.[69] Competition for places in her household continued beyond its initial appointment and may even have been more intense than usual, for the evidence suggests that Anna's female household was somewhat larger than those of her predecessors. Not only did she have the usual six English maids of honour and mother of the maids, as livery lists make clear, but ambassadorial correspondence shows that she still had at least some German maids too, as well as their governess Mother Lowe, or Frau von Loo.[70]

Even so, the king was not minded to make any exceptions to the number of women ordinarily recruited to a consort's service, as Lady Lisle found early on. Having successfully placed her daughter Anne Basset in royal service, Lady Lisle now resumed the battle for Anne's older sister Katharine, who remained in the Countess of Rutland's retinue. Chancellor Olisleger himself was approached but could do nothing, explaining that Anna's household had been made before she arrived and every space was taken. Perhaps Mother Lowe, the 'mother of the Dutch maids' – Anna's German women – might have more influence.[71] The suit continued throughout the spring of 1540.

Another Katherine had been luckier. Katherine Howard was appointed as maid of honour sometime in the winter of 1539. The orphaned niece of the Duke of Norfolk, she had spent her adolescence in the household of her grandmother Agnes Tylney, the dowager Duchess of Norfolk, in Sussex and in Lambeth across the river from Westminster Palace. The Howard dynasty remained powerful despite their protégée Anne Boleyn's fall a few years previously, and in fact several Howard relations were members of Queen Anna's establishment. One of them was Jane Parker, Viscountess Rochford, and this was her fourth queen consort. Perhaps she advised her young cousin Katherine on how to behave and what her duties were. Queen Anna's surviving privy purse accounts show that life in her household was not significantly different from life in service to any other of Henry's wives.[72] Anna was quick to cast off her German-style clothing and pick up the French style favoured in England. A lot of time was spent playing cards. Rewards were paid to tumblers and minstrels, and Anna presented 'Mr Cecil' with a gilt cup for a Valentine's Day present. Gifts flooded in from those keen to ingratiate themselves with their new queen. In February 1540 somebody brought her a parrot. Anna's fondness for jewellery was satisfied by London's goldsmiths, one of whom made her a brooch containing an image of the story of Samson and Delilah. Throughout, she learned to speak and understand some English, enough to converse with her ladies at dinner.[73]

Though her upbringing in Cleves had been arguably stricter than an English equivalent in terms of contact between the sexes, there is no sense that she brought any vestige of this into her household in England. The usual flirtations occurred. Anna's

Richmond Palace, showing the towers and turrets that María de Salinas would have known.

A 1525 French tapestry depicting Mary Tudor's marriage to Louis XII in 1514. Mary is in the centre, flanked by her ladies-in-waiting. The woman immediately behind her is thought to represent Anne Boleyn.

Catherine of Aragon and her ladies-in-waiting watching the King joust at Westminster in 1511, a tournament held to celebrate the birth of their short-lived son Prince Henry. Catherine, on the left, has the King's sister Mary next to her.

The Lady of Richmond.

Mary Howard, Duchess of Richmond, sketched by Holbein in preparation for a painted portrait that has not survived. This was probably done in 1533 to celebrate her marriage to Henry Fitzroy, the King's illegitimate son. The bottom of the sketch is a study of her hat, covered in 'M' for Mary and 'R' for Richmond. Her dress was made of red and black velvet.

West Horsley Place, home of Gertrude Blount, Marchioness of Exeter. This is where she received Elizabeth Barton, the 'nun of Kent', in 1533.

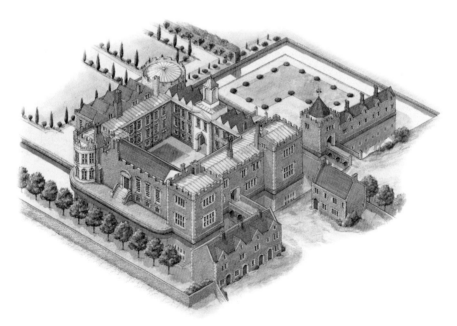

Reconstruction of Kimbolton Castle. María de Salinas, Lady Willoughby, talked her way into the castle after allegedly falling from her horse on her way there at New Year in 1536. She remained in Catherine of Aragon's rooms, at the top of this image in the south range, until the latter's death on 7 January.

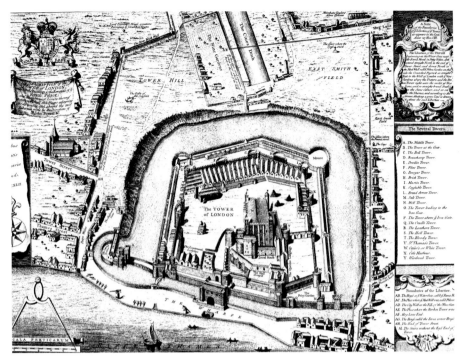

The Tower of London, roughly as it would have been in Anne Boleyn's day. Her apartments are below and to the right of the central White Tower.

Greenwich Palace, where Anne Boleyn was arrested in May 1536. Her chambers were at the back of the palace, overlooking the tiltyard on the left.

Hampton Court Palace, showing the old 'stacked' royal lodgings in the centre. This is where Anne Basset met Jane Seymour in 1537.

The christening procession of Edward VI in 1537, showing Gertrude Blount, Marchioness of Exeter, holding the Prince.

The last page of the letter written by a group of ladies-in-waiting to Henry VIII on 4 August 1539, to thank him for showing them his ships in Plymouth harbour. Anne Basset's signature is at the bottom in the centre.

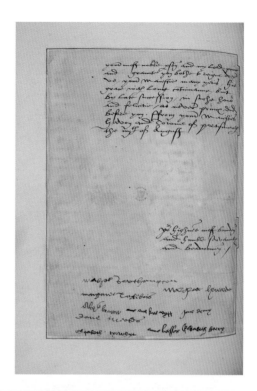

The royal closet in St George's Chapel, Windsor, built for Catherine of Aragon. This is where Katherine Willoughby, Duchess of Suffolk, and Kathryn Parr stood to watch the funeral of Henry VIII in 1547.

The tomb of Mary Howard, Duchess of Richmond, at St Michael's Church in Framlingham, Suffolk. She is buried with her husband Henry Fitzroy, Duke of Richmond.

The tomb of Katherine Willoughby, Duchess of Suffolk, at St James' Church in Spilsby, Lincolnshire. She is buried with her second husband Richard Bertie.

new maid of honour Katherine Howard met, liked and had her
heart broken by Thomas Culpeper, one of the king's gentlemen of
the privy chamber, possibly before Anna had even arrived.[74] Yet
another maid of honour, Dorothy Bray, was conducting an affair
with Sir William Parr that was an open secret.[75] But, broken heart
or not, Katherine Howard soon had a bigger problem, and it was
Queen Anna's problem too. King Henry thought her attractive,
and he also thought it fair to juggle a wife and a mistress. In April
he granted her the goods of two convicted felons.[76] Not a romantic
gesture by most standards, it was nevertheless significant. Women
like Katherine were not given grants in their own right except as
a particular attention, or, indeed, as a precursor to a certain sort
of attention.

This was not the only bad sign for Queen Anna. Increasingly,
the diplomatic situation in Europe did not favour the relationship between Cleves and England either. Henry had hoped that
through Cleves he might find a route to alliance with other
German princes. Unfortunately, they continued to demand that
he subscribe to Lutheranism, which would then place England
in increased danger from both France and Spain and was never
something that Henry had been prepared to countenance.[77] While
the alliance between France and the emperor had broken down,
which was usually a good thing for England, the potential for
England to be dragged into European conflict arguably intensi-
fied. Anna's brother Duke Wilhelm of Cleves remained in uneasy
dispute with Emperor Charles V over the ownership of the Duchy
of Guelders and, to King Henry's indignation, he communicated
with the emperor without keeping England abreast of the changing situation. This was problematic; Henry's marriage to Anna had
included a military alliance. If Cleves drew the emperor's wrath
– if Duke Wilhelm went to war – Henry would be obliged to come
to his defence. This he was not prepared to do, particularly if he
had not been consulted and if Duke Wilhelm ignored his advice.[78]

In March 1540 a new Cleves ambassador arrived. Karl Harst
and Queen Anna immediately put their heads together and worried about the situation.[79] Duke Wilhelm would not give way over

Guelders, and the emperor was hardly likely to let a small German princeling – Wilhelm was not yet thirty – dictate to him. For a while it looked as though a route to peace might be found through a marriage with Christina of Denmark, but this, too, was chancy for England; if Duke Wilhelm and the emperor made peace, that might damage England's renewal of friendly relations with France. By the end of April 1540 all negotiations between Cleves and the emperor had broken down. War was not only feared but even expected. For England, an alliance with Cleves was no longer safe.[80] King Henry felt he had been deceived. He did not know how to balance the military might of the emperor alongside religious considerations, and he did not know how to fit his new wife into any of this. Like Elizabeth Stafford, Duchess of Norfolk, Queen Anna and her ladies-in-waiting were being forced to juggle a world that felt increasingly treacherous.

15

The Principle Occasion of Her Folly

It was 11 July 1540, a Sunday, and a group of the king's privy councillors had just been admitted into Queen Anna's inner chamber
at Richmond Palace.[1] No doubt the women there looked up mis-
trustfully. How often unpleasant things had begun in this way.
For Jane, Viscountess Rochford this might have felt something
like a flashback: another time, another queen, another knife edge.
But would Queen Anna follow her namesake, Jane's sister-in-law
Queen Anne Boleyn, to the Tower? Was anyone seeking to put her
there?

Only a few days ago a similar delegation had arrived to inform
Queen Anna that the legality of her marriage to Henry VIII was
to be examined by a convocation of bishops, and that she must
consent to this. Reduced to tears and bereft of the advice of her
ambassador Karl Harst, who had been summoned to court to be
given the same news separately, Anna had replied that 'for all she
knew, he was given her as a husband, and this was what she saw
in him, and nothing could separate them but death'.[2] Though she
had been brought to consent, Harst thought that she was not fully
aware of what she was signing, since the copies of the documents
had not been translated into German.[3] Now they were back, six
men led by Charles Brandon, Duke of Suffolk. Suffolk explained
that the bishops' convocation had found against Anna's marriage
'by reason of a precontract between lady Anna and the marquis of
Lorraine, that it was unwillingly entered into and never consummated'.[4] They now required her acknowledgement of this also, but
whether she signed or not the annulment was a fact of law already.

The king's councillors must have been heartily sick of the river journey between Westminster and Richmond. Did Queen Anna know that Richmond was used as a place to send unwanted royal women?[5] It was smaller than the king's favourite palaces and considered to be out of date. The royal lodgings were in the old stone donjon on its own moated island, so that to reach the hall, the chapel or even the gardens Queen Anna had to cross a bridge. The layout had been little altered since King Henry VII's day and followed the old style, the queen's lodgings stacked vertically on top of the king's. The rooms were high-ceilinged but small, and Anna must have felt mewed up at the top of the tower.[6] Queen Anna and her household had been there since 24 June in what amounted to banishment. Though the courtiers with her had done everything possible to help pass the time, it had been a very long seventeen days.[7] The queen was not stupid. Both she and ambassador Harst were well aware of Henry's marital past, and they frequently expressed fears that Anna would end up in a situation like Catherine of Aragon, dying in poverty far from the king.[8]

The annulment at least provided a way out of unbearable uncertainty, though not one that Queen Anna would have chosen. She would be the king's 'dear sister', treated with the highest honour. She would have the manors of Richmond and Bletchingley in Surrey, and a household as befitted her status. She would be nominally free to marry again. Whether she was truly reassured by this or not, Queen Anna must have known that it would be useless to demur. Jane, Viscountess Rochford stepped up amid a small group of ladies-in-waiting: they were to act as witnesses. Jane watched with Eleanor, Countess of Rutland and Catherine, Lady Edgecombe as Queen Anna duly signed the papers. The six privy councillors signed too. Three of Queen Anna's chamberers were also there as witnesses – Dorothy Wingfield, Anne Joscelyn and Elizabeth Rastall.[9] Chamberers were usually of slightly lower status than other women in service with the queen, but that very fact meant that they were often present for more explicitly 'private' episodes than some of the highest-status ladies-in-waiting. They also tended to keep their jobs for long periods, and during Henry

VIII's reign that meant that they had borne witness to an increasing number of difficult moments. Anne Joscelyn, for instance, had been in service with Queen Anne Boleyn before she was queen. She had seen both Anne and Jane Seymour die before coming to Anna of Cleves.[10] Their individual and collective memory was superlative, and their inclusion here may have been an attempt to weaponise this to the Crown's advantage should anybody later question Queen Anna's willingness to sign.

In fact, women's evidence had been a central part of the case made against the marriage. Unravelling the decisions behind the annulment is a difficult task, not least because the evidence that is most easily accessible to us was deliberately created to be very one-sided.[11] The diplomatic situation had much to answer for. European tensions had not eased, and an alliance with Cleves continued to be more of a liability than an asset to an England worried about its position between the large Roman Catholic kingdoms to the south and the Lutheran Schmalkaldic League to the north. This, though, was not what was given out publicly. The official line was twofold: firstly, that Anna's pre-contract of marriage with the Duke of Lorraine had not been properly dissolved and that she had never been free to marry Henry; and secondly, that the marriage had remained unconsummated. One of the depositions given as part of the case was made by three of Queen Anna's English ladies-in-waiting, the very same three who then witnessed her signature on the annulment documents: Jane, Viscountess Rochford, Eleanor, Countess of Rutland and Catherine, Lady Edgecombe.[12]

Their evidence was slightly different to that given by the men around Henry. Jane and the others stated that about a fortnight previously they'd had a conversation with Queen Anna in which it became apparent that she was ignorant of the basics of human copulation. The three of them had 'wished her Grace with child', to which she had replied that she knew she was not pregnant. Lady Edgecombe had asked how she could know this if she lay every night with the king; the others chimed in, perhaps teasingly, perhaps anxiously, perhaps even unkindly, that Queen Anna must still be 'a maid', a virgin. There must be more than mere sleeping, 'or else I had as rather the King lay further', Jane had remarked, implying that it would be better for him to be sleeping with another woman in order to conceive an heir. Famously, Queen Anna is said to have replied that each night the king kissed her to bid her goodnight, and again for good morning: 'is not this enough?' 'There must be more than this,' the Countess of Rutland responded, 'ere it will be long until we have a Duke of York.' Queen Anna said that she was contented with this because she 'knew no more'. Had she spoken to Mother Lowe about this? 'For shame, God forbid,' the queen declared.

This was almost certainly untrue. Queen Anna's upbringing might have been more sheltered than that of an English woman of comparable station, but she had a mother, married sisters and many other women around her in the *Frauenzimmer*. She would have seen pregnancy, perhaps even witnessed childbirth, and it is unthinkable that a woman of her status would have been sent to her marriage without having been told about sex. But Jane and the ladies' reported conversation bolstered other evidence given by King Henry and the men around him, and they were probably used by the king for this purpose. He knew that if Queen Anna's own women claimed that she was ignorant of the mechanics of intercourse they would be believed, and thus his own testimony would appear more plausible. For Henry claimed that he had never liked Anna, and that he had been unable to consummate the marriage with her despite trying many times. A number of his closest male servants corroborated this in their own depositions given to convocation, adding details of derogatory comments made by Henry upon meeting Anna, after the wedding night and on other occasions thereafter; but these statements were all extracted at the time of the annulment, months after Anna's arrival.[13]

The letters of Cleves ambassador Harst, though, suggest otherwise, and present Anna as a far stronger character than do English sources. Harst's letters survive in a German archive but are vastly underused by English-speaking scholars, largely because they were written in Low German.[14] Harst thought that Queen Anna and Henry slept together regularly, because she told him so. She even told him on one occasion that she thought she might be pregnant, though within a few weeks she then doubted this.[15] Harst was appalled that Henry had sworn an oath that he'd never touched Anna. When informed about the convocation assessing the validity of the marriage on these grounds, he even asked Henry angrily whether he thought the Duke of Cleves had sent his sister over here for prostitution or whether this was the custom of this country, to seek a foreign bride and cast her aside after six months.[16] He told Queen Anna not to sign anything that agreed to this, and when he heard that she had done so they had a heated altercation in which he warned her that she was condemning not only her own immortal soul by lying about this but Henry's also; she retorted with vicious pragmatism that she had no choice unless she wanted her head cut off.[17]

Somebody here was lying. We may never know who. Undoubtedly Queen Anna knew what sex involved, and if it wasn't happening one can understand why she might have kept this a secret and lied even to Harst, even to her own women, perhaps deliberately creating an impression of naivety rather than go into the shameful details. It's difficult to see how the conversational testimonies of all of King Henry's men could be entirely fictitious, but equally those very testimonies make it clear that they were all afraid of Henry's caprice, none more so than Thomas Cromwell, who provided the most detailed deposition from the Tower after his recent arrest.[18] Cromwell's fall was one of the most shocking parts of the whole affair, for he had seemed high in the king's favour until suddenly, very suddenly, he was not. Nobody at the time was quite sure what had happened, and historians have struggled to unravel it ever since.[19] What is certain is that Cromwell's fall endangered many others too. All of those who gave testimony were people who had something to lose. Jane, Viscountess Rochford was the widow of an executed traitor. She was only able to survive because Thomas Cromwell had browbeaten her father-in-law into allowing her more money, and both of those male protectors were now dead or disgraced. Catherine, Lady Edgecombe was in a similar position. Her late husband had been a friend and client of Thomas Cromwell's, and on his death a year previously Cromwell had sent for her and then given her a position in the royal household, a move that strongly suggests she too became his client, eyes and ears within the queen's household.[20] With Cromwell in the Tower, Lady Edgecombe was adrift; the king, ever aware of the shifting patterns of clientage, would have known this. Even the Countess of Rutland, with an influential husband and no blemish on her record, was not safe. The earl had been Queen Anna's chamberlain, and he owed most of what he had to the king. That all three women signed to a single deposition rather than individual statements further suggests that it was created for, rather than by, them, and we don't know when they signed it, since their names do not appear in convocation's list of those from whom testimonies were collected.[21]

Jane and her colleagues had little choice. The process of annulment began officially on 6 July, but nobody on the queen's side was informed until two days later, by which point the depositions – presumably including the women's – had already been collected. At no point was Queen Anna given the opportunity to speak in her own defence, or commission anybody to do so for her. Ambassador Harst asked Cleves for experienced envoys, but it was already too late.[22] It must have been more than evident to Jane and the others that the annulment would go ahead regardless of whether they participated or not, and refusal might only bring consequences down upon their own heads.

Queen Anna must have felt very alone in these days. To Harst she described the English as 'a pack of wolves'.[23] It's not clear whether she had ever experienced real friendship with any of her English women. While there is evidence that by June she was able to understand and talk in English with them, translating for ambassador Harst, this did not necessarily dispense entirely with the language barrier.[24] The situation was the more difficult because, according to Harst, even Queen Anna's German women were used against her. He had heard that two German maids had allegedly 'confessed a marriage' between Anna and the Duke of Lorraine, and he thought that they had been 'milking the cash cow'.[25] Her

German mother of the maids, Mother Lowe, had also left the country. First given the king's permission to leave on 1 June, she had still been there in early July, when according to ambassador Harst she was then, extraordinarily, granted permission to depart by the king's mistress, Katherine Howard.[26] If Queen Anna had confided in anybody, Mother Lowe was likely the person, and one would think that her testimony for the annulment case would have been extremely useful. That she was expressly told to leave at just this time suggests that the English sought to have her out of the way so that she could not provide any detail counter to their assertions of non-consummation.

Service to the queen had never been risk-free. But, to a historian's eye, by 1540 the surviving sources give a far stronger sense of its attendant dangers than was the case in 1509. At one stage Queen Anna told ambassador Harst that even the privy councillors were 'weeping bitterly' with her, but that 'everybody is fearing for their heads, nobody is allowed to speak up'.[27] If this was the case for men, how much more so for women? Queen Anna had no choice but to accept her fate, and Jane and the other women around her had no choice but to contribute to it. It would be a brave woman who took on this king.

On Friday, 16 July 1540 Jane, Viscountess Rochford and her colleagues wept as they took their leave of the former Queen Anna of Cleves.[28] They could not remain with her, for Anna would have new ladies of lower rank to match her new status. Jane and the others were to attend the new queen, Jane's first cousin by marriage, Katherine Howard. It's possible that Jane had met her before this time at family gatherings, for Katherine had been living as a ward in the household of her grandmother Agnes Tylney, dowager Duchess of Norfolk, at Norfolk House. She had been a strong and vivacious personality in the household. While not everybody had liked her, nobody had been able to ignore her.[29]

So it proved at court. It was later said that the king had 'cast a fantasy' towards Katherine the first time he saw her and by late spring 1540 she was his mistress, plucked from among

Queen Anna's maids of honour in a wearying repeat of what was becoming King Henry's usual pattern.[30] In June she was discreetly returned to the duchess's household at Lambeth so that the king could visit her there; her family, perhaps including Jane, coached her to amuse and entertain him. Queen Anna knew this, and was both upset and furious, holding forth on the subject to ambassador Harst for a whole hour.[31] Harst called Katherine a whore in his letters back home.[32] And yet she had no more choice in her situation than did Queen Anna. One did not say no to the king, who even had the law changed so that he could marry her after a lawyer pointed out that, technically, the fact that she was the late Queen Anne Boleyn's first cousin meant that they were too closely related to permit marriage. A swift Act of Parliament later and Henry was legally allowed to marry any woman he chose, even one he had slept with before.[33] The marriage took place on 28 July at Henry's newly completed palace of Oatlands in Surrey, designed as a kind of bloated hunting lodge so that the increasingly lame king could continue to partake in the sport that he loved without having to endure long rides. In the kind of bizarre juxtaposition that the king seemed to enjoy, the wedding took place on the same day as his erstwhile chief minister Thomas Cromwell's execution on Tower Hill.[34]

By now, Jane, Viscountess Rochford was an old hand, an experienced courtier who had served four queens and been directly involved in the removal of two of those. She knew how to pivot into a new royal household and how to help a new queen find her way through royal ceremonial. She was a crucial part of the human machinery that kept the wheels of queen consortship turning. Queen Katherine had so little court experience that women like Jane were especially valuable to her, and this is one reason why personnel did not initially change much between Queens Anna and Katherine. Besides, the household had been appointed so recently that it did not make sense to entirely rearrange it. Conveniently, a number of Katherine's relations were already part of the establishment; not only Jane, but Mary Howard, dowager Duchess of Richmond, Margaret Gamage, Lady Howard and Katherine's own half-sister Isabel Legh, Lady Baynton. To these were swiftly added another of Katherine's sisters, Margaret Howard, Lady Arundell and her former room-mate and distant cousin Catherine Tylney.[35]

A few women did remain with Anna of Cleves rather than transferring to Katherine Howard, though it's not clear whether this was their own choice and whether it was perceived as an honour, or a dead-end job with few prospects for the future. Elizabeth Rastall, one of the witnesses to the annulment, was still with Anna in 1547.[36] Otherwise, the letters of Cleves ambassador Harst show that new ladies-in-waiting were sent to her, and indeed he liked them better than their predecessors; they were less 'impudent and free'.[37] The indomitable Lady Lisle's daughter Katharine Basset was among them. Katharine had been in the Countess of Rutland's household for some time while her family tried to secure her a position at court to join her sister, the ambitious Anne. The annulment of Queen Anna's marriage made this possible. Katharine's sister Anne Basset kept her place as a maid of honour and was transferred to Queen Katherine Howard's household.[38] This was just as well, for tragedy had come to the Lisle family. In the middle of May 1540 the Basset girls' stepfather Arthur, Lord Lisle had been arrested while visiting London. A day later their mother Honor, Lady Lisle had been placed under house arrest back home in Calais. The couple's religiously conservative beliefs and connections had placed them increasingly at odds with Thomas Cromwell and other evangelicals, and there had been serious disputes over Calais patronage as well. It was feared that Lisle might be in cahoots with that festering thorn in the king's side, Cardinal Reginald Pole, particularly since one of the household's priests had recently fled to Rome. In fact, the Lisles were innocent of any such involvement. The evidence suggests that Lord Lisle was simply caught up in a general move made by Cromwell against those he perceived to be his enemies in the spring of 1540, a move that was curtailed by Cromwell's own arrest and execution shortly afterwards.[39]

Did the Basset girls know this? The family's papers were seized – this is why their letter collection has survived – and naturally it falls silent at this point. This, coupled with the royal annulment and the doubt cast over her position, must have made it an exceptionally stressful summer for Anne Basset. The weather did not help. England was burning up. No rain fell between June and Michaelmas, and the Thames was so low that the saltwater tides reached beyond London Bridge. The drought gave way to plague in a new form, a 'strange sickness' with 'hot agues and fluxes', and Anne must have feared for her father, imprisoned in the Tower and unable to flee the sickness as the royal court did, safe away on progress.[40]

All eyes were on Queen Katherine as she settled into her new position. The French ambassador, Charles de Marillac, thought her 'rather graceful than beautiful', but conceded that 'the King is so amorous of her that he cannot treat her well enough and caresses her more than he did the others', something which Katherine had no choice but to endure. Anne Basset, Jane, Viscountess Rochford and the rest of the court ladies may have spent some of their summer engaged in the refashioning of their clothes, since Marillac also reported that 'all the Court ladies dress in French style'.[41] While the court was still away the unusually shallow and salty Thames attracted three dolphins, seen playing near Greenwich. Dolphins, like swans, were officially the property of the Crown, which was entitled to any that were captured or washed up within three miles of the shore. The three animals were dutifully caught in nets by local fishermen.[42] They might have done better to heed mariners' superstitions. Dolphins, sailors said, appeared in advance of bad storms. Jane, Viscountess Rochford and the others might hope for security under a new queen; but, by now, was it safe to trust that stability might return to the queen's household?

Margaret Morton and Maud Lovekyn had a grievance. As two of Queen Katherine's chamberers, much of her most intimate and personal care was their responsibility. They helped her to bed and helped her to dress, carried her messages and waited upon her. Though not the highest-status position within the queen's household, it was nevertheless one to which much importance was attached.[43] Chamberers knew many bodily secrets, and they jealously guarded their closeness to the queen. Margaret and Maud felt that closeness threatened, and they were not happy about it. Ever since Catherine Tylney's arrival, Queen Katherine Howard 'could not abide' their presence. Margaret was particularly annoyed by this. She had known both of the Katherines in the dowager Duchess of Norfolk's household at Lambeth before they had all come to court, and she clearly felt that Katherine Howard had no right to shut out one former colleague in favour of another, queen or not.[44] Margaret's words, written down later, suggest that she blamed Jane, Viscountess Rochford for the current politics in the queen's chamber.[45]

Certainly the others had also noticed the queen's extraordinary preference for Jane of late. Jane was always there. Indeed, by the time the court was on progress in the summer of 1541 Jane may have felt like she needed a holiday. The queen continually sent her messages by one or other of the chamberers, or the pages, or her gentlemen ushers. At Chenies, the lord admiral's house, Alice Restwold, another of the queen's Lambeth colleagues, arrived to join her household; the queen, having kissed her and told her to lodge with the other chamberers, then sent Jane with a gift of jewelled edgings for her French hoods and a gold tablet.[46] Jane's presence, evidently, had become a sign of the queen's favour. It's not clear quite when the queen's preference for Jane began. Nor do we know precisely how and why the queen came to favour her, or whose doing this really was. For Queen Katherine had a secret, and by summertime Jane knew the secret too.

It had begun innocently enough during Queen Anna's tenure, when Jane had been one of the queen's gentlewomen and her young cousin Katherine one of the maids of honour. As was usual, the queen's women frequently encountered the gentlemen of the king's privy chamber in the course of their duties. Equally naturally, flirtations sprang up, ran their short course and died as regularly as the waxing and waning of the moon. Among the king's gentlemen in the winter of 1539 was Thomas Culpeper, much in favour with the king. Culpeper was the kind of man who enjoyed useful connections and pretty women, and among the queen's maids of honour he had both. Katherine and Culpeper had got along well. But Katherine was not a stranger to flirtation, and apparently held firm against him: there would be nothing else unless he promised her something more concrete. This was not part of Culpeper's plan, and he turned instead to other women. Katherine, unused to rejection, was shocked, sad and no doubt had to watch these other relationships blossom in front of her. 'Her grief was such', she later told him, 'that she could not but weep in the presence of her fellows', the other girls. But soon the king himself made his interest clear and it was not long before she was elevated above her wildest dreams, and far above Thomas Culpeper.[47]

Queen Katherine chose to make him smart for his earlier rejection. One of his new conquests was Bess Harvey. Bess had previously served Queen Anne Boleyn, and had been among the group of women who had been to view the king's ships at Portsmouth in August 1539. At some stage in the spring or summer of 1541, Queen Katherine gave Bess a gown of damask and sent Jane, Viscountess Rochford to Culpeper with a pointed message: 'he did ill to suffer his tenement' – Bess – 'to be so ill-repaired' and so Katherine 'for to save his honesty' had covered the cost on it.[48] It was a bold and relatable, if petty, triumph and says much about Queen Katherine's personality. We don't know precisely when Katherine played this card, but at some stage after she became queen Katherine and Culpeper reconnected. Of itself this wasn't necessarily a problem. Queens naturally encountered men who were not the king. They had to work with them: the queen's council, over half of her household and the entirety of the king's were men. To interact with men for the sake of politics, patronage and even friendship was normal, but Queen Anne Boleyn's execution five years previously had shown that such relationships might be all too easily, even wilfully, misinterpreted.

Nobody knew this better than Jane. Queen Anne had been her sister-in-law, George Boleyn her husband, and their executions had left her bereft and poor, reliant on Crown patronage. We don't know whether Jane knew about her young cousin Katherine's flirtation with Thomas Culpeper back in 1539, but somehow she became, or was made, aware of its reprisal in the spring of 1541. She then became its facilitator. She was 'the carrier of all messages and tokens' between them. Queen Katherine claimed that Jane persuaded her into the relationship, that she had sworn upon a book that Culpeper's intentions were 'nothing but honesty', and Culpeper also deposed that Jane 'provoked him much to love the Queen'. Chamberer Margaret Morton self-righteously called Jane 'the principle occasion of her [Katherine's] folly'.[49] Yet Jane declared the queen the driving force behind their liaisons, that 'three or four times a day since she was in this trouble would ask what she heard of Culpeper'.[50] In facilitating the queen's adultery Jane became proof of the value of loyal ladies-in-waiting. It must often have been frightening, sometimes exhilarating, always exhausting, and we may never know why she did it.

The court was on its summer progress, heading for York. It was late August, and they were at Pontefract Castle just south of Leeds, considered the principal royal castle in the north of England, though it had gone unoccupied for so long that it had required repairs ahead of the king's arrival.[51] The court on progress was a very different place to the court in London. The king's London palaces were specifically designed to accommodate both his own and the queen's households, but this wasn't the case in all the places where they stayed on the route north. Some places – old monasteries, for instance, or bishops' palaces – had only one grand set of rooms worthy of the king, so the queen and her ladies sometimes found themselves accommodated in makeshift royal apartments, curtains taking the place of walls and servants tucked into odd corners. The normal rules of access were difficult to maintain, and thus easy to break. Anybody who was found somewhere they shouldn't have been could simply claim that they didn't know, that they hadn't realised this space was being used as a private chamber, or that they had got lost in an unfamiliar house.[52]

This made it easier than usual to arrange illicit liaisons. At each stopping point the queen, or Jane, or both searched for 'back doors and back steps' through which Culpeper could enter without being seen.[53] When the queen was worried that the king had set the night's watch in an inconvenient place, Jane sent her own servant to the courtyard each night to check. They found rooms that were empty, or out of the way, with easy access in and out; in the bishop's palace at Lincoln a chamber underneath Jane's, at York Lady Rochford's chamber itself, and at Pontefract a chamber at the bottom of the donjon in which the queen was lodged, mercifully a separate building from the king's own rooms.[54] The risk of discovery was enormous. One night at Lincoln Jane and the queen stood at a back entrance watching for Culpeper when the watch came along with a light. Hearts in their mouths, the women hid inside as he closed and locked the door, and were startled when suddenly Culpeper himself appeared, jubilant: he and his manservant had picked the lock.[55]

If there was a point at which Jane considered that things had got out of hand, it might well have been one night in Pontefract Castle. Queen Katherine had brought Jane downstairs to chaperone and to guard the inner door, while the queen and Culpeper 'did together' out of sight at the other end of the room behind a window, the queen at the top of the steps leading outside and Culpeper on the steps themselves, a convenient position for kissing as well as for swift escape.[56] Their relationship was sometimes one of teasing and banter. At York Queen Katherine had laughingly told him that she had 'scores of other lovers at other doors as well'; 'it is like enough', he replied.[57] At Lincoln Jane had watched and listened until three in the morning as they had a long and intimate conversation in which, vulnerable, Queen Katherine had told him of her heartbreak a year and a half ago when he had told her he loved her, only to pursue another woman, and he assured her that he had only gone elsewhere after her marriage had made her unattainable, that he loved only her and always would. Then, he had kissed only her hand, saying that he would 'presume no further'.[58] What did they do in the dark at Pontefract? What else did Jane hear?

We will never know for sure. Under the pressure of questioning and in fear for her life, Jane stated that 'she thinketh that Culpeper hath known the Queen carnally considering all things that this deponent hath heard and seen between them', but she also said that she could neither see nor hear them that night at Pontefract. Culpeper said only that he had 'intended' to 'do ill' with the queen, not that he had done so.[59] Their lack of clarity was partly a result of the law itself. Since the Treason Act of 1534, intention alone was sufficient to bring a charge of high treason. Legally it did not matter whether the act had occurred or not, and so the later investigation did not waste its time trying to prove that it had.[60] Naturally, Culpeper was not going to admit to having had intercourse with the queen of England if he thought there was a chance of survival, but it's just as possible that they had never actually consummated their relationship, or that even Jane simply did not know whether or not they had.

It is surprising that they weren't discovered sooner. But the summer progress wound its way back to Hampton Court, and Jane was still arranging liaisons between the queen and her paramour. The first blow fell in early November, and ironically was not to do with Culpeper at all, but with Queen Katherine's past. A woman who had been in the dowager duchess's household at Lambeth with Katherine told her brother about certain antics in the maidens' chamber there. This brother – an evangelical, and not a fan of Katherine's family's conservatism – suddenly developed a suspiciously outsized conscience and passed these tales to the king's council. From there the story unravelled alarmingly quickly, fuelled by fear of a king whose capacity for judicial murder seemed increasingly limitless.

Katherine, it transpired, had had two sexual affairs while still in her grandmother's household, one with her music teacher Henry Mannox and one with Francis Dereham, a gentleman in her grandmother's service. This was where Katherine had learned how to keep such things a secret. She and Mannox, who was already married, met at night and out of doors, wherever they could find some measure of privacy, in the same way as she would later do with Culpeper. The Dereham affair had gone even further, to full intercourse, and they had called each other husband and wife. Katherine had not been the only girl engaged in sexual contact in that household, but she had been something of a ringleader, stealing the keys to let the boys in and telling them to hide in the little gallery when the duchess, tipped off, stormed into the room one night. When Katherine broke off the affair because she was entering court service, Dereham had betaken himself to Ireland in a fit of pique.[61]

Many of her family members had known about this, particularly the women. It's often said that Katherine was placed at court precisely so that she could catch the king's eye and become the next queen, but this is sheer impossibility. Nobody could have known in the autumn of 1539 that the marriage with Anna would not prove a success, nor that Henry would fasten, limpet-like, onto Katherine. Her relatives must have had many sleepless nights since then, for if Henry found out that his 'jewel' was tarnished they would all suffer. The best that they could do was to try to limit the damage. This is why so many former members of the duchess's household found their way into Queen Katherine's establishment, including, astonishingly, Francis Dereham himself. Given a vested interest in her success as queen, perhaps they would keep their mouths shut.[62]

We don't know whether Jane, Viscountess Rochford knew about Katherine's former life, but she must in any case have lived in a state of unbearable dread while it was investigated, knowing that there was worse to find. In the end it was Queen Katherine herself who gave away the Culpeper affair. She was questioned by Thomas Cranmer, Archbishop of Canterbury. The archbishop was kind and patient with her, giving her space to cry, offering comfort, but returning inexorably to the details over and over. In a moment of panic and confusion Katherine spoke of a visit that Francis Dereham had made her at court before she became queen, and how he had asked her whether she was married to 'Mr Culpeper' as he had heard reported.[63] Cranmer, never slow-witted, knew that he had something. Queen Katherine, swiftly confined to her chambers at Hampton Court, knew it too.

Within days she was removed to the former convent at Syon Abbey, her household dismissed. Katherine knew that Queen Anna had been sent to Richmond Palace to be out of the way while the king and council had ended her marriage. Syon was only a mile away from there and had recently held another disgraced royal woman, the king's niece Margaret Douglas, in trouble yet again for carrying on a dalliance with another Howard boy.[64] More secure than the nearby palace, Syon nevertheless offered appropriate accommodation for a queen, for it had been the wealthiest abbey in England at the time of its suppression in 1539. Queen Katherine was permitted three chambers, 'hanged with mean stuff, without any cloth of estate'.[65] The first was for her staff to dine in, and the other two for her own use.[66] Like her cousin Queen Anne Boleyn, she was permitted only a few female attendants but, unlike Anne, she was allowed to choose them: four gentlewomen and two chamberers 'at her choice, save that my Lady Baynton shall be one'.[67] Lady Baynton was Isabel Legh, Queen Katherine's half-sister. Her husband was the queen's vice-chamberlain, as he had been to all of the king's wives so far. That the king specified Lady Baynton's inclusion is unlikely to have been an act of kindness, and suggests that despite the family relationship Isabel was probably more of a Crown agent, a spy, than a friend or ally, much like Lady Kingston had been for Queen Anne Boleyn.

Queen Katherine also had Anne Parr, Lady Herbert and Elizabeth Oxenbridge, Lady Tyrwhit.[68] If Jane was also among them, it surely cannot have been for long. Once Culpeper's name became a part of the investigation the queen's women were questioned and gave further details in turn, and Jane's role in the whole affair was soon uncovered. Witness depositions are tricky sources to work with. Preserved as paragraphs written in the third person, they were actually given as first-person answers to leading questions, making it difficult to know what the scribe had chosen to prioritise or truncate. The women's depositions give the impression that there was little love lost between Jane and the rest of Queen Katherine's household, but Jane was also a convenient scapegoat for frightened people, since her involvement was already certified. The abundance of surviving evidence here is in contrast to the lack of evidence we have for Queen Anne Boleyn's fall, which must once have existed. The statements given by the queen's women were crucial, particularly those of the chamberers. Margaret Morton – she who had not liked being pushed aside after Catherine Tylney's arrival – had seen the queen look out of her privy chamber window onto Culpeper in the garden below at Hatfield Chase and had 'thought in her conscience that there was love between them'.[69] Catherine Tylney herself had been sent with 'such strange messages' to Viscountess Rochford that 'she could not tell how to utter them'.[70] But they had not known for sure that anything was going on. Queen Katherine had not confided in any of her women except Jane, and Jane had perhaps told her to keep it this way, knowing from prior experience that it wasn't safe for a queen to confide too much in her ladies-in-waiting.

The ways in which the secret was kept, however, raised suspicion, and this tells us a lot about the norms of access for ladies-in-waiting. They noticed when the queen remained closeted for long periods with only Jane, and they thought it odd. They noticed when she stayed up unusually late, and made comments to one another about it. They were surprised when they were ordered not to come into her bedchamber unless called for, and even more when they found her chamber door bolted from the inside. Whereas the king's bedchamber was indeed sacrosanct to all except his groom of the stool, the queen's women were apparently used to going in and out of hers: chaperones indeed.[71]

The investigation continued its wearying course. The maids of honour were to return home, 'save Mistress Basset, whom the King, in consideration of the calamity of her friends, will, at his charges, specially provide for'; Anne Basset's parents were still under arrest.[72] Hampton Court, 'where the ladies are', remained closely guarded, and questioning continued.[73] The women were asked what they had seen and heard, where, when had the queen left her chamber late at night, with whom, when had she returned? In the minds of the king's councillors the queen's chamber took on monstrous proportions, its very femininity and the fact that they couldn't enter it meaning that anything could happen there; as the French ambassador reported ominously, the queen had met with men in 'secret and suspect places'.[74]

By 19 November Dereham and Culpeper were in the Tower, and so was Jane. Queen Katherine's Howard relations were trying every trick they knew. Her grandmother, Duchess Agnes, sharp and quick-witted, pulled many strings to find out what was happening, burned evidence and checked for legal loopholes, but eventually even she was forced to submit to arrest and imprisonment in the Tower.[75] Their goods were inventoried. Jane's silver plate, her jewels – 'a fair brooch, black enamelled with six small diamonds', 'a flower of rubies', a gold brooch with a fashionable 'antique' head – and other treasures were taken, and even her clothes, all black, of velvet, satin, damask and taffeta, were seized.[76] Rumours spilled out of ambassadors' ready pens and across the continent. Jane, the French ambassador Marillac pronounced, 'all her life had the name to esteem her honour little, and has thus in her old age shown little amendment'.[77]

Culpeper and Dereham were tried and found guilty on 1 December and executed on the 10th. Culpeper, as a noble, was beheaded, but Dereham suffered the traditional traitor's death and was 'hanged, [dis]membered, [disem]bowelled, [be]headed, and quartered'.[78] On the 22nd the rest were arraigned and indicted for misprision of treason, knowing of treason but doing nothing about it: eleven members of Queen Katherine's family and their Lambeth associates, seven of them women. Of these, Margaret, Lady Howard, the wife of Lord William, and Catherine Tylney had been in Queen Katherine's service at court. Neither had known about the Culpeper affair and both had given up all they knew of Katherine's pre-marital relationships. That knowledge, not their court service, was why they were attainted. All eleven could now look forward to the confiscation of their goods, lands and titles, and a lifetime of imprisonment. So full was the Tower that even the royal apartments were used, with new locks installed because the king could not find his key.[79] The king spent Christmas at Greenwich, dining on rage and self-pity.[80] Queen Katherine remained at Syon, her mood swinging between terror, depression and forced hilarity. In a final measure of the cruellest of uncertainties, she was forced to wait until Parliament opened on 16 January for a decision to be made as to her future. Her grandmother the Duchess of Norfolk was in the same position.[81]

So too was Jane. According to Imperial ambassador Chapuys, a few weeks into her imprisonment in the Tower she 'went mad'.[82] Her arrest, imprisonment and intense questioning on top of the strain of the summer, carrying such deadly secrets, became intolerable. Jane had seen this play before, and she knew how the last act was supposed to end. Five years ago she had not only witnessed the arrest, trial and execution of another queen, her sister-in-law and mistress, but played a part in it, been interrogated by councillors, seen her words used against those she loved and watched her husband, her sister-in-law and her friends die on the block as a result. To see it repeated with herself at the centre was indescribably traumatic. Unable to process what was happening and what was likely to happen, it is by no means surprising that Jane's mind simply ceased its normal function.

This, though, was no good to the king. He needed reprisals handed down and examples made, for his own satisfaction and for the audience watching his humiliation. Perhaps he also sought to enact specific vengeance upon Jane herself. Her words, her conversations with Queen Anne Boleyn about his inability to perform in the bedroom, the sense that she and the others were laughing at him had been among the worst elements of that entire affair. The very same woman had helped another of his wives to sleep with another man. In Henry's mind she had connived, been privy to his most intimate sexual secrets, laughed at him and made him a laughing stock in front of the whole world, and it was utterly unbearable. But as things stood, the law did not allow for the execution of the mad. Jane must recover her reason.

She was removed from the Tower and sent instead to be with Lady Russell, the lord admiral's wife, at their home on the Strand far west of the Tower.[83] Even in her distressed state, it must have been something of a reprieve. There were fewer locked doors and a return to the kind of luxury she was used to. She could hear the bells of St Mary Le Strand and the Savoy Hospital chapel nearby, and the restful sounds of the city going about its usual business. Lady Russell herself was a familiar face, perhaps even a friend. Older than Jane, she had survived two husbands and nursed her third through at least one bout of serious illness, and she had borne and buried children. She had been in and around the queen's household since Queen Anne Boleyn's day.[84] She knew grief and she knew trauma, and one hopes that she was kind to Jane even as she and her husband were loyal to the king.

Parliament opened on 16 January. Adultery on the part of a queen was not technically within the remit of the treason law, and though in 1536 it had been allowed to be judged thus under the clause of 'imagining the death of the king', in 1542 the king's lawyers would not allow it a second time.[85] Queen Katherine, the Duchess of Norfolk and 'that bawd', Viscountess Rochford, were condemned by parliamentary Act of Attainder instead, an Act that contained a change to the treason law to make a queen's adultery an act of high treason for the future.[86] On 29 January the Commons agreed that the Duchess of Norfolk was guilty of misprision, and the queen and Jane of high treason. Jane had not recovered from her breakdown. Though her reason returned every now and then, she was not of sufficient mental capacity to permit her execution. In a characteristic act of single-minded selfishness, the king forced through a change in the law. If any had thought that Jane might escape, this must have disabused them of that thought. Now the mad could die regardless.[87]

On Thursday, 9 February Jane was taken from the Russells' house and returned downriver to the Tower.[88] The next day she was joined by the queen, whose control had finally broken when she was faced with the journey. Queen Katherine had frozen, unable to move, and the councillors had had to manhandle her into the boat with her ladies.[89] On Saturday the 11th they were officially condemned to death, but not informed until the evening of the 12th, at which point – according to ambassador Chapuys – Jane suddenly ceased to show 'symptoms of madness'.[90] Perhaps the shock had penetrated her dissociation, or perhaps the knowledge that there was an end in sight even came as a comfort.

At seven the next morning they were led separately to the scaffold, set up on the same spot as Queen Anne Boleyn's six years previously, to the north-east of the White Tower in the centre of the palace complex. Queen Katherine died first, and Jane had to watch. The queen 'was so weak that she could hardly speak' and did not say much, merely confessing her guilt and praying for the king before the blindfold was fastened and she laid her head on the block. The axe fell. Her body was covered with a black cloak and her four women, including her sister Lady Baynton, stepped forward to carry it to the chapel, just as Queen Anne's women had done for her all those years ago.[91]

It was Jane's turn. One account said that she spoke little, but another that she gave 'a long discourse of several faults that she had committed in her life'.[92] Commending her soul to God and exhorting prayers for the king, she too was killed.

We will never know why Jane did the things that she did in the service of Queen Katherine Howard. The possible explanations are almost limitless and the drive to speculate has proved irresistible to most historians. She could have come across Katherine and Culpeper in an unchaperoned situation and been bribed or threatened into keeping silence. Maybe she had arranged one meeting for what seemed an innocent purpose and then become implicated before she was able to extricate herself. Perhaps she really was as guilty as her colleagues made her out to be, encouraging the affair for nefarious reasons of her own: revenge on her family or on the king who had taken and twisted her words to kill her husband and to annul his own previous marriage, ruining her life and condemning her immortal soul. Perhaps she simply misjudged the situation and made some bad decisions. Perhaps, perhaps, perhaps.

Regardless of the reasons, Jane no doubt thought that the worst would never happen to her, and in this she was not unjustified. Though the king had killed noblewomen before – most recently the elderly Margaret Pole, Countess of Salisbury, in the spring of 1541 – their crimes had been ones of conspiracy, of religion, or related to international politics. Queen Catherine of Aragon's women had been harried and imprisoned and lost their jobs for their loyalty to her, but they had not lost their lives. Queen Anne Boleyn's women, Jane included, had not even been accused of any crimes. No lady-in-waiting had ever been killed as a direct result of her service to the queen.

Jane's death changed this. Giving evidence had not saved her as it had saved the others. There was no sating this king, and no lady-in-waiting would ever be safe in service again.

16

When Women Become such Clerks

If impulsive Mistress Anne Basset ever communicated directly with her gentler sister Katharine, the winter of 1541–2 must have seen an anxious flurry of notes between them.[1] Both were in unenviably precarious positions. Their mother Honor, Lady Lisle remained under house arrest at their home in France. Their stepfather Arthur, Lord Lisle was imprisoned in the Tower of London on suspicion of treason. Anne had reprised her role as maid of honour to Queen Katharine Howard, but this came to an end with the latter's fall and the dismissal of her household in November 1541. Anne was yet again without a position or even a clear home, and her ambitious soul loathed feeling aimless and adrift. Katharine, the less conventionally successful sister, had been taken into the former Queen Anna of Cleves' household, probably in the summer of 1540.[2] Though Katharine's position was now more secure than her sister Anne's, the winter after Queen Katharine Howard's execution was not an easy time to be in Anna of Cleves' service either. She spent most of this time at Richmond Palace, lodged in its innermost donjon, lead-topped turrets overlooking the Thames. Rumours abounded. Many thought that the king would take Anna back and make her queen again. In mid-December, Cleves ambassador Karl Harst was even instructed to seek reconciliation between Anna and the king.[3] This could not be kept from her household. The relationship between Anna and some of her English women was not altogether easy. Although Harst preferred the women who served Anna now to those she had had while she was queen, he reported that she was still watched, and that her English women searched her belongings while she slept and showed her letters to the king. Though Anna did not want to return home, Harst told her that she would be better off with her brother and only one maid than here in this way and manner with fourteen.[4]

Katharine Basset, though, was loyal. At some point during the summer or autumn of 1541 she unguardedly praised Anna at Queen Katherine Howard's expense. Soon, she told her colleague Jane Rattsey, she would 'see a change', information she seemed to have gleaned from the maids of the queen's household – her sister Anne? Jane, startled, exclaimed, 'What a man is the King! How many wives will he have?' and wondered aloud, 'What if God worketh this work to make the lady Anna of Cleves queen again?' In December 1541 Jane was hauled before the Privy Council to explain this – if she could – and to be closely questioned on her opinion of the king's annulment from Anna.[5] Both she and Katharine must have panicked, for there was no telling how such comments might be taken by a king paranoid about his marital status and his masculinity.

Nothing seems to have happened to either of them, though Jane Rattsey was held in custody for a short time. Perhaps it was thought somewhat ridiculous to attempt to prosecute anybody for having 'dispraised' Queen Katherine, given the revelations about her infidelity to the king. The rumours about Queen Anna continued regardless, even that she was pregnant or that she had had a child. Her household officers, along with Dorothy Wingfield from her privy chamber, were examined by the Privy Council but speedily dismissed after they assured the councillors that there was no truth to the report.[6]

Ambassadors watched the king for hints not only that he might take Anna back, but for signs of interest in any woman. They did not have long to wait. At the end of January 1542, after Queen Katherine's condemnation, Imperial ambassador Chapuys reported that King Henry gave a banquet, probably at Westminster, with many ladies present and that three had been singled out for royal attention. The king seemed most animated by Elizabeth Brooke, Thomas Wyatt's recently repudiated wife; 'She is a pretty young creature', Chapuys remarked cynically, 'and has sense enough to do as the others have done should she consider it worth her while.'[7] Not only was Henry's penchant for ladies-in-waiting fully understood by those around him, but commentators still expected them to play up to this despite the risks involved. Lucy Somerset, another of the maids of honour, was also said to suit the king's 'fancy'. Last but not least, Chapuys thought that Mistress Anne Basset herself was in the running, partly because her stepfather Lord Lisle had recently been given his liberty within the Tower of London complex, a sign that he would likely be released.[8] If Anne heard this – if, indeed, there was any substance to it – surely she cannot have been pleased about it even if she had sought to appease the king on her family's behalf. Anne might be ambitious, but she was no fool, and she cannot have thought that marriage to this king would be a good idea.

In the meantime, Princess Mary's household was the pre-eminent female establishment once more, welcomed to court 'in default of a Queen'.[9] Mary's relationship with Katherine Howard had not been overtly positive – Queen Katherine had threatened to dismiss some of her women because she did not think Mary had treated her with sufficient respect – but some of the late queen's servants, notably those who had given evidence against her, found their way into Mary's establishment over the course of the 1540s, not least those two gossips Margaret Morton and Maud Lovekyn.[10] Princess Mary also kept up relationships with many of the decade's most prominent noblewomen. Her privy purse expenses across these years are full of gifts flowing back and forth, expensive gestures of goodwill and of patronage. Gertrude Blount, Marchioness of Exeter received a puncheon of wine; Gertrude had been pardoned for her role in the 'Exeter conspiracy' that had seen the execution of her husband and had been released from her imprisonment in the Tower in the autumn of 1539.[11] She remained attainted, which meant she had no access to her jointure lands and must live on an allowance from the Crown.[12] Elizabeth Stafford, Duchess of Norfolk was given a brooch of garnet and gold.[13] Elizabeth, too, remained in difficult straits, still under house arrest in Hertfordshire, still at odds with her bullish husband, and still struggling financially on what money he allowed her.

Gertrude, Elizabeth and many other noblewomen had cultivated a relationship with Princess Mary for years. Katherine Willoughby, Duchess of Suffolk was one of these. Married to Charles Brandon, Duke of Suffolk, Katherine was often called upon to represent and even reinforce Crown policy. She had helped her husband to suppress the Pilgrimage of Grace rebellion in 1536 and had formally greeted Anna of Cleves when she arrived in Kent at the end of 1539. But though Katherine played her part in toeing the party line, she also stayed in touch with Princess Mary, whether or not the princess's actions aligned with the royal will. She sent her regular gifts. She visited, and played cards with her. Early in 1543 she lent the princess horses to bring her women from Hampton Court to Syon Abbey, and then to Westminster.[14] The bond between the two was one born of kinship and service, for Katherine's mother María de Salinas had served Princess Mary's mother Queen Catherine of Aragon throughout her time in England. Nor was the relationship one-way. Princess Mary's privy purse expenses show that she made a point of keeping up with her mother's former servants and friends.[15]

Over the freezing winter of 1542–3, then, when Kathryn Parr, Lady Latimer came to London to nurse her husband through his final illness, she soon made contact with Princess Mary.[16] Kathryn's mother Maud, Lady Parr had likewise served Catherine of Aragon for many years. Kathryn and Mary may even have been childhood friends.[17] Soon, Kathryn had joined the princess's household as one of her ladies-in-waiting and was even ordering clothes for her, directing the tailor to send his bill to the king.[18] By February, though, her new position had had an unforeseen effect. The king was visiting Mary's chambers twice, even three times a day, and one suspects he was not only there to see his daughter.[19]

The king assented to his sixth marriage with a hearty 'Yea!'. Katherine, Duchess of Suffolk, sandwiched between Lady Margaret Douglas and the Countess of Hertford, may have felt a little less optimistic. It was a warm July day and there were over twenty people squeezed into the queen's holy day closet above Hampton Court's chapel, a space that was most definitely not designed to hold so many. Katherine will have watched as King Henry slid a ring onto her friend's finger, her delicate hands swallowed by his larger, fleshy paws. Perhaps Katherine marvelled at the new queen's composure, since she herself was notoriously poor at keeping her feelings and opinions hidden. This was not a marriage at which a woman could easily rejoice, and yet quite calmly Kathryn Parr had promised – among other things – to be bonny and buxom in bed with a man who had already had five wives and had killed two of those. If her assent was less cheerful than Henry's, one could easily ascribe that to womanly modesty.[20]

Katherine must surely have sympathised with Queen Kathryn's plight. The two women had orbited one another for years and were probably long-standing friends. They had much in common. Both were goddaughters of Queen Catherine of Aragon. Both had mothers in her service and were raised by strong female role models, because both lost their fathers at a young age. They were even connected to some of the same Lincolnshire people and places, through natal family and through their respective marriages.[21] But Katherine, Duchess of Suffolk had married only once, to Charles Brandon, Duke of Suffolk. Kathryn Parr, seven years older than her friend, was twice widowed already at the age of thirty-one and had hoped to please herself the third time with the young, handsome, charismatic Thomas Seymour. Though Mary Howard, Duchess of Richmond had turned up her nose at a marriage with him in 1538, Kathryn fell like a ninepin before his charm when she met him early in 1543.[22] Yet the king had intervened. Seymour was sent away on an embassy, and Kathryn was now married for a third time against her desire.[23]

Katherine, Duchess of Suffolk had been lucky by comparison. Her marriage to Charles Brandon appears to have been a success; she was his 'entirely beloved wife'.[24] The couple embodied the companionate model of aristocratic marriage, working seamlessly together as a team to manage their enormous estates, promote clients and friends, fulfil their obligations to the king and, most importantly, to procreate. Their two sons Henry and Charles were now rising eight and six. For all that Suffolk and the king were contemporaries, Suffolk was affable and remained physically active, though with bouts of poor health. The king, lamed from a jousting accident many years ago, was overweight, stank of the pus from his leg, was irritable and unpredictable. Of the two, Henry was not the man a woman would want in her bed.

Katherine, Duchess of Suffolk may have been one of those to whom the new queen unburdened herself. Certainly she swiftly became part of the queen's inner circle, attested by her inclusion in the small group who witnessed their marriage, packed like sardines into the queen's closet on that July day. Like most queens consort, Queen Kathryn filled her household with friends, family and like-minded associates, most of whom Katherine, Duchess of Suffolk also knew. Many were experienced, having served previous queens; Jane, Lady Denny, Jane Dudley, Viscountess Lisle and Anne Seymour, Countess of Hertford were all old friends. Anne Basset became maid of honour for the fourth time. The queen's sister Anne Herbert came from Princess Elizabeth's household, and her cousin Maud, Lady Lane also became one of her trusted confidantes.[25]

Queen Kathryn needed all the emotional support that she could get. The court remained at Hampton Court Palace, but the queen's chambers were over the kitchen, and the king visited often. The zeal with which Queen Kathryn ordered 'perfumes' not only for her chambers but for her bed suggests that both were a noisome problem.[26] And yet she could hardly do other than perform her marital duty with the king, who remained desperate for a second male heir. Her expenses show that she regularly consumed water 'ad provocandum menstruum', to bring on menstruation.[27] Such purgatives were thought to increase fertility by cleansing the womb.[28] If Queen Kathryn failed to fall pregnant she risked being cast aside, but if she did conceive the king would surely turn his attentions elsewhere and she could relax, her duty done.

The mid-1540s were a stressful time at home and abroad. The

weather, capricious as the king's temper, stormed, froze and scorched England into plague and scarcity.[29] War, too, was a certainty even before Queen Kathryn's marriage, as the king had signed a treaty with Emperor Charles V agreeing to an invasion of France within two years.[30] For Katherine, Duchess of Suffolk the 1540s were correspondingly laced with anxiety for her husband Charles. He had not been present at the king's marriage in July 1543 because he was serving as lieutenant of the north, defending the northern border against Scottish incursions and handling a thousand and one details of civilian as well as military business. This was not a job that he enjoyed. More to his taste was the planning of a Scottish invasion, which he was asked to do six times between February 1543 and March 1544.[31] Six times Katherine's heart must have been in her throat, and six times relief as the invasion was called off. In the event, the Earl of Hertford eventually led the Scottish invasion in May 1544. Suffolk returned south to the court, where he was a jovial presence in Privy Council meetings as the promised invasion of France was planned. The king had shocked his councillors by declaring that he would personally lead the army to France in a repeat of his antics in the 1520s. Suffolk now had to make this happen: namely, to place the town of Boulogne under siege so that the king might come and accept its surrender. An experienced commander, he did this beautifully and the king's participation in the French campaign ran like clockwork.[32]

At home, Katherine, Duchess of Suffolk performed double duty in soothing both her own and the queen's worries. Queen Kathryn had been appointed regent of the kingdom while the king was away in France. Like Queen Catherine of Aragon in 1513, Queen Kathryn Parr took this responsibility seriously; it was, after all, a chance to show that she could handle the job if there should be a royal minority in due course. Her wisdom was compared with that of Penelope, a classical reference to a woman who had governed her husband's estates during the Trojan War.[33] The king returned home in October and the royal couple embarked on a short progress into Kent.

Katherine, Duchess of Suffolk had to wait a little longer. Her husband the duke did not return until the end of November, but he did at least return whole, and was well rewarded for his efforts.[34] Unfortunately, Katherine's time with her husband was short-lived. She was with him in Rochester on 19 July 1545 – the same day as the *Mary Rose* sank, a tragedy witnessed by not only the king but by Lady Carew, the wife of the ship's captain.[35] The records don't tell us whether she was still at his side while he attended Privy Council meetings in Guildford in Surrey in mid-August. There, on 22 August 1545 at the age of sixty-one, he died.[36] Katherine, now twenty-six, was a widow.

Her feelings, like her presence, were not recorded. As a woman she probably did not attend his funeral, a grand, heraldic affair at St George's Windsor, paid for by the king.[37] By the terms of Suffolk's will she received 500 marks' worth each of cash, plate, jewellery, household stuff and all of his sheep in the county of Lincoln. She was also bound by him to 'keep her sole and marry not', a device often used with a wife's consent in order to keep the inheritance whole for their sons, and she was made one of his executors, responsible for carrying out his last wishes.[38] No doubt she grieved. But Katherine, like her mother, was also practical. Her sons were both minors, and Henry, the elder, was now a Crown ward. If she wanted to retain control of his upbringing and of the estates she needed to purchase his wardship. This wasn't only a matter of money, but of patronage. The king needed to be persuaded that this was a good political move.

Fortunately, Katherine was well connected. Since entering Queen Kathryn's household she had been exposed to a network of men and women who espoused religiously progressive views, and had gradually become one of them.[39] She exchanged letters, gifts and visits with Anne Seymour, Countess of Hertford; she stood godmother to Jane Dudley, Viscountess Lisle's baby daughter in November 1545, hosting a gathering for friends at her own house in London after the ceremony.[40] Suffolk had not been strongly religiously conservative, but he had not been of a strongly evangelical persuasion either.[41] Now Katherine rearranged her household to suit her as a widow and began employing those whose beliefs were closer to her own, evolving faith. Her jointure estates included a number of Church benefices, and she was able to begin appointing evangelical priests to the churches on her lands.[42] Within a year she was able to secure her son Henry's wardship for the princely sum of £1,500, and of the seven men who stood as guarantees for her payments to the Crown, six were among the most prominent religious reformers at court.[43]

The handle was turned and the ropes creaked. Thomas Wriothesley, the lord chancellor, spoke again, raising his voice over the noise of the rack and of a woman in pain. She must tell them who maintained her in her heresy. Who was part of her 'sect'? Were they privy councillors? Who had sent her money? Which gentlewomen? The Duchess of Suffolk? The Countess of Sussex? Of Hertford? Lady Denny? Lady Fitzwilliam?[44]

Anne Askew remained silent. They had been through this already, and she had denied that any of these elite courtier women had had anything to do with her or her beliefs. For hours, Wriothesley and Sir Richard Rich had interrogated her in this small room. So often the mere sight of the rack was enough to inspire prisoners to speak. Not so for Anne. Though it was a bright July day the only light came from candles, flickering into dark corners, glinting malevolently on the whites of the men's eyes and the gold touches on their clothing. Anne did not want to die, but since it seemed to be God's will that she should, at least she would not die apostate with lies on her tongue.

So she 'lay still and did not cry'. The men were so infuriated with her silence that they stood over her and turned the handle on the rack themselves until she was 'nigh dead'. When – eventually – the lieutenant of the Tower loosed her bonds, she lost consciousness. She came to on the bare floor, cold against the burning pain of her body, unable to move. Lord Chancellor Wriothesley was sat on a chair, a looming spectre. For two more hours he 'reasoned' with her, trying to persuade her, through a haze of pain, to recant her heretical opinions.[45] Though she knew that she faced death by burning, she would not give way.

274 THE WAITING GAME

By rights Anne should not have been racked at all. She was a woman, for a start. Women were not tortured. She was also of gentry status, an ancient Lincolnshire family, her brothers in service with the king at court.[46] An educated woman, she had come to London after the breakdown of her marriage and had become part of a growing evangelical community there at a time when religious divisions were growing increasingly fraught.[47] Back in the mid-1530s, many with progressive views had thought that their time had come: they could finally follow in the footsteps of Martin Luther and other continental reformers. The legislation passed had initially appeared to confirm this. The monasteries were dissolved, shrines and relics desecrated, and the Bible was printed in English for everybody to read. But there it had stopped. On the face of it, religious policy had even appeared to backtrack. Where the Ten Articles of 1536 had laid emphasis on scripture as the foundation of faith and had accepted the doctrine of justification of faith alongside the efficacy of good works, the Six Articles of 1539 – his father's 'six fists', as Edward VI would later call it – firmly reasserted the centrality of the mass and of transubstantiation alongside other more traditional doctrines. Appalled by the audacity of lay people to interpret the Bible in ways that did not support the royal supremacy, an Act was passed in 1542 which restricted its reading.[48] Katherine, Duchess of Suffolk and the other women at court were no longer permitted to read the Bible together in groups, only silently as individuals; there was to be no discussion of scripture. Women below the rank of nobility were no longer allowed to read it at all.

Whether the king was trying to steer some sort of middle way or whether there were factions bouncing him from pillar to post is difficult to ascertain, and was perhaps even difficult to fathom for those who lived through this time.[49] But despite the increasingly draconian measures, at the beginning of 1546 there were plenty of people in the queen's household who were keen to discuss religion. The entire day was structured around it. There was scriptural study, study of the Psalms and the gospels, and afternoon sermons.[50] By this time Queen Kathryn herself had written and anonymously published two religious texts.[51] Katherine, Duchess of Suffolk was at the forefront of the circle of reformist believers around the queen. In fact her own former chaplain, John Parkhurst, who would later go into exile under the Catholic Queen Mary I, was now in the queen's employ.[52] Katherine was a patroness of reformist writers like John Bale, and by those who liked her she was called a 'godly woman', a 'great professor and patroness of true religion'.[53] There were plenty who did not like her at all. Katherine's sharp tongue did not endear her to her conservative peers. She had long been at loggerheads with Stephen Gardiner, Bishop of Winchester, one of the architects of Anne Askew's arrest. At a dinner given by Katherine and her husband in 1545, Suffolk had enlivened the occasion by asking the ladies to choose the man they 'loved best' as their dinner partner, and then refused all invitations himself. Katherine, deprived of her own husband, asked Gardiner to partner her; if she couldn't have the man she loved best, she declared, she would have the one she 'loved the worst' instead.[54]

Paradoxically, the experience of formal religion in the chapel royal at court was much the same as it had been before the break with Rome. Holy days remained in place. Traditional ceremonies remained, too; there were palms on Palm Sunday, ashes on Ash Wednesday, and the king even crept to the cross, literally crawling down the nave of the chapel while meditating on the wounds of Christ, on Good Friday. The king was resistant to changing the pattern of religious ceremony that provided such a stage for royal majesty and magnificence.[55] But Anne Askew's arrest and interrogation shows that the atmosphere was a little different in the city of London. In fact, Anne had already been arrested once previously, in March 1545, but Edmund Bonner, Bishop of London had let her go. Then Askew was only a small fish in a bigger pond of heresy. In April 1546, though, prominent evangelical preacher Edward Crome had given a provocative and public sermon at St Paul's Cross in London in which he openly denied transubstantiation, the Real Presence in the bread and wine of the mass. This precipitated a crackdown on evangelical heresy in the city, and this was the context in which Askew was arrested for the second time, this time by the Privy Council, in May 1546.[56]

The Privy Council was not only interested in heresy in London, but in those at court who might be encouraging it. Katherine, Duchess of Suffolk's nemesis Bishop Gardiner led the charge. He and others with similar views were keen to remove evangelical influence from around the king, knowing that this would be crucial to the balance of power in the next reign, the inevitable minority of the eight-year-old King Edward VI. They knew that much of this centred on Queen Kathryn Parr, who had proved her mettle as queen regent once already, and it's probable that Gardiner and his cronies would have liked to remove the queen herself if only they could find a way to do so. They had thought that Anne Askew might be the way. Perhaps certain of the king's councillors had learned lessons from the rest of the reign, because they sought to use Askew not to target the queen herself – too obvious – but the women around her. Some of them no doubt remembered the case of Elizabeth Barton, the nun of Kent, who had had so many noble supporters back in the 1530s; or else, perhaps more likely, they had heard rumours that certain female courtiers had been in contact with Askew.[57] This was too opportunistic to have been a carefully laid plot, and moreover, they were not wholly wrong about Askew's connections. According to Askew's maid, the Countess of Hertford and Lady Denny had indeed sent her money.[58] Her links to Katherine, Duchess of Suffolk were even stronger. Katherine also hailed from Lincolnshire. She was a patron of Hugh Latimer, a leader in the London network of reformers. Askew's sister Jane was married to George St Poll, a lawyer in the duchess's service. Damningly, Katherine was later said to have arranged interviews between Askew and the queen before Askew's arrest.[59]

If true, this might be why Askew bravely refused to implicate the Duchess of Suffolk even under torture, an echo of the way in which the nun of Kent had protected Gertrude, Marchioness of Exeter back in 1534. The Privy Council got nowhere with its interrogation. Askew was sent to the pyre in early July 1546, her body so damaged from the rack that she had to be carried there on a chair.[60] She was viewed by her evangelical peers as a martyr, killed for refusing to surrender her denial of transubstantiation. We can't be sure whether Katherine, Duchess of Suffolk or any of the other court women also believed this. At this stage in 1546 none had yet directly stated that they did not believe in the Real Presence – not surprisingly, given Askew's end – but only a year later many were openly sympathetic. For Katherine, her colleagues and the queen it didn't end there. Askew's death did not stop them from discussing and sharing religious books. Katherine was thought to be a particularly strong influence with the queen in this regard. By 1546 she had a copy of Tyndale's New Testament, and her library included many other evangelical texts. Protestant martyrologist John Foxe and Jesuit Robert Persons both later wrote that she was instrumental in disseminating many of these.[61]

By now King Henry was often ill and in pain from his ulcerated leg and excruciating headaches. Henry's pain was never only his own; he made it into a problem for those around him. To distract him, Queen Kathryn did what she did best, discussing religion and disputing with the king on knotty theological points. After one sharp discussion in the presence of Stephen Gardiner, Henry waited until Queen Kathryn had left and exclaimed sarcastically, 'A good hearing it is when women become such clerks, and a thing much to my comfort, to come in mine old days to be taught by my wife.'[62]

Gardiner was never one to lose an opportunity. He stoked the king's rage, and obtained his permission to draw up articles charging the queen with heresy. Well aware of the religious activities of her ladies-in-waiting and confident of finding illegal texts, he also ordered a search of the belongings of three of her women 'who they knew to be great with her, and of her blood': the queen's sister Lady Anne Herbert, her cousin Lady Maud Lane and Lady Elizabeth Tyrwhit, all reformist sympathisers. This, along with their arrest, ought to provide enough ammunition to justify an arrest of the queen herself. Like a spider in its web, the king rarely left his chambers, and so Queen Kathryn continued to visit with him and to debate religious matters. Now keen to see how far she would go, the king encouraged her. He even told his physician Dr Wendy about it. While the queen suffered a bout of illness brought on by discovering the articles against her, Dr Wendy confided the king's plot to her.

Katherine, Duchess of Suffolk and the rest of the queen's women were immediately ordered by her to 'convey away their books, which were against the law'. On her next visit to the king Queen Kathryn discussed instead the inferiority of women, and declared that she had only ever seemed to dispute with Henry to distract him from his pain, and because she sought to learn from his wise answers. Forgiven, she concocted a new plot with the king: on the next day, the day on which she had been due to be arrested, she came to the king's privy garden with the three women who had likewise been in danger. When the lord chancellor arrived to arrest them the king shouted at him, calling him 'arrant knave, beast and fool'.

The story comes to us from John Foxe, writing during Mary's and Elizabeth's reigns. Its veracity has been a matter for debate, not least because it's the earliest account of these events, which were not mentioned by anybody writing contemporaneously. But Foxe's source, he stated, was 'certain of her ladies and gentlewomen being yet alive, which were then present about her'. Of the three women specifically targeted in this episode, Elizabeth Tyrwhit is the most likely source, since she was the only one still alive when Foxe published his account in 1570, and was linked to him through John Field, another Protestant writer. But Foxe spoke of ladies in the plural. This could easily have been Katherine, Duchess of Suffolk, in whose household Foxe sojourned during 1550, and who would most certainly have known of these events from the queen.[63]

Where once the queen's ladies-in-waiting had been mere scenery, important in their role as the queen's confidantes and companions but perceived merely as window-dressing, they were now understood as political players in their own right. They functioned as a route to the queen for patronage purposes; but, more nefariously, they were now also perceived to be legitimate targets for arrest, questioning, even execution. Where once employment in the queen's service had been merely a route to a better marriage, now it was, quite literally, a matter of life and death.

The summer and autumn passed a shade more calmly. Katherine, Duchess of Suffolk remained at court with the queen among her 'ordinary' ladies-in-waiting. In that capacity she was present at the banquets held for the French embassy in August, arranged for the official ratification of the treaty between England and France concerning the future of Boulogne.[64] As ever, the king was determined that the English outshine the French. The queen and the royal children received new clothes and jewels for the occasion, and no doubt Katherine and the rest of the queen's women wore their finest. Chronicler Edward Hall wrote with world-weariness, 'to tell you of the costly banquet houses that were built, and of the great banquets, the costly masques, the liberal huntings . . . you would much marvel and scant believe'.[65] Perhaps Katherine as well as Hall found it indescribable.

At some stage after this, Katherine was given permission to leave the court temporarily and return home to Lincolnshire to her two small sons.[66] No doubt she needed a rest, and it was understood that noblewomen like Katherine had responsibilities outside the court that must periodically be dealt with in person. She and her husband had enlarged and renovated their home Grimsthorpe Castle a few years previously. Now it was an impressive two-storey building faced in pale limestone, with crenellated towers and four wings around a courtyard. It was soaked in Katherine's family history; she had inherited Grimsthorpe from her father, and the great hall was hung with tapestries given to her late husband by his first wife Mary, the French queen, by whom Katherine had been raised.[67] Christmas and New Year were spent quietly. Katherine will have given and received gifts from friends, family and associates, and she may well have welcomed many of her local clients and tenants to the hall at Grimsthorpe for a holiday meal. There would be accounts to check and sign off, petitions to answer, instructions to give to her estate officers.

Katherine was still in Lincolnshire in mid-January 1547 when a messenger from the queen arrived.[68] This, in itself, wasn't unusual. Katherine and the queen were friends, and messages regularly passed between them when they were apart.[69] But this messenger almost certainly carried bad news. The king's health had been concerning for over a year. The ulcer on his leg gave him periodic attacks of fever. While Anne Askew was racked in the Tower in early July 1546, Henry was sick all night with colic.[70] By November he could no longer walk and was wheeled about his palaces in a chair.[71] Shortly after removing to Whitehall in late December, he had his worst episode yet: a fever that raged for thirty hours and left him exhausted and weak.[72] The royal couple had spent Christmas separately, probably at the king's instigation, and this may well have caused Queen Kathryn considerable anxiety. Since her almost-arrest in the summer she had spent little time away from her husband, knowing that her presence by his side was her best chance of avoiding a repeated threat.[73] At the end of December the king had dictated a new will.[74] By 10 January, Queen Kathryn had sent servants to move her things to Westminster to join her husband, only to find that he would not allow her to see him.[75] It was shortly after this that she sent her messenger to Katherine, Duchess of Suffolk.

It's likely that her message was a summons. If Queen Kathryn thought she might be in danger, or if the king was dying, she needed her closest friend. And things did not look good. The king did not leave his private chambers. He gave no audiences, granted no access except to his doctors, those of the privy chamber who saw to his bodily needs, and certain of his privy councillors. On 23 January he revealed the names of those he had chosen to form a regency council after his death; at night on the 27th, he died.

The king's death was kept secret for three days. We don't know whether the queen and her women knew about it before it was made public on 31 January. On that same day, the names of those appointed to the regency council were also announced, and the queen was not among them. One of Henry's last acts had been to shut his wife out of power. Instead, Edward Seymour, Earl of Hertford – the new king's uncle, and a friend of both the queen and the Duchess of Suffolk – proclaimed himself Lord Protector of England and Duke of Somerset. He had fetched Prince Edward from his house in Hertfordshire the previous Friday, and the new king was now lodged in the Tower for security's sake.[76]

The death of a king was not a time to pause and breathe, no matter the circumstances. While the new king was publicly proclaimed across London and the council began preparations for the funeral, the queen's household immediately went into mourning. Queen Kathryn had her jewels sent to the Tower and donned black clothing.[77] Changes were inevitable for the queen and the women around her. Queen Kathryn was now the queen dowager. Her household would be downsized accordingly: Katherine, Duchess of Suffolk was probably out of a job. Nor could the queen remain at Westminster or, in the long term, any of the royal palaces. Katherine probably helped her as she made preparations to move the short distance from Westminster to St James's Palace, where her servants draped the chambers and galleries in black cloth.[78]

Peers and peeresses were summoned to London, lodged, and clothed in black. Seventy-four London suppliers provided 33,000 yards of black cloth. The king's body lay in state in its coffin in the privy chamber at Whitehall and mourners held vigil, overlooked by the alarmingly life-sized mural of the king painted on the wall there by Holbein. The king had requested burial in St George's Chapel at Windsor, next to his third and favourite wife Jane Seymour, mother of the new king. All of the roads between Westminster and Windsor were mended, overhanging trees and hedges cut back so as not to catch and tear the banners as they passed. The king's coffin was draped in black cloth of gold and topped with an effigy of the king in life, dressed in rich fabrics and jewels and wearing an Imperial crown 'of inestimable value'. The whole travelled on a large gold chariot, drawn by seven horses trapped in black.[79]

Katherine, Duchess of Suffolk was not part of the lengthy funeral procession that accompanied the king's corpse first to Syon, and then the next day to Windsor. Queens did not play an active part in kings' funerals, and so Queen Kathryn and her women travelled separately to the chapel. After days of masses and offerings, the time for burial drew nigh. Katherine, outfitted in sixteen yards of black cloth, stood close to the queen in the royal closet above the chapel.[80] They had a discreet bird's eye view of the entire spectacle, watching through the oriel windows along-side the rest of the queen's women, nobles and 'notable strangers', foreign visitors to the realm.[81] The closet had been built for Queen Catherine of Aragon. It was still covered in her cipher and her pomegranate badge, proclaiming the king's first marriage. Katherine had been named for this queen. Did she notice these now as she stood with Queen Kathryn Parr, watching the committal of the man who had caused such anguish to so many women? Did she think about the bonds between those women? Her own mother, María de Salinas, had come over from Spain with Catherine of Aragon for her marriage to the king, and had attended her as he married another and betrayed her. Now María's daughter helped that queen's successor to bury that same king.

Ashes to ashes, and dust to dust. The snaps of a dozen staves of office rang through the chapel, and they were thrown into the vault. The circle was complete. Katherine and her mistress had survived the waiting game.

Epilogue

A king without a queen was not in need of ladies-in-waiting, and a king who was nine years old was most certainly not yet in need of a queen. It was time for Kathryn Parr's household to disperse. Most of the ladies-in-waiting were dismissed to wend their way home. A wages list covering the second quarter of the year from March to midsummer 1547 shows that ten women remained, all of whom were already in Queen Kathryn's service. A degree of kinship connection was maintained. The list was headed by 'Mistress Cobham', who was in fact Elizabeth Brooke, the daughter of Baron Cobham and the mistress of the queen's brother William Parr.[1] By Michaelmas, ten women had become thirteen, and the divisions between household ranks were reinstated correctly: four gentlewomen, seven maids of honour and two chamberers.[2]

But this didn't mean that Katherine, Duchess of Suffolk's job was done. Though she was no longer among the queen dowager's ladies-in-waiting, she was still her friend. After King Henry's funeral she remained in London at her own house, the Barbican. Even if Queen Kathryn had not needed her, her own son Henry, now Duke of Suffolk, did; he had been given a prominent role in Edward VI's coronation on 20 February, carrying the orb in the procession. Both of her sons were made Knights of the Bath in the traditional night-long ritual before the coronation itself.[3]

By the middle of April, Queen Kathryn was packing up at St James's Palace. A queen dowager must live on her own dower estates, and Kathryn had chosen to move to her house at Chelsea.[4] Her reason for staying close to London was clear: he was tall, handsome, and his name was Sir Thomas Seymour. She had wanted to marry him before the king intervened in 1543. Now the relationship resumed and went further. Before long they were lovers. Katherine, Duchess of Suffolk, as the queen's closest friend bar her sister Lady Herbert, was soon brought into the secret. Messengers went between Chelsea and the Barbican with regularity. In a letter reassuring Seymour that she had wanted to marry him back in 1543 but God's will, in the form of marriage to the king, had intervened, Queen Kathryn remarked, 'I can say nothing but, as my lady of Suffolk saith, "God is a marvelous man."'[5] A little later Seymour wrote to Kathryn, 'I presume I have my lady of Suffolk's goodwill touching mine own desire of you'; the other day she had told his friend Sir William Sharington 'that she would that I were married to their mistress'.[6]

The marriage took place in secret, probably in May.[7] Katherine, Duchess of Suffolk, probably knew about it; she was probably present. But things were complicated. A queen was supposed to spend time in mourning for her husband, the late king. To marry again so soon – less than six months after the king's death – would be considered indecent, dishonouring his memory. And so it transpired. They got permission from the young king retroactively but without telling him that the marriage had already occurred, and he was not pleased. The king's uncle Edward Seymour, Protector Somerset's initial enthusiasm likewise turned to strong disapproval.[8]

It took time for the furore to settle down, and for most of that time Katherine, Duchess of Suffolk seems to have remained in London, visiting the queen regularly.[9] London was full of noblewomen, for though there was no longer a queen's household at court there were still female courtiers, and it was still important to stay in touch with the centre of power. The households of Princesses Mary and Elizabeth remained significant. Kathryn, as queen dowager, still had a complement of women. And Protector Somerset's wife, Anne Stanhope, Duchess of Somerset built up something like a rival court as the wife of the man at the head of governance.[10] Anne had been one of Queen Kathryn Parr's most senior women, alongside the Duchess of Suffolk and others. She has gone down in history as a 'shrew', partly because she was portrayed in that way by Elizabethan writers like John Foxe.[11] The fact remains that she and Kathryn Parr did not like one another, and this developed into a genuine feud in the spring of 1547. One of Kathryn's letters to Thomas Seymour suggested that Anne had taught her husband Protector Somerset to break promises, 'for it is her custom to promise many comings to her friends, and to perform none'.[12] Their mutual dislike could not have been openly expressed while Kathryn was queen and Anne was in her service, but it was spat out now like a sour cherry and shows how the relationship between mistress and lady-in-waiting could turn bitter.

Katherine, Duchess of Suffolk, though, remained close to Queen Kathryn even after they were geographically further distant. By June 1548 Queen Kathryn was six months pregnant with Seymour's child, and on Wednesday the 13th the couple travelled west to Seymour's new country residence, Sudeley Castle, on the northern edge of the Cotswolds.[13] After a gentle, golden summer, she was brought to bed on 30 August and gave birth to a healthy baby girl whom she named Mary. But all was not well. Like her predecessor Jane Seymour, Queen Kathryn's health worsened in the days following the birth. She told her attendant Lady Tyrwhit that she was sure she could not live. On 5 September, 'between two and three of the clock in the morning', she died.[14]

Did Katherine attend her friend's funeral? We don't know. She will have watched, however, as Thomas Seymour went off the rails, his wife's death leaving him without anchor. He began plotting a coup against his brother, Protector Somerset, whom he blamed for his own exclusion from the king's Privy Council. In his wild state he lost all caution. The plot found its way to his brother's ears. Arrested on 17 January 1549, he was executed on Tower Hill on 20 March. One of his last requests was that his baby daughter Mary might be raised by her mother's friend, Katherine, Duchess of Suffolk.[15] Katherine duly took baby Mary into her household at Grimsthorpe, though not without several plaintive letters to secretary William Cecil and Protector Somerset about the need for

money to support the child.[16] This notwithstanding, she kept Mary
in her household for a full year or more, until the child disappears
from all surviving records.[17] Almost certainly, she had died before
her third birthday.

Edward's reign did at least bring with it the fresh wind of further religious reform. By 1547 it is clear that Katherine no longer
believed in transubstantiation, the Real Presence in the Eucharist,
and was prepared to say so publicly now that this was increasingly
permissible. In 1547 alone she encouraged and then sponsored the
publication of her friend Queen Kathryn's most reformist work
yet, *The Lamentation of a Sinner*.[18] She also continued to be rude
to Stephen Gardiner; walking past the chamber in which he was
imprisoned in the Tower of London in 1550, she commented loudly
that 'it was merry with the lambs when the wolf was shut up'.[19]

What of the other women we have met? Greater religious
reform under Edward VI was a boon to Mary Howard, Duchess of
Richmond too. The transfer of power between monarchs had been
a difficult time for Mary and her family. She had not served Queen
Kathryn Parr as a lady-in-waiting 'in ordinary', though she had
appeared from time to time in 'extraordinary' service. She spent
the last years of King Henry's reign living in her father the Duke
of Norfolk's home in Kenninghall in Suffolk, which chafed her
independence. Mary never remarried, and though she received her
jointure she appears to have lived in debt.[20] In 1546 her father and
brother had come under royal suspicion, in no small part because
of her brother the Earl of Surrey's unguarded and ill-advised use
of royal arms at a time of royal paranoia over the succession,
alongside his boasts about his father's likely pre-eminence in the
forthcoming royal minority. Reported by one of his friends, Sir
Richard Southwell, the earl was arrested in December 1546. Those
of the Privy Council who did not relish the thought of Norfolk's
conservative presence for the future did not hesitate to make the
most of this, with the result that Norfolk too was arrested.[21]

Mary learned of this when royal commissioners arrived at Kenninghall to turn them out and to inventory their belongings. A
consummate courtier, she fell to her knees, trembling, and vowed

to keep back no piece of information that might aid the investigation. When questioned, though, she did precisely this: used obfuscation and vagueness to turn questions about her brother's heraldry and to save her father, who she understood was the prime target here. Her brother was executed on 19 January 1547. Her father's death warrant was signed on 27 January, the night of the king's death; but the new regime thought it best not to begin with bloodshed and he was allowed to live, albeit imprisoned in the Tower.[22]

Her father's imprisonment paradoxically allowed Mary greater freedom to explore her religious convictions, and she took full advantage. Like the Duchess of Suffolk, she spent time raising children: she was given custody of her nephews and nieces, her brother the Earl of Surrey's children. In line with her beliefs, she appointed the evangelical John Foxe as their tutor. While in her household he wrote his first draft of his infamous *Book of Martyrs*. Mary also harboured writer John Bale on his return from exile in 1547, and had many Protestant works dedicated to her.[23] Mary died sometime in 1555 and was buried alongside her husband Henry Fitzroy in St Michael's Church in Framlingham, Suffolk.

For Mary's mother, too, the Duke of Norfolk's arrest proved freeing. Elizabeth, Duchess of Norfolk had spent the rest of Henry's reign in her house at Redbourn, Hertfordshire, resigned to her 'prisonment'. She, did, however, welcome some of her nieces into her household, and she remained in touch with family and friends by letter. After her husband's arrest her allowance was paid instead by the Privy Council, and she was given permission to visit London. The accession of Mary I in 1553 saw her return to something of her old prominence; she carried the queen's train at her coronation. Elizabeth finally did gain access to her jointure estates after her husband's death in 1554 and was restored to the bosom of her family, standing godmother to her grandson Philip, the future Earl of Arundel, at St Clement Danes Church in London in 1558. She died the same year, only weeks after Elizabeth I's accession, and was buried in the Howard family chapel at St Mary's, Lambeth under a stone with a laudatory inscription composed by her brother Henry, Lord Stafford, who circumspectly wrote nothing about his sister's headstrong nature.[24]

Gertrude Blount, Marchioness of Exeter followed a similar path. Having been imprisoned during the years of the Exeter Conspiracy in the late 1530s, she was released by the end of 1539, and it's unclear quite how she spent the reign of Edward VI. Her own son Edward remained imprisoned in the Tower, as he had been for most of his young life. He was too valuable a pawn and had too much Yorkist blood in his veins to be allowed to run loose and create a new royal line. Everything changed, though, on Mary I's accession in 1553. Gertrude featured prominently in the procession at her entry into the city of London in early August, riding only a few places behind the queen herself and directly following the Princess Elizabeth. Then, joy: on reaching the Tower, the queen publicly released and pardoned Edward along with other political prisoners. Mother and son were summoned to court and honoured.[25] The golden days had arrived.

Gertrude's influence during the beginning of Mary I's reign was considerable, sought by her friends and distrusted by her enemies, and many thought that her son Edward was a natural husband for the queen. Unfortunately, the queen disagreed. Appalled by this refusal, Gertrude left court. Edward was shortly sent abroad to Charles V's court, a means to keep him away from the English throne. After a time, Gertrude, always wily and strategic, was readmitted to the queen's service where she worked hard to restore Mary's goodwill towards her son, whom she missed unbearably. She became afraid she would die before she saw him again, but in the event it was the other way round: Edward died unexpectedly in Italy on 18 September 1556. Gertrude's last years are shadowy. Her health continued to decline, and she made a will on 25 September 1557. Before 8 January 1558 she had died, and was buried in Wimborne Minster in Dorset.[26]

The two Basset sisters, Anne and Katharine, also continued their roles as female courtiers. Anne Basset, the bold, ambitious, younger sister, received clothing from the Crown by warrant throughout 1546, but she did not remain in Queen Kathryn Parr's service after King Henry's death.[27] She was, however, granted an annuity of £26 13s 4d by King Edward, which was to be paid half-yearly during the king's minority.[28] She reappeared in royal service at Queen Mary's accession as a lady of the privy chamber – an elevation in rank likely down to her age, since she was now in her early thirties, and experience – and was granted the same annuity by the new queen. Within a year, she had finally obtained the goal of so many ladies-in-waiting: a good marriage. On 7 June 1554 she married Walter Hungerford, one of the gentlemen pensioners twelve years her junior, in the queen's chapel at Richmond Palace. Within three years she had died.[29] Her older, gentler sister Katharine remained in Anna of Cleves' service for the remainder of King Henry's reign, but on 8 December 1547 she married Henry Ashley, Esquire, of Hever in Kent, a man she had evidently met while in Anna's household there. Her death is not recorded, but was after 1558 when she was mentioned in her brother James's will.[30]

The longest-lived of all of the women we have met was Katherine, Duchess of Suffolk, of the sharp tongue, fiery temper and progressive religion. With little recourse to the royal court after Queen Kathryn Parr's death in 1548, she spent much of her time at Grimsthorpe, her home in Lincolnshire. Her two sons, Henry and Charles, were educated along reformist lines at St John's College, Cambridge, but in 1551 disaster struck. Sweating sickness broke out in the university city, the same disease of which chronicler Edward Hall wrote that one might be 'merry at dinner and dead by supper'.[31] Katherine had been staying at her home in Kingston, Cambridgeshire. Knowing the danger, she immediately had her sons removed to the Bishop of Lincoln's palace at Buckden in Huntingdonshire – the same house in which Queen Catherine of Aragon had once been imprisoned – but she herself fell ill, albeit not from the sweating sickness. By the time she had recovered sufficiently to visit her sons on 14 July, Henry was dead and Charles was dying. In the space of a few hours she had lost both her children.[32]

It is hard to imagine the depth of her grief. She may have found consolation in an unlikely quarter; at some point in 1552 she married for a second time, to her gentleman usher Richard Bertie. Like her former mistress Queen Kathryn Parr she had made a love match to please herself, but, unlike the queen's, Katherine's proved fruitful and long-lasting. Bertie's religious sympathies matched her own, and the accession of Mary I was not good news for them. Under pressure to accept the return to Catholicism, they chose exile instead.

This was not an easy option. For all that the queen did not want Protestants in her realm, she did not want them to leave and spread their heresy either. Bertie left first. To get out of the country, Katherine disguised herself and her baby daughter Susan and one of her maids and left the Barbican in the darkness of the very early morning. The Barbican was next door to Garter House, the home of the Garter herald, and he had been set to keep watch on her by her enemies. Hearing noise as she and her small company left the house, he came out of his own with a torch. Horrified, Katherine sent the men of her company ahead and took only her daughter and the two women with her. Followed by the herald, she stepped into a doorway of Garter House so that he could not see her. Thinking she had already left, the herald returned to his own entrance and Katherine got safely away.

The couple's time abroad was chronicled by Richard Bertie and incorporated into John Foxe's *Book of Martyrs* in its 1570 edition.[33] Their son, born during that time, was named Peregrine in honour of their travels. From Wesel to Strasbourg to Frankfurt, they travelled Europe's most Protestant provinces, winding up as guests of the Polish king at the time of Queen Mary's death in England in November 1558. Returning to England a year later, it soon became clear that Katherine's Protestant – even Calvinist – beliefs had outstripped those of most other English reformers. Though Queen Elizabeth restored the Protestant state to a degree, it did not go far enough for those who had experienced a more stringent form of Protestantism on the continent. Katherine never returned to service as a lady-in-waiting. By the late 1570s her health was deteriorating, and she died at Grimsthorpe on 19 September 1580.

Surviving the waiting game took courage, audacity, talent and a degree of luck. At the start of Henry VIII's reign it was broadly the same game it had always been: ladies-in-waiting attended the queen as she moved between the birthing chamber, diplomatic audiences and courtly entertainments. By the end of the reign in 1547 it had evolved into something darker and more dangerous. The choices that ladies-in-waiting were forced to make could put their very lives at risk.

In such challenging circumstances different individuals made different choices. The stories uncovered here show how many factors went into a woman's experience as a lady-in-waiting during this era, and how her connections, her principles and her character might shape her life differently from those of her colleagues. Much of women's history leans on a trope of 'exceptional' women: 'girlbosses' who achieved incredible things against the impossibly patriarchal odds of their day. Such women did, of course, exist, and we should celebrate them. But we could easily describe all women in the past in this way. All of the women in *The Waiting Game* existed close to the centre of power and acted in ways that influenced the broader historical narrative. All occasionally stepped outside the boundaries that society allegedly dictated for their sex. And perhaps this is the point. These boundaries were less rigid in practice than in theory, and in many cases 'exceptional' women were, in fact, not so exceptional. *The Waiting Game* shows that if we simply allow women to exist in the past on their own terms there is no need for explicit 'girlbossification'; they are a fascinating historical lens in their own right. Women's history does not need to be exceptional to be relevant.

All the ladies-in-waiting we have met here were strong, determined, intelligent women whose experiences shine light onto the varying aspects of a lady-in-waiting's role. María de Salinas, Lady Willoughby shows us how women could mobilise their contacts to fight complex legal suits and manage their lands, but that they could just as easily be 'bad' landlords as good. Women could be villains as well as victims, sometimes both simultaneously, and could simply make bad decisions like everybody else; Jane Parker,

Viscountess Rochford's involvement in Queen Anne Boleyn and Queen Katherine Howard's downfalls could be read as an example of all three things. Some were thoughtful, cautious and wily, seeking ways to achieve their own ends while remaining on the right side of royal favour; this was Gertrude Blount, Marchioness of Exeter's usual *modus operandi*, standing godmother to royal children and toeing the line while also passing information to the king's enemies. Others found it impossible to be so politically or personally circumspect. Elizabeth Stafford, Duchess of Norfolk suffered many years of ostracism for speaking too freely in support of Queen Catherine of Aragon, and for refusing to accept her own husband's infidelity. Her daughter Mary, Duchess of Richmond used the same determination more effectively, to shine in her cousin Queen Anne Boleyn's household, to successfully defy the king in the matter of her remarriage, and to pursue reformed religion in the face of her father's disapproval. Katherine Willoughby, Duchess of Suffolk followed the new reformist religion too, while Honor, Lady Lisle found herself in trouble for adhering to the old ways.

After the hiatus of Edward VI's reign, ladies-in-waiting returned under queens regnant Mary I and Elizabeth I in turn. Their father's reign had shown how significant, even dangerous ladies-in-waiting could be; now both of his daughters capitalised on this, using the women in their service to further their own political ends. Ladies-in-waiting had always functioned as a connection between the queen and the world outside her privy chamber, acting as barometers of her mood. Now the queen's mood was more important than ever before, since she ruled the whole country by herself, and so the role of her ladies-in-waiting as 'information brokers' correspondingly rose.[34] Spanish ambassador Simon Renard fretted about what advice Queen Mary's ladies were giving her about marriage. Queen Elizabeth deliberately used her women as private diplomatic agents in her many marriage suits; they would, apparently on their own initiative, covertly mention Elizabeth's keenness to the relevant ambassador, who would therefore continue to press the suit, maintaining a diplomatic alliance until it suited the queen to break it off, at which point she would claim innocently that her ladies had acted without her authority. The queen's secretaries deliberately cultivated relationships with particular ladies-in-waiting so that they might know when best to approach the queen over any given issue, and when it would be better not to walk into a storm of the queen's temper. The ladies themselves used their close connection to the queen to further their own ends, assured of her favour in lawsuits, family disputes and matters of debt. To be the queen's lady-in-waiting was to be a person of significance, and everybody knew it.

These women's long-standing ability to fade into the background has served them well. To follow them as a historian is often to see them slide out of view as soon as one tries to focus the lens. But allowing light into the darker corners of any history illuminates more than just one frame. To tell Henry's reign from the perspective of ladies-in-waiting is to see the familiar become unfamiliar. We were never supposed to know these stories like this. It's important that we do.

Acknowledgements

This is the book I have wanted to write since I was a teenager, reading history books and wondering where all the girls were. I'm incredibly lucky to have been able to do it like this, and have enjoyed (almost) every moment of it (footnotes aside). Like all books, it's been years in the making, and a huge number of people have helped it and me on our way. Numerous colleagues and friends read chapters, advised on the publishing process, shared and discussed source material and general writing wisdom; thanks particularly to Sophie Ambler, Nicole Bertzen, Kirsten Claiden-Yardley, Vanessa de Cruz Medina, Heather Darsie, Caroline Dunn, Joanne Edge, José Escribano Páez, Catherine Fletcher, Rafael M. Girón Pascual, Steven Gunn, Courtney Herber, Eva Johanna Holmberg, Lauren Johnson, Lauren Mackay, Rocío Martínez López, Paula Martínez Hernández, Joseph Massey, Shannon McSheffrey, Aidan Norrie, Joanne Paul, Laura Richmond, Gareth Russell, Alexander Samson, Jade Scott and James Taffe. I owe a debt, too, to the many non-Tudor friends who have put up with me and it and me writing it, and cheer-led the whole process: Jennifer and Peyma Barekat, Dion Georgiou and Rachel Topham especially.

My agent Adam Gauntlett and editors Maddy Price and Kate Moreton 'got' what I was trying to do from the beginning and have helped me shape it into the best book it could be – collaborative processes for the win!

To those unnamed souls who made me keep at it out of spite, thank you; rage-writing is surprisingly effective. To the cats who blessed the endeavour by walking over me, my papers and my laptop at various points, we all know that no book is fully complete without feline assistance. Nor could I have kept going without regular doses of caffeine and conversation in Fred's coffee shop in Crofton Park, especially with Annie.

To my sister Lyndsey, here we are yet again. There's no goat in this book as requested because, astonishingly, I couldn't find one. BUT there is a parrot – a different parrot this time – and a nice spaniel.

If I've missed anyone out here it's entirely my own fault for failing to keep track of the many amazing people I have in my professional and personal lives. Any errors that remain in the text are unequivocally my own.

Illustration Credits

Page 7
Above – From the British Library archive / Bridgeman Images
Below – Steve Vidler / Alamy

Page 8
Above – Bill Gloyn
Below – Alex Oliver

Notes

List of Abbreviations

AGS: Archivo General de Simancas, Spain

BL: British Library

CSP Spain: *Calendar of State Papers, Spain*, ed. G. A. Bergenroth et al. (London, 1862–1954), available at British History Online

CSP Venice: *Calendar of State Papers Relating to English Affairs in the Archives of Venice*, ed. Rawdon Brown et al. (London, 1864–1947), available at British History Online

Hall: *Hall's Chronicle; containing the History of England, during the Reign of Henry the Fourth, and the succeeding monarchs, to the end of the reign of Henry the Eighth, in which are particularly described the manners and customs of those periods*, ed. Henry Ellis (London, 1809)

HMC Rutland: *The Manuscripts of His Grace the Duke of Rutland, G.C.B., preserved at Belvoir Castle*, HMC Twelfth Report, Appendix, Part 4 (London, 1888)

Lisle Letters: *The Lisle Letters*, ed. M. St Clare Byrne, 6 vols (Chicago, 1981)

LP: *Letters and Papers, Foreign and Domestic, of the Reign of Henry VIII*, ed. J. S. Brewer et al. (London, 1862–1932)

LRO: Lincoln Record Office

NRO: Norfolk Record Office

ODNB: *Oxford Dictionary of National Biography*

Statutes of the Realm: *The Statutes of the Realm*, ed. T. E. Tomlins and W. E. Taunton, 9 vols (London, 1810–25), III

TNA: The National Archives, Kew

Preface

1   AGS, Estado, 347, no. 68 (Letter of Marquis of Cañete, viceroy of Navarre, to royal secretary Juan Vazquez. Pamplona, June 5th, 1536). The original Spanish is as follows: '[The empress Isabel] me hizo merced con las nuevas de Inglaterra, que aunque acá se habían dicho no tan particularmente, como yo fui hijo de quien fue aya de la reina doña Catalina, no puede suceder caso que pueda ser castigo para aquél rey que no huelgue de ello.' My thanks to José Escribano-Paez for the reference, and to Rocío Martínez López for help with translation.

2   *CSP Spain* I, 288. 'The son of Francisca de Silva' is also on this list as chief cupbearer, so it's possible that Mendoza himself had come to England, though more likely one of his brothers or surely he'd have mentioned that here.

3   For more on this see Barbara Harris, *English Aristocratic Women, 1450–1550* (Oxford, 2002).

4   As the Countesses of Oxford and Worcester did for Anne Boleyn at her coronation in 1533 (BL Harley MS 41, fol. 10). Worcester was Elizabeth Browne; Oxford was most like Anne Howard.

5   John Bellamy, *The Tudor Law of Treason* (London, 1979), pp. 12, 15, 22.

6   There have been article-length studies of groups or individual ladies-in-waiting, such as Harris, *English Aristocratic Women*, pp. 210–40, or Olwen Hufton, 'Reflections on the Role of Women in the Early Modern Court', *Court Historian* 5 (2000), 1–13, or Nicola Clark, *Gender, Family, and Politics: The Howard Women, 1485–1558* (Oxford, 2018), pp. 92–115. Ladies-in-waiting are garnering increasing attention; see, for example, Nadine Akkerman and Birgit Houben, eds, *The Politics of Female Households: Ladies-in-Waiting Across Early Modern Europe* (Leiden, 2013).

7   See Charlotte Merton, 'The Women Who Served Queen Mary and Queen Elizabeth', unpublished PhD dissertation, University of Cambridge (1990).

8   Tim Stretton and Krista Kesselring, eds, *Married Women and the Law: Coverture in England and the Common Law World* (Montreal, 2013).

9   See Nadine Akkerman, *Invisible Agents: Women and Espionage in Seventeenth-Century Britain* (Oxford, 2018), pp. 23–5.

Chapter 1: Brittle Fortune

1   *The Receyt of the Ladie Kateryne*, pp. 45–7.

2   Barbara Harris, 'Vaux [married names Guildford and Poyntz], Lady Jane', *ODNB* https://doi.org/10.1093/odnb/9780198614128.013.900003690

99 (accessed July 2023).

3   Theresa Earenfight, *Catherine of Aragon* (University Park, Pennsylvania, 2021), pp. 55–8, 73–4.

4   Jane's mother was Katherine Peniston. See A. R. Myers, *Crown Household and Parliament in the Fifteenth Century* (London, 1985), pp. 135–210, and A. D. K. Hawkyard, 'Vaux, Sir Nicholas (*c.*1460–1523), of Great Harrowden, Northants.', *The History of Parliament: the House of Commons 1509–1558* https://www.historyofparliamentonline.org/volume/1509-1558/ member/vaux-sir-nicholas-1460-1523#footnote4_6dlr251 (accessed July 2023).

5   On life for women in Queen Isabella's court see Álvaro Fernández de Córdova Miralles, *La Corte de Isabel I* (Madrid, 2002), pp. 160–67. See also Elizabeth Teresa Howe, *Education and Women in the Early Modern Hispanic World* (Aldershot, 2008).

6   María's parents are usually erroneously given as Martín de Salinas and Josefa González de Salas, or simply listed as unknown. See, for instance, Retha Warnicke, 'Willoughby [née de Salinas], Maria, Lady Willoughby de Eresby', *ODNB* https://doi.org/10.1093/ref:odnb/68049 (accessed July 2023) and more recently Theresa Earenfight, 'Raising Infanta Catalina de Aragon to be Catherine, Queen of England', *Anuario de Estudios Medievales* 46:1 (2016), 417–43, and 'A Precarious Household: Catherine of Aragon in England, 1501–1504', in idem., ed., *Royal and Elite Households in Medieval and Early Modern Europe* (Leiden, 2018), pp. 338–56.

7   See forthcoming article by Nicola Clark and Vanessa Cruz de Medina.

8   *CSP Spain* I, 288.

9   *The Receyt*, p. 4.

10 Ibid., pp. 5–8.

11 Ian Mortimer, *The Time Traveller's Guide to Medieval England* (London, 2008), pp, 16–23.

12 *The Receyt*, pp. 9–11.

13 Ibid., pp. 32–3.

14 Imtiaz Habib, *Black Lives in English Archives* (London, 2008), pp. 275–6.

15 *CSP Spain* I, 288.

16 Earenfight, *Catherine of Aragon*, p. 67.

17 *The Receyt*, pp. 39–44.

18 College of Arms MS M8, fols 38v–39; see Lauren Johnson, *Shadow King: The Life and Death of Henry VI* (London, 2019), pp. 242–3.

19 TNA SP1/65, fols 18v–19r (*LP* V, 6 (9)).

20 According to testimony later given by his attendants: TNA SP1/65, fol. 22v (*LP* V, 6 (9)).

21 *Crónica del rey Enrico Octavo de Inglaterra*, Vol. 4, ed. Mariano Roca de

Togores Molíns (Madrid, 1874), pp. 336–7.

22　TNA SP1/65, fols 18v–19r (*LP* V, 6 (9)).

23　*CSP Spain*, Supplement to I and II, no. 1.

24　*CSP Spain* I, 319.

25　*The Receyt*, p. 91. For more on the speculative theories around Arthur's illness and death see Sean Cunningham, *Prince Arthur: The Tudor King Who Never Was* (Stroud, 2016), pp. 167–78.

26　'Item to John Cope of London Taillour for the lynyng and covering of a lyttur of blake veluet with blake cloth for the quene wherein the princes was brought from Ludlowe to London fryngged aboute with blake valance and the twoo hed peces of the same bounden aboute with blake Rebyn and fryngged abowte with blake valance v s' in Elizabeth of York's privy purse account for 1502–3, TNA E36/210, fol. 94.

27　For detailed discussion of the negotiations see Patrick Williams, *Katharine of Aragon* (Stroud, 2013), Chapter 7.

28　AGS, CSR leg. 11, fol. 306.

29　By June 1502 Henry VII was paying a monthly sum for the maintenance of Catherine's household, initially slightly variable, then set at £83 6s 8d until July 1503, when it was raised to £100. The first clear monthly payment is for June 1502 at 100 marks (TNA E101/415/3, fol. 98v). For July, August, September and October 1502 the account specifies 125 marks per month, or £333 6s 8d (ibid., fol. 101r); for November 1502 it is set at £83 6s 8d (BL Add. MS 59899, fol. 3r) and does not change again until July 1503 when there is another lump payment for July, August and September 1503 of £300, i.e. £100 per month (ibid., fol. 27v). Elizabeth of York's privy purse account for 1502–3 documents receipt of £3585 19s 10d *ob* (TNA E36/210, fol. 17).

30　*CSP Spain* I, 394.

31　Ibid., 400.

32　https://dbe.rah.es/biografias/15442/juan-manuel (accessed July 2023).

33　*CSP Spain* I, 439.

34　Ibid., 440.

35　Ibid.

36　Ibid., 431.

37　Ibid., 448.

38　AGS, CSR leg. 11, fol. 314.

39　The last monthly payment of £100 for Catherine's household was made in December 1505. After that date the king's payment books show occasional payments to specific people in her retinue, such as her confessor and the man in charge of her wardrobe, and then in August 1506 he paid the board wages of 'diverse of my Lady Princess's servants' at 51s. This arrangement continued, with him paying for their lodging usually several months at a time, in arrears. TNA E36/214, fols 9v, 24r, 32v, 34v, 39r, 47v, 66v.

40 *CSP Spain* I, 427, 459.

41 AGS, CSR leg. 9, fol. 288 and leg. 11, fols 302–18. Currently in preparation for publication by Nicola Clark and Vanessa de Cruz Medina. With thanks to Paula Martínez Hernández for so kindly sharing her images, and to José Escribano Páez and Vanessa de Cruz Medina for help with transcription and translation.

42 See Martínez Hernández, *El Tesorero Vitoriano Ochoa de Landa: Las cuentas de la casa de Juana I de Castilla (1506–1531)* (Vitoria-Gasteiz, 2020).

43 AGS, CSR leg. 11, fol. 306.

44 *CSP Spain* I, 444, 446. These six women were most likely María de Salinas, María de Salazar, Francisca de Cáceres, Catalina Fortes, Inés de Vanegas and María de Guevara.

45 *CSP Spain* I, 532. It isn't wholly clear which of the previous six women had left by this point. María de Rojas did indeed depart in 1506, but was probably of higher status and not a maid of honour. It may have been María de Salazar, as she was not listed at the coronation in 1509. The chamber account of Henry VII for January 1506 records a payment of 10s for alms for 'the Spanisshe Lady late Decessed', so it is also possible that one of Catherine's maids passed away while in England. TNA E36/214, fol. 16r.

46 *CSP Spain* I, 448.

47 Simon Thurley, *Houses of Power: The Places That Shaped the Tudor World* (London, 2017), pp. 47–53.

48 Earenfight, *Catherine of Aragon*, p. 79.

49 *CSP Spain* I, 513.

50 AGS, CSR leg. 11, fols 306, 317.

51 Ibid., fol. 308.

52 Ibid., fol. 302.

53 Ibid., fol. 306.

54 Ibid., fol. 314.

55 J. Froude, ed., *Life and Letters of Erasmus* (London, 1906), p. 49.

56 AGS, CSR leg. 11, fol. 315.

57 Ibid., fol. 318.

58 Ibid., fol. 306.

59 *CSP Spain* I, 413.

60 Ibid., 439.

61 Her return is often placed earlier, in 1504 or 1505, but she was given £20

'in reward' by Henry VII on 24 April 1506, which shows that she was still in England at that time, and perhaps suggests that that is when she departed. TNA E36/214, fol. 28v.

62 AGS, CSR leg. 11, fol. 302. The Gaona family had a business exporting wool to northern Europe, but they also lent money to the Spanish monarchs, which is probably how María's family knew them. See Javier Goicolea Julián, 'Mercaderes y hombres de negocio: el poder del dinero en el mundo urbano riojano de fines de la Edad Media e inicios de la Edad Moderna', *Hispania: Revista española de historia* 67, no. 227 (2007), 947–92.

63 AGS, CSR leg. 11, fol. 302.

64 Ibid., fol. 306.

65 Ibid.

66 Ibid., fol. 307.

67 *CSP Spain* I, 529.

68 AGS, CSR leg. 11, fol. 314.

Chapter 2: So Much Loyalty

1 Raúl González Arévalo, 'Francesco Grimaldi, un mercader-banquero genovés entre Granada, la corte e Inglaterra (siglos xv–xvi)', *En la Espana Medieval* 39 (2016), 97–126.

2 AGS, CSR leg. 11, fol. 310.

3 Ibid.

4 Ibid., fol. 315.

5 Ibid., fol. 310.

6 Ibid.

7 Ibid.

8 *Correspondencia de Gutierre Gomez de Fuensalida*, ed. the Duke of Berwick and Alba (Madrid, 1907), p. 533.

9 Williams, Kindle edn. loc. 3160.

10 Real Academia de Historia 9/317, fols 86r–87r. My thanks to Rafael M. Girón Pascual for this reference and transcription.

11 *Correspondencia*, pp. 533–40.

12 Ibid., p. 536.

13 Ibid., pp. 536–7.

14 *CSP Spain*, Supplement to I and II, no. 3.

15 Arévalo, p. 114.

16 *The Great Chronicle of London*, ed. A. H. Thomas and I. D. Thornley (Gloucester, 1983), p. 340.

17 Alice Hunt, *The Drama of Coronation* (Cambridge, 2009), pp. 12–38.

18 TNA E36/315, fols 18, 20.

19 Of the twenty-nine women on the list of 'the Queen's chamber' for coronation livery (TNA LC9/50, fols 204r–204v) – discounting the five countesses, who were more usually in 'extraordinary' service – four had come from first Elizabeth of York's and then Princess Mary's households (Lady Anne Percy, Lady Eleanor Verney, Mrs Denys and Mrs Weston); another six straight from Elizabeth of York's (Lady Elizabeth Stafford, Lady Margaret Bryan, Lady Darell, Lady Peche, Mrs Butler and Mrs Brews); one from Princess Mary's alone (Mrs Jerningham); two from Margaret Beaufort's (Mrs Clifford and Mrs 'Stannap' or Stanhope); and four were already with Catherine of Aragon or, like Margaret Pole, had previously served her in Ludlow (María de Guevara, Inés de Vanegas, Catalina Fortes and Lady Margaret Pole).

20 AGS, CSR leg. 11, fol. 306.

21 *LP* 1, 127.

22 *CSP Spain* II, 20. In 1512 Mountjoy became Catherine's chamberlain, which meant both he and likely his wife returned to live at court. Between 1509 and 1512, however, Mountjoy travelled extensively on the continent. We don't know whether he took his wife with him, but there are no references to her at court during these years and she must have died before February 1515, when Mountjoy remarried.

23 *CSP Spain* II, 43.

24 There are occasional references to other Spanish women as 'wife of' various male Spanish household officers, but it's not clear whether they were in formal service as ladies-in-waiting and many are not identifiable.

25 Seen most clearly in the wage list from Elizabeth of York's privy purse account of 1502–3: TNA E36/310, fol. 91.

26 As shown in the list made for the funeral of Henry VII in 1509: TNA LC2/1, fol. 95v.

27 TNA E101/418/6, fols 1, 22; TNA E101/418/6.

28 King Henry wrote to King Ferdinand in November 1509 that 'the child in her womb is alive', suggesting that quickening had already occurred. This is usually at the fourth or fifth month, meaning that she must have fallen pregnant extremely quickly after the marriage in June, and can only have been seven months or so advanced by January. *CSP Spain* II, 23.

29 *CSP Spain*, Supplement to I and II, no. 7.

30 K. L. Geaman and T. Earenfight, 'Neither Heir nor Spare: Childless Queens and the Practice of Monarchy in Pre-modern Europe', in Elena Woodacre et al., eds, *The Routledge History of Monarchy* (London, 2019), pp. 518–33.

31   Thurley, *Houses of Power*, p. 17.
32   *CSP Spain*, Supplement to I and II, no. 7.
33   AGS, CSR leg. 11, fol. 306.
34   Ibid., fol. 322.
35   Ibid., fol. 323.
36   *CSP Spain*, Supplement to I and II, no. 8.
37   Ibid.
38   *CSP Spain* II, 122.
39   BL Cotton MS Caligula D VI, fol. 92 (*LP* II, 2120).
40   Arévalo, pp. 115–16.
41   BL Arundel MS 26, fol. 29v; TNA E36/210, fol. 91; TNA LC2/1, fol. 136;
     LC9/50, fols 182v, 189v, 204, 212.
42   Account given in *CSP Spain*, Supplement to I and II, no. 8.
43   Ibid.
44   Ibid.
45   BL Add MS 21116, fol. 40.
46   G. W. Bernard, 'Compton, Sir William (1482?–1528)', *ODNB* https://doi.
     org/10.1093/ref:odnb/6039 (accessed July 2023).
47   TNA PROB 11/23/8.
48   Sean Cunningham, 'Guildford, Sir Richard (c. 1450–1506)', *ODNB*
     https://doi.org/10.1093/ref:odnb/11723 (accessed July 2023).
49   Lauren Johnson, *Margaret Beaufort* (forthcoming).
50   S. J. Gunn, 'Brandon, Sir Thomas (d. 1510)', *ODNB* https://doi.
     org/10.1093/ref:odnb/3268 (accessed July 2023).
51   TNA PROB 11/16/746.
52   S. J. Gunn, *Charles Brandon: Henry VIII's Closest Friend* (Stroud, 2016),
     p. 18.
53   Joanne Paul, *The House of Dudley* (London, 2022), p. 40.

Chapter 3: My Lord, My Husband

1   R. Virgoe, 'The Recovery of the Howards in East Anglia, 1485–1529', in
     Wealth and Power in Tudor England, ed. E. W. Ives, R. J. Knecht and J. J.
     Scarisbrick (London, 1978), pp. 1–20.
2   Elizabeth later wrote that she and Ralph had 'loved to gether ij yeres',
     and that if Howard had not made suit to her father, she and Ralph
     would have been married 'afore crystynmas'. Since Ralph would not
     reach fourteen, the canonical age of consent, until February 1512, this
     must have meant Christmas of that year. BL Cotton MS Titus B I, fol.
     390.
3   On the arrangement of marriage during this period see Chapter 3, 'The

Arrangement of Marriage', in Harris, *English Aristocratic Women*.

4   '. . . & my lorde my husband had not sende immedyatly word after my
     lade an my lordes furst wyff wos ded he mad sute to my lord my father
     or elles I had be[en] maryed afore crystynmas to my lorde off westmer-
     eland & yt was my lord my husbandes sute to my lorde my father &
     neu[er] came off me nor no[ne] off my fryndes: & when he came thether
     at shroft tyde he wold haue no[ne] off my systeres but only me'. BL
     Cotton MS Titus B I, fol. 390.

5   Elizabeth's birthdate is not certain as it was not recorded at the time.
     Her own letters give two possibilities, but neither were phrased in such a
     way as to be definitive. In June 1537 she described herself as 'yonger then
     he [Howard] by xx yeres'; we know that Howard was born in 1473, which
     would place her birth in 1493, making her eighteen or nineteen in 1512.
     In October 1537, however, she described herself as 'xl yeres of age', which
     would place her birthdate in 1497, making her fifteen in 1512. BL Cotton
     MS Titus B I, fols 388, 390.

6   Ibid., fol. 388.

7   Howard's first wife was Anne Plantagenet, daughter of King Edward IV
     and younger sister of Queen Elizabeth of York.

8   Prince Henry was born on New Year's Day 1511, and died of unknown
     causes on 22 February of the same year.

9   BL Cotton MS Titus B I, fol. 390.

10   An account of her sister-in-law Muriel Howard, Lady Knyvett's funeral
     on 21 December 1512 lists Elizabeth as one of the mourners and gives
     her name as 'The lady haward dowght[er] to the duc of bokingh[a]m',
     indicating that the marriage had taken place by this time. BL Add. MS
     45131, fols 69v–71.

11   Neil Murphy, 'Henry VIII's First Invasion of France: The Gascon
     Expedition of 1512', *English Historical Review* 130:542 (2015), 25–56.

12   *LP* I, 1221 (48); TNA SP1/2, fol. 135 (*LP* I, 1286).

13   BL Cotton MS Titus B I, fol. 388.

14   TNA SP1/2, fol. 135 (*LP* I, 1286).

15   *Grafton's Chronicle*, p. 250.

16   TNA PROB 11/17/293.

17   BL Add. MS 45131, fols 69v–71.

18   TNA SP1/4, fols 79–80 (*LP* I, 1965).

19   Hall, pp. 545–7.

20   TNA E36/215, fol. 167.

21   Hall, p. 564.

22   David M. Head, *The Ebbs and Flows of Fortune: The Life of Thomas
     Howard, Third Duke of Norfolk* (Athens, Georgia, 1995), pp. 34–9.

23 BL Add MS 29549, fol. 1.

24 This was Katherine Peniston. See Harris, *English Aristocratic Women*, p. 218.

25 Lauren Johnson, *Margaret Beaufort* (forthcoming).

26 BL Add. MS 21481, fols 15, 27, 41v, 56, 63v, 69, 86v, 103v, 121, 135v, 150, 167v.

27 Anne of Cleves' maids of honour were paid 50s a quarter or £10 per annum, as were most of these women; TNA E101/422/15.

28 The earliest explicit reference I have found to the queen's 'maids' is a livery list dated to 1519, where 'ladi graye and the quenes maydes' were allotted bouche of court; TNA SP 1/19, fol.117.

29 Maids of honour were usually around sixteen. Since we know that most of these women had served Elizabeth of York, they cannot possibly have been young enough to be maids of honour to Catherine of Aragon. Elizabeth Burton, for instance, was described as 'the wife of John Burton' in 1514 (*LP* I, 3324 (13)).

30 Annuities of various amounts were granted to Elizabeth Saxby, Elizabeth Catesby, Elizabeth Burton, Mary Reading, Dorothy Verney and Elizabeth Chamber, all in September 1514: *LP* I, 3324 (8, 12, 13, 14, 18, 36).

31 There are two surviving lists of Mary's retinue in 1514: Leland, *Collectanea* I, ii, p. 703, and BL Cotton MS Vitellius C XI, fol. 155. Both of these refer only to 'Mademoiselle Boleyn', but, as Eric Ives pointed out, a French payment list for October–December 1514 includes 'Marie Boulonne', which suggests that it was Mary and not Anne Boleyn. See Eric Ives, *The Life and Death of Anne Boleyn* (Oxford, 2004), p. 27, n. 27.

32 Erin Sadlack, *The French Queen's Letters* (Basingstoke, 2011), p. 21; TNA LC9/50, fol. 229; BL Add MS 21481, fol. 15.

33 BL Cotton MS Caligula D VI, fol. 201.

34 Ibid.; TNA SP1/9, fol. 114.

35 TNA SP1/230, fols 221–2.

36 The two lists don't match up completely. Anne Jerningham is on both, but Denys is only on the English list preserved in Leland, *Collectanea* I, ii, p. 703; the list made by the French in BL Cotton MS Vitellius C XI, fol. 155 has 'Jeanne Barnesse'. All three appear in payments and clothing warrants as part of Mary's household before 1514.

37 Sadlack, pp. 64–70.

38 Mary's letters to her brother and to Wolsey, both dated 12 October 1514, are transcribed in Sadlack, pp. 167–8. Charles, Earl of Worcester's relation of his conversation with Louis can be found in BL Cotton MS Caligula D VI, fol. 205 (*LP* I, 3416).

39 Sadlack, pp. 73–4.

40   Ibid., p. 168.

41   Ibid., p. 76.

42   *LP* I, 3381, 3440.

43   Hall, p. 570.

44   Sadlack, p. 78.

45   *LP* I, 3499 (59); *LP* II, 569.

46   *CSP Spain* II, 201.

47   Ibid.

48   The precise relationship between him and María is difficult to pin down, in part because of the sixteenth-century habit of describing every relationship beyond parents, siblings, aunts and uncles as 'cousin', and they do not seem to have been straightforward first cousins.

49   Martínez Hernández, pp. 85–6.

50   Ernesto García Fernández, 'Hombres y mujeres de negocios del País Vasco en la Baja Edad Media', en J. A. Bonachía Hernando, y D. Carvajal de la Vega, eds, *Los negocios del hombre: Comercio y rentas en Castilla (siglos XV y XVI)*, (Valladolid, 2012), pp. 139–44.

51   https://dbe.rah.es/biografias/15442/juan-manuel (accessed 18 May 2023).

52   *LP* I, 1683 ; *CSP Spain* II, 119; *LP* I, 2083, 2421; 2502; *CSP Spain* II, 160, 163, 169; *LP* I, 2908.

53   *CSP Spain* II, 201.

54   Ibid., 238.

55   Martínez Hernández, pp. 129–37.

56   Cockayne, *Complete Peerage*, Vol. 12B, pp. 670–73; see also Willoughby's will, TNA PROB 11/23/362.

57   Queen Catherine had had a miscarriage/stillbirth in January 1510; Prince Henry was born in January 1511 and died in February 1511; a stillbirth immediately after Flodden in 1513; another pregnancy lost in the summer of 1514. See John Dewhurst, 'The Alleged Miscarriages of Catherine of Aragon and Anne Boleyn', *Medical History* 28 (1984), 49–56.

58   *LP* II, 1573.

59   TNA E36/215, fol. 449.

60   *LP* II, 1953.

61   LRO 2 ANC 3/A/36; *LP* II, 2172.

62   TNA E36/215, fol. 452.

Chapter 4: Richly Beseen

1   Charles Wriothesley, *A Chronicle of England During the Reigns of the Tudors, from A.D. 1485 to 1559*, ed. William Douglas Hamilton (London, 1875), pp. 10–11.

2   John Stow, *The Annales, Or Generall Chronicle of England*, ed. Edmund Howes (London, 1615), p. 506.

3   A letter from the Duke of Buckingham requesting to joust on the king's side rather than against him shows that preparations were being made as early as February 1517. TNA SP1/15, fol. 22 (*LP* II, 2987).

4   Hall, p. 582.

5   *LP* II, 1501 (Revels Accounts, no. 7).

6   Elizabeth Norton, *Bessie Blount: Mistress to Henry VIII* (Stroud, 2011).

7   The fullest accounts of Evil May Day, as it became known, are found in Hall, pp. 586–91 and Sebastian Giustinian, *Four Years at the Court of Henry VIII*, ed. Rawdon Brown (Cambridge, 2013), Vol. 2, pp. 70–76. See also Shannon McSheffrey, 'Disorder, Riot, and Governance in Early Tudor London: Evil May Day, 1517', *EHR*, 128 (2023) 27–60, and B. Waddell, 'The Evil May Day Riot of 1517 and the Popular Politics of Anti-Immigrant Hostility in Early Modern London', *Historical Research* 94:266 (2021), 716–35. My thanks to Shannon McSheffrey for sending me her article, and for discussion on the queen's role in these events.

8   As described by de Puebla, Imperial ambassador during the reign of Henry VII: *CSP Spain* I, 210.

9   Giustinian, Vol. 2, pp. 71, 76.

10   Waddell, 'The Evil May Day Riot'.

11   McSheffrey, 'Disorder, Riot and Governance'.

12   For more on pregnancy wear see Maria Hayward, *Dress at the Court of Henry VIII* (Leeds, 2007), pp. 167–8.

13   *CSP Venice*, II, 1103.

14   Hayward, *Dress at the Court*, p. 167.

15   *CSP Spain*, Supplement to I and II, no. 8; Tracy Adams and Christine Adams, *The Creation of the French Royal Mistress* (University Park, Pennsylvania, 2020).

16   See, for instance, the example of Alice Perrers, mistress of Edward III: Laura Tompkins, 'The Uncrowned Queen: Alice Perrers, Edward III and Political Crisis in Fourteenth-century England, 1360–1377', unpublished PhD thesis, University of St Andrews (2013).

17   Norton, Chapter 9 'The King's Mistress'.

18   Harris, *English Aristocratic Women*, pp. 68–70.

19   Hall, p. 595.

20   Norton, Chapter 10 'Mother of the King's Son'.

21   *HMC* Rutland, I, pp. 21–2; see also TNA SP1/19, fol.117.

22   David Loades, *The Tudor Court* (London, 1986), pp. 40–41.

23   As is clear from a livery list made in 1519: TNA SP1/19, fol. 117.

24   TNA SP1/37, fol. 53. See also James Taffe, 'Reconstructing the Queen's

Household, 1485–1547: A Study in Royal Service', unpublished PhD
thesis, University of Durham (2021), Appendix 1A, pp. 265–6.

25   In 1529, for instance, the king's councillors had to wait for the queen
to be fetched from within her privy chamber before they were able
to speak with her: George Cavendish, *The Life and Death of Cardinal
Wolsey*, ed. Samuel Weller Singer (London, 1825), p. 227. See also Taffe,
Courting Scandal: The Rise and Fall of Jane Boleyn, Lady Rochford
(2023), pp. 98–9, and N. Clark, 'Queen Katherine Howard: Space, Place,
and Promiscuity, Pre- and Post-Marriage, 1536–42', *Royal Studies Journal*
6:2 (2019), 89–103.

26   *Lisle Letters* IV, nos 864a, 868a and 867.

27   David Cressy, *Birth, Marriage & Death: Ritual, Religion, and the
Life-Cycle in Tudor and Stuart England* (Oxford, 1999), pp. 28–31.

28   Ibid., pp. 50–73; Delores LaPratt, 'Childbirth Prayers in Medieval and
Early Modern England: "For drede of perle that may be-falle."', *Sympo-
sia* 2 (2010), https://symposia.library.utoronto.ca (accessed June 2023); K.
French, 'The Material Culture of Childbirth in Late Medieval London
and its Suburbs', *Journal of Women's History* 28:2 (2016), 126–48.

29   Katherine's birthdate is traditionally given as 22 March 1519 and is
recorded as such in Cockayne's *Peerage*. This is taken from Cecilie Goff,
A Woman of the Tudor Age (London, 1930), p. 9, and I have been unable
to find any contemporary source to corroborate this. However, as a
member of the Willoughby family, Goff may have had access to records
that no longer survive, and had no reason to fabricate this information;
I have therefore followed Goff in placing Katherine's birth in 1519 at
Parham.

30   Cressy, pp. 80–94.

31   Again, following Goff, many genealogies state that there was at least one
son who did not survive to adulthood, but I have yet to find a contemporary source to support this.

32   Norton, Chapter 10 'Mother of the King's Son'.

33   This house was called 'Jericho'. 'Notes to the diary: 1550–51', in *The Diary
of Henry Machyn, Citizen and Merchant-Taylor of London, 1550–1563*, ed.
J. G. Nichols (London, 1848), pp. 313–23. British History Online http://
www.british-history.ac.uk/camden-record-soc/vol42/pp313-323 (accessed
26 June 2023).

34   Grace Coolidge, *Guardianship, Gender and the Nobility in Early Modern
Spain* (London, 2011); Stretton and Kesselring, Introduction, pp. 1–23.

35   Coolidge, p. 85.

36   AGS, CSR leg. 11, fol. 252. A Castilian ducat was worth about 375 maravedis. 800 ducats was just under half of the amount that Queen Isabella

routinely paid to her ladies-in-waiting as dowry (2000 ducats). Conversion between Spanish and English currency was variable and has proved too difficult to attempt with accuracy here; exchange rates depended on the specific date, weight of metal, and type of exchange, and may even have involved a third currency (often Italian). See the introduction to Peter Spufford, *Handbook of Medieval Exchange* (London, 1986).

37 Ibid., fol. 253.

38 Escoriaza was often known in England as 'Fernando de Victoria', quite literally 'from Vitoria', but this was not his actual name. See Julio-Cesar Santoyo, *El Dr. Escoriaza en Inglaterra y otros ensayos Británicos* (Biblioteca alavesa Luis de Ajuria / Institución Sancho el Sabio, 1973).

39 Juan de Pesquera, who was a 'fourrière' of Charles V's household, an office similar to the English 'harbinger', somebody who rode ahead to arrange lodgings for the royal household. He was probably in Dover arranging this for Charles V in advance of his visit at this time. See J. Martinez Millan, *La corte de Carlos V* (Madrid, 2000), 5 vols, Vol. 5, p. 36.

40 *LP* III, 2486.

41 TNA SP 1/20, fol. 41 (*LP* III 806).

42 *CSP Venice* III, 50.

43 Ibid.

44 Bodleian MS Ashmole 1116, fol. 101r.

45 Steven G. Ellis, 'Centre and Periphery in the Tudor State', in Robert Tittler and Norman L. Jones, eds, *A Companion to Tudor Britain* (London, 2004), pp. 133–50.

46 TNA SP60/1, fol. 40 (*LP* III, 940).

47 TNA SP1/29, fol. 293.

48 BL Cotton MS Caligula D VII, fol. 240v.

49 Norton, Chapter 12 'First Marriage'.

50 Sadlack, pp. 91–117.

51 Ibid.

52 TNA SP1/15, fol. 33 (*LP* II, 3018).

53 Ibid.

54 TNA E36/216, fol. 77r.

55 Ives, pp. 18–34.

56 Lauren Mackay, *Among the Wolves of Court: The Untold Story of Thomas and George Boleyn* (London, 2018), p. 143.

57 The names of the parts and of the women involved come from two separate accounts. Historians have tended to match these up according to the order in which the women are listed in the revel account, but this can only be speculation. See Hall, p. 631 and *LP* III, Revels Accounts, p.

1559.

58 Hall, p. 630.

59 Ibid., p. 631.

Chapter 5: Stout Resolution

1   As shown in the kitchen accounts of the Earl and Countess of Surrey: University of California, Berkeley, MS UCB 49, unfoliated (1523–4), Cambridge University Library, Pembroke MS 300, unfoliated (1526–7), and NRO Rye 74, fols 1–14, analysed by Richard Howlett as 'The Household Accounts of Kenninghall Palace in the year 1525', *Norfolk Archaeology* 15 (1904), pp. 51–60. See also C. M. Woolgar, *The Great Household in Late Medieval England* (New Haven, 1999), pp. 111–65.

2   Under the Duke of Albany the Scots had invaded England for the first time since Flodden a decade previously.

3   Christine de Pisan, *The Treasure of the City of Ladies*, trans. Sarah Lawson (London, 1985), p. 130. The fact that there are sixteenth-century copies surviving shows that this text was still owned and used by women of Elizabeth's time.

4   UCB, MS UCB 49. The two were married by May the following year.

5   The kitchen account makes this clear, and it was the custom for the nobility to dine away from the hall by this date. See Woolgar, pp. 145–6.

6   See the account in Hall, pp. 622–3.

7   C. S. L. Davies, 'Stafford, Edward, third duke of Buckingham (1478–1521)', *ODNB* https://doi.org/10.1093/ref:odnb/26202 (accessed July 2023).

8   Clark, *Gender, Family, and Politics*, pp. 52–6; UCB, MS UCB 49.

9   College of Arms MS I.7, fols 56r–60v; Henry Howard, *A defensative against the poison of supposed prophecies* (London, 1583, reprinted 1620), p. 119. My thanks to Kirsten Claiden-Yardley for this reference.

10 BL Cotton MS Titus B I, fols 388–388v.

11 Loades, *The Tudor Court*, p. 45.

12 UCB, MS UCB 49.

13 The earliest mention of Maud Parr in relation to the queen's household is in the Ordinary of 1517: HMC Rutland, Vol. 1, pp. 21–2. It's not clear whether Lady Bryan was Margaret Bourchier, governess to the princess at this time, or her daughter-in-law Philippa Spice/Fortescue, wife of Sir Francis Bryan, courtier and diplomat.

14 The Parkers, Barons Morley lived at Great Hallingbury in Essex.

15 Sally Varlow, 'Sir Francis Knollys's Latin Dictionary: New Evidence for Katherine Carey', *Historical Research* 80:209 (2007), 315–23.

16 Beverley Murphy, *Bastard Prince: Henry VIII's Lost Son* (Stroud, 2001), pp. 41–68.

17 Jeri McIntosh, *From Heads of Household to Heads of State: The Preaccession Households of Mary and Elizabeth Tudor, 1516–1558*, http://www.gutenberg-e.org/mcintosh/chapter2.html#s2.3 (accessed July 2023), pp. 19–29.

18 *A Collection of Ordinances and Regulations for the Government of the Royal Household* (London, 1790), pp. 135–207.

19 Loades, *The Tudor Court*, pp. 62–5.

20 *A Collection of Ordinances*, p. 149.

21 Loades, *The Tudor Court*, p. 88.

22 *A Collection of Ordinances*, pp 162–4.

23 TNA SP1/37, fol. 53.

24 William's deathbed was later described by witnesses: LRO 1 ANC 5/B/e.

25 There are several surviving copies of William's will: TNA PROB 11/23/362, LRO 2 ANC 3/A/41 and 42.

26 Coolidge, p. 4.

27 LRO 1 ANC 5/B/e.

28 *The Register or Chronicle of Butley Priory*, ed. A. G. Dickens (Winchester, 1951), pp. 50–51.

29 TNA PROB 11/23/362.

30 Helen Nader, Introduction to *idem.*, ed., *Power and Gender in Renaissance Spain: Eight Women of the Mendoza Family, 1450–1650* (Chicago, 2004), pp. 1–26.

31 Harris, *English Aristocratic Women*, pp. 17–26.

32 This is outlined clearly in LRO 1 ANC 5/B/c.

33 See, for instance, TNA STAC 2/21/30; STAC 2/21/17; STAC 2/27/169; STAC 2/21/14; REQ 2/4/141; LRO 1 ANC 5/B/c; 1 ANC 5/B/1/g.

34 TNA STAC 2/27/169.

35 Ibid.

36 Harris, *English Aristocratic Women*, pp. 31–2.

37 Coolidge, p. 4; AGS, CSR leg. 11, fols 29–30. María's mother Inés had actually voluntarily relinquished guardianship on grounds of ill-health in 1500.

38 LRO 2 ANC 3/A/46.

39 TNA SP1/44, fol. 130.

40 *LP* IV, 3140.

41 Hall, p. 707.

42 Jessica Sharkey, 'Between King and Pope: Thomas Wolsey and the Knight Mission', *Historical Research* 84:224 (2011), 236–48.

43 TNA SP1/43, fol. 48.

44 *LP* IV, 3318, 3360; Head, *The Ebbs and Flows of Fortune*, pp. 85–8; Sharkey, 'Between King and Pope'.
45 TNA STAC 2/21/30; STAC 10/4/138; STAC 2/21/22; STAC 2/21/17.
46 TNA SP1/47, fol. 37 (*LP* IV, 3997).
47 TNA SP1/42, fol. 252 (*LP* IV, 3327). See also Taffe, 'Reconstructing the Queen's Household', pp. 222–3.
48 BL Cotton MS Vespasian F I, fol. 77 (*LP* IV, 3265).
49 Taffe, 'Reconstructing the Queen's Household', pp. 223–6; *LP* IV, 4685.
50 TNA SP1/42, fol. 252 (*LP* IV, 3327).
51 *LP* IV, 6526.
52 Strype, *Ecclesiastical Memorials*, Vol. 1, p. 190.

Chapter 6: Faithful to Her

1   Cavendish. *Life of Wolsey*.
2   Ibid.
3   The royal lodgings at Bridewell were stacked vertically, the queen's on top of the king's. Thurley, *Houses of Power*, p. 136.
4   We don't know whether this was the same day as Catherine's famous speech on 21 June 1529, but it seems likely. The account of the cardinals' visit to the queen comes from Cavendish, and he doesn't give a specific date save that it happened while the court was in session, and both the queen and the king were at Bridewell. The 21st was the only day that both monarchs appeared before the court and thus might reasonably have been at Bridewell, as neither monarch spent the entirety of the trial period there; Catherine was at Baynard's Castle on the 18th, and by the 26th she had moved to Greenwich. *LP* IV, 5685, 5716.
5   Cavendish wrote that 'we, in the other chamber, might sometime hear the queen speak very loud, but what it was we could not understand'.
6   *CSP Spain* IV, i, 224.
7   Ibid.
8   Ibid., 232.
9   William Carey, Mary Boleyn's husband.
10 TNA SP1/50, fol. 83 (*LP* IV, 4710).
11 *CSP Spain* IV, i, 232.
12 See Lauren Mackay, *Inside the Tudor Court: Henry VIII and His Six Wives Through the Eyes of the Spanish Ambassador* (Stroud, 2015).
13 As in surviving New Year gift lists.
14 *CSP Spain* IV, i, 232.
15 Leland, *Collectanea* IV, p. 259, and I, Part 1, p. 701; BL Harleian MS 3504, fol. 232.

16   TNA E30/1456.

17   TNA SP1/65, fols 18v–19r (*LP* V, 6 (9)).

18   *CSP Spain* IV, ii, Supplement 573, 574, 575; *Crónica del rey Enrico Octavo de Inglaterra*, Vol. 4, pp. 336–7; Júlia Benavent, 'El apoyo de Isabel de Portugal a Catalina de Aragón, reina de Inglaterra. Registro de cartas de la emperatriz (AGS Est. Libro 68)', *Hipogrifo* 9:2 (2021), 431–44.

19   *CSP Spain* IV, ii, 917.

20   Arévalo, pp. 120–22.

21   *LP* IV, 5636.

22   TNA WARD 9/149/28; *CSP Spain* IV, i, 228.

23   *CSP Spain* IV, i, 460.

24   *Statutes of the Realm* III, 357–61.

25   *CSP Venice* IV, 694. See Head, *The Ebbs and Flows of Fortune*, pp. 86–103.

26   BL Cotton MS Titus B I, fols 99r–101v.

27   BL Egerton MS 2623, fol. 7.

28   See Catherine Fletcher, *Our Man in Rome: Henry VIII and His Italian Ambassador* (London, 2012).

29   *CSP Spain* IV, i, 509.

30   Ibid.

31   See, for instance, Neil Murphy, 'Spies, Informers and Thomas Howard's Defence of England's Northern Frontier in 1523', *Historical Research* 93:260 (2020), 252–72.

32   *CSP Spain* IV, ii, 584.

33   Ibid., 608.

34   Ibid., 619.

35   Stanford Lehmberg, *The Reformation Parliament 1529–1536* (Cambridge, 1970), p. 114.

36   *LP* V, 216.

37   Ibid.

38   See Clark, *Gender, Family, and Politics*, pp. 80–81.

39   BL Cotton MS Titus B I, fols 390r–390v.

40   *CSP Spain* IV, ii, 720.

41   Ibid.

42   Ibid.

Chapter 7: On the Queen's Side

1   BL Add MS 6113, fol. 70 (*LP* V, 1274 (3)).

2   See Clark, *Gender, Family, and Politics*, pp. 101–2.

3   Accounts aren't specific as to which room the investiture happened

in, saying only that it was at Windsor, in the morning, in the king's presence: but it's most likely it was in his presence chamber, the room usually used for this kind of thing.

4   *CSP Spain* IV, ii, 756; Hall, p. 781.

5   *CSP Spain* IV, ii, 786.

6   *CSP Venice* IV, 682.

7   *CSP Spain* IV, ii, 786.

8   TNA SP1/81, fol. 95 (*LP VI*, 1642).

9   See Diarmaid MacCulloch, *Thomas Cromwell* (London, 2019), pp. 133–5.

10 G. W. Bernard, *The King's Reformation: Henry VIII and the Remaking of the English Church* (New Haven 2005), pp. 47–8.

11 MacCulloch, pp. 135–7.

12 J. G. Nichols, ed., *Narratives of the Days of the Reformation*, Camden Society First series 77 (1859), pp. 52–7; George Wyatt, 'Extracts from the Life of Queen Anne Boleigne', in Cavendish https://www.gutenberg.org/files/54043/54043-h/54043-h.htm#FNanchor_210_210 (accessed July 2023). See also Thomas Freeman, 'Research, Rumour and Propaganda: Anne Boleyn in Foxe's "Book of Martyrs"', *Historical Journal* 38:4 (1995), 797–819.

13 Henry Savage, ed., *Love Letters of Henry VIII* (London, 1949), p. 37.

14 *LP V*, 421.

15 MacCulloch, pp. 131–55.

16 Head, *The Ebbs and Flows of Fortune*, pp. 103–4.

17 TNA E101/420/15.

18 J. Smyth, *The Berkeley Manuscripts: The Lives of the Berkeleys*, ed. J. Maclean, 3 vols (Gloucester, 1883) Vol. 2, p. 253.

19 Anne Joscelyn was probably either the unmarried daughter of John Joscelyn (d. 1525) and Philippa Bradbury, listed as 'Anne, my daughter' in her mother's will of 1530, or née Grenville, wife of John Joscelyn, Serjeant of the Pantry.

20 Hall, p. 784.

21 Wyatt, 'Extracts from the Life of Anne Boleigne'.

22 Sadlack, pp. 150–51.

23 *CSP Spain* IV, ii, 739.

24 Ibid., 756.

25 Shannon McSheffrey, 'The Slaying of Sir William Pennington: Legal Narrative and the Late Medieval English Archive', *Florilegium* 28 (2011), 169–203.

26 *CSP Venice* IV, 761.

27 Wynkyn de Worde, *The Maner of the Tryumphe of Caleys and Bulleyn and The Noble Tryumphant Coronacyon of Quene Anne, Wyfe unto the*

Most Noble Kyng Henry VIII, ed. Edmund Goldsmid (Edinburgh, 1884), https://www.gutenberg.org/files/32515/32515-h/32515-h.htm#f16.1 (accessed July 2023).

28   Ives, p. 157.
29   *CSP Spain* IV, ii, 980.
30   Ibid., 986.
31   See James Taffe, *Courting Scandal.*
32   In the summer, Venetian ambassador Capello reported that Anne planned to cross the Channel with 'thirty of the chief ladies of this island'. *CSP Venice* IV, 802.
33   Worde, *The Maner of the Truymphe.*
34   Hall, p. 793.
35   The other two women, Honor Grenville, Viscountess Lisle and Elizabeth Harleston, Lady Wallop were the wives of the deputy of Calais and the most recent English ambassador to France, and were there by dint of geography.
36   *CSP Venice* IV, 802.
37   Hall, pp. 793–4.
38   See discussion in G. W. Bernard, *Anne Boleyn: Fatal Attractions* (New Haven, 2010), pp. 24–33 and 65–6.
39   Ibid., p. 794.
40   Thurley, *Houses of Power*, pp. 50–51.
41   Nicholas Harpsfield, *A Treatise on the Pretended Divorce Between Henry VIII and Catharine of Aragon* (Camden Society, 1878), p. 234.
42   *CSP Spain* IV, ii, 1053.
43   On 23 February Chapuys reported that Henry might have hurried with the wedding because Anne was pregnant; she had an insatiable appetite for plums and the king had told her that was a sure sign. Anne was indeed pregnant at this time. Bernard, *Anne Boleyn: Fatal Attractions*, pp. 66–7.
44   The occasion was widely reported. See *CSP Spain* IV, ii, 1061; Wriothesley, p. 17; Hall, p. 795; *CSP Venice* IV, 870.
45   *CSP Spain* IV, ii, 1061.
46   Ibid., 1057.
47   Ibid., 1061.
48   Worde, *The Maner of the Tryumphe.*
49   Bernard, *Anne Boleyn: Fatal Attractions*, p. 67.
50   Ibid., pp. 67–71.
51   The list of women in attendance at Anne's coronation is found in BL Add. MS 71009, fols 58r–58v.
52   BL Add. MS 71009, fol. 58; *LP* VI, 563.

53 Hunt, pp. 39–76.
54 *LP* VI, 585.
55 Ibid.
56 Sadlack, pp. 153–4.
57 *Chronicle of King Henry VIII of England*, trans. Martin A. S. Hume (London, 1889), p. 135.
58 *LP* VI, 723.
59 Sadlack, p. 155.
60 Francis Ford, *Mary Tudor* (Bury St Edmund's, 1882), pp. 34–56 (p. 41).

Chapter 8: Fragility and Brittleness

1 *CSP Spain* IV, ii, 1154; Hall, p. 812.
2 *CSP Spain* IV, ii, 1154.
3 See Genelle Gertz and Pasquale Toscano, 'The Lost Network of Elizabeth Barton', *Reformation* 26:2 (2021), 105–28.
4 Diane Watt, 'The Prophet at Home: Elizabeth Barton and the Influence of Bridget of Sweden and Catherine of Siena', in *Prophets Abroad: The Reception of Continental Holy Women in Late-medieval England*, ed. Rosalynn Voaden (Cambridge, 1996), pp. 161–76.
5 Her earliest recorded appearance was at the Field of Cloth of Gold as the Countess of Devon (TNA SP1/19, fol. 268). While it's possible that Gertrude served at court before her marriage, there is no surviving proof of this.
6 J. P. D. Cooper, 'Courtenay, Henry, marquess of Exeter', *ODNB* https://doi.org/10.1093/ref:odnb/6451 (accessed August 2023).
7 *LP* VI, 1438.
8 BL Add. MS 71009, fol. 58; TNA SP1/80, fol. 180.
9 BL Harl. MS 543, fol. 128.
10 Will Coster, *Baptism and Spiritual Kinship* (Aldershot, 2002), pp. 7–9.
11 *LP* VI, 1125.
12 Alexandra Barratt, *Anne Bulkely and her Book: Fashioning Female Piety in Early Tudor England* (Turnhout, 2009), p. 63.
13 TNA SP1/80, fols 130–130v (*LP* VI, 1468 (7)).
14 *CSP Spain* IV, ii, 1149.
15 Gertz and Toscano, 'The Lost Network of Elizabeth Barton'.
16 As is made clear by Gertrude's reply: BL Cotton MS Cleopatra E IV, fols 94–5 (*LP* VI, 1464).
17 TNA SP1/80, fol. 116 (*LP* VI, 1465). The draft sent to Cromwell has edits in the margins, but these do not appear to be in Cromwell's hand; see MacCulloch, p. 236, n. 8.

18 BL Cotton MS Cleopatra E IV, fols 94–5.
19 Ibid.
20 Gloria Kaufman, 'Juan Luis Vives on the Education of Women', *Signs* 3:4 (1978), 891–6 (p. 893).
21 James Daybell, *Women Letter-Writers in Tudor England* (Oxford, 2006), p. 255.
22 On deferential space in letters see James Daybell, *The Material Letter in Early Modern England: Manuscript Practices and the Culture and Practices of Letter-Writing, 1512–1635* (Basingstoke, 2012).
23 BL Cotton MS Cleopatra E IV, fols 94–5.
24 *CSP Spain* IV, ii, 756.
25 Ibid., 1123.
26 LRO 1 ANC 5/B/1/g; see also 1 ANC 5/B/c.
27 LRO 1 ANC 5/B/1/m; TNA SP1/68, fol. 61; LRO 1 ANC/5/B/1/d (this document is catalogued as 1530, but dated the twenty-first year of the reign of Henry VIII, which was 1540. However, the fact that it is signed by Thomas Elyot, who was only clerk of the Privy Council up until around 1531, suggests that they did indeed mean 1530.)
28 For instance, TNA STAC 2/21/14; REQ 2/4/141; C 1/665/40; C 1/670/9.; C 1/689/32; C 1 691/26; C 4/43/69.
29 TNA STAC 2/20/400.
30 *LP* VI, 1486.
31 Ibid., 1558.
32 Ibid., 1541 (original BL Cotton MS Otho C X, fols 210–12, mutilated).
33 TNA SP1/79, fol. 158 (*LP* VI, 1252).
34 Elizabeth Darrell was the daughter of Catherine's former vice-chamberlain Sir Edward Darrell. Elizabeth 'Ffynes' may have been a relation of the Barons Dacre. Margery and Elizabeth Otwell, Elizabeth Lawrence, Emma Brown, Dorothea Wheler and Blanche Twyford were of gentry status.
35 *CSP Spain* V, i, 60.
36 Ibid.
37 TNA SP1/79, fol. 158 (*LP* VI, 1252). For a more detailed discussion of this see Taffe, 'Reconstructing the Queen's Household', pp. 212–21.
38 TNA SP1/81, fol. 3 (*LP* VI, 1543).
39 *LP* VI, 1558.
40 *LP* VII, 296.
41 *CSP Spain* IV, ii, 1154.
42 Murphy, *Bastard Prince*, pp. 143–5.
43 Clark, *Gender, Family, and Politics*, pp. 100–103.
44 TNA SP1/76, fol. 168 (*LP* VI, 613).

45 Elizabeth Heale, ed., *The Devonshire Manuscript: A Women's Book of Courtly Poetry* (Toronto, 2012), pp. 59–60.
46 See Heale, and A Social Edition of the Devonshire MS (BL Add. MS 17942) https://en.wikibooks.org/wiki/The_Devonshire_Manuscript (accessed August 2023).
47 Heale, pp. 25–8.
48 Baldesar Castiglione, *The Book of the Courtier*, trans. George Bull (London, 1976), Book 3, pp. 207–78.
49 See David Grummitt, 'Plantagenet, Arthur, Viscount Lisle', *ODNB* https://doi.org/10.1093/ref:odnb/22355 (accessed August 2023).
50 *Lisle Letters* II, nos 182, 193.
51 *Lisle Letters* I, no. 67.
52 *Lisle Letters* II, no. 260.
53 Ibid., nos. 109, 114.
54 Ibid., no. 299a.
55 Ibid., no. 421.
56 Ibid., no. 175; *LP* VII, 958.
57 Dewhurst, pp. 54–6.
58 *CSP Spain* V, i, 90.
59 Ibid.
60 Ibid., i, 97.
61 Ibid., i, 118.

Chapter 9: Extreme Handling

1 This event has been variously dated to either 1533 or 1534, but can be firmly placed in 1534. She states more than once that it occurred on the Tuesday of the Passion week, i.e. Easter week. In 1533, this was 8 April. The Spanish ambassador, Chapuys, stated that the day after this – 9 April – the Duke of Norfolk and other noblemen had ridden to the queen at Ampthill, so it seems highly unlikely that he could have been free to ride to East Anglia to deal with Elizabeth the night before, and still less that he could have returned to court in time to receive this instruction and depart with his colleagues (*CSP Spain* IV, ii, 1058). In 1534, however, Tuesday of the Passion week was 31 March and Norfolk had been in London attending Parliament until its prorogation on 30 March (BL Add. MS 4622, fol. 298).
2 This phrase comes from one of Elizabeth's own letters (BL Cotton MS Titus B I, fols 390–390v). It is just about possible for Norfolk to have reached Kenninghall from London in one night, but probably not with his usual retinue, and he would have needed to change horses frequently

and be careful in the dark. It may be that this was simply a figure of
speech.

3   An inventory of Kenninghall taken later shows that the lodgings for
the duke himself were in the inner courtyard. They were part of a
stacked lodging block, with apartments above and below him. Given the
tendency for the lady's rooms to be at a point of greater seclusion, which
in a stacked lodging like this would mean the highest floor, it is very
likely that the apartments occupied by Norfolk's mistress at the time the
inventory was taken in 1546 were originally Elizabeth's. TNA LR 2/117.

4   BL Cotton MS Titus B I, fols 390–390v.

5   See Harris, 'Marriage Sixteenth-Century Style: Elizabeth Stafford and
the Third Duke of Norfolk', *Journal of Social History* 15:3 (1982), 371–82,
and Susan Dwyer Amussen, '"Being stirred to much unquietness":
Violence and Domestic Violence in Early Modern England', *Journal of
Women's History* 6:2 (1994), 70–89.

6   *CSP Spain* IV, ii, 1130.

7   The surviving sequence includes nine letters from Elizabeth to Thomas
Cromwell, between 1534 and 1540. One from Elizabeth to her brother
Henry, Lord Stafford, and one to her brother-in-law Ralph Neville, Earl
of Westmorland; two from her husband, Norfolk, to Cromwell; one
from Lord Stafford to Norfolk, and one from Stafford to Cromwell. BL
Cotton Vespasian F XIII, fol. 151 (Elizabeth to Cromwell, 23 August
1534, calendared *LP* VII, 1083); TNA SP1/91, fol. 23 (E to C, 3 March,
calendared as 1535 in *LP* VIII, 319, but date unconfirmable); BL Cotton
MS Titus B I, fols 392–3 (E to C, 30 December 1536, uncalendared); TNA
SP1/115, fol. 80 (Norfolk to Cromwell, 27 January 1537, calendared *LP*
XII, i, 252); TNA SP1/106, fol. 219 (E to C, 28 September, calendared as
1536 at *LP* XI, 502, but internal evidence places it in 1537); BL Cotton MS
Titus B I, fol. 390v (E to C, 24 October 1537, calendared *LP* XII, ii, 976);
BL Cotton MS Titus B I, fol. 389 (E to C, 10 November 1537, calendared
LP XII, ii, 1049); BL Cotton MS Titus B I, fol. 388v (E to C, 26 June;
calendared as 1537 at *LP* XII, ii, 143, but internal evidence places it in
1538); TNA SP1/144, fol. 16 (E to C, 3 March 1539, calendared *LP* XIV, i,
425); BL Cotton MS Titus B I, fol. 391 (E to C, 29 January, calendared
as 1539 in *LP* XIV, i, 160, but internal evidence places it in 1540); TNA
SP1/158, fol. 201 (E to Westmorland, 11 April, calendared as 1540 at *LP*
XV, 493, but internal evidence places it in 1541). The remainder of the
letters are not obviously datable: TNA SP1/76, fol. 38 (Henry, Lord
Stafford to Norfolk, 13 May, calendared as 1533 at *LP* VI, 474); TNA
SP1/76, fol. 39 (Stafford to Cromwell, 13 May, calendared as 1533 at *LP* VI,
475); Bl Cotton MS Titus B I, fol. 162 (E to Stafford, calendared as 1537 at

LP XII, ii, 1332); BL Cotton MS Titus B I, fol. 394v (Norfolk to Cromwell, no date).

8   BL Cotton Titus B I, fol. 388.

9   TNA SP1/97, fols 120r–120v.

10 Clark, *Gender, Family, and Politics*, pp. 66–72.

11 Elizabeth used at least two different scribes, and sometimes added her own postscripts.

12 BL Cotton MS Titus B I, fols 388–388v, states that it was eleven years since Norfolk had fallen for Bess. Internal evidence dates this letter to 1538, which means the affair with Bess began in 1527.

13 Gunn, *Charles Brandon*, p. 109; *Testamenta Vetusta*, ed. Nicholas Harris Nicolas, 2 vols (London, 1826), Vol. 2, pp. 533–4.

14 TNA SP1/121, fol. 55.

15 See Daybell, *The Material Letter*.

16 TNA SP1/76, fol. 38.

17 Ibid., fol. 39.

18 Cotton MS Titus B I, fols 392–3; 388–388v.

19 BL Cotton MS Cleopatra E IV, fol. 99. The identity of Mistress Amadas is uncertain. It's usually taken for granted that this is Elizabeth Bryce, wife of royal goldsmith Robert Amadas; but he had died early in 1532 and the rehearsal of her crimes from July 1533 makes it clear that her husband was still alive. Sharon Jansen suggests that she was the first wife of John Amadas, a member of the king's household who hailed from Devon. See Sharon Jansen, *Dangerous Talk and Strange Behavior: Women and Popular Resistance to the Reforms of Henry VIII* (Basingstoke, 1996), p. 68.

20 *CSP Spain* IV, ii, 1130.

21 BL Cotton MS Titus B I, fols 394–394v.

22 Ibid.

23 *CSP Spain* V, ii, 70.

24 Amussen, p. 73.

25 Laura Gowing, *Domestic Dangers: Women, Words, and Sex in Early Modern London* (Oxford, 1996), pp. 42–56 and 189–90.

26 BL Cotton MS Titus B I, fol. 390v.

27 Ibid., fols 388–388v.

28 Ibid., fol. 390v.

29 Ibid.

30 TNA LR 2/117, unfoliated.

31 BL Cotton MS Titus B I, fols 390–390v.

32 BL Cotton MS Vespasian F XIII, fol. 151.

33 TNA SP1/158, fol. 201; BL Cotton MS Titus B I, fols 388–388v, 389.

34 BL Cotton MS Titus B I, fols 392–3.
35 Cromwell owed his seat in Parliament to Norfolk's intervention; he witnessed his will a decade later. Michael Everett, *The Rise of Thomas Cromwell* (London, 2015), pp. 59–60; TNA SP1/115, fol. 80.
36 BL Cotton MS Titus B I, fols 390–390v, 389.
37 Recent research shows clearly that the king's divorce had this effect throughout society: Gwilym Owen and Rebecca Probert, 'Marriage, Dispensation and Divorce During the Years of Henry VIII's "great matter": A Local Case Study', *Law and Humanities* 13:1 (2019), 76–94.
38 BL Cotton MS Titus B I, fol. 389.
39 Ibid.
40 'Parishes: Kimbolton', in *A History of the County of Huntingdon: Volume 3*, ed. William Page, Granville Provy and S. Inskip Ladds (London, 1936), pp. 75–86.
41 Bellamy, *The Tudor Law of Treason*, p. 12.
42 BL Cotton MS Otho C X, fol. 171 (*LP* VII, 610). Commissioners like Gardiner had been receiving oaths since March, so the November Act simply formalised what was already occurring.
43 TNA SP1/89, fol. 136 (*LP* VIII, 196). For more examples of female resistance see Jansen, *Dangerous Talk and Strange Behavior.*
44 *CSP Spain* V, i, 45 and 57.
45 *LP* VIII, 566; *CSP Spain* V, i, 138.
46 BL Cotton MS Cleopatra E VI, fol. 243 (*LP* VIII, 963).
47 TNA SP1/96, fol. 83 (*LP* IX, 289). 'Gaunt's Chapel' still stands as St Mark's Church. It was built to serve the adjacent Gaunt's Hospital, standing opposite St Augustine's Abbey, now Bristol Cathedral. It's likely that Lady Guildford lived within the abbey precinct.
48 TNA SP1/95, fol. 8 (*LP* IX, 6).
49 *LP* VIII, 996.
50 TNA SP1/96, fol. 73 (*LP* IX, 274).
51 *CSP Spain* V, i, 75.
52 TNA SP1/96, fol. 172 (*LP* IX, 386).
53 *CSP Spain* V, i, 238.
54 Ibid.
55 *LP* IX, 970.
56 *CSP Spain* V, i, 246.
57 TNA SP1/99, fol. 163 (*LP* IX, 1040).
58 *LP* IX, 1037.
59 The account of her arrival was written by Bedingfield and Chamberlain to Cromwell on 5 January 1536. The original was damaged in the Cotton fire in the eighteenth century, but it was seen by antiquarian John

Strype before this time, who put a version of it in his *Ecclesiastical Memorials*. Using the two together gives a fairly clear picture of the original text. BL Cotton MS Otho C X, fol. 215 (*LP* X, 28); Strype, *Ecclesiastical Memorials*, Vol. 1, Part 1, p. 372.

60   Strype, *Ecclesiastical Memorials*, Vol. 1, Part 1, p. 372.
61   *CSP Spain* V, ii, 3.
62   Ibid., 9.
63   TNA SP1/101, fol. 21 (*LP* X, 37).

Chapter 10: Inconstant and Mutable Fortune

1   *LP* X, 141.
2   Ibid.
3   The fact that María was there when Catherine died on 7 January, and was named as one of the women acting as chief mourners for the masses from around 15 January, strongly suggests that she remained at Kimbolton throughout this time.
4   *CSP Spain* V, ii, 9.
5   *LP* X, 284.
6   Ibid.
7   The noblewomen who performed the role of chief mourner at the masses preceding the funeral were Eleanor Brandon, who was the overall chief mourner; Katherine Willoughby, Duchess of Suffolk; Frances de Vere, Countess of Surrey; Anne Howard, Countess of Oxford; Elizabeth Browne, Countess of Worcester; Margaret Gamage, Lady Howard; María de Salínas, Lady Willoughby; Jane Hallighwell, Lady Bray and 'Lady Gascon', whose identity is unclear. It's likely that the seven ladies who performed the role of chief mourners at the funeral were from this group. *LP* X, 284.
8   There was some debate about whether she ought to have a hearse at St Paul's in London, but the king refused, as Ralph Sadler wrote to inform Cromwell: TNA SP1/101, fol. 50 (*LP* X, 76).
9   *LP* X, 128 (original BL Cotton MS Otho C X, fol. 220, heavily mutilated).
10   There are several copies of Catherine's will; the contemporary copy, BL Cotton MS Otho C X, fol. 216, is mutilated but calendared in *LP* X, 40 and printed in Strype, *Ecclesiastical Memorials*, Vol. 1, Part 2, p. 252. A later copy in BL Cotton MS Titus C VII, fol. 44 is clearer to read.
11   Harris, *English Aristocratic Women*, pp. 46–7.
12   This might be Elizabeth Otwell, who is mentioned in other docs; Isabel is the Spanish form of Elizabeth.
13   *LP* II, 2747.

14   This anonymous account is *LP* X, 284.

15   Ibid.

16   *LP* X, 284.

17   Chapuys claimed that Queen Anne miscarried on the same day as Catherine's burial (*CSP Spain* V, ii, 21). This was repeated by the Bishop of Faenza (the Imperial ambassador in France) to Dr Ortiz (the empress's envoy in Rome), who wrote the same to the empress on 6 March (*LP* X, 427). Wriothesley's *Chronicle* said she miscarried three days before Candlemas, which would have been 30 January, the day after Catherine's burial (Wriothesley, p. 33).

18   *LP* X, 427.

19   There is a theory that Henry's fall may have caused a traumatic brain injury that affected his personality going forward. See Muhammad Qaiser Ikram, Fazle Hakim Sajjad and Arah Salardini, 'The Head that Wears the Crown: Henry VIII and Traumatic Brain Injury', *Journal of Clinical Neuroscience* 38 (2016), 16–19, and also Suzannah Lipscomb, *1536: The Year that Changed Henry VIII* (Oxford, 2009).

20   *LP* X, 352.

21   *CSP Spain* V, ii, 29.

22   Wriothesley, p. 43; TNA E101/421/13.

23   *LP* X, 901.

24   Ibid., 601.

25   Ibid.

26   Historians have debated endlessly whether the surviving evidence points towards or away from plots to get rid of Anne before April 1536. Both George Bernard and Greg Walker have argued that Anne's fall was triggered very suddenly (Bernard's argument is laid out in his *Anne Boleyn: Fatal Attractions*, and for Walker see 'Rethinking the Fall of Anne Boleyn', *The Historical Journal* 45:1 (2002), 1–29). Eric Ives, and more recently Diarmaid MacCulloch, have argued that there is evidence of a longer-standing attempt to remove Anne, whether as a 'plot' by conservatives or at the direction of the king (see Ives, pp. 289–364 and MacCulloch, pp. 292–342). On the scholarly debate about the existence and role of faction more broadly at this time see Janet Dickinson, 'Redefining Faction at the Tudor Court', in Ruben Gonzalez Cuerva and Alexander Koller, eds, *A Europe of Courts, A Europe of Factions* (Leiden, 2017), pp. 20–40. I do not think it should be particularly surprising that the surviving evidence for Anne Boleyn's fall can be read in either direction. Both Henry VIII and his advisors were masters both of keeping their options genuinely open and of dissimulation, and thus it shouldn't be considered odd that we see Henry pushing for European

recognition of his marriage to Anne while simultaneously seeking ways out of that same marriage.

27 TNA SP70/7, fols 3–13 (summarised and translated in *Calendar of State Papers, Foreign: Elizabeth, Volume 1, 1558–1559*, ed. by Joseph Stevenson (London, 1863)

28 For more on Ales's letter and career see MacCulloch, pp. 313–17, and Gotthelf Wiedermann, 'Alesius [*formerly* Allane or Alan], Alexander', *ODNB* https://doi.org/10.1093/ref:odnb/320 (accessed August 2023).

29 SP70/7, fol. 6v: 'Dilatores, quia nehementer subi a Regina metuebant, noctu et interdiu obseruant cubientum eius, tentant muneribus favitorum et pedissequarum aios, nihil non pollicentur Virginibus in genicaeo'.

30 Ibid.: 'Affirmant elia Regem odire Reginam, propterea, q hoeredem regni ex ea non sustulisset, nec speraret quidem'.

31 TNA E101/420/15.

32 BL Cotton MS Otho C X, fol. 210 (*LP* X, 799). Both MacCulloch and Ives have thrown a spotlight onto Margery Horsman as playing a role in Anne Boleyn's fall. Both note that she moved seamlessly to the service of Jane Seymour, and MacCulloch adds that she and her family were 'precocious evangelicals with links to Cromwell' (p. 316). See Ives, p. 332.

33 *The Story of the Death of Anne Boleyn: A Poem by Lancelot de Carle*, translation, edition and essays by JoAnn DellaNeva (Tempe, AZ, 2021). All references to the poem itself are to this edition.

34 The identification was made by George Bernard in his *Anne Boleyn: Fatal Attractions*, p. 154, and de Carle's editor JoAnn DellaNeva follows this (pp. 47–50), pointing out that Worcester and her brother Anthony Browne were also given starring roles in an Italian novella written during the 1540s.

35 TNA E36/210, fol. 91.

36 For instance TNA SP1/73, fol. 71v, SP1/233, fol. 263, SP1/19, fol. 149, SP1/37, fols 53, 58, E179/69/20, *LP* IV, 2972, E101/420/11, E101/420/15, SP2/N, fol. 2, E101/421/13, *LP* X, 871. It's possible that some of these references may be to Elizabeth Empson/Catesby/Lucy, Lady Lucy as the two women are largely impossible to unravel in the surviving records.

37 *The Privy Purse Expences of King Henry the Eighth*, ed. Nicholas Harris Nicolas (London, 1827), p. 22.

38 BL Add. MS 71009, fol. 58.

39 TNA SP1/103, fol. 318; Bernard, p. 154; W. R. B. Robinson, 'The Lands of Henry, Earl of Worcester in the 1530s. Part 3: Central Monmouthshire and Herefordshire', *Bulletin of the Board of Celtic Studies* xxv (iv) (1974), pp. 460, 492.

40   Both would soon find themselves in trouble for pushing for Princess Mary's return to the succession.

41   See DellaNeva, pp. 148–9.

42   *Lisle Letters* III, no. 703a and IV, no. 847.

43   De Carle, lines 386–7.

44   Cromwell later identified 18/19 April as the day he decided to 'plot out the whole business' of getting rid of Anne Boleyn. *CSP Spain* V, ii, 61.

45   MacCulloch, p. 336.

46   'not six days before her apprehension'. J. Bruce and T. T. Perowne, eds, *Correspondence of Matthew Parker, D. D. Archbishop of Canterbury Comprising Letters Written by Him and to Him, from A.D. 1535, to His Death, A.D. 1575* (Cambridge, 1853), p. 59.

47   Thurley, *The Royal Palaces of Tudor England* (London, 1993), pp. 48, 232–3, and *Houses of Power*, p. 8; *The History of the King's Works*, Vol. 3, ed. Howard Montagu Colvin (London, 1963), pp. 266–8.

48   Anne told this and many other anecdotes to Sir William Kingston, constable of the Tower, during her imprisonment, and he relayed them by letter to Thomas Cromwell. Many of Kingston's letters survive in BL Cotton MS Otho C X, fol. 225r onwards, but are heavily fire-damaged. The calendared versions in *LP* X are generally clearer and I have used these, supplemented by Strype's versions in his *Ecclesiastical Memorials*, Vol. 1, Part 1.

49   *LP* X, 793.

50   De Carle, lines 491–516.

51   Hall, p. 819.

52   MacCulloch, p. 338.

53   Thurley, *Houses of Power*, p. 82.

54   Their precise identities vary depending on the source. Chapuys wrote that Anne was arrested by Norfolk, 'the two Chamberlains, of the Realm and of the Chamber' – probably Lord Chancellor Audley and Treasurer of the Chamber Fitzwilliam (*CSP Spain* V, ii, 48). Wriothesley's *Chronicle* didn't mention Fitzwilliam, but added Cromwell and Sir William Kingston, constable of the Tower, to that list (Wriothesley, p. 36).

55   According to Chapuys; *LP* X, 782.

56   Wriothesley, p. 36.

Chapter 11: Such about Me as I Never Loved

1   *LP* X, 793.

2   As the king's building accounts show. Bodleian MS Rawlinson D 775, fol. 206.

3   Ibid., fols 204–10.

4   University of Nottingham, Newcastle MS Ne 02 (formerly 65), unfo-
     liated: '[for the] stopping upe of ij other windowed wth tymbr in the
     house where the bowe staves standde whiche was removed oute of the
     hall ayenste the raynement of the Ladye Anne late wyffe to oure said
     souaigne Lorde'.

5   This is how the king's chambers at the Tower were decorated (Thurley,
     Houses of Power, p. 241.) We also know that the lower parts of the
     windows in the queen's lodging on the garden side were 'closed up' with
     plain panelling. Bodleian MS Rawlinson D 775, fol. 210.

6   This is what happened to Thomas More. In extreme cases it could be
     indefinite, as was the case later for Edward Courtenay and Walter
     Raleigh. See Ruth Ahnert, *The Rise of Prison Literature in the Sixteenth
     Century* (Cambridge, 2013), pp. 12–13.

7   TNA LC2/1, fol. 136; E101/417/3, no 2.

8   We don't have a birth date for Mary Scrope, but she must have been
     born before her father's death in 1485. The daughter of Sir Richard
     Scrope of Upsall, Yorkshire, and Eleanor Washbourne, she'd been
     connected to the court since at least 1506, when she received a grant of
     clothing (TNA E101/416/3, fol. 76r). In 1509 she'd married Sir Edward
     Jerningham of Somerleyton, Suffolk as his second wife, and had many
     children, several of whom followed her to court. Widowed in 1515, Mary
     then married Sir William Kingston by 1532.

9   *LP* VIII, 327; *Lisle Letters* I, no. 52.

10   Catharine Davies, 'Coffin, Sir William', *ODNB* https://doi.org/10.1093/
     ref:odnb/70721 (accessed August 2023).

11   Roger Virgoe, 'Boleyn (Bullen), Sir James (c. 1480–1561), of Blickling,
     Norf.', *The History of Parliament: the House of Commons 1509–1558*, ed. S.
     T. Bindoff (London, 1982).

12   There are two candidates for 'Mrs Stonor': either Isabel Agard or
     Margaret/Anne Foliot, her sister-in-law, wife of Sir Walter Stonor. While
     Sir Walter, as the eldest son, was the more prominent courtier, there is no
     other record of his wife having been in court service. Isabel, on the other
     hand, was named as being 'in service with the Queen' on a grant to her-
     self and her husband John in August 1536 (*LP* XI, 253), and later received
     an annuity from Philip and Mary in January 1554 'in consideration of
     her service to Henry VIII and Edward VI and to the queens consort
     of Henry VIII in the place of the mother of his daughters' (*Calendar of
     Patent Rolls, Philip and Mary, Volume 1, 1553–4* (London, 1937) p. 60).
     This strongly suggests that she was the 'Mrs Stonor' described as the
     mother of the maids through the reigns of Henry's last four wives. Isabel

is described in visitation records as the daughter of Clement Agard of Foston Hall, Derbyshire, but this is unlikely to be accurate; Clement was not born until 1515. She may perhaps have been his sister.

13 In his first letter, Kingston noted that Lady Boleyn and Lady Coffin lay on pallets in the queen's bedchamber; Lady Kingston and himself lay at the door outside; and 'the other ij gentlewomen' likewise outside the chamber. One of these must have been Mrs Stonor, whom he mentioned later on, but this leaves one unnamed woman. *LP* X, 793.

14 Ibid., 797.

15 Ibid., 797, 798.

16 Ibid., 797.

17 Sara M. Butler, 'More than Mothers: Juries of Matrons and Pleas of the Belly in Medieval England', *Law and History Review* 37:2 (2019), 353–96.

18 *LP* X, 793.

19 Ibid.

20 Ibid.

21 Ibid.

22 Ibid., 797.

23 Ibid., 797, 798.

24 Ibid., 798.

25 *CSP Spain* V, ii, 54.

26 Ibid.

27 Ibid., i, 138.

28 *LP* X, 798.

29 Ibid.

30 Ibid., 848.

31 Bellamy, pp. 40–41.

32 Wriothesley, p. 37.

33 BL Add. MS 25114, fol. 160 (*LP* X, 873).

34 Ibid.

35 Ibid.

36 As described in the indictment. *LP* X, 876.

37 Wriothesley, p. 38.

38 Ibid., pp. 37–8; University of Nottingham, Newcastle MS Ne o2 (formerly 65), unfoliated.

39 *LP* X, 876.

40 J. H. Baker, ed., *The Reports of Sir John Spelman*, Selden Society (London, 1977), pp. 70–71.

41 TNA SP1/10, fol. 268v.

42 BL Cotton MS Vespasian F XIII, fol. 198.

43 *CSP Spain* IV, i, 345.

44   She gave the king 'a shirt of cambric, the collar wrought with gold'
     (TNA E101/421/13).
45   Taffe, *Courting Scandal*, pp. 141–2.
46   Bellamy, p. 76.
47   That Spelman specifically identifies Lady Wingfield as the one who
     'disclosed this matter' is interesting in light of other sources that have
     the Countess of Worcester as 'the first accuser'. It may be that Wingfield
     was part of the earlier investigation from January 1536, but did not
     say anything that could then have led to a treason charge without the
     corroboration of Worcester's unguarded remarks to her brother in May.
     Alternatively, it's possible that she was being used as a kind of scapegoat
     for Worcester and other women who gave evidence, because her death
     meant that she could not suffer for anything said in court. It's plausible
     that Worcester's brothers, Anthony Browne and William Fitzwilliam,
     had moved to keep their sister's name out of the formal trial for fear of
     repercussions, and that this was a ploy that served the prosecution.
48   Wriothesley, pp. 35–6; *CSP Spain* V, ii, 55.
49   Wriothesley, p. 38; *CSP Spain* V, ii, 55.
50   *CSP Spain* V, ii, 55.
51   Elizabeth Foyster, *Manhood in Early Modern England: Honour, Sex and
     Marriage* (London, 1999), p. 5.
52   Taffe, *Courting Scandal*, pp. 152–4.
53   Ibid., pp. 145–6. Taffe also suggests that Jane had not returned to court
     after her dismissal in the autumn of 1534, and that therefore she knew
     that she could not be incriminated in any more recent events. While it's
     true that there are no extant references to Jane between 1534 and 1536,
     the general dearth of material relating to ladies-in-waiting during those
     years makes it too difficult to rely on negative evidence in this way.
54   For instance, C. Whittingham, ed., *The Life of Cardinal Wolsey: And
     Metrical Visions from the Original Autograph Manuscript*, 2 vols
     (London, 1825), Vol. 1, pp. 71–4; John Foxe, *The Unabridged Acts and
     Monuments Online* or *TAMO* (The Digital Humanities Institute,
     Sheffield, 2011), p. 1210 (marginalia); Wyatt, 'Extracts from the Life of
     Queen Anne Boleigne', p. 447.
55   This is reported by Gilbert Burnet, writing in 1679. Burnet had had sight
     of a journal kept by Anthony Anthony, surveyor of the ordinance at the
     Tower in 1536, which reportedly claimed that Jane had gone to the king
     with 'many stories, to persuade, that there was a familiarity between the
     Queen and her Brother, beyond what so near a Relation could justifie'.
     This journal is no longer extant. Gilbert Burnet, *The History of the
     Reformation of the Church of England* (London, 1679), Vol. 1, p. 189.

56 See Anne Crawford, 'Victims of Attainder: The Howard and DeVere Women in the Late Fifteenth Century', in *Medieval Women in Southern England*, ed. Keith Bate (Reading, 1989), pp. 59–74.
57 *LP* X, 908.
58 Ibid., 890.
59 Ibid., 908.
60 De Carle, lines 1173–82.
61 *LP* X, 910.
62 Lancelot de Carle describes Anne's attendants in the Tower as 'damoiselles', a term denoting a gentlewoman, 'anyone under the degree of lady'. DellaNeva argues that Carle used this 'to suit the rhyme and meter and not to indicate their actual age or status'. DellaNeva, p. 255n.
63 De Carle, lines 1278–95.
64 Samuel Bentley (ed.), *Excerpta Historica* (London, 1833), pp. 261–5.
65 De Carle, lines 1290–91.
66 *Statutes of the Realm* III, p. 317.
67 Arundel Castle MS G1/4; TNA SC12/25/53.
68 TNA SP1/104, fol. 82 (*LP* X, 1011).
69 BL Cotton MS Vespasian F XIII, fol. 199.
70 TNA SP1/105, fol. 5 (*LP* XI, 17).
71 Taffe, *Courting Scandal*, p. 170.
72 Kate E. McCaffrey, 'Hope from day to day: Inscriptions newly discovered in a book belonging to Anne Boleyn', *TLS*, May 2021 https://www.the-tls.co.uk/articles/inscriptions-discovered-in-a-book-owned-by-anne-boleyn-essay-kate-e-mccaffrey/ (accessed August 2023).
73 BL Cotton MS Vespasian C XIV, fol. 266.
74 Alice was a knight's wife, Elizabeth was not.
75 *LP* XV, 477.
76 See Clark, *Gender, Family, and Politics*, pp. 128–9; David M. Head, '"Beyng Ledde and Seduced by the Devyll": The Attainder of Lord Thomas Howard and the Tudor Law of Treason', *Sixteenth Century Journal* 13:4 (1982), 2–16; Kimberly Schutte, '"Not for Matters of Treason but for Love Matters": Margaret Douglas, Countess of Lennox, and Tudor Marriage Law', in James V. Mehl, ed., *Laudem Caroli: Renaissance and Reformation Studies for Charles G. Nauert* (Kirksville, MI, 1998), pp. 171–88.
77 TNA SP1/126, fol. 48.
78 *Statutes of the Realm* III, pp. 655–62.
79 TNA E36/120/65.
80 Ibid.
81 His attainder was one of only three which included clauses extending

the treason law so that in future the crime listed, i.e. marrying a relative of the king without permission, would be legally treasonable. Interestingly, it also stated that in future, anybody advising or aiding in the making of such a match would share the penalties for high treason, a clause which, had it come into immediate effect, would have lost Mary her head. See Head, "'Beyng Ledde and Seduced'", and *Statutes of the Realm* III, pp. 680–81.

82 Lady Margaret remained in the Tower until November 1536, at which point she was moved to Syon Abbey (TNA SP1/110, fol. 186). Lord Thomas died of sickness in the Tower a year later in October 1537 (SP1/126, fol. 48).

83 *CSP Spain* V, ii, 77.

84 *Statutes of the Realm* III, pp. 655–62.

85 *CSP Spain* V, ii, 77.

86 *LP* X, 1087 (17).

Chapter 12: Too Wise for a Woman

1 The original of Lady Hussey's answers is heavily mutilated (BL Cotton MS Otho C X, fol. 254), but calendared in *LP* VII, 1036.

2 Both Lady Hussey and her husband had been involved with the Nun of Kent's prophecies in 1534.

3 *LP* VII, 1036.

4 Passed in July 1536. *Statutes of the Realm* III, pp. 655–62.

5 Her illegitimacy hadn't been officially stated, but it had been officially implied by the annulment of her parents' marriage in 1533 and then the First Act of Succession in 1534.

6 McIntosh, p. 75.

7 *CSP Spain* V, i, 45, 138.

8 *LP* VII, 1036.

9 Ibid.

10 *CSP Spain* V, ii, 70.

11 *LP* XI, 10.

12 *LP* VII, 1036.

13 McIntosh, p. 73.

14 *CSP Spain* V, ii, 70.

15 *LP* VII, 1036.

16 BL Cotton MS Otho C X, fol. 276 (*LP* X, 968).

17 *CSP Spain* V, ii, 61.

18 McIntosh, pp. 101–4; BL Cotton MS Vespasian C XIV, fols 274–275v; Otho C X, fols 266–91.

19 This sum represented over eighteen years' worth of wages for a skilled tradesman, which does demonstrate the comparative wealth of even the smaller monastic houses.

20 See R. Hoyle, *The Pilgrimage of Grace and the Politics of the 1530s* (Oxford, 2001), and Michael Bush, *The Pilgrims' Complaint: A Study of Popular Thought in the Early Tudor North* (Farnham, 2009).

21 LRO 1 ANC 5/B/c.

22 *Statutes of the Realm* III, pp. 596–8.

23 This has been uncovered and laid out by Steven Gunn in 'Peers, Commons and Gentry in the Lincolnshire Revolt of 1536', *Past and Present* 123 (1989), 52–79.

24 TNA E36/118, fol. 7 (*LP* XII, i, 854).

25 Ibid., fol. 3v.

26 Ibid.

27 *LP* XII, i, 946.

28 *LP* XI, 585; TNA SP1/107, fol. 66; *LP* XI 828 i, iii; *LP* XI, 975.

29 Gunn, 'Peers, Commons and Gentry'; *LP* XI, 828.

30 Hoyle, pp. 159–66.

31 TNA SP1/109, fol. 70.

32 TNA E36/118, fol. 7.

33 Jansen, p. 27.

34 Ibid.

35 *LP* XI, 860, 1250.

36 Clark, *Gender, Family, and Politics*, pp. 129–32.

37 TNA SP1/106, fol. 248 (*LP* XI, 533).

38 TNA SP1/107, fol. 100 (*LP* XI, 615).

39 TNA SP1/106, fol. 248 (*LP* XI, 533).

40 Gunn, *Charles Brandon*, pp. 157.

41 Grimsthorpe was technically in María's hands, but Suffolk did not himself have a house in Lincolnshire at this time. After the suppression of the rebellion he was ordered to relocate to Grimsthorpe to keep the county quiet for the future, and in 1540 he had it remodelled. He and Katherine lived there for many years after this.

42 TNA SP1/107, fol. 141 (*LP* XI, 650).

43 TNA SP1/112, fol. 149 (*LP* XI, 1267).

44 BL Cotton MS Vespasian F XIII, fol. 232 (*LP* XII, i, 81).

45 TNA SP1/115, fol. 196 (*LP* XII, i, 345).

46 Those who inventoried her late husband's goods noted that she had taken horses to go into Kenninghall. *LP* XI, 163.

47 TNA LR 2/117.

48 Ibid.

49 Ibid.
50 According to Mary's mother Elizabeth, Duchess of Norfolk: BL Cotton MS Titus B I, fols 390r–v.
51 TNA E36/230/65.
52 TNA SP1/128, fol. 69.
53 See Clark, *Gender, Family, and Politics*, pp. 28–31.
54 TNA SP1/111, fol. 240.
55 Ibid.
56 Head, *The Ebbs and Flows of Fortune*, pp. 135–7.
57 TNA SP1/111, fol. 204.
58 Ibid.
59 Head, *The Ebbs and Flows of Fortune*, p. 143.
60 BL Cotton MS Vespasian F XIII, fol. 144.
61 TNA SP1/114, fol. 48.
62 TNA SP1/115, fol. 80.
63 Head, *The Ebbs and Flows of Fortune*, pp. 144–6.
64 Gunn, *Charles Brandon*, p. 166.
65 Jansen, p. 26.
66 Ibid., pp. 26–7.

Chapter 13: Sworn the Queen's Maid

1   *Lisle Letters* IV, no. 895.
2   Ibid., no. 899.
3   *Lisle Letters* III, no. 578.
4   Ibid., no. 717.
5   TNA SP1/124, fol. 1 (*LP* XII, ii, 379).
6   David Grummitt, 'Plantagenet, Arthur, Viscount Lisle', *ODNB* https://doi.org/10.1093/ref:odnb/22355 (accessed August 2023).
7   Many of John Husee's letters to Lady Lisle are occupied with this question. See *Lisle Letters* IV, nos 850 (ii), 864, 865, 870, 874, 884.
8   Ibid., no. 896.
9   Ibid., nos 850 (ii), 863.
10 *Lisle Letters* II, no. 299a; IV, no. 880.
11 *Lisle Letters* IV, no. 870.
12 *Lisle Letters* III, no. 729.
13 *Lisle Letters* IV, no. 850 (ii).
14 Ibid., no. 868a.
15 Ibid., no. 875.
16 Ibid., no. 867.
17 Ibid., no. 868a.

18   *A Collection of Ordinances*, p. 199. Ordinances routinely specify
      numbers of beds rather than servants themselves. It's difficult to map
      numbers of beds directly onto numbers of servants, since bed-sharing
      was a normal practice.

19   *Lisle Letters* IV, no. 868a.

20   Ibid., nos 871, 872.

21   Ibid., no. 854a.

22   Ibid., nos 875, 868a.

23   Ibid., nos 878, 879, 881, 883, 886, 887, 888, 889.

24   TNA SP1/121, fol. 95 (*LP* XII, ii, 77).

25   Or rather, Lady Lisle thought she was pregnant, but no baby materi-
      alised.

26   *Lisle Letters* IV, no. 889.

27   Ibid., no. 887.

28   Ibid.

29   Ibid., no. 891.

30   Ibid., no. 894.

31   Ibid., no. 895.

32   Ibid.

33   Thurley, *Houses of Power*, pp. 217–24.

34   *Lisle Letters* IV, no. 895.

35   Taffe, 'Reconstructing the Queen's Household', pp. 207–10.

36   *Lisle Letters* IV, no. 895.

37   A. R. Myers, *The Household of Edward IV: The Black Book and the
      Ordinance of 1478* (Manchester, 1959), pp. 92–3.

38   *Lisle Letters* IV, no. 895; *A Collection of Ordinances*, p. 164.

39   *Lisle Letters* IV, no. 895.

40   Hayward, *Dress at the Court*, p. 158.

41   *Lisle Letters* IV, no. 895. It's often said that this was because the French
      style of dress, and hoods in particular, were so strongly associated with
      Queen Anne Boleyn that Queen Jane was actively trying to break from
      that. However, Maria Hayward notes that Jane actually had only French
      hoods in her wardrobe as inventoried after her death. Hayward, *Dress at
      the Court*, p. 171.

42   Ibid., pp. 158–74.

43   *Lisle Letters* IV, no. 896.

44   The use of certain colours, fabrics and furs was regulated by law accord-
      ing to social status, in an effort to maintain social hierarchy despite
      an increasingly rich merchant class, and to prevent people spending
      beyond their means. These were called Sumptuary Laws. Though they
      did not officially apply to women, their clothing was supposed to reflect

the status of their father or husband. See Maria Hayward, *Rich Apparel: Clothing and the Law in Henry VIII's England* (Aldershot, 2009).

45 *Lisle Letters* IV, no. 895.

46 TNA SP1/125, fol. 211 (*LP* XII, ii, 680).

47 College of Arms MS M8, fols 32–3.

48 Wriothesley, pp. 65–6.

49 Ibid., pp. 66–7.

50 College of Arms MS I.14, fols 135–8. This is the draft account; there is a fair copy in College of Arms MS 6, and another version in BL Egerton MS 985, fol. 33. See also *LP* XII, ii, 911.

51 *Lisle Letters* IV, no. 900.

52 Ibid.

53 *LP* XII, ii, 970.

54 Hall, p. 825.

55 *Lisle Letters* IV, no. 905.

56 A full account of Queen Jane's burial can be found in BL Add MS 71009, fols 37–44v. See also *LP* XII, ii, 1060.

57 Hall, p. 825.

58 *Lisle Letters* IV, no. 905.

59 Ibid., no. 904.

60 Ibid., no. 906.

61 TNA SP1/126, fol. 58 (*LP* XII, ii, 1030).

62 *Lisle Letters* V, no. 1086.

63 Mary Shelton was one of the key contributors to the Devonshire Manuscript in the mid-1530s.

64 *Lisle Letters* V, no. 1086.

65 TNA SP1/127, fol. 32 (*LP* XII, ii, 1187).

66 MacCulloch, pp. 422–7, 443–5.

67 Ibid., pp. 444–5; Head, *The Ebbs and Flows of Fortune*, pp. 152–5.

68 Suggestion made by editor of the Lisle letters, Muriel St Clare Byrne, V, pp. 11–13.

69 *LP* XIV, ii, 400.

70 *LP* XIII, i, 995.

71 *Privy Purse Expenses of Princess Mary*, ed. Frederick Madden (London, 1831)

72 Mary Norris, in April 1538. Ibid., p. 67.

73 *Lisle Letters* IV, no. 1038.

74 *Lisle Letters* V, no. 1182.

75 Ibid., no. 1136a.

76 Ibid., no. 1137.

77 Ibid., no. 1154.

78   TNA SP1/128, fol. 11 (*LP* XIII, i, 13).

79   TNA SP1/131, fol. 24 (*LP* XIII, i, 690).

80   Ibid.

81   TNA SP1/131, fol. 67 (*LP* XIII, i, 741); TNA SP1/131, fol. 192 (*LP* XIII, i, 846).

82   Clark, *Gender, Family, and Politics*, pp. 28–31.

83   TNA SP1/134, fol. 160.

84   Ibid.

85   Ibid.

86   TNA SP1/135, fol. 74 (*LP* XIII, ii, 84).

87   TNA SP1/135, fol. 76 (*LP* XIII, ii, 75).

Chapter 14: Juggling

1   Pre-modern priests were often given the courtesy title of 'sir'; this should not be confused with possession of a knighthood.

2   TNA SP1/144, fol. 16 (*LP* XIV, i, 425).

3   See the entry in the *Oxford English Dictionary* at https://www.oed.com/dictionary/juggling_n?tab=meaning_and_use (accessed August 2023).

4   TNA SP1/144, fol. 16 (*LP* XIV, i, 425).

5   TNA SP1/124, fol. 9 (*LP* XII, ii, 469).

6   BL Cotton MS Cleopatra E IV, fol. 55 (*LP* XII, ii, 267).

7   *Lisle Letters* V, no. 1120.

8   BL Cotton MS Cleopatra E V, fol. 300 (*LP* XII, ii, 592). See also Fiona Kisby, '"When the King Goeth a Procession": Chapel Ceremonies and Services, the Ritual Year, and Religious Reforms at the Early Tudor Court, 1485–1547', *Journal of British Studies* 40:1 (2001), 44–75.

9   MacCulloch, pp. 498–501.

10   See T. F. Mayer, 'Pole, Reginald', *ODNB* https://doi.org/10.1093/ref:odnb/22456 (accessed August 2023); MacCulloch, pp. 472–8; Madeleine Hope Dodds and Ruth Dodds, *The Pilgrimage of Grace 1536–1537 and The Exeter Conspiracy 1538*, 2 vols (London, 1971); Sylvia Barbara Soberton, *Gertrude Courtenay: Wife and Mother of the Last Plantagenet* (2021), pp. 97–133.

11   Bernard, *King's Reformation*, p. 542.

12   T. F. Mayer, 'Pole, Sir Geoffrey', *ODNB* https://doi.org/10.1093/ref:odnb/22447 (accessed August 2023).

13   The same Bess who had been in service with Catherine of Aragon at her death in 1536, and who became the mistress of Thomas Wyatt.

14   TNA SP1/138, fol. 180 (*LP* XIII, ii, 804 (3)).

15   Ibid., fol. 183 (*LP* XIII, ii, 804 (6)).

16 Ibid., fol. 181 (*LP* XIII, ii, 804 (5)).

17 Wriothesley, p. 88.

18 TNA SP1/138, fol. 132 (*LP* XIII, ii, 765).

19 Ibid., fol. 172 (*LP* XIII, ii, 802).

20 Wriothesley, p. 92.

21 *LP* XIV, i, 191 (3).

22 BL Cotton MS Appendix L, fol. 77v; see Janice Liedl, '"Rather a Strong and Constant Man": Margaret Pole and the Problem of Women's Independence', in J. A. Chappell and K. A. Kramer, eds, *Women During the English Reformations* (New York, 2014), pp. 29–43.

23 TNA SP1/140, fol. 218 (*LP* XIII, ii, 1176).

24 *LP* XIV, i, 37.

25 Stanford Lehmberg, 'Carew, Sir Nicholas', *ODNB* https://doi.org/10.1093/ref:odnb/4633 (accessed August 2023); *LP* XIII, ii, 830.

26 TNA SP1/144, fol. 16 (*LP* XIV, i, 425).

27 Ibid.

28 David Loades, 'Henry Grace á Dieu', in John J. Hattendorf, ed., *The Oxford Encyclopedia of Maritime History* (Oxford, 2007).

29 *LP* XIV, i, 1260, 1261.

30 Dominic Fontana, 'Charting the Development of Portsmouth Harbour, Dockyard and Town in the Tudor Period', *Journal of Marine Archaeology* 8 (2013), 263–82.

31 BL Cotton MS Vespasian F XIII, fol. 251.

32 There were ten women in all who signed their names to this letter: Mabel Clifford, Countess of Southampton; Margaret Gamage, Lady Howard, wife to Lord William Howard; Margaret Skipwith, Lady Tailboys, wife of George, Lord Tailboys; Anne Pickering, wife to Sir Henry Knyvett; Alice Gage, wife of Sir Anthony Browne; Jane Champernowne, wife of Sir Anthony Denny; Jane Ashley, wife to Sir Peter Mewtas; Elizabeth Oxenbridge, wife of Sir Robert Tyrwhit; Anne Basset; and Elizabeth Harvey.

33 *Lisle Letters* V, no. 1395.

34 Ibid., nos 1436, 1441, 1453, 1457a; TNA E101/422/15.

35 *Lisle Letters* IV, no. 895.

36 *Lisle Letters* V, no. 1513.

37 Ibid., no. 1558.

38 See Retha Warnicke, *The Marrying of Anne of Cleves* (Cambridge, 2000).

39 Bernard, *King's Reformation*, p. 543.

40 See Warnicke, *The Marrying of Anne of Cleves*, pp. 79–93; Nicole Bertzen, 'Mission Impossible? Ambassador Karl Harst, Anne of Cleves, and Their Struggles to Secure the Strategic Alliance between Cleves

and England', unpublished PhD dissertation, University of Kent (2022); Heather R. Darsie, *Anna, Duchess of Cleves: The King's 'Beloved Sister'* (Stroud, 2019).

41 Warnicke, *The Marrying of Anne of Cleves*, pp. 107–11; *LP* XIV, ii, 424, 494.

42 TNA SP1/154, fol. 5 (*LP* XIV, ii, 297).

43 Susan E. James, 'The Horenbout Family Workshop at the Tudor Court, 1522–1541: Collaboration, Patronage and Production', *Cogent Arts and Humanities* 8 (2021).

44 See ibid.; Susan Foister, 'Horenbout, Susanna', in 'Horebout [Hornebolt], Gerard', *ODNB* https://doi.org/10.1093/ref:odnb/13797 (accessed August 2023); Kathleen E. Kennedy, 'Susanna Horebout, Courtier and Artist', *Art Herstory* (1 December 2019), https://artherstory.net/susanna-horenbout-courtier-and-artist/ (accessed August 2023).

45 *The Chronicle of Calais in the Reigns of Henry VII and Henry VIII to the year 1540*, ed. John Gough Nichols (London, 1846), p. 172; BL Harley MS 296, fol. 169v; BL Cotton MS Vitellius C XI, fol. 220v.

46 TNA SP1/155, fol. 85 (*LP* XIV, ii, 634). Wotton gives their names: Swarzenbroch, Brempt, Ossenbruch, Loe and Willik.

47 *Chronicle of Calais*, p. 169.

48 *History of the King's Works*, Vol. 3, pp. 341, 349–50.

49 TNA SP1/155, fol. 108 (*LP* XIV, ii, 677).

50 *Lisle Letters* V, no. 1620.

51 TNA SP1/155, fol. 36; *Lisle Letters* VI, no. 1364; BL Add. MS 45716A, fol. 15v.

52 Mabel Clifford, Countess of Southampton, Margaret Gamage, Lady Howard, Margaret Skipwith, Lady Tailboys, Elizabeth Oxenbridge, Lady Tyrwhit and Elizabeth Harvey were not on the list to serve Anna at this stage. Anecdotal evidence shows that Elizabeth Harvey may have remained at court, but she is not on any relevant official lists during this time.

53 TNA SP1/155, fol. 121 (*LP* XIV, ii, 693).

54 BL Cotton Vitellius C XVI, fol. 227 (*LP* XIV, ii, 754).

55 Melissa Franklin-Harkrider, *Women, Reform and Community in Early Modern England: Katherine Willoughby, Duchess of Suffolk, and Lincolnshire's Godly Aristocracy, 1519–1580* (Woodbridge, 2008), p. 54.

56 *LP* XIV, i, p. 293.

57 LRO 2 ANC 3/A/48. There's also an indenture dated 3 July 1539 that implies she is still alive at that date (2 ANC 3/A/50), so it's possible that the scribe made a mistake with the regnal year on either this or the 20 May document that means we can't certainly verify the date of her

death. My thanks to Steven Gunn for discussion on this point.

58 Neither of these places have parish records that go back far enough to check, and there is no surviving tomb.

59 The rumour seems to have been begun by Cecilie Goff (p. 109). A newspaper article from the Northampton Mercury, 28 August 1891, p. 8, however, shows that it was impossible: 'The workmen engaged in concreting the floor of the choir in Peterborough Cathedral have made an important discovery . . . In the course of events Queen Catherine's tomb was opened. It was found to be a vault over 8ft. long by 3ft. 11in. wide. In the interior was a stone, on which was inscribed the fact that the tomb was opened in 1790. What would probably be the remains of the Queen were enclosed in a large leaden shell, from which all traces of the wood coffin had long ago disappeared.'

60 *Lisle Letters* V, nos 1396a; 1409; 1441.

61 *Chronicle of Calais*, p. 173; Harley MS 296, fol. 171; SP1/155, fol. 27. Lady Cobham (either Anne Bray, wife of the 4th Lord Cobham, or Elizabeth Hart, widow of the 3rd Lord Cobham); Lady Hart (most likely Frideswide Bray, wife of Sir Percival Hart, but possibly Elizabeth Peche, wife of Sir John Hart); Lady Finch (Catherine Gainsford, second wife of Sir William Finch); Lady Hault (probably Margaret Wood, second wife of Sir William Hault); Lady Hales (most likely Elizabeth Caunton, wife of Sir Christopher Hales).

62 Hall, p. 833.

63 Hall says that they stayed in the 'palace' (p. 833) and Wriothesley 'Abbey' (p. 109). It's possible that a combination of lodgings was used, because the number of people then with Anna was large, and also because the king remained one night at Rochester too, but at a separate location. My thanks to Heather Darsie for discussion on this.

64 Wriothesley, pp. 109–10.

65 Hall, p. 833.

66 Bertzen, Part 1, pp. 115–18.

67 Hall, pp. 833–4.

68 Ibid., p. 835.

69 TNA SP1/157, fols 172–4 (fol. 174) (*LP* XV, 243).

70 It's not clear how many German maids remained with Anna. It may be that they didn't stay long in England; there's a payment in Queen Anna's expenses (undated) to somebody for their 'going over' with the 'duche maydes' ('Dutch' and 'German' were often conflated by the English at this time) (TNA E101/422/16, unfoliated). Among those who stayed were one 'Gertrude Willik' and a 'Katherine'; the two are lumped together in a list of rewards to Anna's suit in July 1540 (*LP* XV, 937), and Gertrude's

surname is given on the subsidy list of 1544–5 (TNA E179/69/48). She was still attending Anna at Henry VIII's funeral in 1547 (TNA LC 2/2, fol. 59). Gertrude was no doubt the 'Mistress Willik' named by Wotton, a relation of the Cleves steward Willik.

71   *Lisle Letters* VI, nos 1636, 1649–50.
72   TNA E101/422/15 and 16, both unfoliated.
73   Ambassador Karl Harst relayed an anecdote of Queen Anna translating between himself and Lady Rutland at dinner: see Bertzen, Part 2, p. 51.
74   Nicola Clark, 'Katherine Howard: Victim?', in Aidan Norrie et al., eds, *Tudor and Stuart Consorts: Power, Influence, and Dynasty* (Basingstoke, 2022), p. 127.
75   TNA SP1/167, fols 141–141v (*LP* XVI, 1339).
76   *LP* XV, 613 (12).
77   Bernard, *King's Reformation*, p. 543.
78   Bertzen, Part 1, pp. 78–82.
79   Ibid., Part 2, pp. 5–6, 30.
80   Bernard, *King's Reformation*, pp. 560–69.

Chapter 15: The Principle Occasion of Her Folly

1   *LP* XV, 872.
2   Harst, 10 July 1540, in Bertzen, Part 2, pp. 94–8.
3   Ibid.
4   *LP* XV, 872.
5   Both Catherine of Aragon and Princess Mary had been kept at Richmond Palace during times when they were out of favour.
6   Thurley, *Houses of Power*, pp. 50–51, 136, 256.
7   Harst, 3 July 1540, in Bertzen, Part 2, pp. 84–7.
8   Harst, 19 June 1540, in ibid., pp. 69–77; 13 July 1540, pp. 104–8; 29 July 1540, pp. 121–6.
9   *LP* XV, 872.
10   Dorothy Fitzherbert/Wingfield also had a history of service with Jane Seymour. Elizabeth Rastall appears to have been a new addition, but it is likely that she was the sister of Sir Thomas More, and was therefore no stranger to the dangerous whims of the Crown.
11   For more on this see Darsie, *Anna, Duchess of Cleves*; and Nicole Bertzen, 'Mission Impossible?'.
12   The depositions themselves haven't survived, but were seen and transcribed by Strype in his *Ecclesiastical Memorials*, Vol. 1, Part 1, Appendix CXIV, pp. 452–63. The ladies' deposition is on p. 462–3.
13   Outlined in the depositions above; also see Cromwell's letters to the

king in BL Cotton MS Titus B I, fols 273–274v (*LP* XV, 776); *LP* XV, 823, 824.

14 Harst's letters have been transcribed, summarised and analysed by Nicole Bertzen in Part 2 of her recent PhD thesis 'Mission Impossible?'. My thanks to Nicole for her kind permission to use her work here.

15 Harst, 17 April 1540, in ibid., pp. 32–5, and 6 May 1540, pp. 36–8.

16 Harst, 10 July 1540, in ibid., pp. 94–8.

17 Harst, 18 July, in ibid., pp. 110–20.

18 BL Cotton MS Titus B I, fols 273–274v (*LP* XV, 776).

19 See, for instance, Bernard, *King's Reformation*, pp. 542–79; MacCulloch, pp. 506–31.

20 TNA SP1/154, fol. 95 (*LP* XIV, ii, 455); TNA SP1/155, fol. 36; *LP* XIV, ii, 494.

21 *LP* XV, 860.

22 Harst, 7–8 July 1540, in Bertzen, Part 2, pp. 87–94.

23 Harst, 18 July 1540, in ibid., pp. 110–20.

24 Harst, 12 June 1540, in ibid., pp. 50–59.

25 Harst, 18 July 1540, in ibid., pp. 110–20.

26 Harst, 7–8 July 1540, in ibid., pp. 87–94.

27 Harst, 13 July 1540, in ibid., pp. 104–9.

28 Harst, 18 July 1540, in ibid., pp. 110–20.

29 See Gareth Russell, *Young & Damned & Fair: The Life and Tragedy of Catherine Howard at the Court of Henry VIII* (London, 2017).

30 TNA SP1/168, fols 53–75v (*LP* XVI, 1409). Katherine Howard's age at this time is a matter of considerable debate. We do not know exactly when she was born; estimates of her birthdate range from 1518 to 1527. A date of 1521 or 1522 allows for her parents to have married as late as 1515 and still to have had four children before Katherine, without pushing her mother's childbearing years too far beyond the bounds of reasonable possibility. This would make Katherine around eighteen or nineteen in 1540. See discussion in Clark, 'Katherine Howard: Victim?'.

31 Harst, 3 July 1540, in Bertzen, Part 2, pp. 84–7.

32 Harst, 12 July 1540, in ibid., pp. 98–103; 31 July 1540, pp. 126–35; 11 August 1540, pp. 138–42.

33 *Statutes of the Realm* III, p. 792.

34 Thurley, *Houses of Power*, pp. 262–3.

35 TNA SP1/157, fol. 14.

36 TNA LC 2/2, fol. 59.

37 Harst, 23 August 1540, in Bertzen, Part 2, pp. 148–53.

38 TNA SP1/157, fol. 14.

39 MacCulloch, pp. 449–51, 522; *Lisle Letters* VI, pp. 219–53.

40   Wriothesley, pp. 122–3.

41   *LP* XVI, 12.

42   Wriothesley, p. 122–3.

43   John Husee, when asked by his mistress Lady Lisle which women were
     in Anna of Cleves' chamber, reported not only those of the higher-status
     ladies and gentlewomen that he knew, but thought it important enough
     to include the names of the chamberers too. *Lisle Letters* VI, no. 1642.

44   This all comes from Margaret Morton's deposition, given later on in
     November 1541, when she said that 'afftar catryn tylnay was com that the
     quen crld not a byd mesttrysst loffken nor this deponent'. TNA SP1/167,
     fols 133–4 (*LP* XVI, 1338).

45   Ibid.

46   TNA SP1/167, fol. 136 (*LP* XVI, 1339).

47   Clark, 'Katherine Howard: Victim?', pp. 126–8.

48   TNA SP1/167, fol. 142r.

49   *Calendar of the Manuscripts of the Marquis of Bath Preserved at Long-
     leat, Wiltshire*, Vol. 2 (London, 1907), pp. 9–10; TNA SP1/167, fols 141–2
     (*LP* XVI, 1339); TNA SP1/167, fols 133–4 (*LP* XVI, 1338).

50   TNA SP1/167, fol. 142 (*LP* XVI, 1339).

51   Pontefract had been occupied by Henry Fitzroy, Duke of Richmond, in
     1525–6 and by Lord Darcy during the Pilgrimage of Grace, but not since.
     See Ian Roberts, *Pontefract Castle* (West Yorkshire Archaeology Service,
     1990).

52   Clark, 'Queen Katherine Howard: Space, Place, and Promiscuity',
     89–103.

53   TNA SP1/167, fol. 141 (*LP* XVI, 1339).

54   Clark, 'Queen Katherine Howard'.

55   TNA SP1/167, fols 142–3 (*LP* XVI, 1339).

56   Ibid.

57   Ibid.

58   Ibid.

59   Ibid.

60   Clark, 'Queen Katherine Howard'.

61   Ibid.

62   Russell, pp. 122–9.

63   Burnet, *History of the Reformation*, Vol. 4, p. 504.

64   Queen Katherine's brother Charles, in fact. Margaret was displaced for
     Katherine, nominally forgiven only because her isolated location was
     needed for a more serious purpose. She was sent instead to the Duke
     of Norfolk's house at Kenninghall in Norfolk with her friend, Queen
     Katherine's cousin, Mary Fitzroy, Duchess of Richmond. TNA SP1/167,
     fols 123–124v, 127 (*LP* XVI, 1331, 1333).

65   TNA SP1/167, fols 123–124v (*LP* XVI, 1331).

66   There is no way to know where in Syon Abbey Queen Katherine's chambers were. Though recent excavations and archaeological surveys have gone some way towards reconstructing the abbey before its suppression, the fact that it was largely demolished and rebuilt by the Duke of Somerset in the later 1540s makes it impossible to have an actual room plan. See Wessex Archaeology, 'Syon House, Syon Park, Hounslow: An Archaelogical Evaluation of a Bridgettine Abbey and an Assessment of the Results', (2003), available at https://www.wessexarch.co.uk/our-work/syon-house-syon-park (accessed August 2023).

67   TNA SP1/167, fols 123–124v (*LP* XVI, 1331).

68   Later in 1546, the Duke of Norfolk claimed in a letter that Ladies Herbert and Tyrwhit had been in the Tower with Queen Katherine: 'what malise both my nesys that it plesed the kynges highnes to marry dyd bere unto me is not unknowen to such lades as kept them in this howse as my lady herdberd my lady tirwit my lady kyngston and others'. BL Titus B I, fols 99–101v (fol. 101) (*LP* XXI, ii, 554).

69   TNA SP1/167, fols 133–4 (*LP* XVI, 1338).

70   Ibid., fols 131–2 (*LP* XVI, 1337).

71   Clark, 'Queen Katherine Howard'.

72   TNA SP1/167, fols 123–124v (*LP* XVI, 1331).

73   *LP* XVI, 1332.

74   Bradley J. Irish, '"The secret chamber and other suspect places": Materiality, Space, and the Fall of Katherine Howard', *Early Modern Women* 4 (2009), 169–73; *LP* XVI, 1342.

75   Clark, *Gender, Family, and Politics*, pp. 135–8.

76   TNA SP1/167, fols 147–147v (*LP* XVI, 1340).

77   *LP* XVI, 1366.

78   Wriothesley, p. 132.

79   TNA SP1/168, fol. 112 (*LP* XVI, 1443).

80   Ibid., fol. 164 (*LP* XVI, 1472).

81   Clark, 'Katherine Howard: Victim?', p. 136.

82   *LP* XVI, 1401.

83   Ibid.

84   This was Anne Sapcote. See Diane Willen, 'Russell, John, first earl of Bedford', *ODNB* https://doi.org/10.1093/ref:odnb/24319 (accessed August 2023).

85   Bellamy, pp. 40–41.

86   *Statutes of the Realm* III, pp. 857–60.

87   *LP* XVII, 28 (15).

88   Wriothesley, p. 133.

89 Ibid.; *CSP Spain* VI, i, 232.
90 Ibid.
91 *LP* XVII, 100.
92 Ibid.; *CSP Spain* VI, i, 232.

Chapter 16: When Women Become such Clerks

1   It's reasonable to suppose that Katharine and Anne Basset did write to one another, but there are no surviving letters to prove it. This is very often the case for correspondence between women, as personal letters were not routinely kept and their survival is often a case of chance.
2   She was certainly there by July 1541: *LP* XVI, 1023.
3   *CSP Spain* VI, i, 207; *LP* XVI, 1445, 1449, 1453.
4   Harst, 23 August 1540, in Bertzen, Part 2, pp. 148–53.
5   TNA SP1/168, fol. 50 (*LP* XVI, 1407). Though the source refers to 'Elizabeth' Basset, it's far more likely that Katharine was meant; the women talked about the 'maids' room' being 'sadly down', which is information that only those with a close connection to the queen's household would have known, and there is no 'Elizabeth Basset' in any other court records.
6   TNA SP1/168, fols 100–103, 112–113 (*LP* XVI, 1425, 1433).
7   *CSP Spain* VI, i, 230.
8   Ibid.
9   *CSP Spain* VI, ii, 94.
10 Ibid., i, 143; TNA E179/69/41; *Privy Purse Expenses of Princess Mary*, pp. 99, 144.
11 *Privy Purse Expenses of Princess Mary*, p. 111.
12 *LP* XIV, ii, 427, 780 (32); *LP* XV, 436 (87).
13 *Privy Purse Expenses of Princess Mary*, p. 177; McIntosh, pp. 39–44.
14 BL Royal MS 17 B XXVIII, fol. 5v; *Privy Purse Expenses of Princess Mary*, pp. 50, 51, 55, 58, 68, 69, 82, 96, 102, 134, 138, 143.
15 For instance, Lady Kingston (p. 178); and Dorothy Wheler (pp. 53, 123, 159).
16 Wriothesley, p. 141, says that the winter of 1542–3 saw 'greate cold and frost' following an unusually wet summer.
17 Susan James, *Catherine Parr: Henry VIII's Last Love* (Stroud, 2009), p. 77.
18 Ibid.
19 *CSP Spain* VI, ii, 105.
20 *LP* XVII, i, 873.
21 Franklin-Harkrider, p. 48.

22 James, pp. 78–9.

23 Ibid., p. 80.

24 TNA PROB 11/31/456.

25 Kathryn Parr's household is comparatively well documented. See Dakota Hamilton, 'The Household of Katherine Parr', unpublished D.Phil thesis, University of Oxford (1992); and, for example, subsidy lists for the queen's household, TNA E179/69/41, 44, 47, 48, 55; lodging list BL Cotton MS Vespasian C XIV, fol. 107; household accounts and expenses, TNA E101/424/3, 12, 13, 15, E315/161, 340.

26 TNA E315/161, fols 22, 23.

27 Ibid., fol. 22v.

28 J. Evans, '"Gentle Purges corrected with hot Spices, whether they work or not, do vehemently provoke Venery": Menstrual Provocation and Procreation in Early Modern England', *Social History of Medicine* 25:1 (2021), 2–19.

29 Wriothesley, p. 141.

30 *LP* XVIII, i, 144.

31 Gunn, *Charles Brandon*, pp. 197–236.

32 Ibid., pp. 205–9.

33 James, pp. 153–4; Retha Warnicke, *Elizabeth of York and her Six Daughters-in-Law* (Basingstoke, 2017), pp. 147–152; Micheline White, 'Katherine Parr: Wartime Consort and Author', in Norrie et al., eds, *Tudor and Stuart Consorts*, pp. 139–61 (pp. 149–51).

34 Gunn, *Charles Brandon*, p. 208.

35 *LP* XX, i, 1220.

36 *CSP Spain* VIII, 126, 128.

37 Bodleian MS Ashmole 1109, fols 142–6. My thanks to Kirsten Claiden-Yardley for this source.

38 TNA PROB 11/31/456.

39 See Franklin-Harkrider, pp. 46–58.

40 Ibid., p. 49; *CSP Spain* VIII, 174; *LP* XX, ii, 900.

41 Gunn, *Charles Brandon*, pp. 118–20.

42 Franklin-Harkrider, p. 51.

43 TNA WARD 9/149, fol. 136; Franklin-Harkrider, p. 51.

44 Strype, *Ecclesiastical Memorials*, Vol. 1, Part 1, pp. 597–8; Foxe (1583), p. 1263 at https://www.dhi.ac.uk/foxe/index.php?realm=text&goto-type=&edition=1583&pageid=1263&anchor=violet#kw (accessed August 2023) (*LP* XXI, i, 1181).

45 Ibid.

46 Franklin-Harkrider, p. 50, n. 19.

47 Diane Watt, 'Askew [married name Kyme], Anne', *ODNB* https://doi.

org/10.1093/ref:odnb/798 (accessed August 2023).

48 For more on religious policy during the 1530s and 1540s see Alec Ryrie, *The Gospel and Henry VIII: Evangelicals in the Early English Reformation* (Cambridge, 2003) and Peter Marshall, *Religious Identities in Henry VIII's England* (Aldershot, 2006).

49 See Bernard, *King's Reformation*.

50 Franklin-Harkrider, p. 49.

51 See Janel Mueller, ed., *Katherine Parr – Complete Works and Correspondence* (Chicago, 2011).

52 Ibid., p. 112, no. 12.

53 Strype, *Ecclesiastical Memorials*, Vol. 2, Part 1, p. 200; Franklin-Harkrider, p. 50.

54 TNA SP10/10/46, 10/11/4.

55 See Kisby, '"When the King Goeth a Procession"'.

56 Watt, *ODNB*.

57 Strype, *Ecclesiastical Memorials*, Vol. 1, Part 1, pp. 597–8.

58 Foxe (1583), pp. 1262–3.

59 Franklin-Harkrider, p. 50. n. 19.

60 Watt, *ODNB*.

61 Franklin-Harkrider, pp. 49–53.

62 Foxe (1583), p. 1267.

63 See Thomas S. Freeman, 'One Survived: The Account of Katherine Parr in Foxe's "Book of Martyrs"', in Thomas Betteridge and Suzannah Lipscomb, eds, *Henry VIII and the Court: Art, Politics and Performance* (Aldershot, 2013), pp. 235–52.

64 BL Cotton MS Vespasian C XIV, fol. 107; Cotton Appendix XXVIII, fol. 104v.

65 Hall, p. 867.

66 TNA E101/424/12, Part 2 (195).

67 Thomas Fuller, *History of the Worthies of England* (1662), p. 151; https://historicengland.org.uk/listing/the-list/list-entry/1062823?section=official-list-entry.

68 TNA E101/424/12, Part 1 (72).

69 For example, E101/424/12, Part 2 (195); E101/424/12, Part 2 (178); E101/424/12, Part 1 (97); E101/424/12, Part 2 (178).

70 *LP* XXI, i, 1237.

71 *CSP Spain* VIII, 331.

72 Ibid., 370.

73 James, pp. 253–4.

74 Suzannah Lipscomb, *The King is Dead: The Last Will and Testament of Henry VIII* (London, 2015), p. 65.

75   TNA E101/424/12, Part 1 (55, 76, 78).

76   Lipscomb, *The King is Dead*, pp. 121–2.

77   James, p. 259.

78   TNA E101/424/12, Part 2 (20, 118, 120–21).

79   See Ian W. Archer, 'City and Court Connected: The Material Dimen-
     sions of Royal Ceremonial, ca. 1480–1625', *Huntingdon Library Quarterly*
     71:1 (2008), 157–79, and Jennifer Loach, 'The Function of Ceremonial in
     the Reign of Henry VIII', *Past and Present* 142 (1994), 42–68; Strype,
     Ecclesiastical Memorials, Vol. 2, Part 2, pp. 289–311.

80   TNA LC 2/2, fol. 44.

81   Strype, *Ecclesiastical Memorials*, Vol. 2, Part 2, pp. 289–311 (p. 306).

Epilogue

1   TNA E315/340, fol. 82.

2   Ibid., fol. 88. In the first list there is no separation between gentlewomen
     and maids of honour, but by the second list this has been reinstated.
     Chamberer Mistress Skipwith had left by Michaelmas, but another Mis-
     tress Skipwith, perhaps her daughter, had joined as a maid of honour,
     replacing Mistress Guildford, who had also left. Carew, Copley, Bridges,
     Stafford and Aglionby were also new among the maids by Michaelmas.

3   S. J. Gunn, 'Brandon, Charles, first duke of Suffolk', *ODNB* https://doi.
     org/10.1093/ref:odnb/3260 (accessed August 2023).

4   TNA E101/424/12, Part 1 (82, 86), Part 2 (18).

5   Mueller, p. 131.

6   TNA SP10/1/43.

7   James, p. 269.

8   Ibid., pp. 267–8.

9   TNA E101/424/12, Part 1 (2, 7, 23); TNA E315/340, fols 27v–28.

10   See Helen Graham-Matheson, '"All wemen in thar degree shuld to thar
     men subiectit be": The Controversial Court Career of Elisabeth Parr,
     Marchioness of Northampton, *c.*1547–1565', unpublished PhD disserta-
     tion, UCL (2015), pp. 90–137.

11   See James, pp. 272–3, and Retha M. Warnicke, 'Seymour [née
     Stanhope], Anne, duchess of Somerset', *ODNB* https://doi.org/10.1093/
     ref:odnb/68053 (accessed August 2023).

12   Mueller, p. 131.

13   James, pp. 289–91.

14   Ibid., pp. 292–4.

15   Ibid., p. 299.

16   Mueller, pp. 184–7.

17 James, pp. 299–300.
18 Franklin-Harkrider, p. 50.
19 Foxe (1583), p. 2078.
20 The commissioners who inventoried her possessions at Kenninghall in 1546 described her closet and coffers as 'soo bare as your maiestie wolle hardlie think' and stated that her jewels had been sold to pay her debts. TNA SP1/227, fol. 84.
21 Clark, *Gender, Family, and Politics*, pp. 161–5.
22 Ibid.
23 Ibid., pp. 146–8.
24 Ibid., p. 166.
25 Wriothesley, pp. 94–5.
26 J. P. D. Cooper, 'Courtenay [née Blount], Gertrude, marchioness of Exeter', *ODNB* https://doi.org/10.1093/ref:odnb/6450 (accessed August 2023).
27 *LP* XXI, i, 148 (27, 28), 1165 (58), *LP* XXI, ii, 475 (118).
28 TNA E101/426/5, fols 39–39v.
29 *Lisle Letters* VI, pp. 277–9.
30 Ibid., pp. 276–7.
31 Hall, p. 592.
32 Franklin-Harkrider, p. 57.
33 Foxe (1570), pp. 2884–6.
34 See Natalie Mears, 'Politics in the Elizabethan Privy Chamber: Lady Mary Sidney and Kat Ashley', in James Daybell, ed., *Women and Politics in Early Modern England 1450–1700* (London, 2004), pp. 67–82. See also Merton, 'The Women Who Served Queen Mary and Queen Elizabeth'.

Bibliography

Primary Sources

Manuscript Sources
Archivo General de Simancas, Spain
Casa de Sitio Real, legeras 8, 9, 11; Estado 347

Arundel Castle, Sussex
MS G1/4

Bodleian Library, Oxford
Ashmole MS 1109, 1116; Rawlinson MS D 775

British Library, London
Additional MSS 4622, 6113, 21116, 21481, 25114, 29549, 45131, 45716A,
    59899, 71009; Arundel MS 26; Cottonian MSS Appendix
    XXVIII, L, Caligula D VI, VII, Cleopatra E IV, V, VI, Otho C
    X, Titus B I, C VII, Vespasian C XIV, F I, XIII, Vitellius C XI,
    XVI; Egerton MSS 985, 2623; Harleian MSS 41, 296, 543, 3504;
    Royal MS 17B XXVIII

Cambridge University Library
Pembroke MS 300

College of Arms, London
MSS 6, I.7, I.14, M8

Lincoln Record Office
1-ANC, 2-ANC

The National Archives, Kew
C1, C4, E30, E36, E101, E179, E315, LC2, LC9, LR2, PROB 11, REQ 2,
    SC12, SP1, SP2, SP10, SP60, SP70, STAC 2, STAC 10, WARD 9

Norfolk Record Office
Rye 74

Real Academia de Historia, Madrid
9/317

University of California, Berkeley
MS UCB 49

University of Nottingham
Newcastle MS Ne 02 (formerly 65)

Printed Primary Sources
*A Collection of Ordinances and Regulations for the Government of
    the Royal Household* (London, 1790)
Baker, J. H., ed., *The Reports of Sir John Spelman*, Selden Society
    (London, 1977)
Bentley, Samuel, ed., *Excerpta Historica* (London, 1833)
Bruce, J. and T. T. Perowne, eds, *Correspondence of Matthew
    Parker, D. D. Archbishop of Canterbury Comprising Letters
    Written by Him and to Him, from A.D. 1535, to His Death, A.D.
    1575* (Cambridge, 1853)
Burnet, Gilbert, *The History of the Reformation of the Church of
    England* (London, 1679–1715)
Calendar of Patent Rolls, Philip and Mary, Volume 1, 1553–4
    (London, 1937)
*Calendar of State Papers Relating to English Affairs in the Archives
    of Venice*, ed. Rawdon Brown et al. (London, 1864–1947), avail-
    able at British History Online

Calendar of State Papers, Foreign: Elizabeth, Volume 1, 1558–1559, ed. Joseph Stevenson (London, 1863), available at British History Online

Calendar of State Papers, Spain, ed. G. A. Bergenroth et al. (London, 1862–1954), available at British History Online

Calendar of the Manuscripts of the Marquis of Bath Preserved at Longleat, Wiltshire, Vol. 2 (London, 1907)

Castiglione, Baldesar, *The Book of the Courtier*, trans. George Bull (London, 1976)

Cavendish, George, *The Life and Death of Cardinal Wolsey*, ed. Samuel Weller Singer (London, 1825), Gutenberg ebook https://www.gutenberg.org/files/54043/54043-h/54043-h.htm

Chronicle of King Henry VIII of England, trans. Martin A. S. Hume (London, 1889)

Correspondencia de Gutierre Gomez de Fuensalida, ed. the Duke of Berwick and Alba (Madrid, 1907)

Crónica del rey Enrico Octavo de Inglaterra, Vol. 4, ed. Mariano Roca de Togores Molíns (Madrid, 1874)

de Pisan, Christine, *The Treasure of the City of Ladies*, trans. Sarah Lawson (London, 1985)

de Worde, Wynkyn, *The Maner of the Tryumphe of Caleys and Bulleyn and The Noble Tryumphant Coronacyon of Quene Anne, Wyfe unto the Most Noble Kyng Henry VIII*, ed. Edmund Goldsmid (Edinburgh, 1884), https://www.gutenberg.org/files/32515/32515-h/32515-h.htm#f16.1_

Froude, J., ed., *Life and Letters of Erasmus* (London, 1906)

Fuller, Thomas, *History of the Worthies of England* (1662)

Giustinian, Sebastian, *Four Years at the Court of Henry VIII*, ed. Rawdon Brown (Cambridge, 2013)

Grafton, Richard, *Grafton's Chronicle: or, History of England* (London, 1809)

Hall's Chronicle; containing the History of England, during the Reign of Henry the Fourth, and the succeeding monarchs, to the end of the reign of Henry the Eighth, in which are particularly described the manners and customs of those periods, ed. Henry Ellis (London, 1809)

Harpsfield, Nicholas, *A Treatise on the Pretended Divorce Between Henry VIII and Catharine of Aragon* (Camden Society, 1878)

Heale, Elizabeth, ed. *The Devonshire Manuscript: A Women's Book of Courtly Poetry* (Toronto, 2012)

Howard, Henry, *A defensative against the poison of supposed prophecies* (London, 1583, reprinted 1620)

Leland, John, *Collectanea*, 6 vols (London, 1715)

Letters and Papers, Foreign and Domestic, of the Reign of Henry VIII, ed. J. S. Brewer et al. (London, 1862–1932)

Mueller, Janel, ed., *Katherine Parr – Complete Works and Correspondence* (Chicago, 2011)

Myers, A. R., *The Household of Edward IV: The Black Book and the Ordinance of 1478* (Manchester, 1959)

Nichols, J. G., ed., *Narratives of the Days of the Reformation*, Camden Society First series 77 (1859)

Privy Purse Expenses of the Princess Mary, ed. Frederick Madden (London, 1831)

Savage, Henry, ed., *Love Letters of Henry VIII* (London, 1949)

Smyth, J., *The Berkeley Manuscripts: The Lives of the Berkeleys*, ed. J. Maclean, 3 vols (Gloucester, 1883)

Stow, John, *The Annales, Or Generall Chronicle of England*, ed. Edmund Howes (London, 1615)

Strype, J., *Ecclesiastical Memorials*, 3 vols (Oxford, 1822)

Testamenta Vetusta, ed. Nicholas Harris Nicolas, 2 vols (London, 1826)

The Chronicle of Calais in the Reigns of Henry VII and Henry VIII to the year 1540, ed. John Gough Nichols (London, 1846)

The Diary of Henry Machyn, Citizen and Merchant-Taylor of London, 1550–1563, ed. J. G. Nichols (London, 1848)

The Great Chronicle of London, ed. A. H. Thomas and I. D. Thornley (Gloucester, 1983)

The Life of Cardinal Wolsey: And Metrical Visions from the Original Autograph Manuscript, 2 vols, ed. C. Whittingham (London, 1825)

The Lisle Letters, ed. M. St Clare Byrne, 6 vols (Chicago, 1981)

The Manuscripts of His Grace the Duke of Rutland, G.C.B., pre-served at Belvoir Castle, HMC Twelfth Report, Appendix, Part IV (London, 1888)

The Privy Purse Expences of King Henry the Eighth, ed. Nicholas Harris Nicolas (London, 1827)

The Receyt of the Ladie Kateryne, ed. Gordon Kipling (Oxford, 1990)

The Register or Chronicle of Butley Priory, ed. A. G. Dickens (Winchester, 1951)

The Statutes of the Realm, ed. T. E. Tomlins and W. E. Taunton, 9 vols (London, 1810–25), Vol. 3

The Story of the Death of Anne Boleyn: A Poem by Lancelot de Carle, trans., ed. and with essays by JoAnn DellaNeva (Tempe, AZ, 2021)

Wriothesley, Charles, *A Chronicle of England During the Reigns of the Tudors, from A.D. 1485 to 1559*, ed. William Douglas Hamilton (London, 1875)

Online databases

A Social Edition of the Devonshire MS (BL Add. MS 17942): https://en.wikibooks.org/wiki/The_Devonshire_Manuscript

British History Online: https://www.british-history.ac.uk/

Diccionario Biográfico Español: https://dbe.rah.es/

John Foxe, *The Unabridged Acts and Monuments Online or TAMO* (The Digital Humanities Institute, Sheffield, 2011): https://www.dhi.ac.uk/foxe/

History of Parliament Online: https://www.historyofparliamentonline.org/

Oxford Dictionary of National Biography: https://www.oxforddnb.com/

Oxford English Dictionary: https://www.oed.com/

State Papers Online: https://www.gale.com/intl/primary-sources/state-papers-online

Tudor Chamber Books: https://www.tudorchamberbooks.org/edition/

Secondary Sources

A History of the County of Huntingdon: Volume 3, ed. William Page, Granville Provy and S. Inskip Ladds (London, 1936)

Adams, Tracy and Christine Adams, *The Creation of the French Royal Mistress* (University Park, Pennsylvania, 2020)

Ahnert, Ruth, *The Rise of Prison Literature in the Sixteenth Century* (Cambridge, 2013)

Akkerman, Nadine, *Invisible Agents: Women and Espionage in Seventeenth-Century Britain* (Oxford, 2018)

Akkerman, Nadine and Birgit Houben, eds, *The Politics of Female Households: Ladies-in-Waiting Across Early Modern Europe* (Leiden, 2013)

Archer, Ian W., 'City and Court Connected: The Material Dimensions of Royal Ceremonial, ca. 1480–1625', *Huntingdon Library Quarterly* 71:1 (2008), 157–79

Barratt, Alexandra, *Anne Bulkely and Her Book: Fashioning Female Piety in Early Tudor England* (Turnhout, 2009)

Bellamy, John, *The Tudor Law of Treason* (London, 1979)

Benavent, Júlia, 'El apoyo de Isabel de Portugal a Catalina de Aragón, reina de Inglaterra. Registro de cartas de la emperatriz (AGS Est. Libro 68)', *Hipogrifo* 9:2 (2021), 431–44

Bernard, G. W., *The King's Reformation: Henry VIII and the Remaking of the English Church* (New Haven, 2005)

Bernard, G. W., *Anne Boleyn: Fatal Attractions* (New Haven, 2010)

Bertzen, Nicole, 'Mission Impossible? Ambassador Karl Harst, Anne of Cleves, and Their Struggles to Secure the Strategic Alliance between Cleves and England', unpublished PhD dissertation, University of Kent (2021)

Bush, Michael, *The Pilgrims' Complaint: A Study of Popular Thought in the Early Tudor North* (Farnham, 2009)

Butler, Sara M., 'More than Mothers: Juries of Matrons and Pleas of the Belly in Medieval England', *Law and History Review* 37:2 (2019), 353–96

Clark, N., *Gender, Family, and Politics: The Howard Women 1485–1558* (Oxford, 2018)

Clark, N., 'Queen Katherine Howard: Space, Place, and Promiscuity, Pre- and Post-Marriage, 1536–42', *Royal Studies Journal* 6:2 (2019), 89–103

Cockayne, G. E., *Complete Peerage of England, Scotland, Ireland and Great Britain*, 12 vols (London, 1910–59)

Coolidge, Grace, *Guardianship, Gender and the Nobility in Early Modern Spain* (London, 2011)

Coster, Will, *Baptism and Spiritual Kinship* (Aldershot, 2002)

Crawford, Anne, 'Victims of Attainder: The Howard and DeVere Women in the Late Fifteenth Century', in *Medieval Women in Southern England*, ed. Keith Bate (Reading, 1989), pp. 59–74

Cressy, David, *Birth, Marriage & Death: Ritual, Religion, and the Life-Cycle in Tudor and Stuart England* (Oxford, 1999)

Cunningham, Sean, *Prince Arthur: The Tudor King Who Never Was* (Stroud, 2016)

Darsie, Heather R., *Anna, Duchess of Cleves: The King's 'Beloved Sister'* (Stroud, 2019)

Daybell, James, *Women Letter-Writers in Tudor England* (Oxford, 2006)

Daybell, James, *The Material Letter in Early Modern England: Manuscript Practices and the Culture and Practices of Letter-Writing, 1512–1635* (Basingstoke, 2012)

Dewhurst, John, 'The Alleged Miscarriages of Catherine of Aragon and Anne Boleyn', *Medical History* 28 (1984), 49–56

Dickinson, Janet, 'Redefining Faction at the Tudor Court', in Ruben Gonzalez Cuerva and Alexander Koller, eds, *A Europe of Courts, A Europe of Factions* (Leiden, 2017), pp. 20–40

Dodds, Madeleine Hope and Ruth Dodds, *The Pilgrimage of Grace 1536–1537 and The Exeter Conspiracy 1538*, 2 vols (London, 1971)

Dwyer Amussen, Susan, '"Being stirred to much unquietness": Violence and Domestic Violence in Early Modern England', *Journal of Women's History* 6:2 (1994), 70–89

Earenfight, Theresa, 'Raising Infanta Catalina de Aragon to be Catherine, Queen of England', *Anuario de Estudios Medievales* 46:1 (2016), 417–43

Earenfight, Theresa, 'A Precarious Household: Catherine of Aragon in England, 1501–1504', in idem., ed., *Royal and Elite Households in Medieval and Early Modern Europe* (Leiden, 2018), pp. 338–56

Earenfight, Theresa, *Catherine of Aragon* (University Park, Pennsylvania, 2021)

Ellis, Steven G., 'Centre and Periphery in the Tudor State', in Robert Tittler and Norman L. Jones, eds, *A Companion to Tudor Britain* (London, 2004), pp. 133–50

Evans, J., '"Gentle Purges corrected with hot Spices, whether they work or not, do vehemently provoke Venery": Menstrual Provocation and Procreation in Early Modern England', *Social History of Medicine* 25:1 (2021), 2–19

Everett, Michael, *The Rise of Thomas Cromwell* (London, 2015)

Fernández de Córdova Miralles, Álvaro, *La Corte de Isabel I* (Madrid, 2002)

Fletcher, Catherine, *Our Man in Rome: Henry VIII and His Italian Ambassador* (London, 2012)

Fontana, Dominic, 'Charting the Development of Portsmouth Harbour, Dockyard and Town in the Tudor Period', *Journal of Marine Archaeology* 8 (2013), 263–82

Ford, Francis, *Mary Tudor* (Bury St Edmunds, 1882)

Foyster, Elizabeth, *Manhood in Early Modern England: Honour, Sex and Marriage* (London, 1999)

Franklin-Harkrider, Melissa, *Women, Reform and Community in Early Modern England: Katherine Willoughby, Duchess of Suffolk, and Lincolnshire's Godly Aristocracy, 1519–1580* (Woodbridge, 2008)

Freeman, Thomas S., 'Research, Rumour and Propaganda: Anne Boleyn in Foxe's "Book of Martyrs"', *Historical Journal* 38:4 (1995), 797–819

Freeman, Thomas S., 'One Survived: The Account of Katherine Parr in Foxe's "Book of Martyrs"', in Thomas Betteridge and Suzannah Lipscomb, eds, *Henry VIII and the Court: Art, Politics and Performance* (Aldershot, 2013), pp. 235–52

French, K., 'The Material Culture of Childbirth in Late Medieval London and its Suburbs', *Journal of Women's History* 28:2 (2016), 126–48

García Fernández, Ernesto, 'Hombres y mujeres de negocios del País Vasco en la Baja Edad Media', en J. A. Bonachía Hernando, y D. Carvajal de la Vega, eds, *Los negocios del hombre: Comercio y rentas en Castilla (siglos XV y XVI)*, (Valladolid, 2012), pp. 101-40

Geaman, K. L. and T. Earenfight, 'Neither Heir nor Spare: Childless Queens and the Practice of Monarchy in Pre-modern Europe', in Elena Woodacre et al., eds, *The Routledge History of Monarchy* (London, 2019), pp. 518-33

Gertz, Genelle and Pasquale Toscano, 'The Lost Network of Elizabeth Barton', *Reformation* 26:2 (2021), 105-28

Goff, Cecilie, *A Woman of the Tudor Age* (London, 1930)

Goicolea Julián, Javier, 'Mercaderes y hombres de negocio: el poder del dinero en el mundo urbano riojano de fines de la Edad Media e inicios de la Edad Moderna', *Hispania: Revista española de historia* 67, no. 227 (2007), 947-92

González Arévalo, Raúl, 'Francesco Grimaldi, un mercader-banquero genovés entre Granada, la corte e Inglaterra (siglos xv–xvi)', *En la Espana Medieval* 39 (2016), 97-126

Gowing, Laura, *Domestic Dangers: Women, Words, and Sex in Early Modern London* (Oxford, 1996)

Graham-Matheson, Helen, '"All wemen in thar degree shuld to thar men subiectit be": The Controversial Court Career of Elisabeth Parr, Marchioness of Northampton, c.1547–1565', unpublished PhD dissertation, UCL (2015)

Gunn, Steven, 'Peers, Commons and Gentry in the Lincolnshire Revolt of 1536', *Past and Present* 123 (1989), 52-79

Gunn, Steven, *Charles Brandon: Henry VIII's Closest Friend* (Stroud, 2016)

Habib, Imtiaz, *Black Lives in English Archives* (London, 2008)

Hamilton, Dakota, 'The Household of Katherine Parr', unpublished D.Phil thesis, University of Oxford (1992)

Harris, Barbara, 'Marriage Sixteenth-Century Style: Elizabeth Stafford and the Third Duke of Norfolk', *Journal of Social History* 15:3 (1982), 371-82

Harris, Barbara, *English Aristocratic Women, 1450–1550* (Oxford, 2002)

Hayward, Maria, *Dress at the Court of Henry VIII* (Leeds, 2007)

Hayward, Maria, *Rich Apparel: Clothing and the Law in Henry VIII's England* (Aldershot, 2009)

Head, David M., "'Beyng Ledde and Seduced by the Devyll": The Attainder of Lord Thomas Howard and the Tudor Law of Treason', *Sixteenth Century Journal* 13:4 (1982), 2–16

Head, David M., *The Ebbs and Flows of Fortune: The Life of Thomas Howard, Third Duke of Norfolk* (Athens, Georgia, 1995)

Howe, Elizabeth Teresa, *Education and Women in the Early Modern Hispanic World* (Aldershot, 2008)

Howlett, Richard, 'The Household Accounts of Kenninghall Palace in the year 1525', *Norfolk Archaeology* 15 (1904), pp. 51–60

Hoyle, R., *The Pilgrimage of Grace and the Politics of the 1530s* (Oxford, 2001)

Hufton, Olwen, 'Reflections on the Role of Women in the Early Modern Court', *Court Historian* 5 (2000), 1–13

Hunt, Alice, *The Drama of Coronation* (Cambridge, 2009)

Irish, Bradley J., "'The secret chamber and other suspect places": Materiality, Space, and the Fall of Katherine Howard', *Early Modern Women* 4 (2009), 169–73

Ives, Eric, *The Life and Death of Anne Boleyn* (Oxford, 2004)

James, Susan, *Catherine Parr: Henry VIII's Last Love* (Stroud, 2009)

James, Susan E., 'The Horenbout Family Workshop at the Tudor Court, 1522–1541: Collaboration, Patronage and Production', *Cogent Arts and Humanities* 8 (2021)

Jansen, Sharon, *Dangerous Talk and Strange Behavior: Women and Popular Resistance to the Reforms of Henry VIII* (Basingstoke, 1996)

Johnson, Lauren, *Shadow King: The Life and Death of Henry VI* (London, 2019)

Johnson, Lauren, *Margaret Beaufort* (forthcoming)

Kaufman, Gloria, 'Juan Luis Vives on the Education of Women', *Signs* 3:4 (1978), 891–6

Kennedy, Kathleen E., 'Susanna Horebout, Courtier and Artist', *Art Herstory* (1 December 2019), https://artherstory.net/susanna-horenbout-courtier-and-artist/ (accessed August 2023)

Kisby, Fiona, '"When the King Goeth a Procession": Chapel Ceremonies and Services, the Ritual Year, and Religious Reforms
at the Early Tudor Court, 1485–1547', *Journal of British Studies*
40:1 (2001), 44–75

LaPratt, Debora, 'Childbirth Prayers in Medieval and Early
Modern England: "For drede of perle that may be-falle."', *Sym-
posia* 2 (2010), https://symposia.library.utoronto.ca (accessed
June 2023)

Lehmberg, Stanford, *The Reformation Parliament 1529–1536* (Cambridge, 1970)

Liedl, Janice, '"Rather a Strong and Constant Man": Margaret Pole
and the Problem of Women's Independence', in J. A. Chappell
and K. A. Kramer, eds, *Women During the English Reformations* (New York, 2014), pp. 29–43

Lipscomb, Suzannah, *1536: The Year that Changed Henry VIII*
(Oxford, 2009)

Lipscomb, Suzannah, *The King is Dead: The Last Will and Testament of Henry VIII* (London, 2015)

Loach, Jennifer, 'The Function of Ceremonial in the Reign of
Henry VIII', *Past and Present* 142 (1994), 42–68

Loades, David, *The Tudor Court* (London, 1986)

Loades, David, 'Henry Grace á Dieu', in John J. Hattendorf,
ed., *The Oxford Encyclopedia of Maritime History* (Oxford,
2007)

MacCulloch, Diarmaid, *Thomas Cromwell* (London, 2019)

Mackay, Lauren, *Inside the Tudor Court: Henry VIII and His Six
Wives Through the Eyes of the Spanish Ambassador* (Stroud,
2015)

Mackay, Lauren, *Among the Wolves of Court: The Untold Story of
Thomas and George Boleyn* (London, 2018)

Marshall, Peter, *Religious Identities in Henry VIII's England*
(Aldershot, 2006)

Martínez Hernández, Paula, *El Tesorero Vitoriano Ochoa de
Landa: Las cuentas de la casa de Juana I de Castilla (1506–1531)*
(Vitoria-Gasteiz, 2020)

Martinez Millan, J., *La corte de Carlos V* (Madrid, 2000)

Mattingley, Garrett, *Catherine of Aragon* (London, 1950)

McCaffrey, Kate E., 'Hope from day to day: Inscriptions newly discovered in a book belonging to Anne Boleyn', *TLS*, 21 May 2021 https://www.the-tls.co.uk/articles/inscriptions-discovered-in-a-book-owned-by-anne-boleyn-essay-kate-e-mccaffrey/

McIntosh, Jeri, *From Heads of Household to Heads of State: The Preaccession Households of Mary and Elizabeth Tudor, 1516–1558* http://www.gutenberg-e.org/mcintosh/index.html

McSheffrey, Shannon, 'The Slaying of Sir William Pennington: Legal Narrative and the Late Medieval English Archive', *Florilegium* 28 (2011), 169–203

McSheffrey, Shannon, 'Disorder, Riot, and Governance in Early Tudor London: Evil May Day, 1517', *EHR*, 138 (2023), 27–60

Mears, Natalie, 'Politics in the Elizabethan Privy Chamber: Lady Mary Sidney and Kat Ashley', in James Daybell, ed., *Women and Politics in Early Modern England 1450–1700* (London, 2004), pp. 67–82

Merton, Charlotte, 'The Women Who Served Queen Mary and Queen Elizabeth', unpublished PhD dissertation, University of Cambridge (1990)

Mortimer, Ian, *The Time Traveller's Guide to Medieval England* (London, 2008)

Murphy, Beverley, *Bastard Prince: Henry VIII's Lost Son* (Stroud, 2001)

Murphy, Neil, 'Henry VIII's First Invasion of France: The Gascon Expedition of 1512', *English Historical Review* 130:542 (2015), 25–56

Murphy, Neil, 'Spies, Informers and Thomas Howard's Defence of England's Northern Frontier in 1523', *Historical Research* 93:260 (2020), 252–72

Myers, A. R., *Crown Household and Parliament in the Fifteenth Century* (London, 1985)

Nader, Helen, ed., *Power and Gender in Renaissance Spain: Eight Women of the Mendoza Family, 1450–1650* (Chicago, 2004)

Norrie, Aidan et al., eds, *Tudor and Stuart Consorts: Power, Influence, and Dynasty* (Basingstoke, 2022)

Norton, Elizabeth, *Bessie Blount: Mistress to Henry VIII* (Stroud, 2011)

Owen, Gwilym and Rebecca Probert, 'Marriage, Dispensation and Divorce During the Years of Henry VIII's "great matter": A Local Case Study', *Law and Humanities* 13:1 (2019), 76–94

Paul, Joanne, *The House of Dudley* (London, 2022)

Qaiser Ikram, Muhammad, Fazle Hakim Sajjad and Arah Salardini, 'The Head that Wears the Crown: Henry VIII and Traumatic Brain Injury', *Journal of Clinical Neuroscience* 38 (2016), 16–19

Roberts, Ian, *Pontefract Castle* (West Yorkshire Archaeology Service, 1990)

Robinson, W. R. B., 'The Lands of Henry, Earl of Worcester in the 1530s. Part 3: Central Monmouthshire and Herefordshire', *Bulletin of the Board of Celtic Studies* xxv (iv) (1974)

Russell, Gareth, *Young & Damned & Fair: The Life and Tragedy of Catherine Howard at the Court of Henry VIII* (London, 2017)

Ryrie, Alec, *The Gospel and Henry VIII: Evangelicals in the Early English Reformation* (Cambridge, 2003)

Sadlack, Erin, *The French Queen's Letters* (Basingstoke, 2011)

Santoyo, Julio-Cesar, *El Dr. Escoriaza en Inglaterra y otros ensayos Británicos* (Biblioteca alavesa Luis de Ajuria / Institución Sancho el Sabio, 1973)

Schutte, Kimberly, '"Not for Matters of Treason but for Love Matters": Margaret Douglas, Countess of Lennox, and Tudor Marriage Law', in James V. Mehl, ed., *Laudem Caroli: Renaissance and Reformation Studies for Charles G. Nauert* (Kirksville, MI, 1998), pp. 171–88

Sharkey, Jessica, 'Between King and Pope: Thomas Wolsey and the Knight Mission', *Historical Research* 84:224 (2011), 236–48

Soberton, Sylvia Barbara, *Gertrude Courtenay: Wife and Mother of the Last Plantagenet* (2021)

Spufford, Peter, *Handbook of Medieval Exchange* (London, 1986)

Stretton, Tim and Krista Kesselring, eds, *Married Women and the Law: Coverture in England and the Common Law World* (Montreal, 2013)

Taffe, James, 'Reconstructing the Queen's Household, 1485–1547: A Study in Royal Service', unpublished PhD thesis, University of Durham (2021)

Taffe, James, *Courting Scandal: The Rise and Fall of Jane Boleyn, Lady Rochford* (2023)

The History of Parliament: The House of Commons 1509–1558, ed. S. T. Bindoff (London, 1982)

The History of the King's Works, Vol. 3, ed. Howard Montagu Colvin (London, 1963)

Thurley, Simon, *The Royal Palaces of Tudor England* (London, 1993)

Thurley, Simon, *Houses of Power: The Places That Shaped the Tudor World* (London, 2017)

Tompkins, Laura, 'The Uncrowned Queen: Alice Perrers, Edward III and Political Crisis in Fourteenth-century England, 1360–1377', unpublished PhD thesis, University of St Andrews (2013)

Varlow, Sally, 'Sir Francis Knollys's Latin Dictionary: New Evidence for Katherine Carey', *Historical Research* 80:209 (2007), 315–23

Virgoe, R., 'The Recovery of the Howards in East Anglia, 1485–1529', in *Wealth and Power in Tudor England*, ed. E. W. Ives, R. J. Knecht and J. J. Scarisbrick (London, 1978), pp. 1–20

Waddell, B., 'The Evil May Day Riot of 1517 and the Popular Politics of Anti-Immigrant Hostility in Early Modern London', *Historical Research* 94:266 (2021), 716–35

Walker, Greg, 'Rethinking the Fall of Anne Boleyn', *The Historical Journal* 45:1 (2002), 1–29

Warnicke, Retha, *The Marrying of Anne of Cleves* (Cambridge, 2000)

Warnicke, Retha, *Elizabeth of York and Her Six Daughters-in-Law* (Basingstoke, 2017)

Watt, Diane, 'The Prophet at Home: Elizabeth Barton and the Influence of Bridget of Sweden and Catherine of Siena', in *Prophets Abroad: The Reception of Continental Holy Women in Late-medieval England*, ed. Rosalynn Voaden (Cambridge, 1996), pp. 161–76

Wessex Archaeology, 'Syon House, Syon Park, Hounslow: An Archaeological Evaluation of a Bridgettine Abbey and an Assessment of the Results', (2003), available at https://www.wessexarch.co.uk/our-work/syon-house-syon-park (accessed August 2023)

Williams, Patrick, *Katharine of Aragon* (Stroud, 2013)

Woolgar, C. M., *The Great Household in Late Medieval England* (New Haven, 1999)

Index